SOCIOLOGY *of* CHILDHOOD

SOCIOLOGY SERIES
Edited by John F. Cuber

SOCIOLOGY *of* CHILDHOOD

OSCAR W. RITCHIE

MARVIN R. KOLLER

Kent State University

APPLETON - CENTURY - CROFTS

Division of Meredith Publishing Company

New York

To Edith and Pauline

Preface

The decision to write this book resulted from the convergence of our separate, personal and academic interests and activities. In addition to our personal involvements with children, we have for many years indirectly concerned ourselves with children through our classroom contacts with thousands of students preparing for careers in teaching and child welfare. Thousands of other students came to our classes to enlarge their general perspectives in the areas of marriage, family, and children. Their chief concern was to find whatever useful information and insights they could, to be applied eventually in their own adult lives. As a result, we recognized that although many of these students were relatively knowledgeable regarding the developmental, psychological, and educational approaches to childhood, they had not been sufficiently sensitized to the total or the segmental social and cultural contexts in which children grow and develop.

Our efforts to supplement our students' knowledge of children and childhood have been approached principally through two courses: (1) The Sociology of Childhood, and (2) Marriage and the Family. In the first course, the initial and main emphasis is upon the child within the family setting; in the second, the family as a social unit is the principal point of concern. Implicit in the emphasis upon the component parts of the family and their over-all unity in the family course is the vital role of children. Largely because of our common interest and our teaching experiences in subject-matter areas that are complementary, we frequently found ourselves comparing notes, so to speak. And as we explored the subject of childhood and examined the relevant social science literature, we recognized the need for greater attention to this subject.

Although childhood and the family can be viewed as separate areas of study, they can also be seen to constitute an integrated whole. Despite the gap that separates children from adults, there is a recognizable continuity that links them together. This continuity is, of course, not observable in all its minute details. Moreover, in the course of development from child to adult, some personality traits of the former are modified, some fall into disuse, and some are expunged and replaced. Yet, we know that the adult is never totally different from the child he once was. This fact alone suggests that a systematic study of the child is likely to prove fruitful in our efforts to understand the adult and his world.

It may help the student to keep in mind, throughout the reading of this text, that the central thread that binds the several parts and the specific chapters together is the desire to present a sociological analysis of childhood. The deliberate exclusion of other possible emphases is not to be construed as negative judgment of the contributions of other disciplines. Rather than selecting an eclectic approach, which has its values, we chose to draw as much data as we could from the field of sociology alone. This ever-expanding, scientific field of inquiry is broad enough to explore the structures and processes whereby children move to take their place in society. Putting chiefly "sociological" data on childhood together in a meaningful way is a task which we feel is worthy enough to claim the attention of serious students of childhood who wish to work on advanced levels.

The writing of a textbook is perhaps never totally the result of the efforts of its authors. Certainly this work is no exception. Countless persons, including our students and colleagues at Kent State University, our own teachers, and the many authorities we have consulted have all had a part in it. To all of these contributors, known and unknown, direct and indirect, we express our gratitude.

O.W.R.
M.R.K.

Contents

SOCIOLOGY *of*
CHILDHOOD

I

INTRODUCTION AND BACKGROUND

1

Approaches to
the Study of Childhood

If there is one single segment of the life span that has captured and sustained attention, it is childhood. Some insist that the earliest period of childhood, namely infancy, is the most significant part of life. Others imply that the toddler or pre-school child deserves much more attention. Still others tend to stress the lifetime imprint of the experiences of the school-child or the pre-adolescent. The over-all consensus remains, however, that the period from birth to twelve years of age is one of the most meaningful portions of time in any life-history. It is with this first dozen years in the total life of individuals that this text in concerned.

At the heart of this interest in childhood is the recognition that the earliest experiences of an individual form the basis for all that develops in later life. It is commonplace to speak of an adult male as being "father to the child," an expression which credits adults as primary persons in the molding of children. Empirical evidence, however, supports the contention that "the child is father to the man." This expression suggests that adulthood may be viewed as the unfolding of qualities developed in childhood. It is childhood that vitally affects adulthood as well as adulthood that affects childhood. The relationship is reciprocal and mutually reinforcing.

In terms of numbers alone, children constitute a large proportion of the world's population. Because of the infrequent, and often inaccurate, censuses of various nations, one has to rely upon rough estimates or approximations to determine the magnitude of childhood populations. Nevertheless, their numbers are impressive. One reliable source, the Mid-century White House Conference on Children and Youth,[1] reported that

[1] *Children and Youth at the Mid-century*, Mid-century White House Conference on Children and Youth, Chart 75.

3

at about mid-point in the twentieth century there were approximately 844 million children in the world. Of these, 37 million were in the United States, 172 million in Europe, including all of the U.S.S.R., 493 million in Asia, 76 million in Africa, 61 million in South America, 3 million in the South Pacific, and 2 million in Canada.

In a global population of about three billion, children comprise almost one third of the people of the world. By sheer weight of numbers then, children represent an important category. If those who are entrusted with the care of children and those who are affected by children were added to the already large number of the world's children, the sum total would embrace practically the entire human family. It is not surprising, then, to find that serious study of childhood is growing because of the quantitative immensity and qualitative impacts of childhood.

There are a number of different approaches that have been taken by students of childhood and the following descriptions of these should prove helpful to those who wish to sharpen their appreciations of the momentous early years of life.

APPROACHES TO THE STUDY OF CHILDHOOD

General Background

Each approach to the study of childhood has its dedicated advocates as well as its skeptical antagonists. It will be useful, then, for an objective analysis to examine the supporting evidence and judgments, particularly where there are polarities of views. The study of juxtaposed viewpoints may challenge the neutral position of the uncommitted student as well as reminding him that exploration in only one direction often leads to intense commitment and loyalty—earmarks of the closed mind.

An *approach* constitutes "a frame of reference," which implies that an observer looks at his subject from a specific point of view or vantage point. The chief value of a frame of reference lies in its utility in focusing attention upon selected areas without distractions from presumably extraneous matters. Its chief defect, however, stems from this same attempt to concentrate only upon the selected phenomena. The emphasis or high attention paid to one segment of knowledge may understandably lead to relative neglect of other details which merit consideration. Evaluation of each approach will be directed, therefore, to what has been selected for special examination and what it has consequently lost by such a selection.

The very fact that there are numerous approaches to the study of childhood is mute testimony of its multi-faceted nature. Childhood is a complicated area of study and it will not be mastered by the simultaneous use of every approach by courageous, but uninitiated, students who take a course in childhood. The limitations of one lifetime will not permit the marching upon the citadel of childhood by all roads at once. Certainly there is value to be found in eclecticism because this procedure seeks to view the entirety of childhood and to treat children as total individuals. The all-embracing, all-encompassing eclectic intention, however, is not the one which will be employed in this text. The integration of the many approaches to the study of childhood remains a challenge to the most able scholars of the day. The accumulated data pertaining to all aspects of childhood will not be found within the covers of any single volume. At best, each approach has its merits and its shortcomings and we can devote our attention briefly to a short appraisal of the most prominent approaches. Inevitably, of course, the sociological orientation of the authors will assert itself and set the course.

Historical Approach

An approach that should yield great insight is one which makes use of historical materials. There is a sound logic that follows the premise that to understand the present there is need to first understand the past. Treatment of children has varied in time, and a tracing of the earliest interest in youngsters from prehistory, through ancient, medieval, European, colonial, and modern circumstances would be a rewarding experience for students of childhood. It should, at best, constitute a needed antidote to the all too common ahistoricity of so much contemporary social research.

One discovery, in the search for historical changes, would be to find that certain attitudes and certain behaviors have remained relatively unchanged. The ancient laments about the reluctance of children to devote long hours to academic studies have a familiar and modern ring. One ancient Egyptian pupil wrote to his tutor, "I was with thee since I was brought up as a child. Thou didst beat my back and thy instructions went into my ear."[2] James Breasted[3] explains the Egyptian theory of severe punishment for failure to learn by the maxim, "A boy's ears are on his back and he hearkens when he is beaten." Margaret Murray[4] notes that even in ancient Egypt ". . . there were many moral books written for the young, full of copybook maxims. They were painfully like some of those which afflict youth in all countries and in all periods." Recurrent

[2] Adolf Erman, translated from German by Helen M. Tirard, *Life in Ancient Egypt* (New York, The Macmillan Company, 1894), p. 329.

[3] James H. Breasted, *A History of Egypt* (New York, Charles Scribner's Sons, 1924), p. 99.

[4] Margaret Murray, *The Splendour That Was Egypt* (New York, Philosophical Library, Inc., 1949), p. 107.

themes that appear regardless of shifting historical circumstances are valuable by-products of the historical approach.

There have been changes, of course, and these have evolved slowly, laboriously, almost inperceptibly throughout human history. One such change would be the increasing value placed upon children. Far back in the past, children were not generally esteemed or accorded special attention other than general service and obedience to their elders. In time, however, children have come into a modern period of tremendous concern for their well-being to such an extent that the American society, for instance, has been described as chiefly "youth-oriented." In contrast, the vigorous growth of the field of social gerontology, which specializes in the study of aging individuals and their impact upon society, has occurred only as growing numbers and proportions of aging persons in the population have forced scientists to modify their preoccupation with the relatively young.[5]

A third pattern, which represents a distinctively different distillation derived from an historical approach to childhood, is cyclical or wave-like relationships. Instead of remaining constant or slowly developing, conditions occur in time which lead to a reversal of previous conditions. These new conditions, however, may soon be displaced by the reappearance of the formerly predominant behavior patterns. Children, for example, have been historically treated as practically depraved individuals who were sorely in need of adult guidance and pressure. In time, children came to be viewed as particularly precious beings who must be loved and tenderly reared in terms of their own needs and capacities. Reaction to this occurs, however, when children appear to some to be over-demanding, unappreciative, and unworthy of all the attentions heaped upon them. Then the cycle begins all over again; it seems, when one treatment procedure is carried to extremes, repercussions soon manifest themselves.

A search of the literature dealing with the rearing of children makes it abundantly clear that child rearing practices run in fashionable and even faddish cycles. The run of attention appears to move first in one direction and then in another, often only to return again to an older, formerly popular procedure.[6]

In brief, the historical approach to a study of childhood does yield invaluable insights in terms of former conditions which lead to current

[5] See Clark Tibbitts, ed., *Handbook of Social Gerontology* (Chicago, University of Chicago Press, 1960); James Birren, ed., *Handbook of Aging and the Individual* (Chicago, University of Chicago Press, 1959); Ernest Burgess, ed., *Aging in Western Societies* (Chicago, University of Chicago Press, 1960).

[6] See Orville G. Brim, Jr., "Changes and Trends in Child-Rearing Advice," *Child Study*, Vol. 36, No. 4 (Fall, 1959), pp. 23–27; Grace Langdon and Irving Stout, *The Discipline of Well-Adjusted Children* (New York, The John Day Company, Inc., 1952), pp. 3–47; Urie Bronfenbrenner, "Changing American Child: A Systematic Analysis," *Journal of Social Issues*, Vol. 17, No. 1 (1961), pp. 6–18.

circumstances. Further, those patterns that are unaffected by time and those that are subject to change can be observed. Finally, the patterns of change may take the form of constant growth or cyclical growth-decline-growth. When there is a need to clarify a point in the ensuing exposition, historical evidence will be cited to illuminate that point. The more comprehensive analysis and synthesis of historical data as it relates to children, however, will not occupy a central place in this discussion, but will be left in the hands of historians.

Developmental Approach

One of the most popular frames of reference has been that which emphasizes the various phases and/or stages of growth through which children pass. From the moment of conception, this miraculous creation of life in the fertilized ovum, first a microscopic speck which gradually unfolds into adult maturity, is a process that has attracted attention through the years. Its dramatic appeal, its down-to-earth nature, and its universality encourage investigation.

The developmental approach to the study of children rests upon the biological processes that occur automatically in all living things. Applied to children, the increasing refinement of muscles, nerves, glands, and other physical organs is the foundation for age-grading of children in various cultures.[7] If the child is in the infantile stage, little is required of him. Typically as the child moves on to more mature phases, however, social pressures or cultural demands arise which require more compli-cated conformity.

While internal changes are going on within the body of the growing child, it is the external changes that excite the greatest comment from observers of the developing child. Increasing height and weight, increas-ing abilities in sensory perception, greater skill at communicating, walk-ing, grasping, and, most important of all, understanding are noted and taken into account when dealing with the child. The growth of youngsters from a state of complete helplessness to a condition of adult control is anticipated, but, nevertheless, remarkable. How often elders remark when they meet a child who is growing up, "My, how you have grown since the last time I saw you!" Obviously, this condition is predictable and should not necessarily elicit comment. Yet, most individuals can recall occasions when their biological development drew declarations of sheer amazement from adults.

Thus, growth and change characterize the developmental study of

[7] See Nathan Miller, *The Child in Primitive Society* (New York, Brentano's, 1928); Oscar Chrisman, *The Historical Child* (Boston, Golden Press, Inc., 1920); Margaret Mead and Martha Wolfenstein, eds., *Childhood in Contemporary Cultures* (Chicago, University of Chicago Press, 1955).

children. The Gesell studies [8] of the physical or biologically based performances of children at various stages of growth is an example of a research approach to childhood from this point of view.

The developmental approach is related significantly to health or medical problems. Because of previous and current neglect of physical developments during childhood, adults have grown to maturity with needless deformities and handicaps. Farseeing men and women in the medical profession have taken their skills and medicines to under-developed countries and emerging nation-states to combat death-dealing, painful, or crippling diseases, congenital defects, or accidents. Men like Albert Schweitzer, Tom Dooley, and Gordon Seagraves have won worldwide acclaim for their humanitarian and sacrificial services to the people of remote areas. The hospital ship, U.S.S. Hope, is a more recent product of the desire of many American people to share medical knowledge with the world's people. The only criticism that these efforts have encountered is that they are minimal when weighed against the urgency and abundance of cases that exist. A policy of "helping others to help themselves," may provide the long sought answer to the problem.

Psychological Approach

Under the aegis of psychology, there are subsumed such specializations as psychiatry, psychoanalysis, and social psychology. All of these share the common denominator of concern with individuals despite apparent attention to collectivities. Whenever an attempt is made to generalize about a group of people, an almost inevitable counter-observation is made that the generalization does not apply to certain individuals who represent the exceptions to the generalization. Persons are unique, and the psychological approach does caution observers of childhood to avoid over-generalizing from limited samples. The central theme that unites the various components of the psychological approach may be summarized in the expression "individuals differ." Applied to the study of childhood, the psychological approach heightens awareness that each child is not exactly the same as any other child.

Conditioning and learning have long held important places of interest in psychological circles. Psychological study of childhood, thus, leads to much discussion about the place of intelligence and habituation. Psychologists and kindred affiliates have developed productive techniques

[8] See Arnold L. Gesell, *Infancy and Human Growth* (New York, The Macmillan Company, 1928); Arnold L. Gesell, *Atlas of Infant Behavior* (New Haven, Yale University Press, 1934); Arnold L. Gesell, *How a Baby Grows* (New York, Harper & Row, Publishers, Inc., 1945); Arnold L. Gesell and Frances L. Ilg, *The Child from Five to Ten* (New York, Harper & Row, Publishers, Inc., 1946); Arnold L. Gesell and Frances L. Ilg, *Child Development* (New York, Harper & Row, Publishers, Inc., 1949).

which concentrate on how children acquire new behavior, and which have helped educational psychologists to uncover some of the intricacies of the learning processes.[9] In addition, children who are deviants, either as exceptionally gifted or exceptionally retarded individuals, have been the subjects of significant case studies of great depths.[10]

Certainly one of the most important themes stressed by those who utilize the psychological approach is the warning not to deal solely with the "outer environment" of children, but to examine the "inner environment" as well. By this theme, psychologists have reference to the feeling states of youngsters which lead to particular interpretations of external stimuli. We shall refer to this "inner environment" shortly as a desirable counterbalance to any tendency towards an overzealous sociological interpretation.

Educational Approach

The key concept in the educational approach is the thesis that children are "school processed." Children are viewed as entities who enter at one end of the formal process somewhat lacking in human knowledge and are released at the other end of the process somewhat saturated with as much of the accumulated know-how of mankind as possible. While the educational focus tends to be upon the formal experiences of school, there is also keen appreciation of the influence of informal experiences occurring simultaneously outside the school structure. Educationists do pay attention to the influence of home, church, and community. They are among the first to recognize their contributions and seek to incorporate them in the total school processing. The use of parent-teacher organizations, field trips, outside speakers, charity drives, and numerous other school activities outside the general curricula testify to this awareness. Nevertheless, educationists continue to give priority to the various school experiences formally prepared for children.

While non-school experiences are valuable aids to formal school experiences, they may also nullify much that has been laboriously taught during formal school training. Instruction in the acceptable practice of English grammar can easily be undone if there is poor use of English within the homes and community of learners. Such training will be voided if formal instruction is not brought to life by daily usage. Educators who are conscious of this problem work for the day when education will not be regarded as something for young learners merely in an

---

[9] See John W. Tilton, *An Educational Psychology of Learning* (New York, The Macmillan Company, 1951), pp. 63–128.

[10] See, for sample studies, Samuel A. Kirk, *Early Education of the Mentally Retarded* (Urbana, University of Illinois Press, 1958); Joseph L. French, *Educating the Gifted* (New York, Holt, Rinehart & Winston, Inc., 1959).

elementary school, but when education will be broadly regarded as a process which continues throughout life.

The rigidity of formal class sessions when "learning" takes place has given way somewhat to a newer approach among educators who take into account the total informal life of a school. This new point of view is concerned with schools as communities in which young people live, play, and work together. The corridors, lunchroom, gymnasium, playground, offices, dispensary, and auditorium are locales of learning which may be incorporated into the educational program instead of incorporating only the facilities and activities within the confines of classrooms.

Frequently when perplexing human problems confront men, they seem inevitably to conclude that with "more and better" education their problems will dissipate. There seems to be unbounding faith in the efficacy of education. Within the ranks of professional educators, however, there remains a sobering realization that current practices fall far short of idealistic goals.[11] Educators, themselves, are in the forefront of efforts to retain whatever is deemed worthy in their tradition and yet to discard obsolete procedures in favor of new methods which give promise of improved instruction.

Therapeutic Points of View

Some professional persons are concerned with children as individuals who are in need of help. This perspective may not necessarily rank as "an approach," but, more likely, it is a combination of approaches. The unifying principle underlying the therapeutic point of view is that knowledge is drawn from any legitimate study of children and is subsequently practically applied. Depending upon the orientation of the therapy-minded person, children are "helped" to achieve some preconceived "desirable" goal. The emphasis in adopting this point of view is upon action or reform rather than with objective descriptions of reality as it currently exists.

At the outset of life, children lack the ability to protect themselves from whatever dangers or difficulties may exist. Their state of complete helplessness has prompted some persons to become their self-appointed champions to shield them from any misuse or abuse. Children are, thus, regarded as persons in need of placement, guidance, and care from their elders. All children may be viewed as having certain inalienable rights which must be granted regardless of circumstances surrounding particular cases. Essentially, this point of view is warm, sympathetic, and characterized by humane treatment of children. Talented persons dedi-

[11] See E. E. Snyder, "Weaknesses of Public Education, A Social Point of View," *Journal of Educational Sociology,* Vol. 34 (October, 1960), pp. 91–93; S. M. McMurrin, "Real Weakness in American Schools," *U.S. News and World Report,* Vol. 51 (August 28, 1961), pp. 58–60.

cate their lives to the care of children and they render inestimable comfort and kindness to sustain and enrich children's lives through such dedication. The care and treatment of children, however important, will not be the point of view adopted in this book.

The Sociological Approach

The approach utilized in this book is basically *sociological.* In the context of the study of childhood, children will be studied *as persons being introduced to and interacting within social systems.* By virtue of their birth to members of a specific human society, children are viewed as being gradually brought into contact with social structures and made increasingly aware of how these social structures function. Human infants are regarded as creatures who are treated in such a manner that they will eventually fit well into social schemes laboriously developed by their predecessors. Their survival and the survival of their group are dependent upon how well they can become integral parts of a particular human society. Their society looks at children as the means to perpetuate itself against all internal and external threats. In turn, children are sustained and can be future-oriented to the extent that they participate in the ways of adults.

The central concept in the sociological approach to childhood is the process of *socialization.* A synonym for this process may well be *acculturation* because this term implies that children acquire the culture of the human groupings in which they find themselves. Children are not viewed as individuals fully equipped to participate in a complex adult world, but as beings who have the potentials for being slowly brought into contact with human ways.

Sociologists and students of sociology are just as capable of assuming too much for their discipline as are other specialists or students of specialties. In a recent thought-provoking article, Dennis Wrong[12] cautions sociologists and their followers that they should guard against an overzealous dedication to the efficacy of the socialization process. While no pun is deliberately sought, we cannot resist agreeing that Wrong is essentially right. He points out that man is a social animal without being entirely socialized. He writes:

'Socialization' may mean two quite distinct things; when they are confused an over-socialized view of man is the result. On the one hand socialization means the transmission of the culture; the particular culture of the society an individual enters at birth; on the other hand the term is used to mean the 'process of becoming human,' of acquiring uniquely human attributes from interaction with others. All men are socialized in the latter sense; but this does

---

[12] Dennis H. Wrong, "The Oversocialized Conception of Man," *American Sociological Review,* Vol. 26, No. 2 (April, 1961), pp. 183–193.

not mean that they have been completely molded by the particular norms and values of their culture.[13]

We shall keep this legitimate criticism in mind and shall present socialization as subject to certain limitations which will be discussed in ensuing chapters.

Sociologic inquiry focuses upon the human group or human groupings. Consequently, sociologic study of children will examine closely the means by which children become members of human groups. Any and all groups that impinge upon children form the substance of the sociologic diet. Initially, children are confined to their immediate families. In time, however, there is an intricate network of groups through which children pass. Each group through which children pass tends to leave its imprint upon them until they emerge as participant adults in their own society. Finally, with technological knowledge accelerated, the barriers of time and distance are diminished and children will predictably be brought into contact with a variety of societies and their variant cultures. All these group contacts will be examined in the materials that lie ahead.

Within every society, there are common or universal situations such as the phenomena of birth, marriage, death, sexual roles, aging, and a multitude of other conditions that are derived from human interaction. The manner in which each of these situations is defined provides each society with its particular unique quality. While much of the sociologic study of children that follows will have reference to the American society, there will be a deliberate effort to lift the discussion out of a strictly American context and to try to deal with the infinite variety of children and definitions of children which are found in the societies of the world. By this procedure, it is hoped that sociologists and students of sociology will broaden their perspective to include the entire human family and not narrow it to a single society or a single referent group.

SUMMARY

The following chapter, "The Sociology of Childhood," will more fully develop the general ideas contained in this initial presentation of the approach adopted in this text. It should be clear, at this juncture, that the student needs to be aware of the many possible approaches to the study of childhood. These have been identified as being historical, developmental, psychological, educational, therapeutic, and sociological. The merits of each approach were briefly suggested and, where applicable, observations were made about certain problems that were associated with a particular approach.

Data derived from different approaches will be utilized to some extent

[13] *Ibid.*, p. 192.

throughout the body of this text to illustrate or illuminate certain points. There may be times when the various approaches may yield conflicting information and these, too, will be noted. By deliberate choice the sociological approach to the study of childhood will be the frame of reference employed. The contributions resulting from this approach will be noted, but appropriate criticisms or cautions will also be included to avoid undue sociologic bias. By persisting in the sociological approach, the anticipated result should be a more complete and objective understanding of children's efforts to become full participants in human societies.

READINGS

BECK, Lester, *Human Growth* (New York, Harcourt, Brace & World., Inc., 1949).

BOSSARD, J. H. S. and BOLL, Eleanor, *The Sociology of Child Development,* 3rd ed. (New York, Harper & Row, Publishers, Inc., 1960).

BRIM, Orville, *Education for Child Rearing* (New York, Russell Sage Foundation, 1959).

COOLEY, Charles H., *Human Nature and the Social Order* (New York, Charles Scribner's Sons, 1902).

DAVIS, A. and HAVIGHURST, Robert, *Father of the Man* (Boston, Houghton Mifflin Company, 1947).

HURLOCK, Elizabeth, *Child Growth and Development* 2nd ed. (New York, McGraw-Hill Book Company, Inc., 1956).

POLLAK, Otto, "Relationships Between Social Science and Child Guidance Practice," *American Sociological Review,* Vol. 16 (February, 1951), pp. 61–67.

STRAUSS, A. and SCHUESSLER, K., "Socialization, Logical Reasoning, and Concept Development in the Child," *American Sociological Review,* Vol. 16 (August, 1951), pp. 514–523.

THOMAS, W. I. and THOMAS, Dorothy S., *The Child in America* (New York, Alfred A. Knopf, Inc., 1928).

2

The Sociology of Childhood

INTRODUCTION

In broad terms, the sociology of childhood refers to the systematic application of the knowledge, concepts, methods, and techniques of sociology to the study of children. In approaching this objective, special attention will be directed to socialization, the process whereby children become participating members of the societies into which they are born. At the same time, the relevant structural, functional, interactional, and cultural aspects of these societies will be analyzed.

In the remainder of this chapter, an *overall* description of the more important perspectives of the sociology of childhood is presented. The intent is to call attention to those aspects of child development and behavior which are more significantly related to the social and cultural context in which childhood is experienced. In the main, these perspectives are

1. Childhood as a significant phase of society
2. Variations in the social definitions of childhood
3. Socialization as process, practice, and structure
4. Child-centered, child-oriented, and child-dominated systems
5. Children and near-age siblings
6. Children and other age-level categories
7. Adolescence as threshold and transition to adulthood

CHILDHOOD AS A SIGNIFICANT PHASE OF SOCIETY

In every known human society, biological variations related to sex and age are to some extent incorporated into the social structure. That is to say that the statuses and the corresponding roles of the members of the

14

society are based largely upon the participating person's sex and age. Although such differentiations need not rest entirely upon maleness or femaleness, the distinctiveness of the sexes along with socially formulated rationales tend to constitute sufficient justification for such status differentiations.

In like manner, age is a basis for the allocation of statuses. Unlike sex, the person's age is not a constant, therefore, societies provide a series of age-connected statuses into which the person moves as he progresses from one age-level to the next. But as in the case of sex-connected statuses, the statuses occupied by persons of a particular age level need not be directly dependent upon attributes of the person which are inherent in his age. To illustrate, the sixteen-year-old may be capable of self-support, self-determination, marriage, and parenthood; yet, he may be required to continue occupying the status of the adolescent.

Implicit in the above example is that in utilizing age (and sex) as a basis for the ascription of statuses, certain age-based limitations are imputed to the person and then reified by the society. Thus, limitations which are said to exist because of age sometimes exist not because of inherent incapacity but because of the lack of social recognition or because of the failure of the society to permit or stimulate development along certain lines. Often, the result of this is that the sixteen-year-old has limited abilities for self-support, self-determination, marriage, and parenthood only because he has had no chance to develop these abilities.[1]

This tendency of societies to recognize limitations which are, at times, the result of societal definition rather than of biological inadequacy, is not completely representative of the distorted definitions of the individual sometimes made by societies. In some instances, persons are assigned tasks or given roles that are at variance with their biological or age potentials. But whether ascribed statuses are consistent with biological potentials or not, societies are faced with the necessity of dealing with the consequences. An extreme case of imputing and reifing "inability" is reflected in the social definition of adolescence. Generally, the maturities of adolescents are inhibited and the imposed inhibitions become the source of personal and social problems. This is rather specifically illustrated in marriage laws which hold, in effect, that sixteen-year-olds are "not ready" for marriage. In such a case, the girl is certainly capable of reproduction, yet she is likely to be "not ready" for marriage only because she has not been prepared psychologically and socially for it.[2] Clearly, then, the biological nature or, more specifically, the physical development of the person is less important in the ascription, or achieve-

[1] For an excellent and classic discussion of status and role see Ralph Linton, *The Study of Man* (New York, Appleton-Century-Crofts, 1936), pp. 113–131.
[2] See "The Self-Fulfilling Prophecy," in Robert K. Merton, *Social Theory and Social Structure* (New York, The Free Press of Glencoe, 1949), Chapter XII.

ment, of statuses, than is the person's actual social development; i.e., his real knowledge and skills. On the other hand, the biological nature or immaturities of the individual set certain limits which cannot be exceeded regardless of demands by society.

Status and role ascription based on age is a worldwide practice. In every society there are at least three age-related statuses: childhood, adulthood, and old age.[3] Many societies, however, subdivide these into many more age levels. In the United States, there are five generally recognized age-level statuses; they are infancy, childhood, adolescence, adulthood, and old age. The first two, infancy and childhood, are the principal concern throughout this book.

In the United States, the term "child" often refers to both infants and children. At times—in the law, for example—it also includes persons under twenty-one years of age. Not uncommonly, children are referred to as toddlers, pre-school children, teenagers, and youth. For present purposes and unless otherwise noted, child, children, and childhood will refer principally to infants and to children under twelve years old.

Childhood, as a structural component of society, constitutes one of several age-level statuses. It involves patterns of values, attitudes, norms, and behavior that govern social relations among children as well as those between children and persons in other age-level statuses. Although these are patterns of childhood, they are nonetheless important to others. For since all persons are first introduced to the patterns of childhood, they retain their familiarity with many of those patterns. Otherwise, they could not transmit the appropriate aspects of the culture to succeeding generations of children. When, therefore, the present generation of children become adults, their earlier acquaintance with child culture will enable them to pass it on to other children.

The activities of children, especially infants, are kept highly selective and limited. But these limitations are not permanent; for as children approach adult maturity their activities are progressively expanded. These changes do not occur automatically, however; they are socially stimulated and directed. Essentially, this movement is a partial reflection of Benedict's "cycle of growth from infancy to maturity"; it is the socialization process.

Functionally viewed, socialization is more than child-rearing or growing up. Its primary function is indispensable to the continuity of society. For since a society is, by definition, a continuing entity which spans generations; and since the persons constituting a society live but a very brief time, it is imperative that these units of society shall be continually replaced. In this replacement process, both reproduction and socialization are necessary. The first results in individuals with the potential to adapt to the culture of any society; the second determines the specific

[3] Linton, *op. cit.*, p. 118.

culture to which they adapt. Hence, the sociological significance of this latter process.

Through socialization, the individual acquires the values, attitudes, norms, knowledge, and skills appropriate to his status and role. The nature of these status-role components will, of course, change as he meets the relevant criteria of his society, such as age or occupation. However, since the status-role components of a society are structurally and functionally interrelated, he must acquire a familiarity with statuses and roles other than his own. Otherwise, reciprocity, an essential attribute of the status-role concept, could not occur and effective interaction would be precluded. It follows that when the child is behaving strictly within the bounds prescribed by his role, he is at the same time acting in terms of another role which is not yet available to him. Frequently, such situations constitute preparation for the performance of roles which will be ascribed to him in the future.

Variations in the Social Definitions of Childhood

Infants are much the same the world over. They are completely dependent upon others for care and protection. Before they can begin to learn to care for themselves or to behave in distinctly human ways, they must experience a degree of physical maturation. In the final analysis, however, and within biologically imposed limits, the society determines the degree of maturation necessary for social learning. Basically, this fact underlies the wide variations in the roles of the children of the world.

As infants pass beyond the stage of infancy into childhood, their potentials come to be expressed in differences which are mainly of a cultural order. Despite this "learning to be different," the biological forces inherent in the human organism contribute toward a continuing degree of similarity in young children. For example, children of five or six, regardless of their society, must still depend largely upon others for their physical well-being.

Whatever the degree of sameness among children, the fact remains that historically their statuses have not been universally the same. There is apparently no considerable body of literature on the history of childhood. Yet, the wide divergences in the statuses accorded children can be inferred from descriptive accounts of the cultures of various peoples.

Although there are wide gaps in our knowledge about the life of children in past ages, there is information on certain specific points that is helpful in our efforts to gain a historical perspective for our modern studies. One such specific topic is the status of childhood, by which is meant the position of children in relation to their parents and the larger social group of which they are a part. Possibly it is because the question of their status, rather than the children themselves, touched the interests of their elders that relatively more information is available on this subject.[4]

Childhood Among Primitives

Historical and anthropological accounts of primitive peoples clearly indicate that children often occupied statuses significantly different from the statuses of children in most modern societies. The social significance of children among some primitives is suggested by their attitudes either toward the children or toward parenthood. "A carefree childhood is generally the lot of Toda children. Parents tend to be indulgent, exhibiting great fondness for their offspring."[5] In contrast to the Toda, "in some Madagascar tribes children not only begin to work at an incredibly early age but also enjoy full property rights."[6]

On the whole, primitives seem to have placed a high value on children. Apart from their emotional attachments to their offspring, there were perhaps other considerations involved. Among these, a sense of dignity and pride in parenthood, children's contributions to the day-to-day family life, and the prospect of security in old age were distinct possibilities.

This positive reaction to children on the part of primitives was apparently not limited to parents and their children. A considerable non-parental interest in children is suggested by the fact that "primitive folk are constantly adopting children and lavish upon them as much emotion as upon their own issue."[7] Perhaps the members of the community recognized that children performed an important social function. For in the absence of the written word, they were the only future or potential carriers of the culture.

A final indication of how primitive children were regarded is implied in the treatment accorded the erring ones. Generally, adult reactions to such children were marked by tolerance, even patience. Regarding this, Lowie reports that "there is rarely any form of corporal punishment; in many tribes never."[8] To be sure, there were instances of harsher treatment, of disinterest, and even of rather complete rejection, but these seem not to have been at all representative. It is also true that abortion, infanticide, and child labor were not totally non-existent; yet, these too were uncommon. What is more, it is highly probable that such reactions were not indications of negativism toward children; rather, they were perhaps dictated by certain needs of the group as they saw them.

[4] James H. S. Bossard and Eleanor Stoker Boll, *The Sociology of Child Development*, 3rd ed. (New York, Harper & Row, Publishers, Inc., 1960), p. 585.
[5] Stuart A. Queen, Robert W. Habenstein, and John B. Adams, *The Family in Various Cultures* (Philadelphia, J. B. Lippincott Co., 1961), p. 32.
[6] Linton, *op. cit.*, p. 474.
[7] Robert H. Lowie, *Are We Civilized?* (New York, Harcourt, Brace and Company, 1939), p. 136.
[8] *Ibid.*, p. 138.

It seems that the importance of childhood in primitive societies was determined by societal considerations. On the whole, children were not regarded as important, in and of themselves. The rights and privileges which they enjoyed in no way interfered with the prior rights and privileges of their elders. Thus, they tended to be submissive without being servile, and subordinate without being slavish. Despite their subordinate status, however, theirs was not a harsh nor a difficult social life.

Childhood in Early Civilizations

The social definitions of childhood in early civilizations such as China, India, Egypt, Greece, and Rome varied widely. Yet in the history of these peoples some common reactions toward children are discernible.

On the whole, children were desired and the new-born was a welcome addition to the household. But, as in the case of primitive societies, the ancients looked upon children as potential contributers to the common good. They were expected to make their contributions to family subsistence, and later to care for their parents during their years of decline. Until such time as they could become productively employed, children were under continuing, complete, and rigorous parental control.

In Greece and Rome, for example, children had almost no rights save those bestowed upon them by their fathers. "While, generally speaking, fathers loved their children and did not desire to kill them or sell them or rule them in an arbitrary or selfish way, they had the right to do so and the state enforced this right instead of interceding in behalf of the child."[9] This absolute authority of the Roman father over his child continued even after the offspring reached his majority. Thus, the father had the right to choose a marriage partner for his son or daughter. Under Roman law the father's right to this complete control ended only upon his loss of Roman citizenship or with his death. Although in public life the adult son of a Roman citizen-father exercised the rights of any other citizen; in his father's house he was no longer his own master. "Neither age, nor rank, nor the consular office, nor the honors of a triumph, could exempt the most illustrious citizen from the bonds of filial subjection."[10]

Infanticide, child abandonment, and child selling were widely practiced in early civilizations. The first of these, infanticide, was principally a device for population control. To some extent, it was also an eugenic measure. For example, the Twelve Tables of Rome forbade the rearing of a deformed child.

Although abandonment was a modified form of infanticide, it was far less direct or certain in its effects than were drowning and suffocation,

[9] Grace Abbott, *The Child and the State*, Vol. 1 (Chicago, University of Chicago Press, 1938), p. 3.

[10] Edward Gibbon, *The Decline and Fall of the Roman Empire*, Vol. 4 (New York, The Macmillan Company, 1938), p. 473.

which were widely used. To some, the use of abandonment as a form of infanticide was regarded as a progressive change because of the possibility that at least some of the children who were abandoned would not die. As a matter of fact, these children were often found before they died and were cared for and "adopted" by those who found them.

Child selling was another common practice among the peoples of early civilizations. "The sale of children early attained extensive proportions in the orient. Both Chinese and Japanese reports bear witness to its prevalence and to efforts to suppress it." [11] Aside from the transfer of children along with the sale of their slave parents, children were often sold in order to satisfy creditors' claims upon their parents. In addition, the selling of children was facilitated by the productivity of child labor.

From this brief outline it would appear that in early civilizations, no less than in primitive societies, the status of children was one of submissiveness. Furthermore, in early civilizations, even among primitives, children were compelled to fit into the existing order ultimately for the benefit of their adult superiors. When these two types of societies are compared, however, the preponderance of generosity and affection for children as children, seems to have rested with the primitives rather than the early civilizations.

Childhood in Europe and America

The medieval world of Europe derived much of its culture, including the definitions of childhood, from the early civilizations, especially Greece and Rome. In like manner, the peoples of modern western society, including America, have patterned their thinking and behavior regarding children after those of early European life. Thus, when one views the broad span of the history of the western world certain attitudes and practices toward children can be seen to have existed, with minor variations, throughout long periods of time.

The definition of childhood in medieval Europe was much the same as in ancient societies. The notion that "children are to be seen, not heard" was not only widely prevalent in medieval Europe; it was rigidly insisted upon. As a general rule, children, by necessity, reached social maturity at an early age. Those who lived among the masses were frequently forced to shift for themselves with little hope of solicitude or aid from those in the higher levels of society. Thus it was that hundreds, even thousands of children existed with a bare minimum of the necessities of life. As the life patterns of these societies changed, the depressing circumstances under which children existed apparently changed for the worse.

Medieval definitions of childhood seem not to have gotten better until

11 James H. S. Bossard and Eleanor Stoker Boll, *op. cit.*, p. 593.

well into modern times. This situation is to be seen in the writings of social critics and reformers such as John Howard, perhaps the greatest of the penal reformers; Elizabeth Fry, the famous English lay prison visitor; and Charles Dickens, famous novelist-social historian of childhood in England. In nineteenth century England,

boys and girls, naked to the waist, worked in the coal mines thirteen hours a day pulling loads of coal. At first only pauper children were 'apprenticed' to the factory owners by the overseers of the poor who wanted to get rid of the burden of supporting them; as the need for labor increased, non-pauper children were employed, their only wages being food and clothes of the coarsest kind. These children, some only five or six years old, were obliged to live in dormitories near the factory, where they were treated like slaves.[12]

Conditions such as these provided social reformers with a powerful weapon with which to attack the imperfections of the existing social order. Through the protest writings of these reformers, many persons became interested in the plight of underprivileged children and remedial programs began to be inaugurated in many areas. In England, some of the earliest organizations and prominent persons in this movement were, The Marine Society, founded in 1756; also Elizabeth Fry, Quaker reformer; Matthew Davenport Hill, Recorder of the City of Birmingham; and Mary Carpenter, Superintendent of Red Lodge Reformatory for Women. In Switzerland, there was Johann Heinrich Wichern; and in France, Frederic Auguste Demetz, all of whom were actively engaged in reducing the harshness with which children, both offenders and non-offenders, frequently were treated.[13] To a considerable extent this was the social heritage of countless numbers of children who lived in Europe at the beginning of and well into modern times. But the protest writings of such social reformers contributed to an interest in the plight of underprivileged youngsters. More than this, it was people such as these who initiated programs designed to improve the life conditions of these dependent and neglected children.

Childhood in America

From the standpoint of the present status of childhood in much of the modern world, and especially in the United States, the social changes wrought through the efforts of early social reformers loom large. Although their expressed interests were mainly in the problem children of their day, the impetus and momentum which these reformers gave to the re-

[12] J. Salwyn Schapiro, *Modern and Contemporary European History* (Boston, Houghton Mifflin Company, 1946), p. 119.
[13] See Negley K. Teeters and John Otto Reinemann, *The Challenge of Delinquency* (Englewood Cliffs, N.J., Prentice Hall, Inc., 1950).

definition of childhood have carried over and have been enlarged upon in the present-day world.

Perhaps the best example of this enlarged—and enriched—definition of childhood is to be found in the United States. Historically, in the colonies and during the early years of the Union, children were largely a depressed category. As in Europe at that time, many children were dependent, neglected, and even abandoned. Sometimes the penalty for those who deviated too far from community norms was flogging, imprisonment, or hard labor. Indenture was often forced on them and on those unfortunate enough to be bereft of parental guidance and/or support.[14]

The reforms being instituted in Europe about this time had their counterparts in the United States. Increasingly during the latter part of the seventeenth century, programs and agencies were being organized to deal with the numerous problems which beset the children of that time. Prominent among these developments were the adoption of more liberal policies regarding the treatment of child offenders, and later, the establishment of separate facilities for the differential handling of delinquent and neglected or orphaned children.

Gradually, the concern for the welfare of problem children expanded until reformers and philanthropists were no longer alone in their efforts to improve the life chances of these unfortunates. Little by little, and one after another, individual states made provisions for child care and protection. A notable example of this development was the convergence of an emerging humanitarianism, a broader application of the concept of the rights of man, and new treatment practices, such as probation, parole, and a previously non-existing socio-legal mechanism called the juvenile court.[15] This court, which was established in Chicago, Illinois in 1899, was a clear manifestation of the community's acceptance of its responsibility for the welfare of children, who, in many instances through no fault of their own, were faced with difficulties against which they and their parents could not successfully contend.

Although the juvenile court was part and parcel of the legal machinery, its policies, methods, and techniques were not confined to the traditional rules and practices of law. Rather, a central component of the new court was its adoption of the concept of *parens patriae*. In essence, the adoption of this concept imposed upon the state—through its juvenile court— the responsibility of ultimate parenthood. To some extent, then, the state, through the court, was to be "father to the child." To meet this responsibility, non-legal techniques and methods were required. These were

[14] Harry Elmer Barnes and Negley K. Teeters, *New Horizons in Criminology* (Englewood Cliffs, N.J., Prentice-Hall, Inc., 1943), p. 899.

[15] There are numerous accounts of the founding of the juvenile court; see Negley K. Teeters and John Otto Reinemann, *op. cit.*

sought and found in the newly developing profession of social work.[16]

The utilization of social work practices in connection with children under the jurisdiction of the juvenile court did much to improve the life-chances of certain categories of children. The results of this joint juvenile court social work effort were much more far reaching. For as a profession based upon scientifically derived knowledge, it was not enough that social workers were involved with problem children; they recognized that a non-problem child might well become a problem child. Thus, they turned their attention to the accumulation and the development of techniques applicable to both problem and non-problem children.

To a considerable extent this expanding body of knowledge which was being utilized by social workers was the result of the research efforts of social scientists, especially in psychology, anthropology, and sociology. Because of this, it may be said that these disciplines were involved in and made some contributions to the expanding interest in problem children such as that manifested by the juvenile court. Of course the impact of the social sciences was not confined to the problem areas of childhood, rather, research activities in the social sciences were directed toward the broader area of human social behavior.

Increasingly, as new knowledge and insights were derived through the social sciences, it became apparent that man could, in large measure, control his own destiny. It became apparent also that not only was social change inevitable and continuing, but that such change could be directed. As social scientists understood more clearly the continuities involved in the life span of the individual, the concept of "the child being father to the man" gained greater ascendancy, and the role of the child in societal continuity was more clearly understood and appreciated.

Meanwhile, certain basic values, such as the rights of the individual, and the dignity of the human personality, were being increasingly extended to all persons, including children. This trend toward a more general and liberal interpretation of these values was largely the result of a long developing humanitarianism coupled with the growth and communication of scientific knowledge of human nature and social life. The net result of this trend has been a re-definition of childhood which places children in a position in which they are highly valued, protected, cared for, and guaranteed full opportunity for physical, emotional, intellectual, and social development.

In contrast to the definitions of earlier societies the definitions of childhood in modern societies, especially the United States, represents a rather successful attempt to bridge the wide gulf which historically separated children from certain fundamental societal rights, privileges, and opportunities which tended to be available to their elders. The bridging of this

[16] *Ibid.*

gulf, which came only after a long and difficult struggle on the part of humanitarians, philanthropists, professionals, and scientists, is well illustrated in the formal declaration of the rights of childhood so eloquently expressed by the conferees at the Mid-century White House Conference on Children and Youth in December, 1950, at Washington, D.C.

Out of this conference came a pledge regarding the rights of childhood. This pledge is an expression of consensus regarding the recognition and implementation of these rights. That the framers of this "bill of rights" recognized and accepted the concept of "the child being father to the man" is well implied in their promise that "as you grow from child to youth to adult, establishing a family life of your own and accepting larger social responsibilities, we will work with you to improve conditions for all children and youth." [17]

SOCIALIZATION AS PROCESS, PRACTICE, AND STRUCTURE

Ideally, the socialization process in the United States involves the implementation of an implicit "bill of rights" for children. It provides care and protection, health and security and full opportunity and encouragement for the creative development of every child as he grows toward adult maturity.

Socialization is the process whereby the neonate is fitted progressively into various social systems within the society in which he lives. The particular systems into which a given individual is introduced through this process will, of course, depend upon a number of considerations such as age, sex, social class, personal attributes, and special social demands. Thus viewed, socialization is a life-long process, involving Benedict's "cycle of growth from infancy to adulthood" (see p. 16). As already indicated, the time dimension of the socialization process is, for present purposes, less than the entire "cycle of growth." Rather, socialization is viewed principally as the period of childhood, up to but not including adulthood.

The socialization process is carried on in accordance with accepted theories of the nature of the human organism, the nature of human nature, as well as certain theories of learning. This is not to say that socializers —parents for example—are necessarily knowledgeable regarding these theories. Nonetheless, the socializers utilize their relevant beliefs, impressions and expectations, some of which during recent times may be somewhat derived from the experts. In effect, socialization tends to proceed in accordance with certain broad theories and through the utilization of conventional methods and techniques of child rearing.

[17] Hazel Fredericksen, *The Child and His Welfare* (San Francisco, W. H. Freeman & Co., Publishers, 1957), p. 352.

Frequently, in discussions of the socialization process, social and cultural factors are emphasized to the relative exclusion of physical, physiological, and psychic forces. In this text social and cultural factors are given prime consideration, however, this should not be construed as rejection of the importance of non-social and non-cultural factors.

The importance of non-social and non-cultural factors in the socialization of the person has not been overlooked by social scientists.

The human being develops through the *interplay* of three sets of influences which impinge upon him—*his inherited organism and all of its functions* (Authors' italics), the culture which he contacts, and the unique personal experiences he undergoes. It cannot be stressed too emphatically that both the culture and *the original nature* (Authors' italics) are significant for human behavior as *reservoirs of potentials* and *not as behavior per se.*" [18] . . . the individual, his needs and potentialities, lies at the foundation of all social and cultural phenomena. . . . It may be assumed that it is the needs of the individual which provide the motivations for his behavior and which are, through this, responsible for the operation of society and culture.[19]

Careful examination of the socialization of the child will reveal that, like other social behavior, child-rearing practices tend to follow certain predictable patterns. For example, middle-class mothers in the United States tend to rear their children in accordance with certain characteristic techniques, methods, and principles. These practices may be regarded as facilitating devices in socialization. Whether or not their effects are positive or negative depends upon what particular techniques, methods and principles are utilized and how they are utilized. If, for example, toilet training is begun too early, say at nine months, and harsh and threatening measures are employed, learning is likely to be retarded and psychological damage might result.[20]

More often than not, socialization is viewed as process. However, it is possible and profitable to view it as structure. Ultimately, the *process* of socialization necessarily requires initiating, directing, and facilitating agents or agencies. In addition, it requires the employment of skills, techniques, methods, and materials. Finally, all of these are combined or systematized into the structures in which and through which the process of socialization is carried on.

[18] *Sociology, A Synopsis of Principles,* 4th ed., by John F. Cuber. Copyright © 1959, Appleton-Century-Crofts, Inc. Reprinted by permission of Appleton-Century-Crofts. p. 165. For a discussion of the need for sociologists to give greater attention to non-social and non-cultural factors in socialization, see Dennis H. Wrong, "The Oversocialized Conception of Man in Modern Sociology," *American Sociological Review,* Vol. 26, No. 2 (April, 1961), pp. 187–193.

[19] *The Cultural Background of Personality* by Ralph Linton. Copyright © 1945, D. Appleton-Century Company, Inc., pp. 5–6. Reprinted by permission of Appleton-Century-Crofts.

[20] See W. Allison Davis and Robert J. Havighurst, *Father of the Man* (Boston, Houghton Mifflin Company, 1947), especially pp. 97–106.

Once some socialization has taken place, the problem of further socialization becomes one of providing a structure that motivates people to give up or modify their old definitions and accept new ones. . . . The assumption underlying this focus is that, holding individual psychology constant, effective socialization may be facilitated or impeded by the structure of the socialization situation.[21]

The significance of the structural dimension of socialization is well pointed up in the transitional adjustment experiences of the child who moves to a new neighborhood, joins an organized group for the first time, or enrolls in school as a new student. In any one of these situations, the ease and rate of the child's adjustment might depend, among other things, on the nature of the formal structure, the informal structure, the status system, status mobility, and systems of incentives and rewards.

CHILD-CENTERED, CHILD-ORIENTED, AND CHILD-DOMINATED SYSTEMS

The structure of socialization can be profitably examined by placing the social systems involving children on a continuum. If this continuum of systems is viewed in terms of the organizers, the participants, and the source of direction, three ideal-type children's social systems emerge. They may be defined as "child-centered systems," "child-oriented systems," and "child-dominated systems."

Child-centered systems are adult-designed. Although adults are participants, it is the child who is the center of attention and concern. In this system, more than in any other, the child's total personality is involved. However, because adults provide these systems for the promotion of the child's best interest, they maintain continuing supervision and control within them. Among these systems, the family, and the nursery school are prime examples.

Closely allied with, but in some respects divergent from, the child-centered systems are collectivities such as the play groups of younger children and some peer groupings among children of elementary school age. Generally, adults supervise these groups only indirectly; and while the children themselves are the creators of these systems, their characteristics and composition are largely determined by adult inspired circumstances.

Child-oriented social systems are formal organizations in which children are the principal participants; or they are general systems which make special provisions for the participation or the servicing of children. These are adult-created, adult-sponsored, and adult-controlled systems.

---

[21] Harry C. Bredemeir and Richard M. Stephenson, *The Analysis of Social Systems* (New York, Holt, Rinehart and Winston, Inc., 1962), pp. 91–92.

Unlike the child-centered systems, children join or are otherwise formally inducted into or served by these systems. In addition, the nature of these systems is such that individual spontaneity, creativity, interests, and behavior of the child participants are channeled principally toward adult-defined ends. Some examples of these systems are the school, the scouts, and the Junior Achievement groups. Non-child specialty systems such as the church, the library, and certain welfare organizations are also included.

As is to be expected, child-dominated social systems involve older children. Except for the impact of the normative system and, where applicable, the intermittent attempts at intervention by adult sponsors, children dominate these systems. They organize, utilize, and control them. As a result of participation in these structures, children are relatively free to make their own decisions, pursue their own interests, and thereby venture alone into areas not yet known by them. The best example of this type of children's social system is the boys' gang. Other examples which are to some extent extensions of these systems, are adolescent cliques and college fraternities.

These social structures exert varying degrees of impact upon children and are among the principal agencies of socialization. Added importance is given to them because they often tend to be the initial social situations in which children are involved. The significance of such structures is that children's participation in them is not an end in itself, but rather a facilitating experience for induction and integration into other and more general structures in the social system.

It is important, therefore, that a rather thorough examination of the nature and operation of these structures should be undertaken. From such an examination one may expect to receive greater insight and understanding concerning the character of the socialization process and its implications for those who socialize as well as those who are socialized.

Certain other results which can be expected to accrue from the study of these organizations are important also. Not the least of these is an increased understanding of the characteristic adult-child interaction patterns which are of the essence in some of these structures. Moreover, when these patterns are viewed longitudinally, the course of change can be discerned more clearly and the forces which facilitate such change can be isolated somewhat more easily and precisely. Finally, insights such as these can contribute to the prediction of probable future change in the socialization process and in the structures that facilitate that process. In following the approach outlined here, the derived knowledge and insights regarding the entire range of socialization, including the processual and structural aspects, should broaden the student's knowledge and increase his understanding of other social and cultural phenomena.

CHILDREN AND NEAR-AGE SIBLINGS

No two children are born into the same family; perhaps not even twins. The first-born enters a family system comprised of two interacting persons. The second child enters a system comprised of three, and so on. Thus, the contacts and relationships of siblings within a family become progressively more numerous and complex with each succeeding child.

Obviously, however, siblings of approximately the same age are exposed to many common experiences. They share the same parents, the same home, and ideally, the same advantages and opportunities. Yet, there are instances in which one child might be given preferential treatment by parents. Such treatment may be based on the child's age—he's the oldest child, or the "baby"—or it may be due to an unconscious preference of the parents or a parent. Conceivably, the preferential treatment of a child may be a figment of a sibling's imagination.

Children of the same family may gain security from their relationship. They can learn from each other. In their play and other collective activity they have opportunities to cooperate and apply the rules of competition. Often, they provide mutual protection against outsiders and not uncommonly they conspire against their own parents. However, closeness or cooperativeness is not the whole story of sibling relations. With the coming of a new child into a family the next older one has to make certain adjustments. The former baby must relinquish, at least to some extent, his position of preference. The child who thus loses his status as "the baby" might react in any one of a number of ways, including neurosis, bottle sucking, or physical aggression which is veiled as affection toward the new baby.[22] Regardless of the exact nature of the sibling relationship it is a significant experience in the personal development and social adjustment of the child. Generally, this relationship is not one which involves continuous cooperation and accord, nor is it likely always to be dominated by disageement and conflict. Instead, sibling relationships, like any other human relationship, are likely to involve a complex of discord, accommodation, and accord. Perhaps the extent to which any of these exist is related to variables such as family situation, sex, age, order of birth, and personality.

CHILDREN AND OTHER AGE-LEVEL CATEGORIES

Earlier, some brief references were made to social differentiation based on age. It was pointed out that childhood as an age-level status involves a series of behavior patterns which standardize and regulate interaction

[22] D. M. Levy, "Studies in Sibling Rivalry," *Research Monographs of the American Orthopsychiatric Association,* No. 2, p. 397.

between children and persons in other age-level statuses (see p. 15). These behavior patterns are socially designed and approved pathways of interactions. They set the boundaries within which children are expected to give expression to their needs and interests. They are, ideally, manifestations of the legitimate status and role of childhood.

It should be emphasized that roles always involve reciprocity. That is to say, in a given childhood role the socially expected behavior is always predicated by a socially expected reaction consistent with the role of the person toward whom the child is behaving. In like manner, the same expected reciprocity prevails when the interaction is initiated by the latter. This means that children must learn not only the expectations involved in their statuses and roles, but also the expectations associated with the statuses and roles of persons in the other age-level categories with whom they interact.

Essentially, these role expectations of children relate to the rights and duties ascribed to them because of their particular status: childhood. It is inevitable, however, that they will not occupy the status of childhood permanently. This means that they must progressively adapt themselves to the different expectations or requirements of a series of roles, including adolescence, adulthood, and old age. Meanwhile, they learn and play the role of childhood, and they learn, to some extent, the other age-level roles. This knowledge of other roles is essential to the successful performance of their own childhood role. Furthermore this acquaintance with the roles of other age-level categories facilitates the bridging of the gap between childhood and the succeeding age-level status.

Although the role of childhood contains a bridge over which children may pass on to the next age-level status, barriers are also involved. Thus, mainly because of their knowledge of other statuses, children may have certain interests and self-defined needs which they are not permitted to satisfy. Here lies the potential for conflict. This conflict may be generational—between children and adults—and thus lead to one type or set of results. Or it can prevail between children and those who occupy the next age-level status; in this event, another type or set of consequences will probably follow. Regardless of whether adults or adolescents are parties to the conflict the results are likely to have appreciable significance, especially for the children involved.

The relationships between children and those in other age-level statuses involve interaction which runs the gamut of the social processes. For example, there may be competition for attention or affection, or there may be cooperation in the pursuit of commonly sought-after goals. Whatever form this interaction might take, the results often have far-reaching implications for the parties involved. Moreover, the results sometimes relate to those not directly involved in the situation. For example, parents sometimes become involved in disputes between their respective children. Or again, parents sometimes make invidious comparisons of the results of their respective children's competitive efforts. For these reasons, a close examination of such interactional patterns can be most instructive.

In examining the relationships and consequent interaction between children and persons in other age-level statuses, the following sets of relationships have been selected: children-parents, children-adult non-family authority figures, children-adolescent siblings, and children-adolescent non-siblings. This proposed examination of these relationships can serve a variety of purposes. It can result in greater comprehension of the relationships that bind children to persons in the various age-level statuses. It can lead to a deeper appreciation of the reciprocal impact inherent in the interaction which these relationships imply. It can contribute to a clearer understanding of the socialization process. Finally, it can provide a clearer perspective regarding the final stages of childhood as a point of departure for a new and different status.

ADOLESCENCE: THRESHOLD AND TRANSITION TO ADULTHOOD

Several considerations warrant the inclusion of a discussion of adolescence in the sociology of childhood. In the first place, the status of adolescence is not clearly defined, however, it is noticeably different from that of adulthood. Adolescents are often expected to act responsibly, but on the other hand, are not given complete responsibility (as under the law, for example). They are in a period of transition from childhood to adulthood and intermittently show signs of both.

As the child grows toward adult maturity he reaches a point where physical changes become quite evident. These are changes in body size, contour, and coordination. They are accompanied by changes in physiological functioning. The impact of these changes and the child's reactions to them often lead to new and strange feelings and sensations. In addition, the responses which adults make to these developments sometimes lead to greater consciousness of them and sensitivity to them on the part of the child. These changes in the structure and functioning of the child's body, coupled with the reactions of self and others to them, constitute a new dimension in the life experience of the child.

Taken as a whole, these changes evidence the child's emerging power to procreate. They are the flowering of his sexual potential; they are the sign that he has reached the onset of puberty. Because of its nature and because of its definition by the child and others, the arrival at puberty tends toward separation; this is to say, the child is now less a child. In some societies, notably America, he continues to be less and less a child. This is true in the physical sense; but socially, he is still likely to be regarded as a child, even though he may be criticized when he acts like a child. This situation of being no longer a child but not yet an adult, plus the recurring conflicting definitions of what he is or should be, tends to develop in him an ambivalence toward self. Despite the uncertainties concerning what he is or should be and the expectations regarding his relations with others, he manages to fashion patterns for himself, or more likely, adapt to the patterns followed by those who share his predicament.

By the time children reach preadolescence, their social experiences and learning have been quite varied. Their dependence upon others is decreasing and their reliance upon themselves is correspondingly increasing. They are learning to adjust to changes in types and sources of authority. They are witnessing changes in the kinds and degrees of social subordination imposed upon them. They are being incorporated into a wide range of divergent social situations or structures. In a word, they are acquiring effective—though not always approved—skills for dealing with new social structures and cultural phenomena.

Eventually, children come to recognize and anticipate the new and, to them, more meaningful possibilities which the future holds. The exercise of increasing self-dependence has often given them great satisfaction, and they look forward to even greater satisfaction so derived. At the same time, these children come to recognize various authority figures to whom they must submit, and are progressively experiencing socially imposed or implied limitations upon the exercise of autonomy. Finally, they become more aware of the decreasing rigidity of the social subordination imposed on them.

Meanwhile, other aspects of self-development and new personal involvements are being experienced by these children. Their self-concepts are becoming more crystallized as the realization that they are growing up becomes evident. Their interests and activities are far from being family-, or even school-centered. New vistas are opening up to them. They are finding new and meaningful reference groups. Their chums, their gangs, and their clubs are relationships which are becoming increasingly absorbing and time-consuming. In these groups, children play, talk, and learn together. Together they entertain visions of things to come in the new status that awaits them.

Perhaps more than any other social structure, the gang symbolizes and facilitates this new departure in children's orientation. Apparently, this applies to boys much more than to girls. To some extent, however, girls at this stage of development do move away from strict parental or adult control and association, and at least in some social circles they form their own preadolescent and gang-like age groupings. At first this gang development tends to involve "twosomes"; later these twosomes interlock and form larger groupings which crystallize into relatively highly organized and rigidly structured gangs.

Out of these gang situations emerge consequences of great and frequently lasting import. First, the gang, by its very nature is a conflict-producing group. As a general rule, its members are continually at odds with various segments of adult society. They represent perhaps the most highly organized and successful effort directed toward the reduction and even elimination of adult control and supervision. Consequently, children who are being integrated into gang life are, at the same time, beginning the transition which leads ultimately to adult status.

Contrary to popular opinion all gangs cannot be legitimately defined as socially destructive or anti-social. Gang children can and do learn much that is personally and socially useful. The experiences of gang life afford its participants unique opportunities to become better acquainted with the requirements of new and future role components. Leadership, the ability to follow, and social skills, all of these are valuable lessons which are taught within the context of the gang. Finally, the arena or life-space of the gang provides a proving ground for those pre-adolescents who by this time are anxiously looking forward to the enjoyment of the rights, privileges, and advantages, if not to the responsibilities and difficulties of adult life.

SUMMARY

This chapter began with a definition of the sociology of childhood. Generally, the sociology of childhood was said to focus upon the interaction between children and other age-level categories; upon the reciprocal impact resulting from this interaction, and the social structures in which such interaction is experienced.

In elaborating on this conception of the sociology of childhood, attention was directed to the importance of the social and cultural context in which childhood is experienced. In this connection, it was emphasized that although age is essentially a biological phenomenon, it is ultimately the social definition of age that is a principal basis for the allocation of statuses and roles.

Social definitions of age, and consequently of childhood, vary in time and place. Thus, the varying definitions of childhood in primitive, ancient, and modern societies were discussed. As a result, the differential rights, responsibilities, privileges, and immunities of children in different times and places were outlined.

Socialization was examined from three points of view: process, practice, and structure. Thus, attention was called not only to the ideal and the reality of socialization, but to the significant social structures involved in it as well. These structures were classified and discussed as child-centered, child-oriented, and child-dominated social systems. Some consideration was given to relationships between children and their near-age siblings, and between children and persons in other age-level categories. Finally, the relevance of adolescence for childhood was discussed.

READINGS

BENEDICT, Ruth, "Child Rearing in Certain European Countries," *American Journal of Orthopsychiatry* (April, 1949), pp. 342–350.

BOLL, Eleanor S., "The Child," *Annals of the American Academy of Political and Social Science* (September, 1943), pp. 69–79.

EARLE, Alice Morse, *Child Life in Colonial Days* (New York, The Macmillan Company, 1899).

ERIKSON, Erik H., *Childhood and Society* (New York, W. W. Norton & Company, Inc., 1950).

MACARDLE, Dorothy, *Children of Europe* (Boston, Beacon Press, 1951).

MEAD, Margaret, and WOLFENSTEIN, Martha, *Childhood in Contemporary Cultures* (Chicago, University of Chicago Press, 1955).

II

SOCIAL SETTINGS
FOR CHILDHOOD

3

The Social-Cultural
Context for Socialization

No child lives his entire life within the confines of his immediate family circle. Furthermore, the life experiences of the child in modern, complex societies almost always extends beyond his family, peer group, neighborhood, and frequently his local community. Indeed, even the child whose contacts are somewhat limited to family and neighborhood will nonetheless be influenced by forces and circumstances which prevail far from his immediate social milieu. Witness, for example, the child who lives in a geographically isolated farm community. He is likely to visit town or the city periodically, or contact visitors or passers-by from outlying areas. Or, perhaps, he will hear stories of "far-away" places and long to see them, or wonder about them. In no event is he likely to believe that his community is "the world"—not today, at least.

Generally, the community into which the infant is born is to a considerable extent a reflection of a larger, more extensive, "super-community." Therefore, the patterns of life to which he is exposed at home are likely to be, in many respects, similar to those in neighboring and even far-off communities. Such similar and interrelated communities, taken as a whole, constitute a society.

Within the societies of the modern world, subways of life sometimes appear. These subways of life may develop relatively complete systems of institutions which may order the individual's whole life from birth to death. They may affect the way the person is handled at birth; they structure the peculiar family into which he is born; they may determine how he will be educated (as in either a public or parochial school), how he will make a living, marry, and be handled at death. The concept of a community was used for these

37

subways of life which are less than a society. "Society" could be defined simply as the largest and most comprehensive of the modern communities.[1]

THE CHILD, SOCIETY, AND CULTURE

Although each community tends to be somewhat unique, there are common threads running through each so that the totality of communities of a particular society comprise a unified whole. Ultimately, the child reared or socialized in a particular community will be influenced initially and even principally by that community, but he will also feel the impact of the total society of which his community is a part. By way of illustration, consider the case of a child reared in a Christian home in a small New England town. Although he may be a member of the local Congregational church, and although his church or Sunday School experiences may not extend—so far as he is conscious—beyond his own local community, the value system, the characteristic attitudes and practices of his local church, of its national organization, and indeed of the entire Christian community all, to some extent, combine in their influence on him. A similar case can be made regarding other institutional patterns such as the public school system.

The several communities of a given society constitute a social-cultural pattern which continues over time. Thus, except for social and cultural changes and allowing for variations in the perceptions and conceptions of individuals, a given social and cultural context can be expected to retain its essential characteristics indefinitely. Stated differently, both society and culture are continuing phenomena; they span generations. Manifestly, the units or people of society must be replaced, and these new units must learn the culture. The replacement of the people of society is not achieved merely through reproduction; the learning of the ways or culture of the society is essential to the completion of this process. "The human infant comes into the world as a biological organism with animal needs and impulses. From the beginning, however, the organism is conditioned to respond in socially determined ways. The individual learns group-defined ways of acting and feeling, and he learns many of them so fundamentally that they become part of his personality." [2]

Despite the characteristic unity or wholeness of a society, it is not identical throughout. To say that a society and its culture constitute an all-inclusive whole is not to say that its constituent parts are completely integrated, nor that they are identically experienced by all of its mem-

[1] *American Social Structure* by Don Martingale. Copyright © 1960, Appleton-Century-Crofts, Inc. p. 486. Reprinted by permission of Appleton-Century-Crofts.
[2] Leonard Broom and Philip Selznick, *Sociology* (New York, Harper & Row, Publishers, Inc., 1958), p. 79.

bers. Every society has its internally conflicting forces as well as its separate divisions. In like manner, the culture of any society is likely to include contradictory elements, and differential opportunities for participation. Despite the divergences and differentials in a society and culture, there are forces of accommodation at work which assure an effectively high degree of unity and continuity. This accommodation is reflected, for example, in caste and class relations and often in adolescent-adult relations. In addition there may be patterned regional differences in values, attitudes, and behavior so that rather definite and significant sub-cultures come to exist. When this occurs, as it has in the United States, the impact is likely to be felt in many areas of life, including that of childhood.

Sub-groups and Sub-cultures

In socializing the infants into membership in their society, the intent is to prepare them for and fit them into certain segments and facets of the whole. "Each member of a society need only acquaint himself with as much of its total culture as he needs to fit himself to fill a particular place in the life of the community." [3] Generally, the segment or place in society into which one must fit is determined by various factors such as sex, family, and social class. In a dynamic and democratic society, the person is not socialized necessarily for a predetermined place, but often to fit into places that become available by choice, change, circumstances, or chance. [4] Examples of this are to be found in the poor boy who becomes an industrial tycoon, the constitutionally weak child who becomes a world famous athlete, and even the young female who grows up to be a famous political personage.

Limited or selective socialization of the child means that he is not involved with nor does he participate in the total society. He interacts in or comes to be a member of a limited number of sub-groups, [5] and, at times, aspires to or has contact with certain others. Meanwhile, the extent of his knowledge of the culture must be sufficient at least for his group participation, and of course may extend beyond this limit.

Among the first groups into which the child is progressively introduced are his family, play group, peer group, and inter-generational school groups. Participation or adjustment in these groups require some knowledge of the culture, and this adjustment, in turn, makes a contribution to his further learning of the culture. At first, the child learns to behave as a member of his family group. This requires adjusting to the human

[3] *The Study of Man* by Ralph Linton. Copyright © 1936, D. Appleton-Century Company, Inc., p. 85. Reprinted by permission of Appleton-Century-Crofts.

[4] An exception to this observation is to be found in the United States where one's racial identity is in certain areas a determinant of the limits of one's mobility.

[5] The term *sub-group* is used here to contrast a part of society from the whole. Hereafter, in this chapter, the shortened version *group* is used.

and non-human elements encountered in his home. Thus, for example, he learns to depend upon and obey his parents, to share with his siblings, to play with and care for his toys, and perhaps to avoid certain objects such as a sharp knife or a hot stove. With these lessons learned in the home, he soon becomes involved with his peers and with adult non-family members. In such situations, he acquires additional knowledge and skills and is thereby better able to conform to new and changing social expectations.

Since the different groups with which the child becomes involved are interrelated components of a single society, they share some common and unifying cultural characteristics. For example, honesty, competition, fair play, and property rights are important considerations in all of these groups. Furthermore, the child's role expectations based on sex tend to remain the same in the several groups to which he belongs. In this latter instance, once the little male understands the meaning of masculinity, or being "a little man," he usually fashions his group behavior accordingly. Thus, he runs, jumps, wrestles, and "skins the cat" but hastens to inform "little sister" that she may not do likewise because "you're a girl." When he is older and in school, he will continue to regulate his behavior in terms of what is appropriate for boys. In like manner, girls learn and continue to act "as girls." Sometimes a boy or a girl may deviate from socially approved sex-linked behavior. Although this is occasionally tolerated in the very young, this tolerance declines as the child gets older. Thus it is that roles based on sex not only have a continuity over time, but usually extend into all situations of each succeeding age-span.

Social Differentiation and Stratification

As already indicated, all members of any given society do not experience all aspects of their culture. The character and extent of the participation of one person or collectivity of persons often varies widely from that of others. The population is differentiated because of the great variety of societal needs and tasks and because of the wide differences in individual capacities, abilities, and interests. Broadly viewed, this differentiation reflects (and determines) the bases for differential training as well as the criteria for preferential opportunities. Universally, therefore, variations in sex and age, for example, are bases for differential training. Although the fact that a person is male or female, child or adult may have no significant bearing upon the ultimate life-chances of that person, it does indicate some degree of differential socialization and status-role access. Thus, males and females are socialized toward different ends and children and adults are ascribed different positions in the social structure.

As used here, social stratification is a special form of the process of social differentiation. It implies status gradations, and the differential distribution of goods, services, and life-chances generally. In effect, it is the process through which people of a society are separated into categories and accorded or denied access to certain areas of social life. The separation, placement, and access dimensions of social stratification are usually applied without regard to the personal attributes of the individual concerned. Unlike mere social differentiation, organic factors such as sex and age are not pertinent in the stratification process. Furthermore, neither individual intelligence or personal achievement is a necessary consideration in the determination of one's place in the stratification system. Although mobility may be achieved, the tendency is for the person to remain in his initial position in the system. The net result is that people occupying different positions in the stratification system are exposed to and manifest differentials in wealth, income, education, and occupation.

A child's placement in the stratification system is that of his family; it is part of his social heritage. As such, the impact of social stratification is often likely to be an extremely significant and permanent force in his life experiences. Because the child's position in the stratification system is ascribed to him as part of his social heritage, he is socialized to occupy that position. Thus the values, attitudes, and behavior which characterize his segment of the stratification system constitute, in the main, the culture which is transmitted to him. Since all children are not born into the same social position, they are not all exposed to the same socializing experiences, substantively viewed. With regard to American society, this situation is reflected in the wide contrast between the life experiences of the rich and the poor. Children born into rich or even moderately "well-to-do" families are assured of the physical necessities, of adequate educational opportunities, of contact with the "finer things of life," and of certain luxuries; in contrast, children of the poor sometimes subsist on inadequate diets, are denied optimum educational advantages, experience the more degrading facets of life, and almost never know even the minimum luxuries of living. These contrasting situations reflect not only the extremes in the life experiences of children, they imply differentials in the substantive character of socialization. For the child of the rich must be socialized to lead the life of the rich; and the child of the poor must, in like manner, be prepared to experience his heritage.

SOCIALIZATION AND SOCIAL SYSTEMS

In a society the relationships and behavior of the people involve regularities and are thereby predictable. Consequently it may be expected that groups of the same order, say the Jones, Smith, Brown, and other families will exhibit, within limits, the same overt and covert behavior. Stated differently, there is a complex of common, patterned behavior which is socially approved and prescribed for family life. When the study of groups is directed not toward the member but toward the patterns governing their relationships and behavior, a new dimension of the group emerges; namely, the social system. "The sum total of the ideal patterns which control the reciprocal behavior between individuals and between the individual and society constitute the social system under which the particular society lives." [6] Just as a society includes numerous sub-groups, a social system of the society contains segments or divisions appropriately referred to as sub-systems. Thus, one may speak of the family, the peer group, the gang, the clique, and the school as systems or more precisely, sub-systems. For simplicity sub-systems will be referred to merely as systems or social systems.

The importance of social systems is that they perform a function in the continuity of society and culture that can hardly be over-estimated. "Social systems serve as a guide to the shaping of individuals and to their arrangement in certain relations to each other, this combination of shaping and arrangement making it possible for the mutually adjusted individuals to function together as a society." [7] Social systems also provide the prescriptions for the person's behavior in parts of the society (groups) as well as in situations of casual, intermittent, or momentary interaction. This means that although one may have guests in the home infrequently, when he does he is prepared to follow a behavior pattern different from that which prevails among family members. Or, when he interacts with the "cop on the beat" or is in the presence of Santa Claus he knows what is expected of him and what he can expect from the other.

After the initial period of socialization in the family, the child becomes progressively involved in other systems. While in the family, however, he acquires attitudes and knowledge regarding the patterns to be found in the play group, the neighborhood, and the school systems. Although some of what the child learns in the family is not directly applicable to family living, it may nonetheless be consistent with family functions. For example, parents may teach their children to be wary of strangers, to be polite to other adults, and, to say "no" to certain proposals made by their playmates. The admonition, "Remember, Bill, when you go to school sit still in your seat and pay attention to the teacher," is the kind of instruction often given children as they are being prepared for their first school experience.

Although socialization occurs concurrently in several social systems, preparation for such involvements is cumulative and introduction into

[6] Linton, *op. cit.*, p. 105.
[7] *Ibid.*, p. 107.

systems tends to occur progressively. First, there is the immediate family, the larger family, the family and guests, the family and functionaries who come into the home, the play situation, the neighborhood and so on until the child becomes involved in or makes contact with a variety of systems in the community. It is somewhat in this order that social systems of different orders come to be foci for the child's expanding behavior.

Although the attitudes and knowledge that the child gains from the family often aid him in making the transition into other systems, his roles in these other systems may require much more of him. The child from the family on "the wrong side of the tracks," for example, may find that some of his ideas and practices in the use of language, in his personal grooming, or in his handling of property are "all wrong" in the school system. Indeed, he may find that participation in non-family social systems imposes strange, new, and conflicting demands upon him. Whatever his social background, as the child moves into these new situations, his values, attitudes, knowledge and skills are almost certain to be modified and enlarged.

Social systems are comprised not so much of persons as of statuses and their corresponding roles. The nature and the extent of the person's involvement in these systems are determined by the role requirements of the statuses they occupy. In reality, however, the system sets forth *ideal* patterns for the regulation of human interaction. These patterns are applicable to all who become involved in the system. This means that countless numbers of widely divergent personalities may at any given moment, or over time, be involved in the same social system. A social system may require that many people behave similarly—to play the same role—but there is almost always varying degrees of deviation from the role expectations. Furthermore, social systems involve changing memberships. To take a common example, the child is socialized to participate in and is socialized within the classroom as a social system rather than a group. He may or may not know the other members of the class or the teacher. Even if he does, he must soon move into a series of different classes where he will meet many new and different children and teachers. To adequately deal with the changing membership of the classroom situations he must be acquainted with the appropriate and prevailing patterns, including values, attitudes, norms, and behavior. In view of the instability of the personal make-up of groups, social system analysis can be expected to facilitate meaningful observation and understanding of human behavior. Moreover, by utilizing the social system concept in the study of socialization, one can derive insights regarding the effectiveness of that process upon the socializee as well as the impact it makes upon those who socialize.

VALUES AND THE CHILD

Although a society is a whole, it is comprised of different parts—groups, classes, and other collectivities—that are interrelated. To a considerable extent, these different parts perform varying functions, involve only some people, and operate according to dissimilar norms. Despite this, however, the several parts of a society ultimately constitute an integrated and functional unit. Even though differentiation, stratification, and a division of labor exist, and conflict and cross purposes prevail in a particular society, there are always certain ideas regarding what is right, desirable, or important that are common to the several groups and social systems of that society. These ideas constitute the society's dominant or major values, and it is around these values that societal consensus is organized.

Values, like other components of culture, exist on several levels. Thus, different groups or classes may, to some extent, subscribe to different values. But apart from these specialized values there are those which tend to be most highly regarded and most widely accepted, and thereby involve, in varying degrees, the whole society. These are the dominant or major values and are the ones that are of concern at this point. Not only are they the principal unifying force in the society, but they give both the society and the culture a distinctiveness or uniqueness all its own.

With regard to the personalities involved, values serve to regulate, channel, and mold. They set directions for socially sanctioned aspirations and development. They delineate those ends and means that are highly approved, those that are tolerated, and those that are rejected. Finally, they serve as ultimate guidelines throughout the person's entire life-span.

Values are relevant to the child even before birth, for they relate to whether or not parenthood is important and desirable. They are significant considerations in the choice of techniques and methods of child rearing; and, they must be communicated to the child in the course of his socialization. "In the complex interaction between parents and child, the person not only learns about the conventions and standards that govern social life, but he also internalizes them, that is, incorporates them in his own personality. The process by which values and specific rules are internalized is complex, but it is usually tied closely to the intimate relations between children and parents."[8] Although the values inculcated into the child in his family setting are sometimes contravened by what he learns in outside groups, they are nonetheless frequently supported and promoted by these groups. For example, the school, the church, and

[8] Eli Chinoy, *Society: An Introduction to Sociology* (New York, Random House, Inc., 1961), p. 336.

various other group situations teach the child many of the same values to which he was introduced by his parents.

In a highly differentiated society in which individualism, competition, and certain middle-class values are dominant, value consistency is not likely to prevail equally throughout. Furthermore, among certain categories and classes the commitment to the dominant values may be more verbalized than internalized. When, therefore, the dominant values are denied, distorted, or discarded in certain segments of society, the child involved in such situations might well be disaffected, disillusioned, or otherwise deterred from following the more socially sanctioned paths of life.

SUMMARY

The foregoing discussion is a descriptive overview of the all-inclusive social and cultural context for the socialization of the child. It is an attempt to set forth in bare outline the social and cultural boundaries within which countless different individuals and categories of different types of individuals become socialized and participate in various segments of the same society.

It was emphasized that the transmission of culture to the new-born is a necessary prerequisite to effective social participation. It was pointed out that since people are perceived to differ in organic traits such as sex, they are differentiated into various categories.

Apart from the process of mere differentiation, social stratification was referred to as a process in which people are further differentiated without reference to personal attributes. Stratification, it was shown, is part of the child's cultural heritage. Further, it was suggested that escape routes from this heritage tend to be closed.

The concept "social system" was introduced as a tool for the study of social behavior. Social systems and social groups were differentiated and certain advantages of each of these heuristic devices were suggested.

In view of the divisions, distinctions, sources of differences, and conflicts explicit and implicit in the discussion of the above subject-matter areas, the chapter was concluded with some comments on the unifying force of values. Despite the divisions and differences found in a society, the unity which the term society implies was said to derive principally from its value orientation. Although values, like other cultural components, are not shared equally, it was pointed out that every society has certain dominant or major values to which its people generally subscribe. These values provide the basis for the character or distinctiveness of the society.

With this descriptive account as an introduction or point of departure, attention is now directed to a more detailed and analytical account of the relative impact exerted upon children by the various segments of society.

READINGS

BROWN, Francis James, *The Sociology of Childhood* (Englewood Cliffs, N.J., Prentice-Hall, Inc., 1939).

DAVIS, Kingsley, *Human Society* (New York, The Macmillan Company, 1948).

HILLER, E. T., *Social Relations and Social Structures* (New York, Harper & Row, Publishers, Inc., 1947).

KOHN, Melvin L., "Social Class and Parent-Child Relationships: An Interpretation," *American Journal of Sociology,* Vol. XLVIII, No. 4 (January, 1963), pp. 471–480.

LEIGH, Minturn Triandes and LAMBERT, William W., "Pancultural Factor Analysis of Reported Socialization Practices," *Journal of Abnormal Social Psychology,* Vol. 62, No. 3 (May, 1961), pp. 631–639.

LINTON, Ralph, *The Cultural Background of Personality* (New York, Appleton-Century-Crofts, Inc., 1945).

PARSONS, Talcott, "The School Class as a Social System: Some of Its Functions in American Society," *Harvard Educational Review,* Vol. 29, No. 4 (Fall, 1959), pp. 297–318.

WILLIAMS, Robin M., Jr., *American Society* (New York, Alfred A. Knopf, Inc., 1951).

4

Impact of Social
Stratification Upon Children

Children are brought into a world prepared to receive them into a prescribed social system. Depending upon fortuitous circumstances, children may be afforded every opportunity to bring forth their personal capabilities or have considerably less or minimum chance to do so. A plausible parallel to the situation imposed upon children is the example of actors in a play, who will perform in given settings, who must carry out certain roles, who will be observed by certain expected audiences, and who must recite certain memorized lines designed to carry out the intentions of the playwright. Both actors and children are expected to learn what is set before them—and little else. They, of course, may interpret their roles somewhat variously, but only within the limits imposed by some external authority. While the ideal of equal opportunity is held in esteem by those who value democracy, an objective reality is that *differential opportunity* is the lot of infants. At birth, one infant is welcomed as a future prince; another infant will, most likely, have little real choice but to become a pauper.

Every human society has evolved social systems that accord high status to some of its people and lower position to the greater bulk of its people. Men everywhere accord their fellows certain privileges or dis-privileges in proportion to their social rank. In some societies, it may be merely the possession of a family name, or the ownership of land, cattle, heads, women, crops, or even ritual that confers status and social role. It may suffice to have had some remote ancestor or to be a future inheritor from one's immediate kin. It may be sex, birth order, or "pure" whimsy," but whatever the criteria used to place children into social orders, they are binding and potent in their impact.

The wide range and variety of social class criteria suggests that the higher or lower ranking of individuals is done arbitrarily. That which one society holds in esteem may be evaluated in another part of the world as degrading. While one society may define one bit of behavior as trivial, another society may be found which views such behavior as filled with significance. In the American society, for instance, personal freedom is idealized and one's behavior in certain respects may acceptably be highly individualized. In a contrasting society, however, children must learn as soon as possible that the group takes precedence over all personal desires and this is the "proper" way of life. An American caused an uproar in a foreign courtroom not long ago because he crossed his legs in public. From an American point of view, such behavior is inconsequential. In the eyes of others, this same behavior was judged to be rude and disrespectful and may have led to a death sentence for the accused.

The arbitrary nature of social status, however, is more apparent than real. Each society has its own logical structure and it is within this context that observations make sense and can be viewed as meaningful. Children are not born into some mystical, universal society, but into a specific society with its orderly restrictions and with its own rationales for the imposed inhibitions.

Benefits and Restrictions of Social Class

Social rank implies both rights and duties. In the United Kingdom, one of the few European societies in which remnants of an ancient feudalism still survive, a child born "a commoner" in Liverpool may follow his father on the docks, and loyally support "the Throne," whereas a child born to the royal family may become "By the Grace of God of the United Kingdom of Great Britain and Northern Ireland and of His Other Realms and Territories, King, Head of the Commonwealth, Defender of the Faith" and recipient of all due respect and homage. In America, a child born to an upper class family will be duly registered and readily accepted at some exclusive school, travel comfortably around the world, and find a corps of attorneys carefully administering his future holdings and funds. In contrast, a child born to a middle class family will attend a public high school, possibly experience a vacation with his family in a mortgaged car for a limited tour of the West for a few weeks, and probably grow up to puzzle over his income tax return to the federal government.

In more remote locations, a child will be schooled to suffer hunger and pain without complaint and to hunt and gather the means of subsistence as his ancestors before him. Some will live in palaces and many will continue to live in straw hovels plastered with cow dung. Some children will be exhorted to propitiate a pantheon of spirits who will smile upon them and favor them with bountiful harvests. Still other youngsters will be instructed that they are either members of a priestly class or the personifications of a diety, and will receive the adulations of faithful worshippers as a matter of course.

In brief, what has been pointed out is that children are free to behave only within the limits of social class systems and that this freedom may be very broad or very narrow. Further, it has been implied that concomitant with freedoms come responsibilities. One is never so free that he may overlook his duties in relationships with others. The leader must consider his followers, the king must watch carefully the needs of his subjects, the upper classes must be, in various ways, charitable to the poor, the officer must be able to carry out his own orders to his men, and so on. An insightful priest recently remarked that while he was an honored man among his people, he must never forget for an instant that he must conduct his life in a manner acceptable to them or he will be rejected and scorned by these same people.

While there are privileges and responsibility that accompany social status, the reverse is also true. Because the prestige surrounding higher levels of society is visible, the lack of it is felt strongly in the lives of the many who are located in the lower echelons of the same society. Children, particularly, suffer from lower class positioning because they are less sheltered from harm. One of the most sensitive barometers of the level of living of a given society is the infantile mortality rate, the number of infants under one year of age dying per thousand. Almost without exception, unless counter measures are instituted, lower class children die in great numbers before the first year of life is over. Disease, nutritional neglect, accidents, improper rest and exercise, lack of attention to warmth or heat, and fundamental ignorance take a tremendous toll of young lives in the lower levels of a society. Within the United States, for example, there has been improvement, but much remains to be done. The overall infant mortality rates within the United States have been steadily falling, for instance, but they do not reflect the variations in class levels that are known to exist.

If disprivileged children can survive the rigors of infancy, there remain many more hazards that they must overcome. In their formative years, they cannot help but witness future examples of what their own lives may be by noting the conditions of ever-present adults. Life can understandably be judged as one long struggle to survive. Food, shelter, and clothing are sufficient goals to attain for a typical lower class child. The trouble is that these essentials are often lacking and can be attained only after considerable effort and good fortune.

Hopelessness is familiar to the lower class child. He sees no way out of his condition and, indeed, may never have even thought of some way to improve it. As he becomes aware of other levels of society, he certainly cannot feel akin to them. His attitude may be described as "irresponsible"

	Infant Deaths Under One Year
Year	Per 1000 Live Births, U.S.A. 1915–1955 [1]
1915	99.9
1920	85.8
1925	71.7
1930	64.6
1935	55.7
1940	47.0
1945	38.3
1950	29.2
1955	26.4

by his superiors. If children of the lower classes are to be understood, observers must grasp the idea that such children cannot easily take a positive, cooperative, helpful stand in a society that holds them in a form of social bondage. One has nothing to lose when he is on the bottom rung of the social ladder. One can readily take a devil-may-care attitude which sooner or later may run counter to attitudes held by those enjoying the privileges of higher status. Scrapes with the law and legal authority become more commonplace in the lower classes and its origin is highly related to the matter of so-called irresponsibility.

Consequences of Social Class in the Life of Children

By reason of class position, then, the child is accorded relatively full or limited participation in his society. He will, on the higher levels, be granted access to the best that his society can provide, whether it be material goods or the non-material satisfactions derived from public adulation. Descending in the social order, the child is granted that much less of what is available in his social world. He may be given a slow, painstaking education to eventually take a high position in life or he may be thrust into earning his keep as soon as possible without too much interest in gradual preparation for maturity.

For those who value human life and the concomitant potentials wherever it is found, this condition of limited participation in a given society is regarded as a serious loss. By stifling the opportunity to participate, the society has limited the potential contributions of the disprivileged. A counter argument presented by those who defend differential status systems is that a society does not require the services of all its people at high levels. It needs, in fact, the services of its people mainly at lower levels to do the menial tasks and to perform the perfunctory jobs to keep the society operative.

[1] *Historical Statistics of the U.S., Colonial Times to 1957*, Bureau of Census, p. 25.

Social Mobility and Children

Social class structure varies from those which permit the maximum degree of vertical mobility to those which fix the individual's station in life from the moment of his birth. Children introduced to conditions which originally may be harsh soon recognize that even this stringent diet is palatable if the chance to improve one's self is present. If, however, a child is made aware that there is a ceiling to his social life and he can do no more than repeat the life of his parents, then he will possibly either adopt their ways as the only feasible way to live or harbor suspicions and resentments that color his every move.

Many years ago, one of the writers visited a slum area in a major city and noted the many unkempt children, dressed in rags, playing quite happily with some discarded tin cans beside a muddy pool of water on a vacant, debris-filled lot. Their home was an unpainted wooden structure which lacked a front door, but which boasted windows with broken panes of glass or torn oilskins. The entire neighborhood was in a state of disrepair as if, after a bombing or some disaster, the entire area had been abandoned. When this scene was described to a friend with much disgust and summed up by saying that running away would have been preferable, the friend indicated that no such "solution" would occur to these children because such conditions are accepted without repulsion. The point, of course, is that under-privileged children throughout the world accept conditions that are imposed upon them and find their lot quite tolerable. If, in time, they can discover *contrasting* levels of living, then and only then, can young people acquire the notion that they may wish to explore a different mode of life from that of their parents and friends.

Hypothetically, there are two circumstances which can markedly alter living conditions among persons at deprived social levels. One of these would be conditions in which persons have moved away from their earlier depressed status and yet retain a certain sympathetic identification with those who remain behind. The other circumstance would be those conditions in which persons, who never participated in lower socioeconomic levels, vicariously know the nature of lower class life. In the former category, there are many socially mobile individuals who did not always have their present high level of living and who desire to do something for those who continue to experience the minimal comforts available in their society. The philanthropies of "poor boys who made good" are examples of this former type. In the latter category, there are those like Ghandi or Franklin D. Roosevelt, who were members of upper levels of their respective societies, but whose life-histories are concerned with dedication to improvements in conditions experienced by the economically depressed and socially rejected.

Both sources of class change come, however, from outside the disprivileged classes under discussion. They, alone, were in the position to note *contrast* and to do something about it. The social climate of lower class children, thus, will probably not be changed either by themselves or by their parents, but solely by the good offices of members of the outgroup. This, of course, does not adequately account for those people who lift themselves by their own bootstraps. Such types will be discussed in ensuing chapters in more specific circumstances.

Further Reaction to Class Structures

It has been the dream of certain students of human society to achieve what is tantamount to a classless society or utopia in which everyone lives at the highest levels possible. Such persons strongly resent the restrictions of class and have sought to create a social order that would free humanity from such systems. The ideological division of the known world into opposing camps on this issue threatens whatever world security now exists.

It is not the purpose of this chapter to argue for one side or the other of this issue. Interest in this matter exists because it is an extremely significant area in the lives of children who are caught up in it. The life of a child in the U.S.S.R., Communist China, and in Hungary is far different than the life of a child in the U.S.A., Canada, England, and France chiefly on the basis of this clashing ideology. It is practically the daily diet of a child in the communist world to hear about class consciousness, class conflict, and the ultimate triumph of the working class, while the child in the western world may be either unaware of class divisions or can accept his class level with a minimum of trauma or discomfort. By any approach, the pervasive nature of class cannot be set aside in the daily living experiences of thousands and millions of children.

Descriptions of Upper, Middle, and Lower
Class Children in America

Sociologists and other social scientists have devoted many years to research projects calculated to describe the actual conditions associated with various class levels. We are indebted to them for much of the data that follow. The limitations of their studies, however, become the limitations of generalizations derived from them. Thus, the usual criticisms of limited samples, minimum information, tests of significance, reliability, validity, and the like apply. There will always be notable, individualized exceptions, and omissions to the word pictures that follow. The generalizations that follow are attempts to portray typical children at various class levels and not any specific child who obviously was one small unit in total summations. It is not the best that can be done. But, it will be an attempt to do the best we can with what we have.

UPPER CLASS CHILDREN.[2] Upper class children belong to a select circle into which they have been admitted to maintain and perpetuate family traditions. Ordinarily, few children are in a family unit and so the emphasis is upon quality and not quantity. Their whole purpose in life will be to consolidate, guard, entrench, and deepen the rich heritage of their past. Horizontal mobility will be their chief activity. The only possible fear that overshadows their life is the spectre of descending vertically in the social scale. An upper class child is born into a proud heritage and he must not bring shame to the escutcheon.

In a patrilineal society, the upper classes are particularly sensitive to the desirability of a male heir to carry on name and family fortunes. Girls are welcomed for lending beauty and grace to the household. Both sexes are carefully trained to associate with their upper class peers and to minimize contacts with lower echelons. Carefully screened employees are utilized to achieve this goal of seclusion and privacy. Consequently, the children's experiences are away or apart from the masses of people.

Because upper class families are at the pinnacle of society economically and socially, the use of parental supplements in the form of nurses, servants, governesses, guards, chauffeurs, tutors, and companions is quite common. Upper class parents may act as overseers and determiners of policy, but much of the parental influence is indirect. The emotional life of the child is closely tied to these parental supplements rather than to the distant parents who are too busy in other realms to be burdened with the constant attention a child may need. Children of royal families, for example, have developed some strong attachments to their nurses and governesses. Children of planters in the colonial South likewise developed strong attachments to their "mammies." Servants were the confidants of upper class children rather than their own parents who were preoccupied elsewhere.

The economic well being and, indeed, the high prestige enjoyed by children of the upper classes stem from the work and reputation of past ancestors. Like Moslems who face Mecca, the upper classes bow in the direction of the glorious past and the near-divinity of their forebears. Portraits; records of their achievements or exploits such as collections, citations, medals; and even personal possessions are carefully preserved as heirlooms for the edification of the young. The linkage with the past is reified to such an extent that the upper class child is extremely conscious

[2] See James T. Adams, *The Adams Family* (Boston, Little Brown and Company, 1930); Cleveland Amory, *The Proper Bostonians* (New York, E. P. Dutton & Co., Inc., 1947); August Hollingshead, *Elmtown's Youth* (New York, John Wiley & Sons, Inc., 1949); Ferdinand Lundberg, *America's Sixty Families* (New York, Vanguard Press, Inc., 1937).

of his ancestral ties. Genealogical studies are quite popular among the upper classes provided they do not uproot matters which are best kept quiet and buried. Ancestry is to be revered, emulated, and its heritage must be carried on into the future. Even symbols, such as a family crest, have meaning and are given prominence at family gatherings.

The health of upper class children is carefully guarded under the best medical attention the family can command. Not only the young survive against biological assaults, but so can all members of the upper class family. Thus, a condition that is common among upper class families is for a child to have few siblings, but by contrast, to have an abundance of adult and even aged persons in contact with him. The result is a world relatively devoid of the influence of other children, but heavily affected by the wishes of elders.

There is a stability to the upper class family that is comparatively unknown in lower levels. Having greater investments in the family estate and considerable insulation from the more rapidly changing outside world, the upper class child generally has one home which serves as an anchor throughout his life. He does not experience the constant moving about that other children go through as their parents try to climb the social ladder. He is rarely uprooted to adjust to a variety of neighborhoods and unpredictable new neighbors as is the lot of middle class children. A notable exception occurs, however, in the extensive travels that are possible for him as excursions away from homesteads can and do take him into new cities, regions, and countries.

Proper manners are the hallmark of the upper class child. He is carefully schooled in courtesy, respect, and dignity. Vulgarity, loud talking, temper tantrums, uncleanliness, and awkwardness are to be avoided. Upper class children are to be charitable, but not overly concerned with the needs of lower class people. Parent surrogates are not of their class, but they are to be treated courteously as participants within the family circle. A child may express himself, but never in a crude manner. He must cultivate the dress, the taste, the speech, and the gentility of his class. One must learn to be "a gentleman" or "a lady." One must observe the amenities or suffer the consequences of rejection and isolation. Acceptability is the highest accolade an upper class child can acquire.

W. Lloyd Warner and his associates have been acclaimed for their work of subdividing the trichotomy of classes of upper, middle, and lower into upper and lower divisions within each class level.[3] A brief discription of the upper class child's life would be incomplete if distinctions between the upper-uppers and the lower-uppers were not made.

The lower-upper class family has *arrived*, but not quite. By this is im-

---

[3] See W. Lloyd Warner and Paul S. Lunt, *The Social Life of a Modern Community* (New Haven, Yale University Press, 1941).

plied the observation that lower-upper families are close to the upper-uppers, but not close enough. The lower-upper child takes on renewed importance because it will probably be through his life that the lower-uppers may affect a liaison with the upper-uppers. The lower-upper elders can provide the necessary boost to make the final step upward, but will probably never themselves have entree. One is reminded of the situation imposed upon Moses who was permitted to see the Promised Land from afar, but was never allowed to enter it. The lower-upper elders share this condition, but have the satisfaction of providing opportunities for their children to enter the upper-upper levels.

The lower-upper class child is frequently born to wealth far superior to that of an upper-upper child. This wealth is not rooted in the past, but more likely was recently acquired by economic good fortune and skillful maneuvering based upon huge capital investments. Perhaps the child's father accumulated great wealth because of the demand for his products or services during wartime; or perhaps the wealth was gathered by wise stock market purchases or by rising real estate values. At any rate, the economic gains are relatively recent and lend substance to the descriptive expression that these people are, indeed, the *nouveau riche*. Because his heritage is recent, the lower-upper child is more likely to be in contact with the latest innovations or advantages the society can provide. His home will have the latest devices and aids to personal comfort. In all probability, his home will be comparatively new, whereas the home of an upper-upper class child may have been built many years back.

The lower-uppers resort to the power of money to purchase the linkage with the past which is naturally bestowed on the upper-uppers. They buy an estate, mansion, castle, summer home, servant quarters, or other accoutrements usually associated with the established families. When it comes to lavish display, this can be accomplished with greater dispatch than even the upper-uppers. Ostentation might best describe this quality of the lower-uppers in contrast with the reserved, aloof, quiet dignity that pervades the typical upper-upper class home.

To be consistent with their ultimate objective, entry into the upper-upper class, the lower-upper class family will bring their child into contact with children of the upper-upper class whenever possible. This may be accomplished by enrollment in exclusive, private schools, finishing schools, or academies, attendance at concerts, parties, operas, shows, or other functions in which upper-uppers may participate. Eventually, the carefully planned campaign to enter the ranks of the upper-uppers does result in success by an upper-upper class invitation to a lower-upper child to join various affairs. Friendships and contacts develop which may eventuate in marital and familial ties. The goal of upper-upper class status is very important and while not everyone may enter their ranks, the lower-upper classes are willing to try again and again through the lives of their children.

MIDDLE CLASS CHILDREN. The great balance wheel of society is the numerous and yet nebulous people known as the middle class. They live their lives far from the rarified atmosphere of the upper classes and stand apart from "the huddled masses" of the lower classes. Successful or upwardly mobile members of the lower classes replenish their numbers, but these find that they have merely reached "the halfway house" as there is still another class to reach well beyond the middle class.

The middle class philosophy consists of *getting ahead,* to try to do better than one's mother or father. This does not necessarily mean that children are to try to climb into the upper classes, but it does mean that they are to improve their conditions whenever and wherever possible. Middle class children are trained to be proud of their middle class morality, but they are also urged or prodded to keep moving along and not to become too self-satisfied. Hard work, industry, and high energy output are the formulas for success.

There is a keen interest in scientific child rearing in order to realize the maximum capacities of young children. The middle class is the chief supporter of Parent-Teacher Associations and child study groups. Its constituents are avid readers of *how-to-rear-your-child* books, and are highly sensitized to any lack of inter-personal harmony. One must "win friends and influence people." This will come by personal magnetism or know-how. In general, middle class children are told that they must be self-reliant, study diligently, work hard, save carefully, and keep alert. The rewards of such effort will eventually be realized.

Middle class children are taught to be cooperative, to share, to take turns, and to be considerate of the rights of others. The *good* middle class child is obedient and behaves himself. He is not to fight unless it be for self-defense. To resort to any form of physically enforcing his will on others is disapproved because it is too similar to certain lower class people who tend to refuse to think. This middle class viewpoint pervades much of American life. American foreign policy has been for some time to remain strong, but not to fight unless forced to do so. America's entries into the two major world wars were both based upon provocative acts of overt aggression; the sinking of the Lusitania and the bombing of Pearl Harbor. Only in recent times has the policy been altered somewhat into forms of "brinkmanship" or "blockades." Even here, another rationale for war is provided. This desire to avoid controversy and to achieve harmony through negotiations has some relevance to middle class background for many American children.

Because working together is held as a virtue among the middle classes, each person is expected to do his share in the family unit. The father will continue to act as the chief economic mainstay, but when conditions demand it, the wife and mother will seek employment away from the home to supplement the income. The enforced absence of the father and, possibly, the mother tends to place even greater responsibilities upon younger middle class children. Such children may or may not work outside their homes although token jobs such as cutting the lawn, carrying out groceries at the local market, or delivering newspapers are viewed with pride and as excellent training for the days ahead.

Independence is held in great esteem by middle class people. One of the chief goals of a middle class family is to live independently in their own home. Indeed, the purchase of a comfortable home is probably the greatest single financial transaction in their lives, and they will occupy most of their lives to pay for it. To be one's own landlord, even if the plot of ground is modest and the home is unpretentious, is a deep, abiding satisfaction that is savored by middle class people. The rest of the world may be in ferment, but they have a place that is comparatively secure and pleasant. Stability is respected as a product of home ownership and strong family solidarity.

In general, there is an inverse relationship between social class levels and the number of children in family units. The higher classes generally have fewer children per family unit and the lower classes have more children per family unit. The upper class child would either be an only child or have relatively few siblings with whom to deal. The middle class child, however, would probably have several siblings. Middle class children are thus in a position of sharing their child's world with a number of brothers and sisters. Ordinarily, there would be enough of the world's goods to meet their needs. Competition for attention or outlets for individuality is supported by adequate, although not plentiful, economic goods and services. Only in the lower class levels does the large number of siblings pose a problem of dividing bare essentials among many individuals.

Because equalitarianism is a middle class virtue, the individual wish for recognition is somewhat stifled. Middle class persons would be the last to describe themselves as being exclusive or "stand offish." On the contrary, they would be prone to emphasize their desire to be democratic, altruistic, and self-effacing. Yet the desire to be recognized as someone who is *special* cannot be disregarded. Middle class people, consequently, tend to form cliques, which seem to be the products of steering a middle course between being considerate of everyone and yet being different from others who lack specialized interests.

Middle class children reflect this formation of cliques by developing friendships with a limited number of children and maintaining only a casual acquaintance with all others. This is excellent training for middle class orientations which can profess a love for humanity in the abstract, but which consist of a deep concern for a special circle of a few friends in reality.[4]

LOWER CLASS CHILDREN. To begin life at the bottom of the social class system means to be enmeshed in constant struggle for survival. Life is not easy for lower class children. Each one is another mouth to feed and another life to sustain in a large family. If there is to be a future for lower class children, a certain degree of toughness is required. This toughness will be the child's armor to protect himself from the many dangers that surround him.

A lower class child observes the frequent recourse to violence among his elders. To sit down together and to calmly discuss troublesome matters are the ideal folkways of the middle class. To settle matters by a show of force is much more simple and far more effective than mere talk according to lower class standards. Expression of power cannot be based upon some form of polished diplomacy. Like their parents who respect only muscles and brawn, lower class children generally acquire a physical and psychological toughness, which means survival rather than complete degradation in a rugged world.

For many reasons, a lower class child is likely to experience a family life devoid of the presence of his father. It may be due to desertion, imprisonment, search for work, or, perhaps, death in a hazardous occupation. Whatever the explanation, a lower class child will tend to have minimum contact with his father and maximum contact with his mother. The mother-child relationship is a strong one in lower class families, at least during early childhood. If the mother has preserved some elements of feminine gentility in her own personality, there is stronger chance that her offspring may acquire enough of her qualities to carry him eventually out of the lower classes. If, however, she has acquired an unbending personality born in the rigors of lower class living, the chances are that her children will have the same quality which can nullify any attempts to climb out of lower class levels.

Lower class children must participate in adult life as soon as possible. That is, the tendency is to hurry them along into adult responsibility rather than to indulge them as middle or upper class parents do. Their time of youth is short, because dependency and helplessness are far from desirable characteristics in a world that can sweep aside the weak and dependent. Lower class children, for instance, are asked to contribute to the support of their families as soon as possible. Whereas, in the upper classes the father alone performs the supporting role and in the middle classes the father's work is frequently supplemented by his wife's work; in the lower classes *everyone*, father, mother, and children, are expected

[4] For an excellent description of relationships between social class and family life, see Ruth S. Cavan, *The American Family* (New York, The Crowell-Collier Publishing Co., 1953), Chapters 5, 6, and 7.

to perform some supportative function. One lower class father recently complained to a judge that his eleven year old son was a "no-good" because he had not found some work with which to justify his participation in their family circle.

Since society has not dealt too kindly with them, lower class children have a high potential for anti-social behavior, judged by middle or upper class standards. Children must survive somehow, and if work is not available, which is the usual case thanks to child-labor laws, then other sources of economic support must be found. It may come through relief or the receipt of charity, but if such legal support is not forthcoming, then illegal action might be justified by such people. Their code resembles the jungle law of survival by cunning and strength. Bravado, flaunting the law, and disrespect for established authority yield a certain amount of satisfying notoriety which sustains lower class children.

In the lower class the search for happiness often takes the form of immediate satisfaction of desires, but because this is not often possible, withdrawal from harsh realities is the most frequent behavior pattern. Various forms of escapism such as desertion, alcoholism, drug addiction, and sexual escapades are known to lower class youngsters because they observe them in the lives of the older people near them.[5] The models set before lower class children are those of reaching for immediate, short range pleasures or the alternative of getting away, by escapist means, from the ever-present travail of misery and degradation.

SUMMARY

This chapter is concerned with the impacts that are made in the lives of children because of the universal phenomena of social levels. The lines of social class are invisible and intangible, but they are just as effective in reality as if walls were found keeping one segment of society apart from all other segments. These levels of social distinction mean that human beings are not granted equal opportunity in life, but are afforded differential opportunity to develop their personal capacities. For some children, social class insures full privileges even though they are always accompanied by social responsibilities. Nevertheless, moving down the social scale implies increasing disprivileges and lack of responsibilities. Children experiencing this as their birthright either endure these conditions or seek some means to escape them.

Social class lines may be drawn tightly so that none may enter or they may be drawn loosely in order to recruit newcomers from lower ranks. Children caught up in such social milieu react by developing qualities

[5] In this context, it might be wise to view the film "The Quiet One," available through Compass Film Service, P.O. Box 43, Genesee, New York.

of diligence, flexibility, and intellectual curiosity; or they may descend to the depths of despair, animosity, and negativism. Millions of children are involved in the world struggles which spring from contrasting ideologies concerning social class rigidity.

In this study of social stratification and its imprint upon children, the recurrent theme is heard loud and clear. . . . *Men create their own world.* Their children and their children's children for untold generations take the consequences of their wisdom or their ignorance.

READINGS

DAVIS, Allison, *Social Class Influences Upon Learning* (Cambridge, Harvard University Press, 1950).

DAVIS, Allison, and HAVIGHURST, R. J., "Social Class and Color Differences in Child Rearing," *American Sociological Review*, Vol. 11 (1946), pp. 698–710.

DAVIS, Allison, "American Status Systems and the Socialization of the Child," *American Sociological Review*, Vol. 6 (1941), pp. 345–354.

FAIRCHILD, M. "Social-Economic Classes in Soviet Russia," *American Sociological Review*, Vol. 9 (1944), pp. 236–241.

GREEN, A. W., "The Middle Class Male Child and Neurosis," *American Sociological Review*, Vol. 11 (1946), pp. 31–41.

GRIFFITH, Thomas, *The Waist-High Culture* (New York, Harper & Row, Publishers, Inc., 1959).

HOLLINGSHEAD, A. G., *Elmtown's Youth* (New York, John Wiley & Sons, Inc., 1949).

KOHN, Melvin L., "Social Class and the Exercise of Parental Authority," *American Sociological Review*, Vol. 24 (June, 1959), pp. 352–366.

KOHN, Melvin L., "Social Class and Parent-Child Relationships: An Interpretation," *American Journal of Sociology*, Vol. LXVIII, No. 4 (January, 1963), pp. 471–480.

KORNHOUSER, Ruth, "Warner Approach to Social Stratification," in R. Bendix and S. H. Lipset, *Class, Status, and Power* (New York, The Free Press of Glencoe, Inc., 1953).

ROSENFELD, E., "Social Stratification in a 'Classless' Society," *American Sociological Review*, Vol. 16 (December, 1951), pp. 766–774.

WHITE, Martha, "Social Class, Child Rearing Practices, and Child Behavior, *American Sociological Review*, Vol. 22 (December, 1957), pp. 704–712.

5

Influence of
Social Institutions

Social institutions may be regarded as the main pillars of every society. They consist of the formal systems of human relationships which deal with basic needs of human beings and human groupings channeled through the value system of the current culture. While this definition of social institutions involves a wide variety of associational patterns, it is generally agreed among social scientists that economics, religion, government, education, and the family are basic. Health and recreation might easily qualify as social institutions when described so broadly, but their structures and functions may be subsumed under one or more of the major institutions just enumerated. The vital nature of social institutions becomes increasingly evident whenever some defect, default, or malfunction within any one of these major institutions occurs. Then the entire society is, or feels, seriously threatened and could possibly suffer some dire consequences.

If a society is to survive, and this constitutes one of its most fundamental needs, it looks to its children to come through its processing well versed and well rehearsed in its institutional patterns. Through children, social institutions are intended to be maintained and, if possible, strengthened. Therefore, for present purposes, primary examination of each of the key institutions will be helpful.

ECONOMICS AND ITS SIGNIFICANCE FOR CHILDREN

The area in which men of a society are most active is that of earning a living. Child rearing is usually left to women, especially in the infancy and early childhood period, while men delay the time until they will give serious thought to the future economic capacities and prospects of their offspring. The preoccupation of husbands and fathers with economic pursuits, especially within the United States with its emphasis on the acquisition of goods and services, provokes commonly bitter complaints from wives and children. The economic support provided by husbands and fathers is appreciated, but this is alleged to detract from the amount and nature of the time spent with their family. Indeed, many wives, mothers, and children harbor doubts as to the priority or primary love of their husbands, fathers, and adult male relatives. The male abandonment or relative neglect of their families except in a cursory fashion may, in some cases, be more apparent than real; while in others, it is a simple fact.

Many men can explain how they struggle to acquire economic power and gains for the maintenance and well-being of their families and not for themselves alone. The role of the chief economic supporter of the family remains with men as one of their traditional functions despite increasing employment of women outside the home. The world of work is a demanding one and there are many times in a man's life when he wonders if he can endure the fierce competitive pace. Yet, there persists the problem of fulfilling the role-demands of being a father. Probably many a father secretly castigates himself for his seeming inattention to his family. Of course, children need the attentions of both their parents, but when it comes to the dilemma of being both a *good* father and a *good* provider, men resolve their problem typically by doing the one thing they believe they can do best and that is their almost universal attention to economic activities.

Women, of course, can counter by noting that they have continued to meet their responsibilities as wives and mothers while also increasing their economic participation. However, when they have done so, their problems of role-conflict are not as difficult as men's because they may resort to devices not ordinarily open to men. For example, women may perform many economic functions within their homes and attend to their children as well. They may find part-time work which takes them away from home and children only temporarily. They may provide for other women to take their place when they leave their children for outside work. They may take advantage of such aids as frozen foods, self-regulating stoves and ovens, canned goods, washers and dryers, polishers and vacuum cleaners to help them meet their domestic responsibilities and yet move efficiently outside their homes. Finally, there are numerous employment possibilities open to women, but usually not followed by men, in which women continue to service their homes and children. Nursing, social work, sales work dealing with women's or children's clothing, dietetics, nursery supervision, and home demonstrating are a few of these opportunities. While much has been made of the absenteeism of fathers due to their preoccupation with economic matters, there is a parallel concern that mothers have moved away from their homes and families causing more difficulties than many women would care to admit. An extensive literature has developed on "working mothers" and their positive or negative impacts upon childhood.[1]

Figuratively, the economic world intrudes upon homes and families sufficiently to cause children to learn how to fend for themselves or to develop techniques to deal with persons employed as supplements to their parents. Operating in *loco parentis* (in place of parents) has become the full time economic activity of many individuals and merits fuller discussion in an ensuing chapter. Even though parents delegate authority and responsibilities to others, they can anticipate some effects on the personalities of their children. While popular opinion continues to warn about dire results if parents persist in yielding their traditional prerogatives to parent-substitutes, empiric studies continue to fail to sustain the accuracy of the dire predictions. Perhaps these reassuring results are traceable to the relatively crude measurements currently employed. That is, contemporary devices are possibly not sensitive enough to detect what affects personality development; or the expectation of such may be merely a slavish adherence to older folkways. In the interim, until effects can be objectively determined, students of childhood can properly delay reaching definite conclusions as to the positive or negative impact of employment outside the home.

In under-developed countries the struggle for survival is so severe that no family member is immune to contributing to the support of his family. Mothers, fathers, and children work to sustain their homes. In such places, the economic function of the family has not been transferred into specialized hands. Homes are producing as well as consuming units. The closest equivalent to such families in the United States have been the self-sufficient rural families at the turn of the century when the services of every family member from the smallest child to the oldest adult could be used. Chores for children were commonplace in rural America, and children's problems were concerned with work rather than with what to do with one's free time.

But the older pattern of family farming has been eroding for many years. In a hard hitting, forthright presentation of what is happening in numerous small communities which formerly relied on family farming,

---

[1] See Robert Blood and R. L. Hamblin, "The Effects of the Wife's Employment on the Family Power Structure," *Social Forces* (May, 1958), pp. 347–352; S. Glueck and E. Glueck, "Working Mothers and Delinquency," *Mental Hygiene* (July, 1957), pp. 327–352; Lois Hoffman, "Effect of Maternal Employment on the Child," *Child Development*, Vol. 31, No. 4 (1960); Ivan Nye, "Employment Status of Mothers and Adjustment of Adolescent Children," *Marriage and Family Living*, Vol. 21 (August, 1959), pp. 240–244; F. Lundberg and M. F. Farnham, *Modern Women, The Lost Sex* (New York, Harper & Row, Publishers, Inc., 1947); *Marriage and Family Living*, Vol. 23, No. 4, (November, 1961), entire number devoted to "Women and Work."

Joseph Lyford[2] describes life around Vandalia, Illinois. He uses the example of a farmer, "one of those who live perpetually on the margin of extinction," who speaks about his situation:

I don't know whether to buy more land or not. I've got to have it to stay in business, but I can't afford the price. It's gone from $50 to $300 an acre and even then you can't find land to buy. The doctors and lawyers are buying it up and renting it out. I've been in debt clear up to my ears. The interest on my loans is eating me up and if I don't expand my acreage I'm licked. The cost of carrying a tractor and corn picker and sheller and a truck is just the same, whether I'm farming 200 acres or 600. I've been in debt every year since 1956. My land is just enough to support my family. I've got four more besides these fellows (pointing to his sons). The boys want to be farmers and I've tried to talk them out of it. This is a hard thing for me to do, to tell my oldest son he can't do the thing I wanted to do when I was his age especially when he has the makings of a good farmer. . . . What should I do—tell him to look for a job he can't do as well, a job that doesn't even exist? It takes as much money to start a farm now, with all the equipment we have to have and the prices of feed and fertilizer, as it does to start a good business—$15,000 to $20,000. Where can they get that kind of money? A kid can't start farming these days the way he used to. The only way he can make it is to have his old man turn over everything he has to him free and clear. I'm pinned down. It's been real bad this year, the worst I've ever seen.

Rural and urban people alike are caught up in the profound upheaval, still going on in the United States, in which mechanization, industrialization, and automation are able to produce an abundance of goods with a minimum use of human labor. Displacement by machines and new sources of energy place many people at a disadvantage in finding employment. There are others, however, who are not troubled with the lack of work, but rather with how to manage the abundance available to them by a rich and expanding economy. The children of such persons are not disprivileged, but privileged. They follow a life which is a far cry from the *rugged American* prototype. Such children may vicariously enjoy watching television cowboys struggle against great odds or read about frontiersmen who opened western trails. But their direct knowledge of out-door life may extend to two weeks in summer camps "roughing it" in heated swimming pools, eating three or more meals a day in a screened dining hall, and being entertained by trained counselors.

All this is not a plea to return to the days of hard work and chores for children. This is merely to present the question that plagues many parents who wish to do the *right thing* with their children. Contemporary parents who are able to provide a comfortable life for their children are wondering what personality traits are engendered by providing every toy that suits children's fancy, by shielding children from any economic worries,

---

[2] Joseph P. Lyford, *The Talk in Vandalia*, A Report to the Center for the Study of Democratic Institutions, Copyright 1962 by the Fund for the Republic, Inc., pp. 15–16.

and by catering to every whim that children choose to express. Such personality traits as kindness, generosity, appreciation, honesty, courage, reliability, sacrifice, responsibility, and consideration are qualities that have been valued in the past. Perhaps these qualities are no longer desirable or applicable to contemporary conditions. Society may have to determine new goals for the socialization of some children rather than insisting on the retention of perhaps outmoded personality characteristics.

This presents a problem only to those parents of older, traditional persuasions who continue to value personality traits that they believe are the foundations of success. Such parents are hard pressed to find household tasks for their children under contemporary conditions which provide an abundance of laborsaving devices. Children of such parents are often distressed when they find that they have limits imposed upon their economic demands. It is not uncommon to find them complaining bitterly about the refusal of their parents to provide "just a little thing" for which they asked.

While economic changes have affected the socialization of children so that they enter a different type of world than their parents once did, there are still numerous economic tasks that do require constant vigilance, a willingness to expend energy, a tenaciousness, and to some extent, a sacrifice of personal desires for the sake of getting tasks done. By training children to expect that the outside world will continue to pamper them as their parents once did may lead to some rude awakenings for certain children.[3]

RELIGION AND ITS MEANING IN CHILDHOOD

In searching for answers to the puzzles of life, mankind has developed multiple systems which satisfy his cravings for sense and meaning in the face of awe-inspiring mysteries.[4] Belief that the answers thus provided are the correct ones sustains men in their devotion to religious systems of their own creation. Deep seated emotional overtones cast an aura over these beliefs that does not tolerate much tampering or much skepticism from the uninformed or unconvinced. Traditional ideas and feelings are implemented by bringing children into close contact with religious convictions and ideologies as soon as possible and keeping them involved as long as possible.

The presence of young children, who have yet to acquire the religious convictions of their parents, may interfere with the solemnity, dignity, or

[3] See David Riesman, *et al.*, *The Lonely Crowd*, (New Haven, Yale University Press, 1950). A penetrating analysis of the changing character of Americans.

[4] See Charles F. Potter, *The Faiths Men Live By* (New York, Ace Books, Inc., 1954); J. Milton Yinger, *Religion, Society and the Individual* (New York, The MacMillan Company, 1957).

piety of religious services. Facilities and personnel, however, have been developed to encourage communicants to bring their children to religious services and activities even if they are infants or toddlers. Some places of worship provide nurseries or baby-sitters, while others offer sound-proof, glass enclosed rooms equipped with bottle-warmers, cribs, and playpens. The concern is not necessarily with formal instruction in faiths, but with fostering in children some feelings of identity, close emotional association, and acceptance of religious atmosphere as parts of normal living.

The commitment of a child to his religious background is deepened and enhanced by numerous other activities. Sunday school, Saturday school, Summer Bible school, retreats, picnics, church suppers, dramatizations, choirs, parochial day schools, and holidays share in common the value of binding children ever closer to their parents' faiths.

Pre-literate societies achieve the same ends by forming classes of children who are carefully schooled in their religious obligations. Because religious ceremonies are part of the daily fabric of folk societal life, children have ample opportunity to participate, observe, and imitate their elders. On the plaza of a contemporary pueblo in the Southwest, one of the writers was recently privileged to witness the religious dances of a people intent on praying for good harvests of corn. This was an annual ceremony, not designed to attract tourists, but to pray for good harvests. While the elders sang and young adults carried out a series of intricate maneuvers, some of the youngest children in the pueblo were placed at the end of the procession to perform, as best they could, the dance steps of their parents. No one laughed at any mistakes that they made. They were encouraged by their kinsmen to join the propitiatory rites and they did so with great verve. The promotion of appropriate devotional attitudes is a most serious business which eventually means the survival or the obsolescence of a faith. If children are unconvinced or unprepared, religious dedication dies with each generation.

The popular belief has been that it is older persons who are very religious and who become even more religious as they age. This hypothesis was not sustained in a study made by Harold Orbach[5] in the Detroit metropolitan area. He found that individuals established "life-styles" rather early in their lives. It was in their childhood that people developed religious philosophies. If they achieved some deep religious convictions early in their lives, they tended to continue their religious ideas and feeling-states by engaging in worship services, work associated with promulgation of their faiths, and integration of religious precepts in their daily lives. If, on the contrary, they had divorced themselves

[5] Harold L. Orbach, "Aging and Religion, A Study of Church Attendance in the Detroit Metropolitan Area," *Geriatrics*, Vol. 16, (October, 1961), pp. 530–540.

from spiritual matters while quite young, they tended to become detached from religious organizations, skeptical of all forms of piety, and unconvinced that religious ideologies possessed much merit. Adherents to various faiths have known of these general tendencies from close observation of their co-religionists for some time. They do not hesitate to bring children into communication with their respective faiths as soon as it is feasible. The biblical admonition of antiquity, "As ye sow, so shall ye reap," takes on new significance in the light of these findings.

The Power of Ritual

One of the distinguishing features of religious organizations is the establishment and promulgation of special forms of propitiation at specified times of the year. The religious calendar of each faith is filled with holidays calculated to remind the faithful of their ties to the past. Frequently, symbols have a prominent part to play in rituals which carry with them meanings which are clear chiefly to those who are trained to appreciate them. The term holiday, which in modern guise is considered to be a secular event in which one breaks routines and takes a brief, but welcome, respite from normal activities, originated in the practice of "a holy day," which consisted of a call for worship and appropriate veneration from the faithful.

To the initiated, holiday rituals are filled with meaning and inspiration. They act as bonds which hold them closely to their religious beliefs. The beauty, the pomp, the order, and knowing what to do at the appropriate time in unison with an entire congregation are most satisfying experiences. The achievement of ritual is one of identification with like-minded people. There are those, however, who are not so easily convinced about the power of ritual. They complain or rebel against what they choose to call "empty, meaningless, foolish ritual" or "pious hypocrisy." Such people have become disenchanted with religious ceremonials for many reasons. Among them would be such experiences as being compelled to follow elaborate rituals because of the authoritarian power of older persons. As children, such individuals may have followed the form of a ritual, but never understood the substance of the activity. Or, there are many children who have never been rooted in any single religious tradition because their parents believed rather in a broader, tolerant, all-embracing point of view. The result is like an adult who remains a bachelor, not because he dislikes women, but because he likes them all; it is similar to a person who respects all faiths, but will not invest his time with any one. Still another type is one who values his personal freedom to do as he wishes without the confining requirements of an established ceremony.

But the power of rituals remains. Quite often those who insist that they have an antipathy towards ritualism are in the forefront of those establishing new rituals. Being without traditions, they find it comparatively easy to create new traditions or new forms which they find quite satisfying. A secular example may be found among youngsters who resent the restrictions of their parents or teachers, but who willingly submit to requirements of special dress, manners, and speech developed by their peers. Religious history is filled with instances of dissent with certain religious propitiatory acts and the subsequent development of new forms of worship or adoration. Untold numbers of children were swept along in the tide of emotions that ran from religious upheavals of this nature. They shared with their parents the necessity to move away from former neighbors and friends with whom they had religious quarrels. In new locations, the dissenters were free to begin the building of new traditions. These in turn, easily became the center of new controversy so that the chronology of religious developments appears to take the form of a many branched tree or a vine composed of tendrils which divide and subdivide into seemingly endless patterns.

Ritual does not necessarily imply association with highly spiritual matters of soul-saving or eternal life after death. It frequently touches intimately the daily lives of religious adherents by dramatizing and emotionally heightening certain so-called critical moments in the life-cycle. These are *rites-de-passage* that anthropologists find routinely in societies throughout the world. The arrival of a child, his first tooth, his first successful hunt, his entrance into adolescence, his wedding, and his death are all chosen for special attention to mark off movement into higher levels of social status. Religious faiths, particularly, tend to make much of children's entry into successive stages of religious maturity. The naming of a child, his consecration to his parental traditions, his personal pledge to conduct his life in accordance with religious values are all cases in point. These rituals become increasingly familiar to children as they are repeated over and over again with each successive child. In due time, everyone will take his turn as the focus of religious acclaim. These are ties that bind children to the religious systems of their elders. They are not easily broken or ignored.

THE POLITICAL INSTITUTION AND CHILDHOOD

The relationships between childhood and political structures are more indirect than direct. That is children are *acted upon* rather than being actors with respect to political systems. In general, children are without power, except in such cases as royal children ascending a throne at a tender age. Even in these instances, a regent or a group of older statesmen control the political reins in the name of the child monarch. Children's political roles involve typically those behaviors that bring forward new action or new regulations in the name of the society or they act as catalytic agents which quicken the pace of governmental activities. In the former situation child labor, absence from school, and vandalism, violence, and thievery have brought on child labor legislation, compulsory school attendance, and provisions for rehabilitation of juvenile delinquents respectively. In the latter case, the denial of access to the facilities of schools, buses, and playgrounds has prompted lawmakers, executives, and the judiciary to reawaken their interest in civil rights guardianship and responsibilities. On the local level, it may cause a furor when a school teacher is accused of being brutal to a child or if school authorities require certain gymnasium attire for all their pupils. On the national level, the mental health or the exposure of children to salacious literature or films can lead to White House Conferences on Children and Youth or to congressional investigations. The world of children is, thus, not too remote from the adult world of political controls.

Ideally, system and order are required in the affairs of men and it is the political institution that organizes power in such a way as presumably to insure the well-being of all citizens. In America, children are taught at the elementary grade level to pledge their allegiance "to the flag . . . and to the republic for which it stands." The serious nature of such a pledge comes home later to citizens when they are called upon to serve their military obligations. The defection of a number of soldiers taken prisoner during the Korean "police action" called sharply into question the depth of such pledges of allegiance. No doubt, closer attention to studies in American history has reached into the elementary and secondary schools partially as a result of such incidents. In similar fashion, American children are currently receiving greater emphasis upon scientific training partly because Americans were jolted by the Soviet's successful launching in 1957 of Sputniks I and II. These instances of sensitivity concerning provisions made for American children overlook the fact that most American soldiers taken prisoner in Korea did not become turncoats, or that the scientific training of America's youth has been adequate enough for the nation to take the lead in many areas towards which national attention is directed. It apparently is a common failing to publicize the unusual or unexpected and to miss the obvious stability of much human behavior.

The clash between sovereign political powers or groupings of sovereign states is one of the most dramatic and violent upheavals possible in human experience. Already the world has suffered two world wars and any number of scattered clashes that could easily ignite a third global conflict. It is not necessary to expand upon the accumulated literature that bears upon the effect of wars on families, or more particularly, on children, except to observe that the general impact is devastating, disruptive, and damaging.[6] The far reaching effects of war are carried into the future in the personalities of the youngest generation. Abhorrence of war appears to last as long as those children who have been socialized during wartime. Thereafter, new generations of children may find war less repellent and more exciting until such time as real experience with war brings its sobering tragedies.

The domestic or internal affairs of modern political powers have been handled by a variety of bureaucratic structures which have been created specifically to handle assigned areas of importance to the citizenry. Childhood receives its share of bureaucratic attention. In the United States, for instance, the Children's Bureau serves as a clearinghouse for all information concerning American children.[7] Starting in 1909 and continuing until at least 1960, there have been a series of White House Conferences on Children in which periodic examination of the condition of American children has been accomplished. In these conferences, governmental and civilian authorities and interested persons pool their knowledge to appraise the status quo. Their discussions and conclusions are widely broadcast in order that, ultimately, new legislation and new directions for handling children might result.

Government appears to be the one agency in modern society to which citizens ultimately take their troubles. The American society may be viewed as being split into three separate, but related age divisions. Two of these are *the young* and *the old*. The middle division is *the adult* which must support both young and old in problems over which they have minimal control. The dependency of both young and old upon mature adults appears to be growing heavier and more burdensome. In former times, all segments of the society contributed considerably to their economic support. In contemporary circumstances, the dependency ratios are increasing to such an extent that local, state, and federal agencies receive a flood of appeals to spread the costs and responsibilities among all mature adults. But how shall it be done equitably and democratically? The demands of modern living are many, and those segments of society which make the most noise will probably get the most attention; a modern

[6] See Reuben Hill, *Families Under Stress* (New York, Harper & Row, Publishers, Inc., 1949); Edward C. McDonaugh, "The Discharged Serviceman and His Family," *The American Journal of Sociology*, Vol. LI, No. 5 (March, 1946), pp. 451–454; Martha Eliot, "The Effect of War and Civil Defense on Children, The British Experience," *Social Service Review*, Vol. 16 (1942), pp. 1–36; Willard Waller, *The Veteran Comes Back* (New York, The Dryden Press, 1944); Ernest Burgess and Harvey Locke, "War and the Family," *The Family, From Institution to Companionship* (New York, American Book Company, 1953), 2nd ed. pp. 606–643.

[7] Their publications *Your Child from One to Six* and *Infant Care* have been some of the most popular governmental publications ever produced. The U.S. Department of Health, Education, and Welfare conducts a clearinghouse for research in child life which will enable a student to keep in touch with the growing body of knowledge concerning children or American children in particular.

equivalent of the old rural observation that the creaky wheel on the wagon gets the most grease.

The voices of children or their spokesmen may be lost in the arena of political competition. Recent developments suggest that the aged are coming more and more into the political limelight and the shift in attention from youth may well be on its way. Just as the upswing in births caught the attention of the nation at the end of World War II, so the growing proportion of older people in the country now heralds the development of gerontological interests. In a country that has seen many White House Conferences on Children and Youth, there now has appeared a *first* White House Conference on the Aged.

In the American political system, it is possible to envision a shift in political power from one party or political philosophy to another. This will mean the acceptance of new governmental commitments towards children or it may mean an end to further appeals and support on behalf of children. Whichever way the political pendulum swings, children will be grossly or subtly affected for some time to come. They are no longer solely in the home, but subjects of attention from the highest authorities.

EDUCATION AND ITS RELATIONSHIP TO CHILDREN

In primitive, peasant, or under-privileged societies, the educational process is handled by the family institution. Mothers and fathers are the principal teachers. Only in relatively recent times has formal educational structure reached such an elaborate proliferation that it merits institutional status. Compulsory, publicly supported school systems in the United States involve the bulk of American children. It is a privilege that adults may properly cherish, but its benefits may be less appreciated by children who are compelled to go through the educational processing. The sheer joy of learning is not necessarily endorsed by the current crop of consumers. Homework, examinations, projects, and assignments seem to come in a never-ending fashion and constitute labor to children. Work does not always seem a privilege to the one doing the work. Chances are that many children eventually gain the desired perspective on education, but childhood is often left far behind before that result occurs.

Since education has been extended to all children, a problem has developed: What ends shall be served by universal education? Or, expressed in other terms, children should be educated in the United States, but for what purposes? Whatever answer is given, the educational system will be oriented along this line. Perhaps it should be a broad preparation for life in which general skills and socially sanctioned attitudes are acquired. Or perhaps, the objective to keep in mind is the ultimate ability to perform a useful societal task. The American educational system has typically reacted to dilemmas of this nature by absorbing both goals as legitimate ends to follow. It has tried to please the advocates of vocational training as well as those concerned about liberal education. It has attempted to be all things to all people, a most difficult task. Yet, in a general way, it has succeeded because most control of at least elementary levels remains in the hands of local school boards. However, as the system gathers more and more students at the junior and senior levels, consolidation reduces localism. At the state and federal levels, higher education in the colleges and universities is dealing with a wide, diverse body of students who come to campuses to formally culminate their training in every imaginable subject field. There is something for everyone in these communities of scholars.

The world of going to school is a world all its own. The classmates, the teachers, the administrators, the rivalries, the petty loves and hates, the exciting events, the times of despair, and the welcomed vacations and special holidays all evoke a nostalgia that is never quite overcome. As much as students claim that they count the days and months until they are free from their educational toils, it is interesting to observe their joy in school reunions, homecomings, and returning to their alma mater. It is a time for development and when the educational processing has gone on fairly smoothly, it is a pleasure to relive or recall such days. It may conceivably be a time of great travail for others. In this event certain failures and difficulties along the educational pathways foreshadow problems in later maturity. With a few notable exceptions, such as writers, actors, artists, and practical scientists, those who have difficulties with their educational experiences have unconsciously given notice of their future difficulties with other societal systems. Difficulties within educational systems are predictive of adult behavior only to the extent that the system is in accord with the society it supposedly represents.

In the kindergarten and primary levels, American children, at least, have a great deal to learn in a fairly short time. They are moved from a practically illiterate stage to a literate stage. The rapid absorption of fundamentals is an exciting adventure, especially under modern methods of teaching which uphold respect for individual abilities. It is a rare period of dedication to learning, an event that may not occur again until much later in life, if at all. Evaluation of progress is made, but this usually does not become an end in itself.

It is only with entrance into higher grades that report cards, ratings, and conferences are introduced. Children are slowly made aware that it is possible to "not pass" or be "held back" in the educational world. No one has ever claimed that grading has been developed into a fine science. The emphasis here is that grade consciousness does appear to increase as students move through the schools. In Great Britain, for example, passing a series of difficult examinations at a very early age can determine one's whole life career. In Japan and in the U.S.S.R. this same stress upon early evaluation, with its important impact upon lifetimes, converts what might be a most worthwhile experience into a nightmare of fear and worry. Suicides have been attempted in some cases when failures seem to doom the individuals concerned to a life of hard labor and lowered social status. On a less dramatic level, but nevertheless important one, American children go through numerous evaluations which, for some, become the principal reasons for studying. If this occurs, education and eventually society stand to suffer. For vast numbers of school children, grades may constitute a mild form of threat. Despite these difficulties, children appear to move through the system without too much damage to their personalities. It is for the few who suffer unmeasured anguish because of grading systems that the plea goes out to educators to exercise extreme caution in subjective decisions that could work a lifetime of hardship upon those who are graded.

Every educational system attempts to condition its students to be able to enter the society in which it is rooted. A distinguishing feature of the American educational system is the wide latitude that is permitted each student. Within certain limits each student has the opportunity to work at his own pace and within his own capabilities. He is offered a wide variety of subjects and courses from which he may choose, and he is encouraged to express his individuality in such a way that he is not a carbon copy of every other student. "Think alike," "feel alike," "act alike," and "be alike" are foreign to formal American educational philosophy but omnipresent in the realities of the school as a social system.

One might describe one of the chief trends in American education for some time as "the cult of personality." In recent decades, however, there seems to be a counter current running against the emphasis on personal expression and in the direction of greater stress on mastery of content and techniques to gain more content. As Americans have made solid achievements in the pure and applied sciences, there appears to be a renewed confidence that the American educational system is not as lacking as its critics would have the public believe. Certainly, the educational system in the United States is far from perfect, but it does not follow that it is inadequate or too lenient with its students.

THE PLACE OF THE FAMILY

The place of the family is central in the lives of children. It is from here that children enter into every other institution. Teachers may act as adjuncts to parents for a time, and fellow workers or classmates may become close friends; church, synagogue, or community life may generate a sense of real attachment, but these only supplement the family life of children. Only within the family system is the core personality of the child likely to operate and become well rounded. Little is held back or hidden. One may enter or leave a non-family situation, but normally in the configuration of the family, one has a place for life.

Because of the centrality of family life to children, it merits the fullest possible discussion. This will become the objective of the following chapter. It must suffice, for the sake of brevity within this chapter, to re-affirm the primary importance of families in the socialization of children. All other institutions seem to take a secondary or supplemental position as far as childhood is concerned.

SUMMARY

As pillars that support society, social institutions reach deeply into the lives of everyone. Particular attention is paid to children because these youngsters will ultimately be charged with the responsibilities necessary to keep the society going. The influence of the major social institutions, namely economic, religious, governmental, educational, and familial, cannot be fully treated in a single chapter. At best, this chapter confined itself to suggestions of the many ways in which children are affected by these social structures. The most important institution of all, the family, is not discussed at all, but is reserved for the following chapter. The relationships that were discussed should not be regarded as some sort of social mold into which helpless children are poured. On the contrary, children react to their institutional treatment. When they become adults within their society, they come back to the basic institutions to fortify them, to rebuild what they consider to be weak portions of the systems, and to create new patterns that will enable coming generations to emerge better equipped to cope with human foibles.

READINGS

ABERLE, David, and KASPAR D. Naegle, "Middle-Class Fathers' Occupational Roles and Attitudes Toward Children," *American Journal of Orthopsychiatry*, Vol. 22 (1952), pp. 366–378.

BIGELOW, Howard, *Family Finance* (Philadelphia, J. B. Lippincott Co., 1953).

BROOKOVER, Wilbur A., *A Sociology of Education* (New York, The American Book Company, 1955).

CLARKE, Helen I., *Social Legislation,* 2nd ed. (New York, Appleton-Century-Crofts, 1957).

DUBIN, Robert, *The World of Work* (Englewood Cliffs, N.J., Prentice-Hall, Inc., 1958).

ECKARDT, Roy, *The Surge of Piety in America* (New York, Association Press, 1958).

GETZELS, J. W., and GUBA, E. G., "The Structure of Roles and Role Conflict in the Teaching Situation," *Journal of Educational Sociology*, Vol. 29, No. 1 (September, 1955), pp. 30–40.

GLAZER, Nathan, "Three Possible Contributions of Sociology to Education," *Journal of Educational Sociology*, Vol. 33, No. 3 (November, 1959), pp. 97–104.

GORDON, C. Wayne, *The Social System of the High School* (New York, The Free Press of Glencoe, Inc. 1958).

HENRY, William E., "The Business Executive: A Study in the Psycho-Dynamics of a Social Role," *The American Journal of Sociology*, Vol. LIV (1949), pp. 286–291.

HOLLINGSHEAD, August B., *Elmtown's Youth* (New York, John Wiley & Sons, Inc., 1949).

KOLB, J. H., and BRUNNER, Edmund de S., *A Study of Rural Society* (Boston, Houghton Mifflin Co., 1946).

LOWIE, R. H., *Primitive Religion* (London, Routledge, 1925).

NEISSER, Edith, "Emotional and Social Values Attached to Money," *Marriage and Family Living*, Vol. 22, No. 2 (May, 1960), pp. 132–138.

PERRY, Joseph, "The Mother Substitute of Employed Mothers: An Exploratory Inquiry," *Marriage and Family Living*, Vol. 23, No. 4 (November, 1961), pp. 362–367.

PETERSON, Evan, "The Impact of Maternal Employment on the Mother-Daughter Relationship," *Marriage and Family Living*, Vol. 23, No. 4 (November, 1961), pp. 355–361.

SCHNEIDER, Louis, and DORNBUSCH, Sanford, "Inspirational Religious Literature: From Latent to Manifest Functions of Religion," *American Journal of Sociology*, Vol. LXII, No. 5 (March, 1957), pp. 476–481.

SEELEY, J. R., SIM, R. A., and LOOSLEY, E. W., *Crestwood Heights, A Study of the Culture of Suburban Life* (New York, Basic Books, Inc., Publishers, 1956).

SIEGEL, Alberta, STOLZ, Lois, HITCHCOCK, Ethel, and ADAMSON, Jean, "Dependence and Independence in the Children of Working Mothers," *Child Development* (1959), pp. 533–546.

STOUFFER, Samuel, *The American Soldier* (Princeton, Princeton University Press, 1950).

SUSSMAN, Marvin, "Needed Research on the Employed Mother," *Marriage and Family Living*, Vol. 23, No. 4 (November, 1961), pp. 368–374.

WACH, J., *Sociology of Religion* (Chicago, University of Chicago Press, 1944).

WALLER, Willard, *The Sociology of Teaching* (New York, John Wiley & Sons, Inc., 1932).

6

The Primacy
of the Family Institution
as Culture Carrier

The assumption that the family is a central source of influence on the child will not come as a surprise to anyone. Yet, even platitudes may contain profundities. It is the purpose of this chapter to provide some explanatory materials which support the thesis of the primacy of the family. Since such a position may not be altogether demonstrable, there is the need to qualify and more cautiously describe the limitations and circumstances which comprise the sphere of influence of the family.

THE PRIMARY NATURE OF THE FAMILY

The concept of "the primary group," credited to the insightful Charles H. Cooley,[1] provides the first clue that the family merits high attention from students of the sociology of childhood. While the primary group is an ideal construct, the family meets most of the criteria characteristic of primary groupings. It comes close to involving the whole personalities of its participants, not merely fragments or segments of personalities as secondary groups do. It demands and achieves face-to-face relationships over long periods of time, while secondary groups rely more heavily upon intervening media such as pictures, letters, advertisements, and formal forms of discourse which are utilized more intermittently. There is chiefly a spontaneous, unrehearsed, relaxed informality in family living, whereas in secondary groups one behaves among functionaries who conform to structured, formal procedures which demand guarded or cautious action

[1] Charles H. Cooley, *Social Organization* (New York, Charles Scribner's Sons, 1915), pp. 23–24.

lest one offend others in their assigned duties. Within the confines of the family, a member may feel free to express himself, to literally tell the truth, and if necessary, almost be brutally frank with less fear of major retaliation. In secondary groups, at the opposite extreme, one must be vigilant, sensitive to the reaction of strangers if he is "too frank," and concerned about the repercussions if he says or does something unacceptable. Acquisition of knowledge in secondary groups is rather deliberate or conscious, whereas the socialization processes going on inside family units are frequently unconsciously conducted.

On this latter point, James H. S. Bossard and Eleanor Boll [2] have made much of the opportunity provided the family to socialize the young when they sit down at the same table for their daily meals. While the purpose of such an occasion is ostensibly to renew nutritional strength, the primary qualities of family living come into play at such a time and the personalities of children are affected. It is their contention that social scientists would find in the informal give and take at mealtime many clues as to the nature of the family itself, and much concerning the direction in which they would have their children move.

Ideally, the longer the exposure to others, the greater the impact upon children. The less the exposure to others, or if the relationship is fleeting, passing, or momentary, as is true of many secondary groups, then the more shallow are the results in personality-building. The fact is that family life is a lifetime relationship, one is *always* the son or daughter of a given set of parents, one is *always* a brother or a sister to someone within a family, one *remains throughout life* a nephew, niece, grandson, or granddaughter. This persistent reinforcement of contact and kinship is a cardinal point to remember when one considers the significance of family influence. Parents and other family members thus have ample time in which to operate. Within secondary groups, such as a class of university students who are together for a quarter or a semester at the most, time is at a premium and action must occur quickly or time will run out, and many matters will simply have to remain unsettled or untouched. In the family, however, time seems almost unlimited and very little seems to be untouched when it comes to such matters as ideas, feelings, or shared experiences of growing up.

Secondary groups may be quite large and consist of huge gatherings of people in which individuals become almost indistinguishable from everyone else. Personalities, in such a situation, are submerged or kept dormant except for the few outstanding leaders. In the family, on the other hand, the group is generally quite small and consequently personalities are conspicuous and are the foci of constant attention. One might *hide* in a secondary group, but rarely within the bosom of one's

[2] James H. S. Bossard and Eleanor Boll, *The Sociology of Child Development*, 3rd ed. (New York, Harper & Row, Publishers, Inc., 1960), pp. 229–243.

family. Each person is usually noticed and his slightest behavior is subjected to what may appear to be seemingly endless comment and discussion. The growing child appears to be under almost constant surveillance and he must answer to his relatives for his errors or, on the other hand, contribute to family pride or esteem or prestige by his achievements.

In brief, the family is the initial builder of personality attributes and its handiwork may be seen in the immediate lives of children as well as long afterwards when they are mature adults. It is of course true that secondary-group situations also build personalities, but by comparison with family experiences, they are less profound in their impact and can be more easily nullified by other secondary and especially primary-group circumstances.

It is important to exercise considerable caution in describing the priority of the family institution in child socialization. It would be a grievous error to assume that the family has the total responsibility in child rearing and that all other groupings, by comparison, are inconsequential. It is possible to become overly impressed with the influence of family life and fail to place it in a proper perspective. It is not uncommon, for instance, to hear that racial, religious, or ethnic prejudice originates in homes, thus it is within the family context that bigotry is first learned. Yet, studies have shown that such a hypothesis is not always sustained by the evidence. In one such study, which dealt with the prejudice of lower-class children, no significant differences were found between the openly antagonistic, the prejudiced, or the apparently tolerant when it came to family backgrounds.[3] All varieties of prejudice seemed to be manifested regardless of what the family of the informants happened to be. Thus, there are obviously other experiences which can mark an individual and these may be found in non-family situations.

Clyde Kluckhohn[4] in discussing the infancy and childhood of the Navajo people makes this same point. He writes:

The most striking theoretical question which emerges from this consideration of some of the main aspects of Navajo infancy is this: how can this picture be reconciled with the facts of Navajo witch-craft, on the states of morbid melancholia and endemic uneasiness which have been well documented for adult Navajo? How can the anxiety level be so high among a people where infants are nursed whenever they want to be, where childhood disciplines are so permissive, where there is genuine affection for children? If the writings of certain psychoanalysts were literally true (and the whole truth), adult Navajos ought

[3] William McCord, Joan McCord, and Alan Howard, "Early Familial Experiences and Bigotry," *American Sociological Review*, Vol. 25, No. 5 (October, 1960), pp. 717–722.

[4] Clyde Kluckhohn, "Some Aspects of Navajo Infancy and Early Childhood," *Psychoanalysis and the Social Sciences*, Vol. 1 (New York, International Universities Press, Inc., 1947), pp. 85–86.

to have calm, beautifully adjusted personalities. In spite of the fact that Navajo infants receive a maximum of protection and gratification, they tend to be moody and worry a great deal when they become adults.

The explanation may rest in part upon the frequent ill health of Navajo children, upon teasing, upon refusal of the breast to toddlers, and upon delays in response to crying or upon other factors (such as genetic ones) that have been overlooked. But the main point is probably not that the theorists are utterly wrong, *but that they claim too much for the earliest years* (italics ours) and do not pay enough attention to later events and to the total situation in which the mature person finds himself.

The family, then, is fundamental to personality formation, but is only one of a series of primary and secondary groups which affects acculturation.

The Non-Optional Nature of the Family

If one could choose one's family, perhaps he might have a selection different from the one he actually experiences. It has been reported that in the Samoan society of the past, "children" were given the choice of living with married couples of their own selection when they had reached some point in their lives when they could make intelligent decisions. This choice of "parents," however, did not occur when the youngsters were in the age category of infancy to twelve years of age, the chronological age-span with which we are concerned. In reality, options in the area of choosing parents remain exceptions and are not typical for the vast majority of children. Even in the cases of divorce or separation when the wishes of children to live with one parent or the other may be taken into consideration, the final decision rests with legal authorities and is not determined by children. It is, thus, a near-universal experience to become a part of a family network without personal volition.

Theoretically, one can conceive of human groups arrayed on a continuum ranging from optional to non-optional. The parent-child relationship may be placed closest to the non-optional end, but there is no empiric evidence that *pure* optional groups actually exist. The reason for this conclusion is that there are always social pressures, cultural expectations, and other conditions and modifiers which introduce an element of less than a clear choice in so-called "optional" groups. A child may decide he has a preference for one parent or the other, but his cultural experience leads him to evaluate parents on the basis of what his society determines is a "good" parent. Among the Eskimo, it might be a skillful seal hunter. Among the Bahima, it might be an expert cattleman. Or, among Americans, it might be the one who can provide the most comfortable home.

It has been the experience of millions of children to have their families broken by divorce and desertion. And the general trend in the United States appears to be that more and more children are involved in broken homes. Statistics in support of this contention relate to the increasing percentages of divorces involving minor children, the increase in the absolute number of divorces over the past few decades, the increase in the average number of children per divorce, and the disproportionate numbers of desertions in the lower classes which typically have more children per family unit than the upper or middle classes. Thus, husbands and wives often take steps to terminate their relationships and thereby break up their families. But, their children remain essentially captive or in a non-optional position because they are still minors and live with one parent while remaining tied to both.

For those parents who choose to remain together despite critical lack of concern for each other, their children must endure the pathologies of misalliance as best they can. Their non-optional status becomes painfully clear to those perceptive children who might wish to escape their circumstances, but who cannot do so.

Within so-called optional groups, in contrast, participants have the prerogative of coming and going as they please. Optional-group authorities may be challenged and questioned, their power extending to the person only as long as that individual allows it to be applied.

Essentially, then, membership in a family is fixed by birth and the chief means of exit is death itself. Children may not come and go as they please, but are tied to their families by kinship bonds that hold firm against all expressions of emotion including resentment and hatred. Because the ties to kinsmen are based upon birth and are, in turn, socially reaffirmed within a culture, children may challenge family authority, but with far more caution knowing that they are rather tightly bound to the people they may be criticizing.

There are approximately twenty-five divorces per one hundred marriages annually in the United States. This does not mean that one out of four marriages in the United States is touched by divorce, because the divorces secured in a specific year did not necessarily stem from marriages made that same year. Nevertheless, the ratio of one divorce to every four marriages in a single year does indicate that a great many families have been dissolved and that there are many more families that will probably take the same steps to legally break up their homes. In describing the *solidarity* and *integration* of American family life, there are, then, notable exceptions, and observers of the American scene need to guard against assuming that ideal-typical constructs of family life necessarily square with reality. Many family units do work closely together and take each other's needs into account, including those of children. Such families feel strongly the need to deal with each other and to rise above personal whims or individualistic moods. There are other families, however, in significant and growing numbers, in which individuality and choice are more prized than conformity to cultural norms. These families do not feel bound to behave as others do which would be to remain together regardless of circumstances.

It is from the point of view of children who did not ask to be born to a specific dyad of parents that families may be understood as essentially non-optional. "For better or for worse" is a pledge that applies more to children than to men and women who allegedly take such a vow. It is children who are bound to their parents who enjoy much latitude as to how they will treat their offspring. Some children may be handled with genuine love and affection. Others may be treated as annoying mistakes who *happened* to enter the family and constitute additional burdens in an already troubled relationship. Child neglect and rejection are found in all socio-economic levels. On the other hand, many children who were not exactly "wanted," have been warmly welcomed and tendered care in accordance with the means of their respective families.

The Committee on Human Development at the University of Chicago [5] is credited with the identification and definition of *the developmental task* concept. The developmental task is defined as "a general mode of behavior which arises at or about a certain period in the life of the individual, successful achievement of which leads to his happiness and to success with later tasks, while failure leads to unhappiness in the individual, disapproval by the society, and difficulty with later tasks." This concept implies that the early experiences of children do prepare the stage for roles and responsibilities that lie ahead.

For the child who is smothered, over-protected, or misguided by parents, there is little chance to learn the desired developmental task. For children whose needs may be neglected or minimally treated because their parents are constantly fighting or bickering, there is also lack of opportunity to acquire skills, attitudes, and insights that will profit them in later life. An abused child, a child who has been treated with scorn, a child who has been discouraged in all attempts to express his point of view—these and many more become the misfits, the misanthropes, and the defeated in maturity. On the other hand, those children who are fortunately encouraged to perform within their capacities and interests, who are led to experience some measure of triumph in their formative years, and who are helped to distinguish between productive and non-productive actions, are in the desired strategic position of gaining increasing command of situations when they grow up. The uncompromising nature of the parent-child relationship, thus, moves children in the directions in which they are faced in their respective families.

[5] Robert J. Havighurst, *Developmental Tasks and Education* (Chicago, The University of Chicago Press, 1948), p. 6.

CONTINUITY OF THE FAMILY

When parents are asked for rationales as to why they had the children they did, they may engage in considerable introspection or they may turn to culturally explanations such as "children complete the family," "children make perfect love objects," or "children are necessary to carry forward the ways of their society." Psychological motivations, however, may or may not be consciously understood by couples who have entered into parenthood. For example, many parents seek to have children because these youngsters can possibly become ego extensions enlarging the scope of personal influences. Or, children can provide living proof that men and women are truly masculine or feminine and can function as their respective role conceptions indicate. For a great many parents, the motivation is nothing more than performing as they are expected to perform. Such parents neither probe their psyches nor question cultural expectations, but merely bring forth children because everyone else has them in due time.

From a psychological perspective, parents rarely have children for the sake of the greater society. On the other hand, from a sociological point of view, the end result is the arrival of children within some form or fragment of family structure which does perpetuate the species and forges additional links in the chain of family, cultural, and societal continuity. While the individualistic reasons for having children may remain obscure to certain parents or other parents may hide reasons because the reasons may not be socially approved, it is the overall results with which sociological analysis is chiefly concerned.

Most children enter a family unit which is already ongoing, which has a history, a heritage, a name, and a reputation. Family members are intimately identified with the newcomers and their experiences and the experiences of their children become mutually meaningful. If children seem to be moving in the direction of making drastic errors, older, wiser kinsmen can suggest more efficient procedures because they have already explored a number of alternative avenues of action, some sound, others sterile. Family associates commonly say, "Don't do as I do or did, but do as I say," not necessarily to dominate other individuals' lives, but to share what they regard as their hard-won knowledge which can profit youngsters if they permit themselves to be counseled by it. There is much to be gained by the entire family, it is usually assumed, if the training of the young can be smooth, intelligently guided, and uninterrupted.

Of course, there is another side to this picture. Not all adults have the intelligence, the wisdom, the experience, or even the desire to improve the situations confronting children. They may take the stand that "what was good enough for them is good enough for their children." Such adults themselves may be suffering from mental illness, poverty, inadequate schooling, serious deprivations which they may now consciously or unconsciously employ to ultimately have deleterious effects upon their children. The sufferings or shortcomings of one generation can easily infect the youngest generation and, perhaps, one cannot be reminded of this point often enough.

Social changes do occur, however, and the experiences of older persons are not necessarily pertinent to newer conditions which children face. The experiences of elders, then, are rendered obsolete and dysfunctional, if they become guidelines in a rapidly changing society that has passed them by. The context in which the experiences of older family members may be most useful is in respect to the type of person-to-person relationships which continue to affect the fabric of personality and society through generations.

For certain parents who have long since passed the formative years of childhood, children present opportunities to live again. Such parents vow that their children will not have to suffer the hardships that came when poor decisions were made. These youngsters will be guided past the hazards and ills that hampered their elders. Other parents adopt the attitude that nothing can be done to help children from repeating individual or familistic ways. These parents are extremely limited in their abilities to alter the life-chances of their children by reason of their lower socio-economic status, their insensitivity towards the lives of their children, and their failure to recognize their own shortcomings. Nevertheless, whether by helping children to avoid pitfalls that may have trapped elders or by failing to protect children from repeating the difficult life of parents, there is some semblance of continuity in family life. Families may be viewed as entities with *central tendencies* or moving in certain directions. Perhaps, a better description would be *family inertia*, which implies that some families seek to be upwardly mobile, some are complacent, and others steadily descend. In any event, they sweep their children along the mainstreams of their families' constant nature.

Recognition of the continuity of families may be found in essentially non-family relationships which seek to be family-like or quasi-families. Such associations place some value in the durability of family ties by trying to emulate them. Hence, it is not uncommon to hear such expressions as, "We belong to one big family," "We are all brothers at work on a common task," or "The founder of this organization was like a father to us," repeated frequently in lodges, clubs, camps, and professional societies. On the college campus, college homecomings, brotherhoods, sisterhoods, and housemothers are further examples of family-like references. Or, most sentimental of all, many former graduates can feel closely bound to their schools when they lift their voices to sing praises to their alma mater, their fostering mother.

The Emotional Nature of the Family

In a world that can be cold and forbidding, members of some family circles may rejoice in the warmth of their ties, the closeness of their relationships, the intimacy they enjoy, and the mutually satisfying consideration they give to each other. Genuine expression of affection is permitted such family members as each may unashamedly care for the other. An adult male and an adult female can love each other without restraint, without fear of criticism, and with high approval from society. Mothers may cuddle their babies and give full vent to their feelings of great tenderness. Fathers will also not be considered unmanly if they display great pride in their children. In brief, for some families feelings that are often suppressed, denied, or modified in non-family situations, because they could possibly be misinterpreted, are given freedom within the family.

Of course, emotions do not run strictly in the direction of love, high consideration, and appreciation. Emotions can surge in other directions such as hatred, fear, worry, anxiety, antipathy, boredom, contempt, and dislike. Participants in non-family associations must exercise great caution not to permit these negative emotions from breaking out into open hostilities. In families, however, each person may give vent to these feeling-states. One may cry, one may shout scorn, one may say exactly what is on his mind. Women often describe this aspect of family life as "letting their hair down," in sharp contrast to the stiff, prepared "coiffures" they maintain when in public. And, all this type of emotionality provides a lesson in double standards for children growing up captive in family situations. Children who witness such outbursts learn that there are "public manners" and there are "family manners" and these two behavior patterns are to be kept separate and distinct. For those children who fail to distinguish between displays of temper within their homes and control of feelings outside their homes, there often occurs serious behavior problems in which the greater society becomes involved. Children are, thus, brought into the world and fostered by families which minister to whole personalities, which demand continued face-to-face associations, which seek to hold children in unbreakable bonds, and which expose them to a wide range of emotionality.

A recent report on the relationships between parents and children in the collective settlements of Israel, the Kibbutz, suggests that there is much to learn about the establishment of newer forms of family living which might be beneficial for all concerned:[6]

If there is this alienation from the parental role, as we know it, what accounts for the zestful, enthusiastic relationship of Kibbutz parents with their children?

[6] See Howard Halpern, "Alienation from Parenthood in the Kibbutz and America," *Marriage and Family Living*, Vol. 24, No. 1 (February, 1962), pp. 42–45.

I believe that the notable exuberance of the parent-child interaction is related to this alienation. The parents share all the joys of growing up with their children but little of the pains. When a child is wounded, physically or emotionally, it is the *metapelet,* trained nurse, who responds to the tears and offers consolation and comfort. It is the *metapelet* who engages in the struggle of toilet-training and other struggles in the exasperating process of teaching the growing child to replace the pleasure principle with the reality principle. Should the child become ill, he is sent to the infirmary where the medically trained nurses, not his parents, tend to his needs. In short, the parents and the children have between them a bond of countless hours of warmth, of laughter and of fun, but they do not share a bond based on going through the hell and misery of growing up together. This is the root of the alienation. The relationship between parents and children in the Kibbutz is like that often found between grandparents and grandchildren in our familial framework. Grandparents traditionally have the maximum amount of enjoyment with the minimum of responsibility and turmoil. This often makes for a very happy and affectionate relationship between grandparents and grandchildren, and this is the atmosphere that seems to exist between Kibbutz parents and their children.

The circumstances in Israel which led to the establishment of the Kibbutz pattern have not occurred in the United States, but relevant to these circumstances it is significant to observe that in special cases, troubled and painful shared experiences of parents and children may not bind them closer together, but may serve to drive them further apart.

FUNCTIONS OF THE FAMILY IN RELATION TO CHILDREN

There are probably numerous functions that families perform in relation to children, but in the interests of brevity, about eight different functions can be identified. These are (1) to serve as a culture carrier, (2) to interpret and simplify a complex world, (3) to discipline, (4) to protect, (5) to give freedom to explore, (6) to help solve problems, (7) to provide pleasant family living, and (8) in sum, to develop personalities. These are to be understood as universal functions, unless otherwise specified. Furthermore, they are operational within the same structures which have been described earlier.

As Culture Carrier

Culture, itself, being an abstraction cannot move. It requires agents who have accepted certain formulas for living to activate it and make its impact felt among men. A prime carrier of a given culture is a family unit within a specific society. This is the first human grouping into which a child is brought. In the child's most plastic years, the family is charged with its care and upbringing. Family influence continues well into adulthood and probably never really releases its offspring. The family serves as society's representative and chief spokesman to the child. It must convey the message that eventually he will join the larger group and take his place in society. The family will bring to the child, according to its ability to comprehend, the ways of mankind, detail upon detail, item after item, and part by part until much of the fabric of social life is unveiled. Thus, the child will be acculturated in the same style as his fellowmen. If the process fails, however, the child can easily become a misfit, a threat to the company of men.

There are rules for social living and, before getting into the game of life, the child is schooled by the family to learn what these regulations are. There are things he must do and there are things he should not do. There is a whole language to learn, not only to become technically correct, but the child must even become familiar with the idioms, the subtle meanings behind words, the masks which hide more pointed ideas. There is a cultural logic to pursue from first premise to final conclusion. There is a cultural philosophy to develop which gives rhyme and reason to an otherwise confusing world. There are kinship ties with which to become familiar, as these indicate just how one stands in relationships to others. There are cultural implements to use which can be of considerable help or which can be dangerous to the careless user. There are dangers to avoid and there are worthy cultural goals to seek. These are only some of the cultural items that the family carries from the greater society and attempts to introduce to its children.

To Serve As Interpreter

Families select only portions of a culture to convey to their children and consequently neglect other elements that could have been chosen. The family serves as a screen to the culture of its society and selects only those portions that it deems worthy of attention. In this manner, the family can slant its information to help create the type of person it wants the child to be. It may offer the fine, the spiritual, or the noble. It may, contrariwise, expose the child to the worst, the vulgar, or the most unworthy portions of a culture. These value-laden terms are judged from the point of view of cultural participants and not by outside observers. By this selective process, the family explains to the child the nature of its cultural universe.

Children have been called walking question marks. Their questions are bound to be answered in a family in the manner in which the family already understands the situation. If family members are prejudiced or ignorant about certain matters, it is within this context that the child comes to view the world. If, on the other hand, the family participants are well informed and objective, a calm, adequate, thoughtful interpretation is given for a child's question. Only in rare instances does a culture reach a child untouched, unhampered, or unaltered by the processes of family communication. Like a newspaper, families *twist* the news for the consumer. The presentation of all the facts without bias is an ideal condition that is rarely, if ever, achieved. Families may not be trying deliberately to distort cultural characteristics, but unconsciously, by use of individualistic and highly selected illustrations, this is what occurs. Children see the cultural world from the eyes of their family informants.

To Discipline the Child

Unfettered freedom to do as one pleases does not exist. To create an ego which has no regard for other egos guarantees social conflict. The family is early charged with the social responsibility of getting the child into line, to restrain his natural urges and outbursts, and to rein in behavior that can only lead to a conflict with other people in his society.

Certainly, one does not break a young colt to harness immediately. There must be a time for kicking up the heels and letting others carry the serious social burdens. To place a heavy weight on a fragile back can only serve to break or harm it. But, as a colt gains strength and has had a taste of freedom, there does come a time for understanding that the carefree days in open meadows have passed away. So it is with children. They are often judged to be entitled, and most cultures make it their birthright, to be freed for a time of responsibility, to be allowed to play, and to seek only fun. In time, children do grow up and must put aside childish behavior and childish things. Surely they will rebel as discipline intrudes upon their pursuit of pleasure. But society will have its way and the family is instructed to apply strong measures, if necessary, to prepare the child for his social position.

Discipline does not necessarily imply harshness and cruelties. It can be gentle, persuasive, firm, fair, sensible, and consistent. Its virtue lies in the strength of men who act in concert. It brings to bear pressures in socially approved directions so that paths are cleared and society can proceed. It pools energy rather than disperses it. Society thrives on such a quality.

In fulfilling the obligation of applying discipline, families serve the young well if they impose restraint upon desire and impulse. A child will, once a stimulus has been given, respond as directly as possible to satisfy its needs. As it grows older, however, its family interjects social barriers between stimulus and reaction. One must learn to respond in the socially approved fashion and not in some sporadic, untrained, individualistic manner. Society instructs its youth, through the agency of the family, that humanity cannot operate upon impulse and immediate satisfactions. A child must learn, painfully if need be, that there must be delay, there must be a holding back, there must be great effort before a person may be granted social satisfactions. Many fields of study call themselves disciplines, meaning that there is a requirement of great control, great effort, and great denial to become a recognized adherent. Children learn this lesson of inhibiting natural desires when they enter formal schooling. The school, however, represents only a continuation of the lesson of discipline begun at tender ages within families. That which is socially worthwhile will not be attained by simply asking for it. One has to move along pathways previously blazed. Family discipline provides the means to follow these pathways.

The family has been aptly described as an arena in which there is a "collision of wishes." [7] Reuben Hill and Willard Waller write:

Behind the closed doors and drawn shades of our closed system of family living, the needs and wishes of family members collide and, when friction becomes severe enough, tempers explode, for home is a place where a man can be his worst, and often is. There is about family interplay a brutal and naked incisiveness. One can dissemble little with one's immediate kin. [8]

It is in the reality of family life that children discover that wishes are not freely granted and that human interaction demands some ability to withstand frustrations.

Some wishes may be more easily achieved than others. Children have to acquire a sense of which wishes may be granted and which ones do not have a chance. Some wishes might have to be altered or reconsidered. Some wishes might turn out to be in direct conflict with the desires of others. Still other wishes might be secured if one is willing to bide his time and not demand immediate satisfaction. Viewed from the perspective of colliding wishes, families may be called miniature societies, because they reflect what will surely occur in the greater society. Thus, children in the family are given an opportunity to learn important lessons in getting along with others before it is too late.

To Act as Protector

Unfortunately, there are potential dangers that wait for the day when children may stray or venture away from the guardianship of their families. Some societies live under more precarious circumstances than others, but in all of them, there still lurks serious trouble for vulnerable, naive, unsuspecting children. One of the most vital functions that families perform is to guard children from harm until they have gathered both strength and ability with which to cope with potential threats.

[7] Reuben Hill and Willard Waller, *The Family, A Dynamic Interpretation*, Revised Edition (New York, 1951), p. 26. By permission of Holt, Rinehart, and Winston, Inc., Publishers.
[8] *Ibid.*

In general, female children frequently experience an over-dosage of protection or over-protection. The solicitous care often given to females accounts in some measure for their somewhat more gentle nature, social responsiveness, keener interest in inter-personal harmony, and repulsion against brutal or cruel aspects of human treatment. On the other hand, male children tend to be given the experience of under-protection. Male aggressiveness, rough-and-tumble behavior, direct manner, and seeming unconcern for social niceties have some relationship to this type of handling. Evidence that these qualities are not necessarily sex-linked can be found in the fact that when female children are under-protected, as can and does happen in lower class situations, they display the *male* qualities of toughness, willingness to fight for their rights, and direct attacks upon barriers that prohibit personal achievements. Male children, likewise, begin to display *female* qualities of being shy, sensitive, less belligerent, and more persuasive if they have encountered over-protection in their families.

The problem of protecting children, as it is with so many problems, is to find the happy balance between the extremes of over- or under-protection. Children could probably well utilize certain characteristics of both male and female personality traits, regardless of their own sex. Usually, however, children tend to receive an unbalanced dosage of protection in one direction or the other. Parents are commonly puzzled as to how far they should go in their protective functions. Throughout the socialization process, parents are confronted with matters having to do with granting or denying permission to act. Each decision adds or accumulates pressures on one side of the balance or the other. To equalize them is a rarity.

To Grant Freedom

The function of protection is strongly associated with the granting of personal freedom or its denial. In America, parents are reminded constantly that there is desire for personal liberty. Chains, fetters, denials, and refusals are far from popular. Many Americans point with pride at this heritage which decries restraints. One must not be stopped from assembling, reading, petitioning against grievances, worshiping, or bearing arms. The Declaration of Independence asserted as "self-evident truths" that men are entitled "to life, liberty, and the pursuit of happiness." No person or no government should stand in the way of individual freedoms. Even children, who have been thwarted by what they call unfair restrictions by their elders, are quick to cry out, "It is a free country, isn't it? Why can't I do as I please?"

The answer to such a question is that there is another facet to freedom beside that of no restraint. Americans have been prone to emphasize *negative freedom,* that is, no one should prohibit individual action. The neglected aspect of freedom is *positive freedom* which amounts to the restriction of behavior in order to reach desired goals. This is to say that parents of American children, at least, must do more than say, "We will not stand in your way." They can also say, "If you desire to reach some goal, we will help you reach that goal. It will require you to demonstrate your ability by disciplining yourself to learn whatever society requires of you." Freedom, then, does not relate solely to doing as one pleases. It relates also to the development of individual potentials by acquiring the skills of one's society. Freedom extends only as far as the next individual with whom one lives. These two or more individuals have to acquire a social sense or else society cannot endure.

To Solve Problems

The dilemmas daily faced by parents are commonplace to those who are trying to raise young children. There may be some guidelines to follow from the larger society, but when it comes to day-to-day living, decisions have to be made within the immediate family and nowhere else. It is one thing to talk about granting freedom to children because Americans place a high premium upon this value, but it is another matter to take care of the many difficulties that may develop in specific situations such as at play, in school, or during religious instructions. Unless the society has developed highly particularized roles, many people simply have to interpret social roles as best they can. Just what shall they say or do to and for their children? What will constitute a proper decision? What shall be done in each specific situation? If there could be a written code to follow, as in legal statutes, parents could look up the solution in the proper volume. But, such a tome does not exist. Parents must play their parts by ear, so to speak. Some may say that they do not care what they do and will act upon impulse or whatever suits their fancy. Others may take their roles far more seriously and wonder what will evolve from the decision they make on a given day.

To Enrich Family Life

For many people the struggle for survival leaves little time for the niceties. But for others, especially those who are well above the subsistence level, there is the important function of helping to make family life interesting, exciting, stimulating, challenging, and pleasing. Instead of permitting family life to become routinized, dull, and unimaginative, parents can do a great deal toward filling their family experiences with a wide range of activities. These, in turn, become the springboards to fuller living in non-family activities. There may be, for instance, travel opportunities or interesting guests to bring into the family circle.[9] There may be family newspapers, gatherings, entertainments, or stimulating discussions and readings.[10] Or, there may be family pets to enlarge the vision of life. Variety *is* the spice of life and applies equally well to the family atmosphere provided for a growing child.

The Major Task: Personality Development

The chief function of families, however, may be summarized in the task of creating personality qualities within their children that will be their greatest asset in life. Sociologists have been close to the truth when they have described the family as *the cradle of personality*. It is within the family that personality is first developed and where it is given fundamental direction. There are some who have felt that the family no longer functions as it did in the past and they, therefore, conclude that there is very little utility to family life after all. No doubt, some functions have been lost or changed in their nature for many families. However, the chief function of rearing children to acquire personalities that will enable them to live satisfactorily in a specific society still remains. If the society is competitive, then the family will build into its children such qualities as aggressiveness, decisiveness, self-confidence, and shrewdness. If the society prefers cooperation, the family will labor to erect personality structures of gentility, kindness, dependability and appreciation. If the society is militaristic, then the family concentrates upon such characteristics as bravery, pride, toughness, and cunning. Certainly, children will not remain passive and completely amenable to family pressures; they may frequently rebel against being pressured into societal molds. In the long run, however, many children unconsciously accept their families' efforts to prepare them for the non-family world.

SUMMARY

The central position of the family in achieving the expected socialization of children has been detailed in this chapter. Families were not presented as the sole agency of society, but were conceded to have a maximum and long-lasting effect upon their children. Families were discussed as excellent examples of primary groups which work with the total personalities of their participants because of their close, emotional ties, in-

[9] See James H. S. Bossard and Eleanor S. Boll, "The Role of the Guest: A Study in Child Development," *American Sociological Review*, Vol. 12, No. 2 (April, 1947), pp. 192–201.

[10] James H. S. Bossard and Eleanor S. Boll, *Ritual in Family Living* (Philadelphia, University of Pennsylvania Press, 1950).

formality, involuntary relationships, and attention to the few people who live within their structures.

Both positive and negative influences were discussed. Eight different functions of families were noted. They were (1) to serve as a culture carrier, (2) to interpret a complex world, (3) to discipline members, (4) to protect adherents, (5) to give freedom, (6) to solve problems, (7) to enrich family living, and (8) to develop personalities. In this last function, many of the other functions are involved. By developing personal attributes which become an integral part of children, families set the stage for personal and social consequences. It was emphasized that the family must not be over-rated as an agent of society in the socialization process. The family, nevertheless, merits prime consideration because of its direct and lasting impact upon children.

READINGS

BENNETT, Ivy, *Delinquent and Neurotic Children* (New York, Basic Books, Inc., Publishers, 1950).

BLITSEN, Dorothy, *The World of the Family* (New York, Random House, Inc., 1962).

BOWERMAN, Charles E., "Family Background and Parental Adjustment of Step-Children," *Proceedings of Pacific Sociological Society*, Vol. 24, No. 2 (June, 1956), pp. 181–182.

CALHOUN, A. W., *A Social History of the American Family* (New York, Barnes & Noble, Inc., 1945).

DUVALL, Evelyn, "Where Do They Get Their Ideas of Love and Marriage?" *The PTA Magazine*, Vol. 56, No. 8 (April, 1962), pp. 10–14.

EISENSTEIN, Victor, *Neurotic Interaction in Marriage* (New York, Basic Books, Inc., Publishers, 1956).

ELKIN, Frederick, *The Child and Society, The Process of Socialization* (New York, Random House, Inc., 1960).

GOODE, William J., "The Sociology of the Family," Chapter 7, in Robert K. Merton, Leonard Broom, and Leonard S. Cottrell, Jr., Editors, *Sociology Today: Problems and Prospects* (New York, Basic Books, Inc., Publishers, 1959).

HAWKES, Glenn, "The Child in the Family," *Marriage and Family Living*, Vol. 19, No. 1 (February, 1957), pp. 46–51.

HEINICKE, Christopher, "Some Effects of Separating Two-Year Old Children from Their Parents: A Comparative Study," *Human Relations*, Vol. 9, No. 2 (1956), pp. 106–107.

HERBERT, Otto, "What Is a Strong Family?" *Marriage and Family Living*, Vol. 24, No. 1 (February, 1962), pp. 77–80.

KARDINER, Abram, *et. al.*, *The Psychological Frontiers of Society* (New York, Columbia University Press, 1945).

KENKEL, William, *The Family in Perspective* (New York, Appleton-Century-Crofts, 1960).

LANDIS, Judson, "The Trauma of Children When Parents Divorce," *Marriage and Family Living*, Vol. 22, No. 1 (February, 1960), pp. 7–13.

MARTINSON, Floyd, *Marriage and the American Ideal* (New York, Dodd, Mead, & Company, 1960).

MILLER, D. R., and SWANSON, G. E., *The Changing American Parent* (New York, John Wiley & Sons, Inc., 1958).

MILLER, Nathan, *The Child in Primitive Society* (New York, Brentano, 1928).

MUSSEN, P. H. and CONGER, J. J., *Child Development and Personality* (New York, Harper & Row, Publishers, Inc., 1956).

NYE, Ivan, and MACDOUGALL, Evelyn, "Do Families Have Subcultures?" *Sociology and Social Research*, Vol. 44, No. 5 (May–June, 1960), pp. 311–316.

PARSONS, Talcott, and BALES, R. F., *Family, Socialization, and Interaction* (New York, The Free Press of Glencoe, Inc., 1955).

PERRY, Joseph B., Jr., and PFUHL, Erdwin H., Jr., "Adjustment of Children in 'Solo' and 'Re-Marriage' Homes," *Marriage and Family Living*, Vol. 25, No. 2 (May, 1963), pp. 221–223.

ROWNTREE, Gusilda, "Early Childhood in Broken Families," *Population Statistics*, Vol. 8, No. 3 (March, 1955), pp. 247–263.

SEARS, Robert, "Relation of Early Socialization Experiences to Aggression in Middle Childhood," *Journal of Abnormal Social Psychology*, Vol. 63, No. 3 (November, 1961), pp. 466–492.

SIMPSON, Richard, "Parental Influence, Anticipatory Socialization, and Social Mobility," *American Sociological Review*, Vol. 27, No. 4 (August, 1962), pp. 517–522.

WHITING, Beatrice B., ed., *Six Cultures, Studies of Child Rearing* (New York, John Wiley & Sons, Inc., 1963).

WINCH, Robert F., *Identification and Its Familial Determinants* (New York, The Bobbs-Merrill Company, Inc., 1962).

7

Adult Non-Family Participants

In discussing the larger social and cultural context of childhood in Chapter 3, the principal focus was upon the more formal, structured, and collectivity-oriented systems. Attention was given only implicitly to informal, loosely structured, and somewhat individual-oriented situations. Clearly, however, contact and interaction in these latter situations are both widespread, repetitive, and may be deeply significant. Since the growing child's experiences are not always anticipated, planned, and regulated, those experiences are almost certain to include incidental or intermittent meetings and interactions with persons whose relationships with him seem, on the surface, to be only peripheral. It is contact situations of this sort that constitute the focus of this chapter. To distinguish the persons in these situations from those in the family, peer, and more formally structured groups or social systems, they are, for present purposes, referred to as *adult non-family participants.*

Not all social situations involving the child are clearly and systematically structured for him. In the course of his development, chance or adventitious contacts and interactions occur. For instance, he may have casual contacts with other children while waiting in the Saturday morning movie line, or brief encounters with adults as he goes to and from school, or chance meetings with stranger age-mates or adults while playing in back alleys, vacant lots, or playgrounds. Sometimes, such contacts are fleeting in their temporal duration, nonrecurrent, and negligible in their influence. Sometimes, however, they are of longer duration, recur from time to time, and result in some considerable influence. On the whole, then, the child's contacts and interactions with the adult non-family participant falls within this contextual range.

The importance of the adult non-family participant in the socialization process is implied in the observation that "sociological theory or practice that disregards the dyadic pattern and its influence upon the whole range of social life . . . commits a far-reaching error."[1] Again, "Above all else, this point must be grasped: the pair always behaves otherwise than either member would alone, or at the very least, in cases where one partner is overwhelmingly dominant, than the passive member if left to himself would behave."[2]

The extent to which the child and the adult non-family participant constitute a *true pair* differs in accordance with the character of the latter person in question and the circumstances under which the two meet. Generally, such pairs or *near-pairs* meet infrequently, adventitiously, momentarily, and/or even indirectly. This is to say, the child might merely see but not communicate with the other person.[3] Despite such contacts and relations, the probability that the adult non-family participant might exert influence upon the child should not be disregarded. Furthermore, such meetings might well prove to be the beginning of a continuing reciprocal attachment or relationship.

PARENTS AND ADULT NON-FAMILY PARTICIPANTS

Usually, parents are responsible for determining what social relationships and experiences are best or appropriate for their children. They determine at what point in the child's development certain aspects of the culture shall be presented or what personal contacts shall be made available to him. In complex societies, formally structured organizations or systems such as the school, the church, boys' clubs, and the like, usually supplement and facilitate this selective process. By and large, these systems and the family have consensus regarding what aspects of the culture should be transmitted to the child and when. In large part, this consensus is brought about by the fact that parents usually attempt to expose their children only to those situations in which the prevailing norms and practices are consistent with what they regard as desirable or best. To the extent that this selective process prevails, family-controlled, or family approved relationships and experiences are brought about.

In social situations involving children and adult non-family participants, there tends to be less assurance of consensus and consistency between parental expectations and the type of influence these participants sometimes exert upon children. This may be largely due to minimum contact

[1] Howard Becker, *Systematic Sociology on the Basis of the Beziehunslehre and Gebildelehre of Leopold von Wiese* (New York, John Wiley & Sons, Inc., 1932), p. 508.
[2] *Ibid.*, p. 516.
[3] Such contacts include TV characters, such as the Cartwrights, Superman, Captain Kangaroo, and those adults who conduct programs designed especially for children. Even though the child knows that some of these personages are not *real*, he is likely to respond to the images presented or to whatever commercial appeals are made.

and communication between parents and these persons; or, it may be due to different orientations regarding what is or what is not appropriate in adult-child relationships. In any event, depending upon the particular adult non-family participant involved, the child might be subjected to experiences which approach rather closely to or deviate rather widely from those in which his parents would have him become involved. With regard to some aspects of the child's behavior, the influences of adult non-family participants might well be decisive. To illustrate, these influences may hold the key to mother's question, "Now, I wonder, where did he learn that?"

In highly complex, urbanized, and democratic societies these contacts and relationships are not generally the same for all children. They vary in extent, in duration, in frequency, and even in quality. In a rather rigidly stratified and specialized society, however, such variations are likely to be less widespread. Furthermore, in such societies people tend to be separated into various categories which are socially and frequently geographically isolated. In such instances, the social class to which a child's family belongs will tend to constitute the boundaries within which he may have contact and interact with adult non-family participants. Such class-based limitations tend to be expected and this usually leads to experiences which are consistent with those of the class to which the child belongs. In addition to class limitations, the child's family may impose other limitations based on religious, racial, or ethnic considerations.

The particular experiences a child has with adult non-family participants and the results of these experiences vary with the characteristics of the participants and the circumstances under which interaction occurs or the relationships emerge. It is desirable that these different possible experiences should be examined and their probable results determined, however, the impact of any such interaction is not easily determined or predicted. Nonetheless, it is possible to make certain generalizations which might contribute to an understanding of these forces. To do this, adult non-family participants are classified and discussed under the following headings; distant relatives, friends, neighbors, nigh-dwellers, acquaintances, guests, servants, functionaries, and passers-by.

CONTACT AND INTERACTION WITH DISTANT RELATIVES

For present purposes, distant relatives—either in terms of more remote kinship or separation by geographic space—whose relationships with the child are not clearly structured and whose interactions with him occur only infrequently, are classified as non-family participants. A child's distant relatives include all of his kin who do not live in the same household, who do not live nearby, and who do not interact with him regularly. Although physical distance is a factor in the definition of a child's distant relatives, the more important consideration is the character and regularity of the relationships. For example, a child may live several hundred miles from one of his grandparents whom he visits only infrequently, yet the two may be so emotionally involved that their relationship will be extremely meaningful and mutually satisfying. Such a grandparent is not a psychologically *distant* relative.

It should not be assumed that relationships between the child and his distant relatives are of the same order as those involving persons outside of his family. They are not. Even though a child may be less emotionally attached to a particular distant relative than he is, say, to a friend of the family, he is nonetheless likely to think that he *ought* to feel something because that relative is, after all, a member of the family. By and large, such a relationship is not likely to result in any considerable positive impact upon the child; for the recognition and even the acceptance of this mandate to feel may well be merely a ritual performed without subjective meaning. In some instances, however, this feeling for the family can take on special importance or meaning. This is especially so among members of the upper class where family name and tradition are generally regarded as of prime importance. The fact that outsiders often attach special significance to kinship ties is important, and this tends to influence the child's conception of the connection between the distant relative and himself.

The child's view of his position and feelings regarding the distant relative is but one side of the coin. The character of this relationship also depends upon the reactions of the relative. He too is subject to the meanings and pressures of kinship. If he regards the kinship bond as important, he will perhaps respond to his young relative in a positive manner. However, there is one feature of the kinship system which might interfere with the development of a positive relationship between a child and his distant relative: the latter might have children of his own. Taken alone, this presents no problem, but it is possible that this relative might find it difficult to become involved with the child of his distant kin. The possibility of competition or conflict between the children of distantly related parents might develop to the point where the adult will become alienated from his young distant relative.

Family Visits and Family Reunions

To the extent that family contacts and interactions are formalized and regulated, they tend to be expressed in family visits and family reunions. The former occur more frequently, include fewer people at a time, involve less distant relatives, and are less formal than the latter. In the case of family visits, the child's contacts with distant relatives might give him opportunities to select and become better acquainted with a favorite cousin, for example. This is a probable consequence of relatively frequent visits with a particular relative who is already a favorite with the child's parents. By such visits, the child gets to participate in new situations which may come to be satisfying and enriching. Eventually such visits could lead to the transformation of a distant relative into a close relative, that is, the child and the adult could become emotionally closer.

Although the child might enjoy visiting a particular relative, this could have irritating or disturbing consequences for his parents, if they regard the relative's reactions to their child either as over-indulgent or over-severe. In any event, such visits need not be equally satisfying to both the child and his parents. Indeed, it could prove to be a source of conflict when the family gets back home. Whatever the outcome, be it pleasant and rewarding or dull and painful, such experiences might leave the child with feelings which may or may not be quickly or easily dissolved. Depending upon the specifics of the situation, child visiting with distant relatives is a broadening, though not always a helpful experience. As such, its significance for child development should not be overlooked nor discounted.

In contrast to family visits, family reunions occur rather infrequently. They tend to involve more planning, more people, and more formality. As its manifest function, the family reunion is a family-maintaining and solidifying social device. It is manifestly a situation which brings widely separated kinsmen together to renew and strengthen the bonds that hold them together. Periodically, these family gatherings provide a face-to-face situation which serves to remind the members of their common family tradition. At these meetings, families reminisce about their most memorable experiences, exchange views on some of their common interests, discuss plans for collective action, and pass on information concerning their absent kinfolk.

Of no small importance at the family reunion is the introduction or re-introduction of the children of the several family units. When children were "to be seen, not heard," the child did not occupy a place of importance at the family reunion. Now, however, the display of one's child or children is perhaps one of the principal latent functions of such meetings. To some extent, an opportunity to show-off one's precocious offspring is a consideration underlying attendance at the family reunion.

Generally, family reunions tend to be viewed and interpreted in terms of their significance for the experiences of the adults who attend. It is highly probable that the adult relatives receive some special and even lasting effect from these periodic meetings. To the extent that this is so, they are likely to pass on some of the results of the reunion experience to their children. Today, children, as well as adults, play an important role in the family reunion. Sometimes, parents commend their children or scold them for their behavior in front of the family. They express sympathy for the child who was slighted or rejected at the gathering of the kinfolk. Finally, the impact of the reunion may be expressed through family talk about how well things worked out or through the free exchange of ideas concerning plans for the next meeting.

Parental reactions to the family reunion as illustrated here are perhaps significant cues and aids to the child in his definitions of the total reunion situation as well as of the various relatives in attendance. Furthermore, they may underscore the value of kinship. However, the child's reactions to the reunion need not depend wholly upon parental evaluation of the situation. In such cases where the contact is direct, the interaction face-to-face, and the relationships multiple and varied, even though brief, the child can be expected to have a mind of his own. Thus, he may dislike his cousin Sara, and show it. In the event that his parents have expressed a dislike for this relative (in private), he might behave rudely toward her. In contrast, his favorite relative may be his ne'er-do-well Uncle Bill—least favorite among other members of the kinship—and he lets one and all know it. These examples illustrate two opposite types of reactions which the child might express toward his relatives at the reunion. Conceivably, either or both may cause his parents and other relatives to be critical of him.

Apart from the attachments he might feel for the various distant relatives at the reunion, the child's involvement in this situation can produce various results. He might acquire new information concerning people, places, and events. He might be made to feel important and worthwhile or of little importance and relatively worthless. He might enter into the spirit of the occasion wholeheartedly and enjoy himself immensely, or he might feel uncomfortable and ill at ease, like an unwelcome guest among strangers. Depending upon the nature of the child, of his parents, and their relationships with him, and depending upon the character of the distant relatives and the relations he has with them, the family reunion is a possible source of significant experiences for the growing child.

The following firsthand report on a family reunion is taken from the files of the authors.

The reunion is held the last Sunday in August each year at one of the parks near Danville, Illinois—usually Kickapoo State Park.

This family reunion isn't like those one reads about in books. Ours doesn't include all the relatives. Most of my maternal and paternal aunts and uncles and cousins have been excluded. (It might be more accurate to say that they just aren't invited even though a number of them live within a ten-mile radius of my father.) We had a discussion about this a few years ago and even though many of us thought others should be invited, my father was very much opposed. In the end, his opinion prevailed as did his decision that no liquor should be served.

Since the reunion includes for the most part my brothers and sisters and their children who live fairly close together in mid-state Illinois, it really becomes a family picnic at which there is little new to talk about (except perhaps for the few of us who live farther away and visit less often). There are generally a few informal games—touch football, badminton, horseshoe pitching, and male vs. female softball game. The main event, of course, is dinner; then resting and visiting and playing with the little ones, etc.

. . . I'll try to give my impressions of those attending, starting with my youngest brother and moving to the oldest. (There is bound to be a lot of "hindsight" in this and also prejudice and preference that I've built up over the years.)

Noah (italics signifies brother or sister) and Mattie and their three children didn't attend this year. I include them because there was a good deal of "reasoning why." The consensus was that Mattie has 'influenced' Noah over to her family; she has always acted strange and unfriendly: they attended other years after considerable coaxing.

Herbert and Clara and their three children drove over from Indianapolis. The children were very proud and showed it. Herbert and Clara looked well and seemed relaxed. Greg seemed as quiet as ever.

George and *Odelle* and their two girls. George was upset by the eagerness with which several members of the family approached Jocelyn and Tori. The girls were overwhelmed by so many strangers trying to kiss, hug, or say hello.

Bev and Scotty and their three children. We stayed all day Saturday and overnight with them in Champaign. I could sense strained relationship between them. She admitted that she resented the long hours he spent as president of the local ——— club in addition to those of a full time and a part-time job. She was obviously very tired with all the work entailed in caring for her ten-month-old boy and two other children. Scotty, of course, complained that she never goes out with him anymore.

Alice and Jake and their four children. Most of the family was solicitous of them. Their month-old baby had been born with a hydrocephalic condition. Alice wore a strained smile and seemed to have accepted the situation. Jake said little or nothing. Alice says he would hardly touch the baby.

Beth and her two children. Her eyes seemed so sad; they were always so big and lovely. She was quiet and very much a 'loner' during the day. I talked with her while she sat away from the group smoking (Daddy disapproves). She felt a little outcast because some of the family members disapprove of her choice of a male companion.

Hattie and Bob and their six children didn't come to the reunion but phoned from Massachusetts early Sunday morning and talked at length about themselves. They always seem to be in some difficulty and were, of course, a topic of discussion at the picnic as usual.

Angie and her daughter Pat. She is always so busy—the go-getter, the organizer. My impression—she's going somewhere fast—but where? She puts an overemphasis on the importance of money—especially to Pat—and is dogmatic in her preaching and teaching to Pat about alcoholic beverages.

Helen and Chuck and their two children. Chuck didn't go to the picnic. George and I visited Helen at her new home on Saturday. She was completely entranced with the children; she has always been that way about children. She talked and talked as she showed us the house—hardly giving us a chance to comment. Later she told me how terribly depressed she felt at times and how she felt about the menopause and discussed the fact that Marilyn Monroe had taken her own life—and how one could get the nerve to do it. She was concerned because Angie accuses her of deserting the family and of being selfish with her time and energies. My impression—she is devoted to her children, she loves but is uncertain about her husband; her home which she has looked forward to and worked for all her life has not been the answer to happiness she thought it would be.

Trever and Millie and their three sons. Milledge, the oldest, is in the Army. Trever and Millie and the younger boys were a joy to watch. They were comfortable and honest with each other and with others. The boys were outgoing and robust and the parents were justly proud. This didn't seem the same family that had had such seemingly unsurmountable difficulties years before.

Daddy and Lettie. Daddy looked fairly well but seemed tired and is graying fast. Lettie had an arthritic condition and talked about it much of the time. They seemed to be on good terms with everyone but the conversation is superficial. Everyone seems to know what *not* to talk about with Daddy.

There were others at the reunion—Aunt Ellie and her two unmarried daughters and Aunt Sara (both my mother's sisters) who came for the first time from Indianapolis. My second brother's (Junior) child Art was there. He has been living with Daddy for 6–7 years now. His father lives in Washington, D.C., and hardly corresponds with him. Art is not doing well in school. He seemed uncomfortable in the group except with the older grandchildren. They (the grandchildren) stayed together much of the time as did the other age groups (now that I think of it).

Family reunions such as this can serve to maintain and solidify family ties. In some instances, however, they may represent concessions to the will or interests of some older member or members of the kinship group who are determined to keep the family together. For the child, specifically, the family reunion can point up the importance of kinship; it can facilitate his identification with members of the family or at least with the family name; or, it can involve him in family traditions or with persons who are to some extent part of his past, present, and future.

FRIENDS, NEIGHBORS, NIGH-DWELLERS, AND ACQUAINTANCES

As popularly used, the term *friend* is highly imprecise. It is often used to refer to one who is known only casually. For present purposes, however, a friend is one who is intimately bound to another by an enduring, intimate, but non-kinship tie. Friendship, as here defined, involves mutual respect, esteem, and affection. The interaction between two friends is of a primary-group quality; it tends to be all-embracing, intimate, and lasting. Friendship is, therefore, a source of significant influence for the parties concerned.

As used here, the term *neighbor* is akin to the term friend, but the neighbor and the friend relationships differ qualitatively. The term neighbor has locality implications: a neighbor is one who lives nearby. Although the neighbor relationship is ideally primary-group oriented, it tends to be less emotionally intense and in a highly mobile society less permanent than the friend relationship. Quite commonly, however, a neighbor is, or becomes, a friend.

Frequently, the term neighbor is applied to one who merely lives next door, or nearby, even though the relevant parties are barely on speaking terms or are hardly known to each other. It would seem, however, that a term other than neighbor should be applied to two people so situated. The term here employed to refer to such persons is *nigh-dwellers*. Nigh-dwellers live in close physical proximity, but their contacts, interactions, and emotional ties are, at most, minimal.

Manifestly, an *acquaintance* is a person whom another person knows, at least by name. Usually, they are on speaking terms, and even converse when they meet. Sometimes, acquaintances are also nigh-dwellers; this is especially so in many parts of the large urban communities. Frequently, two people become acquaintances by being introduced to each other by a mutual friend or acquaintance. They may meet from time to time, develop an association independently of the mutual friend, and may ultimately establish themselves as friends, or may remain mere acquaintances.

Friendship, neighboring, nigh-dwelling, and acquaintanceship each implies a relationship which is qualitatively different. The nature and frequency of these contacts differ. As a result, the interaction involved in each of these relationships vary somewhat. For example, interaction between friends or neighbors frequently occurs within the home. Between nigh-dwellers and acquaintances, the interaction usually occurs outside the home. When, as sometimes happens, the latter interact within the home, the occasion tends to be special and somewhat formal.

Up to this point, friends, neighbors, nigh-dwellers, and acquaintances have been viewed from the adult perspective. Such a view of course has significant implications for children. Certainly the parental definition of another person as friend, neighbor, nigh-dweller, or acquaintance will be communicated to the child. And, the child will be expected to behave toward that person accordingly. This could conceivably pose a problem. The child might, for example, react negatively toward the person his parents define as a friend, or overly positive toward the person who is only a nigh-dweller. To illustrate, the child might studiously avoid contact with the friend, but "spend too much time in those people's yard."

Unless parental supervision is strict, continuous, and effective, the child's relationships with these persons might not follow the patterns communicated to him by his parents. When this happens the child is likely to find himself involved in situations which result in experiences which are not approved by his parents. Whatever the parents' reactions may be, these experiences involve the transmission of new ideas and information to the child. Sometimes, of course, parents and their children identify with and react similarly to these persons. In many instances friends and neighbors, especially, are second only to parents in their impact upon children. Directly or indirectly, intentionally or unintentionally, each of these categories of persons stands to play a part—large or small —in facilitating the process of child development.

THE CHILD AND THE GUEST

Until the child enters school (in modern urban societies generally) his life is centered mainly among members of the immediate family. To a considerable extent, his physical life-space may include only his home and its more immediate environs. He may leave his home area at special times and for special purposes, such as spending a holiday with his grandparents. But aside from excursions such as this, home and neighborhood often set the boundaries within which the very young child's principal contacts and associations are carried on.

The boundaries set by home and neighborhood do not necessarily result in the isolation of the child from the outside world. Nor do they insulate him against its influence. In fact, much of the outside world is communicated to the child through his contacts with older persons who, unlike him, are not limited by these boundaries. Of those persons who bridge the gap between the child's experiences in home and neighborhood and the activities of the larger social setting, the guest in the home stands out pre-eminently. As a person who lives outside the child's home, the guest functions as a transmitter, bringing into the world of the child new ideas and information, and new and different opportunities for vicarious participation in the outside world. It must be added, however, that the extent to which any particular guest performs this function will depend, among other things, upon where he lives, what his experiences have been, the frequency of his visits, and the level of his interaction with the child.

Unlike the guest who lives nearby, the one who comes from a distant place is likely to be a source of new and exciting experiences. His tales are likely to be "taller," therefore, the prospect of his visit might be awaited with keen anticipation. It might be preceded by a period—even though brief—of near-exemplary behavior. Such a guest may indeed work wonders with a child. When a guest affects a child in this manner, parental control may be facilitated and mutually satisfying parent-child relationships are likely to be promoted.

Obviously, the child does not welcome all guests equally. Some are highly welcome, some are tolerated, and still others are rejected. In the latter case, the result of the visit may be embarrassing to the guest, irritating to the parents, and upsetting to the child. In fact, the child who is upset by a guest and shows it, or who is negatively disposed toward a guest and is rude, might suffer not only from the presence of the guest but also from his parents' criticism of his unfriendly behavior. From such a situation the child can learn the important lesson, "We must always be courteous and considerate to guests in our home." Should the child reply, "But I don't like him, mommy," the same admonition is perhaps repeated. And if the child responds, "Daddy says Mr. Brown is an old fuddy-duddy," mother might be hard-pressed for an appropriate response. If, however, she parries this point successfully, the child—by this time on the defensive—might argue, "But mommy, you said after he left here last time, that. . . ." From this point on, the issue is no longer courtesy and consideration toward the guest, but obedience and respect toward parental authority. When the storm has subsided, mother might find that the lesson she set out to teach has been deferred.

The situation which prevails when a guest is in the home can be informal or formal. In the former case, there might be little pre-planning by the family, the guest being expected to take "pot luck." The family routine can remain relatively the same. The termination of such a visit might be at the pleasure of the guest who, in this case, is likely to be a close friend of long standing. In this situation, such strain that the visit might involve is perhaps not too considerable for the child. He might not be expected to put on his company manners and whatever child-centered activities are characteristic of the family may continue uninterrupted.

The formal guest situation presents a contrasting picture. The family routine is perhaps modified, although the period of visitation is usually pre-set. In such a situation, the visitor might be a business associate or a former classmate, or a future or at least potential in-law. In the face of such a visit, parents are prone to require that the child display his company manners—that he be on his best behavior. He might even be sent out to play or to visit with relatives. Because guest-centered activities sometimes take priority over child-centered activities, the child's frustration or aggression potential might well be activated. However, the character of the guest and his relations with the child might well forestall or at least minimize such a development.

Largely because parents control the situation, the child-guest relationship is likely to be a positive aspect of socialization. It can facilitate the child's ability to relate himself to new and different personalities. It can offer him the opportunity to learn about people, places, and events. It can provide another potential source of recognition and response. It can stimulate and develop his powers of self-control. It can liberate him from extreme self-centeredness, from over attachment to parents, and indeed from the likelihood of becoming too satisfied, too soon, with too little.

THE CHILD AND THE SERVANT

Domestic service in the United States involves a work force of considerable size and importance. Throughout the country many households include servants, full-time or part-time, among its members. In addition many domestic workers live in their own homes. Although these servants are often employed in work roles not directly related to child-rearing, such as cook, maid, laundress, chauffeur, gardener, and handy man, they are frequently involved in intermittent or continuing relationships with the young children of their employers. In addition, however, many servants are specifically charged with certain aspects of child rearing. The nursemaid, the baby sitter, and the governess are cases in point.

The extent to which children are influenced by the servants in their parents' employ will, of course, vary from one family situation to another. Yet, because of the specific character of their work situations, certain categories of servants may be more influential than others. Generally, nursemaids and governesses are such categories. In a like manner, servants who "live in" can be expected, generally, to exert a greater impact upon children than those who "live out."

Principally because of economic considerations, only the people who live on the higher levels of society are likely to have servants working full-time and living in their homes. An equally general rule is that servants tend to be recruited from the lower levels of society. Among the exceptions are the occasionally poor and distant relative, or the economically unfortunate family friend who volunteered to help out, but stayed on. In the latter cases, however, they tend to be treated somewhat as members of the family. In addition, it is not uncommon for a non-family or the non-friend servant to achieve a family-like status. Such servants sometimes acquire a dominance over their employer's family which is reminiscent of the matriarchate, and which, of course, extends to the children involved.

In part, because their social background differs from that of their employer's, servants often present to children views of a somewhat different and special world. Also significant is the fact that servants are sometimes regarded by children and their parents as prototypes of a different people. This is well illustrated in the United States because a considerably high proportion of domestic servants are Negroes and persons whose nationality backgrounds are not far removed from Europe. Such persons tend to be defined differently and categorically. Consequently, they are likely to be widely regarded as representative of the other persons who constitute these population categories. In this way, certain racial and ethnic stereotypes tend to be communicated to children and are, in part, maintained.

As already indicated, some servants are, to all intent and purposes, integral parts of their employers' family units. Authority to supervise, control, and correct the children may be accorded to, or to some extent assumed by such servants. Often when the parents are absent or even when they are present but too busy to be bothered, these servants exercise authority over the children and make decisions regarding what they may or may not do. In these situations where the child regards the servant as "a soft touch," the exercise of such prerogatives may be welcome, and even sought after by him. If, on the contrary, the servant is defined as a hard task master, conflict, rebellion, and avoidance may follow—unless, of course, strong affectional ties exist between servant and child; then, he may be defined as hard, but fair.

At times, the servant plays the role of companion, confidante, and teacher. When this role is performed as part of a mutually satisfying relationship, the results to the child can be rewarding and enriching. However, one possibility that should not be overlooked is that the servant who is companion, confidante, and teacher might communicate to the child certain ideas and information defined by his parents as objectionable. When this occurs, the situation might be further complicated by the fact that the child is fascinated or intrigued by such ideas and information and thus seeks to continue such learning. In order to cope with this situation, the parent-employers might repeatedly order the servant to cease and desist. If this is not effective, and the servant is not discharged, other results may follow. These might include the development of a *sub rosa* servant-child relationship, an increasingly intense attachment of the child for the servant who is being "mistreated"; or, increasing secretiveness, sullenness, or obstinacy by the child toward his parents.

Wherever it prevails, the servant role is an integral and significant component of the family situation. It is a potential resource for constructive development in the child-rearing process. Yet, whether or not it leads to socially constructive or destructive consequences depends in large measure upon the characteristic orientations and reactions of the servant and the child, as well as upon the particular family situation in which the servant is employed.

THE CHILD AND THE FUNCTIONARY

Initially, the interactional experiences of the child are limited to the members of his own household. Gradually, however, he is thrown into contact with a limited number of outsiders, including his own age-level intimates, neighbors, and members of his larger family. Manifestly, he has to acquire new sets of responses appropriate to non-family situations and relationships. Because interaction outside the home is often necessary, and even potentially helpful, the family usually encourages the cultivation of these relations. Frequently, however, the child is initiated into sets of informal but limited interactional situations long before he spends any considerable time away from his family. Yet, these may be significant experiences for they provide opportunities for the child to experience, sometimes vicariously, certain different aspects of the larger social and cultural context. In addition, the child is enabled to acquire new skills and information and to experiment with their uses.

The informal and limited interactional situations referred to here are limited not only in terms of the range of interaction, but also by the fact that participation is limited to the child and an adult, the latter being referred to as a functionary. For present purposes, the term *functionary* is used to refer to a person who interacts with another in a highly specialized mannner and for the purpose of rendering a specific service or performing a particular job. This interaction situation involves behavior that is direct, face-to-face, brief and recurrent. In addition, the parties that are involved tend to orient their actions and reactions toward the service or job involved.

To further clarify the concept of functionary, as used here, two additional observations must be made. First, the functionary tends to orient his actions principally toward the child's parents. Usually, it is they for whom he performs or works; this is the case even when the job or service is directed specifically toward the child. Because of the primacy of parents with regard to the role of the functionary, it is more precise to say that the child is involved mainly with the peripheral aspects of the functionary role. Secondly, in the functionary-child relationship the adult participant tends to display only a small fragment of his personality. He may, for example, answer the child's questions and offer explanations concerning the service being performed. Frequently, the interaction might be initiated by the child's question, "What are you doing?" Gradually, however, the child's interests may lead to questions and concerns which are not directly connected with the work performed by the functionary. Essentially, this results from the fact that, unlike the functionary, the child is accustomed to involving a relatively wide range of his personality in any situation in which he feels the urge to do so.

This tendency not to limit the range of behavior or personality expression is especially characteristic of the very young child, say between the ages of three and six. During this period of life the child has not yet learned to order his behavior in accordance with the prevailing expectations. He does not yet know what specific behaviors are appropriate and expected in certain situations. He may say and do things, such as speaking out of turn, or divulging family secrets to outsiders. In fact, such behavior has been said to be the bane of the mother's existence. Largely because of the child's lack of perceptiveness concerning what is appropriate to discuss with whom, mothers often maintain close surveillance when functionaries are present. Although the fact that junior might get in the way is perhaps a legitimate reason for watching or removing him, such precaution also minimizes the likelihood that he will speak out of turn.

Functionaries include persons of widely different personal characteristics. They live in different parts of the community, and in different social-class levels. They perform various kinds of services which require a wide variety of information and skills. The result of these differences is that the situations in which they become involved with children cover a wide range of possibilities for interaction. To illustrate, functionaries include mailmen, delivery men, repairmen, and insurance collectors. Although each of these types performs a different service, all of them usually interact with the child in his home. Because of this, these are the types with whom the younger children who stay close to home are likely to become involved. Certain types of functionaries contact children, usually the older children, outside their homes. Among these are policemen, school guards, bus drivers, and store clerks.

Whether children interact with functionaries in their own homes or outside their homes might well make a great difference. In the first instance (as already pointed out), the parents usually have continuing opportunity to observe and supervise the interaction, and are thus enabled to exercise a degree of control. When, however, these contacts take place outside the child's home such control is far more difficult to effect. Since this parental control might be exercised to the point of overprotectiveness, freedom from it might well facilitate opportunities which enable the child to develop self-confidence and self-reliance. However, individual differences must be taken into account.

The role of the functionary in the socialization of the child might well be a significant factor, although its exact meaning is not easily determined. Nonetheless, the implications of learning theory would seem to support the contention that functionary-child interaction is an important aspect of socialization, especially in urban society. For here, many children have regular, and most children have multiple, contacts with a wide variety of such persons. As a result, these children may be exposed to widely differing attitudes, ideas, information, and skills. For some children, these experiences with functionaries will be similar to those they encounter at home. But whether or not such experiences duplicate and complement or counteract and contradict home experiences, some change in the child's personality is almost certain to result when functionary meets child.

PASSERS-BY: THE DISTANT VIEW

The oft' repeated expression, "Isn't it a small world." might well be applied to the world of the child; for, initially, his is indeed a small world. Therefore, he must progressively acquire the knowledge and skills, internalize the attitudes and values, and become aware of the expectations and norms which will enable him to fulfill the role requirements of his ever-widening world.

The child's preparation for behaving effectively in his ever-expanding world is carried on initially in his home and neighborhood. The formal systems appropriate to him, such as the school, also make their contributions to this end. In the final analysis, however, all learning is not transmitted through socially recognized or formally structured systems. Neither does all social interaction proceed in accordance with patterns that are generally shared and approved. In learning the culture the child often "picks up" ideas and skills. Not uncommonly, he may find it necessary or, at least to him, interesting to interact in unexpected and sometimes inappropriate situations. Much of this learning and interaction is of course the result of the informal aspects of social systems. Not all the learning in home and school, for example, conforms to the formal demands of these systems; children do "get together." For children, as for others, there is much learning or interaction that is largely adventitious.

Children often have interactional experiences that are atypical, unstructured, momentary, and irregular. Frequently, they also have significant visual contacts that are similarly characterized. Such minimal interaction and visual contacts might well be a source of significant social participation and learning. These experiences can yield a twofold type of consequence—that which flows directly from the interaction or contact, and that which results when the child's parents are aware of the contact and react to it.

For present purposes, the adult participants in these situations are referred to as *passers-by*. It should be noted that the passer-by is either an active participant, or an object participant. The first is illustrated by the ticket seller at the movie house and the local policeman. The object participant includes the outstanding citizen of the community, the visiting celebrity, and the local drunk. That these two types of participants are not mutually exclusive is well illustrated by the local policeman; one child talks with him and he is an active participant; another child just stares at him, and he is thereby an object participant.

The potential for the active participant to influence children would seem obvious; perhaps it is less so with the object participant. Yet, it is not uncommon for one to react to a person whom he sees from time to time but with whom he never communicates or interacts. Awareness of another through sight, and even through thought, sometimes results in significant reactions, either overtly or covertly. For example, when a child looks at the village drunk he might pity him, fear him, be amused by him, or attracted to him. In a sense, movie and TV stars, as well as heroes in literature, sports, and other areas of life may also be regarded as object participants in the passers-by category.

Whatever the type of passers-by, and whatever the child's reaction to him, repeated contact or interaction with such persons is likely to exert a cumulative impact on the child. The following are influences passers-by might exert on the child: (1) they can illustrate or crystallize stereotypes, (2) they can contribute to the development of attitudes, (3) they can be regarded as examples of persons to be avoided, or emulated, and (4) they can point up the contrast between the type of people whom the child knows well and those whom he might possibly come to know.

Despite the lack of direct, prolonged, or systematic contact and interaction between the child and the passer-by, the former's awareness of the latter is perhaps an important factor in the socialization process. Broadly considered, passers-by demonstrate the wide variations to be found in personality types, in personal behavior, in reputation, in prestige, and in status. As the child comes to view passers-by in these terms, his knowledge and expectations of the world beyond his home and neighborhood develop and expand. Finally, because passers-by often represent that which is different or new, and because they sometimes suggest that things different, new, and exciting are to be found outside his own world, the child might well conclude that the world is indeed a great big place— a wonderful, friendly, exciting, awesome, or even a frightening place in which he must someday find his own particular niche.

SUMMARY

In this chapter, some of the less structured, less formal, but nonetheless significant interactional situations in the socialization process have been discussed. Implicit in this discussion is the notion that adult non-family participants in the child's experiences are often, to him, attractive, satisfying, and influential.

No attempt has been made to point up only the positive aspect of these situations; rather, it has been suggested repeatedly that these situations may lead to negative consequences, for example, parent-child conflict. What is important is not that the interaction experienced in these situations might exert a positive impact upon the child, but that perhaps they exert an impact. Finally, this chapter implies that in any attempt to analyze and understand the course of child socialization, one should not confine his interest and attention to the more formal social structures. Although the formal social structures which deal with children are important focuses in their life-experiences, other less formal social structures or situations play their part too. For whenever and wherever two or more people meet and interact, the personalities of the interacting parties are almost certain to be modified, at least to some small degree. It is largely because of this that the role of adult non-family participants in the socialization process has been discussed.

READINGS

BARKER, R. G., "The Social Interrelations of Strangers and Acquaintances," *Sociometry,* Vol. 5 (1942), pp. 169–179.

BEAVER, Alma P., "The Initiation of Social Contacts by Pre-School Children," *Child Development Monograph,* No. 7 (1932).

BECKER, Howard, and USEEM, Ruth H., "Sociological Analysis of the Dyad," *American Sociological Review,* Vol. 7 (1942), pp. 13–26.

BOSSARD, James H. S., "Process in Social Weaning: A Study of Child Visiting," *Child Development* (September, 1951), pp. 211–220.

HILLER, E. T., *Social Relations and Structures* (New York, Harper & Row, Publishers, Inc., 1947).

NORTHWAY, Mary, and DETWEILER, Joyce, "Children's Perception of Friends and Non-Friends," *Sociometry,* Vol. 18, No. 4 (1955), pp. 527–531.

WOLF, Kurt H., *The Sociology of Georg Simmel* (New York, The Free Press of Glencoe, Inc., 1950).

8

The Child and the Classroom

INTRODUCTION

In the socialization of the child, different social systems deal with different aspects of the total process. Among these systems the school is a principal socializing agency, second only, perhaps, to the family. The school, it is to be observed, is an age-graded system in which children are separated into classes. Functionally, the classroom is the core or central unit of the system. It is the place where the education of the child is centered, especially during the early years. Generally, the classroom is a locality-based unit with compulsory attendance required of all or nearly all local residents of a given age range. Because the school is a significant socializing system, and because the classroom is the central unit of that system, an examination of the classroom would seem to be in order. In the examination that follows, the *classroom* refers to teaching-learning situations in the elementary schools of the United States.

By the time the American child is six years old, he has been introduced into the school system. Thus begins a new and different phase of his socialization in a new and different situation. Although the school is in a few respects like the family, it is vastly different in most respects. Theoretically, the school takes the child as he is. The child's personality as it has emerged in his family setting must be taken as the point of departure for the schooling process. This means that the school's program is designed to meet the needs of the child as an individual, but only so long as those needs are not inconsistent with the needs of other children and with the community's conception of what education ought to be.

In the academic year 1960–61, about 25,265,620 children were enrolled in the public elementary schools of this country. These children were being taught by 857,353 teachers of whom 125,477 were male. Of these children, 380,000 who were living in urban communities in the

1959–60 school year were being taught in classes of more than 40 pupils each.[1] Based on the conservative estimate of the average of 30 children per classroom, the number of elementary classrooms in the public schools of the United States in 1960–61 amounted to about 842,187.

Although there are non-public schools in the United States, they are included in this discussion only by implication. In limiting this discussion to public elementary schools, it is not intended to suggest that all these schools are necessarily the same. Indeed they vary considerably. Fundamentally, however, elementary schools and their classrooms conform to the same general pattern. Usually, there is a single teacher for each class, especially in the first three grades. The curricula encompass essentially the same subject-matter areas, although additions and modifications do not occur at the same rate nor do they involve the same content throughout. For example, a considerable number of elementary schools provide special teachers for subjects such as music, art, speech, and physical education. Finally, the newer schools, especially in the suburban areas, tend to be more modern in terms of architectural design, equipment, teaching aids, and other materials.

THE CLASSROOM: CONTEXT FOR CONTAINMENT

When the child enrolls in school he enters into a situation that is new and vastly different from that to which he has been accustomed. Here, for perhaps the first time, he is relatively on his own. The people around him are for the most part strangers. The norms regulating his behavior are more clearly defined, relate to different considerations, and are apt to be more uniformly enforced than those to which he is accustomed. Now, for the first time, rules, routine, and regularity govern his life. He finds that his needs and interests are not really of paramount concern to anyone but himself. Concessions to his whims or fancy, tolerance of his moods and wishes, and allowances for his inadequacies and failures are less likely to be important elements of this new experience.

He and twenty to forty other children are confined within an enclosure called a classroom. Physically, it is a room quite unlike any he has experienced; it is larger, perhaps lighter and better ventilated; or, it is drab, depressing, and stuffy. Whatever the comparison to rooms he has known, in this one he has a special place to sit; if he is not restricted to continuous sitting, he may stand or walk only with permission and may not leave the room at will. In addition, he is required to do the things required of the other children and failure to conform and perform exposes him to sanctions, direct or indirect from the other children, from

[1] "Facts and Figures," reported from N.E.A. *Research Bulletin*, XXXIX (February, 1961), pp. 26–31, in *The Education Digest*, Vol. 26, No. 9 (May, 1961), p. 43.

his teachers, or from his parents. Such, in brief, are the more immediately observable physical and normative characteristics of the classroom.

The Teacher in the Classroom

In order to understand more fully the impact of the classroom upon the child, the personal, social, and professional attributes and experiences of the teacher must be taken into account. Without the teacher the classroom is incomplete. Usually, the teacher—especially in the first three grades—is an adult female. In spite of the claims, or indeed the actuality of democratic leadership, the teacher is the dominant and controlling figure in the classroom. It is she in whom the ultimate authority is vested, both by virtue of her official rank and because of her status as an adult. Although the class may be said to be governed in accordance with and for the purpose of promoting democratic principles and practices, it is the teacher who ultimately decides, either directly or indirectly, what is or is not consistent with those principles and practices. "In the final analysis it is the classroom teacher who implements the social temperature, school policies to the contrary, notwithstanding. For *no philosophy of education, no curriculum, no method is any more effective than the teacher who implements it.*" [2] Thus, in addition to adjusting their behavior to the physical and normative character of the classroom, school children must remain ever alert to the need to win and hold the approval of the teacher.

The role of the teacher with her authority and superior knowledge, therefore, is a crucial factor in the child's school experience. Whether the child feels accepted and secure, or rejected and alone may be determined largely by how the teacher plays her role. Whatever the ideal definition of a teacher's role may be, her conception of that role and the extent to which her behavior is consistent with that conception are related to her own background and training. Examination of the background and training of the teacher indicate that social class considerations are vitally significant.

Prior to 1920 teachers were recruited mainly from the ranks of the middle classes. [3] For those who were of upper-lower class background the elevation to the status of teacher perhaps represented a selective process whereby they were chosen largely because of their middle-class aspirations. Moreover, upon becoming teachers such persons were in effect becoming members of the middle class. "In current years, there has been a

2 Florence Greenhoe Robbins, *Educational Sociology* (New York, Holt, Rinehart & Winston, Inc., 1953), p. 283.

3 Robert J. Havighurst and Bernice L. Neugarten, *Society and Education*, 2nd ed., (Boston, Allyn and Bacon, Inc., 1962), p. 358.

further increase in the heterogeneity of social backgrounds, with the most pronounced changes being a drop in the number of teachers who came from farm families . . . and an increase in the number who came from urban working-class homes." [4]

The selective process whereby persons move into the field of teaching is, for many, a process of upward social mobility. This change in their status opens opportunities for new contacts and social relationships. Different attitudes and values are often accepted and activated. Although the impact of the teacher's social mobility upon the child in the classroom cannot be precisely determined, the changes in her social circumstances and any personality changes that accompany such mobility might somehow enter into the performance of this newly achieved role.

It is important to know something of the social origin of any given teacher if we are to understand his performance in the teaching role. In this connection, however, we must look at social origin in relation to personality. It has been said, for instance, that social origin is the single most important fact in predicting a teacher's behavior. This is a gross oversimplification. Although a given teacher's social origin may have had an important influence upon his or her personality, it is virtually impossible to cite generalized effects that would be true for all teachers of any single origin. For example, a teacher who comes from a middle-class family is not necessarily ineffective in dealing with lower-class children. Some middle-class teachers, coming from fairly relaxed home environments, may emerge as adaptive personalities, who really take on the color of their social surroundings. For them, it would be relatively easy to get along sympathetically with children and parents quite different from themselves. In another group, for whom a rigid upbringing had the effect of inculcating a tendency to panic when faced with the strange or unusual, prejudices may be easily aroused. Some of these persons may cling to their own ways as the only right or proper ones. They could easily drift toward treating with disdain children or parents who were of different races, religions, nationalities, or economic circumstance. [5]

The role of the teacher, like any role, involves a configuration of behavior patterns which are prescribed independently of the unique personal attributes of those who play that role. With regard to the question "What does it take to make a teacher?", it can be said, in the vernacular, that "It takes all kinds." Each teacher, therefore, can be expected to teach and manage her class not only with regard to the role requirements of the teacher but also in terms of her own idiosyncratic traits. For example, the lower-class person who raises himself through his own efforts and becomes a teacher might so completely reject lower-class values and behavior that he is intolerant toward the lower-class children in his classroom. It is equally conceivable, however, that such a person, remembering his own struggle to get ahead, might assume the responsibility of see-

[4] *Ibid.*, pp. 463–464.
[5] *Ibid.*, pp. 468–469.

ing that the lower-class child who is ambitious gets every chance for self-improvement. In this same vein, the possibilities cited by Havighurst and Neugarten [6] are further instructive:

One, for example, tortured by inner feelings of inferiority, may regard his origin as a thing of shame to be lived down. Another, having a powerful identification with father and older siblings, may so conduct himself as to retain and exemplify his family's social rank, and in doing so ally himself with pupils and parents of similar origin. A third, imbued with strong achievement drives, may seek to deny his origin by accepting middle-class standards and by being unusually strict, if not actually punitive, against the children and parents from whose rank he sees himself as having risen by dint of self-denial.

The heterogeneity of classroom teachers is based on more than social-class differences. Today, more than even a quarter of a century ago, teachers are being recruited from various racial, religions, and ethnic categories. One result of this is that the image of the "old maid teacher" is rapidly coming to be a thing of the past. As teachers are drawn from these various backgrounds both pupils and the community find it necessary to re-examine their conceptions of what a teacher should be like. Perhaps the single, older image of the teacher is being replaced by multiple images which result in teachers being categorized in various ways.

The consequences of the widespread employment of teachers from varying racial, religious, and ethnic backgrounds are felt in the administrative circles of the school system as well as in the classroom. This is especially evident with regard to teachers who are Negroes. In many school systems the common practice is to assign Negro teachers to schools in which student bodies are largely or predominantly Negro. About twenty years ago Myrdal [7] pointed out that "where there are segregated schools the Negro teacher has usually a complete monopoly on the jobs in Negro schools. Where schools are mixed, Negroes have difficulty in getting in." Today this same situation is still widely prevalent. This practice of considering race in the assignment of teachers means that in some instances a new and non-relevant dimension is added to the role of the teacher. This is to say, for example, that instead of assigning qualified teachers to schools where they are needed, superintendents sometimes assign qualified *Negro* teachers to schools *where they will fit*.

The increasing heterogeneity of teachers as an occupational category suggests the difficulty of formulating a meaningful image of *the* teacher. This difficulty, however, is perhaps due to the characteristics which are regarded as significant for formulating such an image. As Havighurst and Neugarten [8] have so correctly pointed out, "As teachers increasingly

---

[6] *Ibid.*, p. 472.

[7] Gunnar Myrdal, *An American Dilemma* (New York, Harper & Row, Publishers, 1944), p. 319.

[8] Havighurst and Neugarten, *op. cit.*, p. 476.

represent all social types, it is increasingly impossible to generalize about 'the' school teacher in terms of social and personal characteristics." It may well be that the perception of the teacher should exclude racial, religious, or ethnic considerations, and even marital, age, or rural-urban characteristics. Perhaps a more meaningful image of the teacher would have at its core those intellectual and emotional attributes which by necessity the role of the ideal teacher requires.

Like other roles, that of the teacher is a configuration of rights, privileges, and duties. Some classroom teachers conform rather closely to the ideal; others are less successful. There are those who are adequately knowledgeable, highly skilled, stimulating, considerate, and accepting in their classroom behavior. And there are those who are less so. From this, it follows that the results of the child's experiences with the teacher in the classroom is necessarily dependent to some extent upon the teacher.

The Teacher as Disciplinarian

Upon closer examination, the role of the teacher in the classroom involves much more than the teaching of subject matter. In their discussion of the "Teacher in the School," Havighurst and Neugarten [9] list a set of sub-roles which are enacted in the classroom. They are:

Mediator of Learning

Disciplinarian

Parent Substitute

Judge

Confidante

Surrogate of Middle-Class Morality

Of all of these sub-roles, perhaps no one gives the teacher, especially the new teacher, more concern than that of disciplinarian. This is perhaps mainly because of a combination of two factors: (1) the teacher's sub-role as Surrogate of middle-class morality and (2) the relatively high proportion of lower-class students in the classroom. For many teachers disorder and conflict within the classroom are somewhat commonplace, and, of course, interfere with the "business" of teaching.

The problem of discipline faced by so many teachers may be caused by an apparently widely held conception of discipline as *keeping order*. Thus viewed, discipline is a matter of externally applied measures of control and is a means to an end. Frequently, teachers can be heard to complain

[9] *Ibid.*, pp. 494–499.

or insist that "You must get them quiet before you can teach them." It must be granted that teachers recognize that keeping students quiet is not really the essence of discipline. Yet, they believe that the attention implicit in a state of quiet is certainly prerequisite to effective teaching. Perhaps, then, the difficulty in maintaining "discipline" to keep children quiet, lies in the direct approach sometimes taken to this objective—an approach which almost raises *quiet* to the level of an end rather than a means to an end. It may well be that the most effective approach is not to get them quiet and teach, but rather to teach to get them quiet in order to go on teaching.

In a larger sense, discipline is more than maintaining order, more than the external application of measures of control. It is, in fact, an end in itself; and as such it is one of the principal objectives of the educational process. Discipline thus viewed is self-discipline.

The discipline employed in our classrooms should be designed to place upon the child more and more responsibility for his own choices, purposes, and behavior as he grows in the ability to shoulder such responsibility. Such "discipline," instead of being repressive and utilizing punishment and reprisals for missteps, will plan with the children the purposes to be achieved and through the social control of group approval and disapproval will teach the child to discharge creditably the responsibilities assigned to him by the group. Such a procedure is consistent with the principles of good learning, with democratic methods, and with the facts of child development.

Classroom control then becomes something for which all members of the class *feel* some responsibility because misbehavior jeopardizes the achievement of purposes *they* have planned. There is also a different conception of "classroom order." In place of the repressive silence once held to be so desirable, it is now recognized that children . . . engaging in worthwhile and cooperative activity will produce a certain amount of natural noise. . . .

The conclusion seems obvious that the maintenance of classroom discipline is a function of good teaching. It is a natural outgrowth of a well-conceived and functional learning situation in which the learners participate in formulating the purposes of their daily activities, and the regulations and conditions within which those purposes will be achieved. The *process* of the daily conduct of the class is in itself a learning experience under these conditions, and is as much a part of the curriculum as is any factual knowledge, and in many respects far more important. It is a type of classroom discipline which is truly educative in self-discipline, and which helps children to become increasingly able to shoulder their responsibilities as democratic citizens of a democratic state. It is no longer simply something which the teacher maintains; it is something she helps children attain.[10]

This conception of discipline is an ideal, the achievement of which involves certain difficulties. Among these difficulties, at least three merit

[10] Willard S. Ellsbree and Harold J. McNally, *Elementary School Administration and Supervision* (New York, American Book Company, 1951), pp. 215–216. A second edition of this work was published in 1959.

discussion at this point. First, the student composition of many classrooms includes children whose cultural backgrounds vary widely. Many children upon enrollment in school have had little or no experience in the assumption of responsibilities, in making choices, or in collective decision-making such as implied in this latter conception of discipline. Thus, they are likely to be unprepared or indeed unable to adapt to such expectations. Instead of actively orienting their behavior toward common objectives collectively determined, they may depend, as they are accustomed, upon the decisions and directions of the teacher who is, in their view, an adult and therefore *the* authority. Another possible reaction is that instead of cooperating with the group, or instead of relying on the teacher, some children will seek to continue to follow their own individual inclinations, thereby creating conflict and disorder in the class. Whatever the specific courses they follow, some children are not prepared, are unwilling, or find it difficult to adapt readily or easily to this conception of discipline.

The implementation of this conception of discipline in the classroom is further impeded by competing forces outside the particular classroom. Such forces may be found to some extent within the school of which a particular classroom is a part. For example, it may be that the teachers differ significantly in the extent to which they are committed to this conception of discipline and vary widely in their implementation of it. When this happens, not only is there inconsistency in the treatment of children in the different grades, but this inconsistency is likely to be experienced by the same children as they move from one grade to the next.

Another difficulty likely to be faced by the teacher who seeks to follow this conception of discipline finds its source outside the school, especially in the child's home. Some children come from homes where they "are to be seen, not heard." In their homes they have few responsibilities and are not permitted to participate in decision-making along with the family. Thus, the requirement of shouldering responsibilities and the chance to express their opinions in the classroom may, so long as their home situations remain unchanged, prove frustrating for them and difficult for their teachers. From the point of view of these children, the rigid treatment they receive at home and the liberal treatment accorded them in the classroom constitute a kind of conflicting regularity which is perhaps upsetting almost to the point of insecurity. For the teacher who seeks to stimulate and promote the development of self-reliance and self-discipline among these children, opposition or the lack of cooperation from their families constitutes a competitive force against which the teacher may find it extremely difficult to prevail.

It would seem, therefore, that despite the ideal conception of discipline as responsible, choice-making, self-regulating behavior the prospect of its successful implementation in the classroom depends largely upon forces over which the teacher and her pupils have no control. To be functional, this conception of discipline must be clearly communicated among teachers and consistently pursued by them. In addition, unless the parents of school children and the community at large accept and cooperate in the implementation of such discipline, this particular objective of the learning process is not likely to be achieved.

The Child in the Classroom

Ideally, the school is the one social system to which all children have access. As a matter of fact, all children, save those who are physically or mentally incapable, are required to attend school. Because school attendance is mandatory, the school child occupies an ascribed status categorically, without regard to individual inclination or performance. At the same time, however, there is an element of achievement in this status which can be either a source of satisfaction or frustration. This is because the school is oriented principally toward the successful performance of certain tasks and to the fact that its rewards are allocated on the basis of the successful performance of those tasks. Moreover, as these tasks are successfully carried out the principal reward is promotion to a higher grade in the system. In this sense, the element of achievement is the central consideration in the status of school child.

Whether this status is viewed as ascribed or as achieved, it is the child's first experience in a system in which differentiation is formally structured and is based not on kinship or friendship ties but on the child's competitive efforts. His rewards come not as a matter of right, but as a consequence of merit. The approval he receives, the attention he gets, and the opportunities available to him all tend to be bound up with his conformity to classroom norms and his performance of the tasks assigned to him.

Children in the elementary school are systematically differentiated primarily on the basis of age. Generally, they are not separated by sex. Although the system of grading is designed to classify them by academic achievement, sometimes children in the same class differ significantly in this respect. All things considered, age, sex, and academic achievement are so managed as to bring about an optimum degree of homogeneity in the class so that learning can take place.

In terms of social and cultural backgrounds and in personality attributes, however, children in the elementary class differ significantly. Within a given classroom there may be children of different races, religions, ethnic groups, and socio-economic levels. Often they come from neighborhoods that differ in physical structure, in prevailing social norms, and in social prestige. Furthermore, the families they represent are sometimes large, poor, broken, disreputable, or a combination of these. On the other hand, they are sometimes small, moderately well-off, highly integrated and/or prestigeful. Some or many of the children in a classroom may be from broken homes in the slums of the city. Among these may be children who fight, or steal, or swear; they may be truant, troublesome, or intractable. At the same time, some pupils may be quiet, self-effacing, or withdrawn. In some instances, there may even be those who are frightened, insecure, or highly disturbed. The presence of such vastly different children within a single classroom poses certain problems both for the children and for their teacher. It constitutes a setting in which conflict and confusion might easily reign. It is a challenge and even a strain upon the teacher and is likely to require much of her time, energy, and effort merely to organize and manage the situation.

Ideally, the classroom is a democratic setting in which the learning process is carried on with regard for individual differences and needs. The diversity of the social and cultural backgrounds and the personality traits of the children complicate and make difficult the realization of this ideal. Further complications and greater difficulty arise, however, from the fact that the classroom tends to be organized in accordance with middle-class values, despite the ideal that democracy shall be its guiding philosophy. The student, according to these values, should be clean, neat, orderly, respectful, truthful, honest, intelligent, and highly motivated. He should value property, be competitive, work well with others, plan to go to college, and aspire to be successful in business, industry, or one of the professions. This middle-class model of the student is in rather direct contrast with what many, perhaps most, students are really like. It would seem, then, that classroom interaction would be disruptive of learning to the same degree that this model is maintained for students who are unable to conform to or approach the ideal.

INTERACTION WITHIN THE CLASSROOM

In some respects the elementary school classroom is like a community. It is comprised of a definite, diverse, and changing population. As a social subsystem, it is comprised of statuses and roles, regulated by sets of social norms, formal and informal, and oriented in the direction of a core set of values. Moreover, the relationships and interaction of the classroom tend to be limited principally to certain definable and observable areas. These relationships are bi-sexual, peer group, and cross-generational. They involve pairs, cliques, and the entire group; at the same time, however, they tend not to be static or permanent but are variable and allow considerable shifting back and forth. As for the interactional processes in the classroom, they run the gamut from competition, to conflict, to accommodation, to cooperation, and to assimilation.

Upon entrance into the classroom, the child is often individualistic and self-seeking. In the course of his involvement with the class, however, he is encouraged or pressured to work with others, to take his turn, to share. At first some are more or less resistant to such efforts; eventually, however, most children accept or at least conform to these requirements. Before some do, and even long after, they continue to be intermittently individualistic. Thus, throwing spit balls, drawing uncomplimentary pictures of teacher or of other students, walking around the room without permission, and talking out of turn are not uncommon.

Gradually—more quickly for some than for others—a state of relative quiet and decorum is established. Yet, from time to time there may be those who will behave impulsively or seek to test the limits of the teacher's tolerance. The reactions of the teacher to such deviations might well depend upon whether she is the authoritarian or the democratic type. If she is the former, her insistence upon strong teacher control might lead to alienation and antagonize not only those who misbehave but some of the better-behaving children as well. If, however, she is the democratic type, there remains the chance that classroom control will be difficult or that she will be taken advantage of by the few. In any event the teacher's handling even of the typical, expected incidents of deviation is a significant determinant of the course and quality of interaction in the classroom.

Cooperation with other pupils, conformity to the rules, respect for the teacher, and high academic performance all involve behavior which leads to rewards. The child who measures up to these standards will be moved readily and regularly through the grades. In addition, his marks are likely to be sufficiently high to lead to the approval of his teacher, the praise of his parents, and pride in himself. Furthermore, because of his successful performance in the more formal aspects of the school system, avenues of leadership are likely to be open to him. Such leadership roles as he may come to play will result from his popularity among his peers or perhaps from his being chosen by the teacher.

In some instances success in the classroom can lead to difficulties. The child who studies to the relative exclusion of being friendly or "horsing around" from time to time may come to be regarded as a bookworm by his peers. If, in addition, he has the definite approval of the teacher he may be defined as teacher's pet. The consequences that sometimes flow from such definitions can be isolating and disruptive of peer-group relations. Indeed, the tendency on the part of many children to compete for the attention or approval of the teacher can also lead to strained relations and even conflict. When this happens the likelihood that the social-psychological climate of the classroom will be conducive to optimum learning may be noticeably reduced.

The attention-approval-getting behavior of the elementary school child is directed not only toward the teacher but toward other children as well. Thus, the child tends to seek the favor of certain other children whom he likes. A given classroom is often comprised of sets of best friends. Sometimes these are pairs of the same sex; in the higher grades they sometimes involve several children, frequently of both sexes. These best-friends relationships are in-groups which tend to provide security and preferential treatment for its members. The process of selecting or electing leaders in the classroom is sometimes dominated by these groups or at least demonstrates how closely they stick together.

Obviously, the curriculum requires a certain degree of formality, regularity, and routine in classroom interaction. The content of such interaction is, of course, related to the various subjects studied and to some extent to the techniques and methods of presentation utilized by the teacher. Generally, however, the teacher makes assignments, explains ideas, reports on events, answers questions, asks questions, and the like. The students, in turn, recite their lessons collectively and individually. They, too, ask and answer questions. They report certain of their experiences to the class. They read, write, spell, recite, draw, and sometimes even dramatize their lessons. In addition, they sing, watch movies and television, listen to recordings, and play games. It is through such intercommunication and activity that the process of formal learning is carried on. But of course the informal aspects of classroom activity and interaction are perhaps equally a part of the learning they experience.

The Child and the Changing Classroom

Like the society it represents, the elementary school classroom is not a static, unchanging situation. It is in a state of change. The nature and the rate of this change of course vary from one school system to another. In fact, innovations are not always introduced at the same time in all the classrooms of a single school system. Thus, French or Russian may be introduced to sixth graders in one elementary school of a community but not in the other.

In recent years experimentation has led to the introduction of new programs and approaches in the elementary school. New programs of testing, classification, and placement of students have been tried. Modifications and new departures in methods of teaching have been employed. Changes in subject-matter have been introduced. Physical plants, teaching aids and materials have been modernized. Modifications in the internal structure relating to personnel, districting, and racial desegregation have been introduced. Although these changes do not directly affect all elementary school children, and although those affected are not influenced to the same degree, the changes themselves are nonetheless significant. For if these changes can be taken as indications of the school's response to a changing society, and if, as seems quite plausible, they represent but an extension of that changing society, then future and continuing changes in the school system can be expected.

SUMMARY

In this chapter the elementary school classroom has been discussed as a major situation for socialization. Although the importance of the non-public elementary school is recognized, the emphasis here is upon the public school system. The classroom was defined as a place of physical containment in which certain norms prevail. The norms set the limits within which the educational process is carried on.

Considerable attention was directed to the teacher because she is the central figure in the situation. The changing social origins and the resultant heterogeneity were discussed. It was suggested that despite their diverse social origins they all tend to evaluate and reward their pupils in accordance with the latter's conformity to middle-class values. The sub-role of the teacher as disciplinarian was examined with a view toward pointing up the different conceptions of discipline and the probable consequences that flow from the relevant behavior.

The children in the classroom were discussed in terms of their social and cultural backgrounds and their personality attributes. Their heterogeneity in these respects were noted, and certain related behavioral differences were taken into account.

The discussion of classroom interaction was divided into the informal and the formal. Both of these were examined in terms of teacher-child and child-child interaction. Reference was made to the roles of leadership, of the bookworm, and of teacher's pet. Attention was also called to the best-friends relationships into which children often enter.

Certain of the broad changes occurring in the school system were outlined. These changes, it was contended, are likely to have a significant and lasting effect upon the school system. Finally, it was suggested that these changes are related to the dynamic nature of the society of which the classroom is a functional unit.

READINGS

BROOKOVER, W. B., "Research on Teacher and Administrator Roles," *Journal of Educational Sociology*, Vol. 29, No. 1 (September, 1955), pp. 2–13.

CANTOR, Nathaniel, *The Teaching-Learning Process* (New York, The Dryden Press, 1953).

CLARK, A. W., and VAN SOMMERS, P., "Contradictory Demands in Family Relations and Adjustment to School and Home," *Human Relations,* Vol. 14, No. 2 (May, 1961), pp. 97–111.

DAVIDSON, Helen, and LANG, Gerard, "Children's Perceptions of Their Teachers' Feelings Toward Them Related to Self-Perception, School Achievement, and Behavior," *Journal of Experimental Education* (December, 1960), pp. 107–118.

DAVIS, Allison, *Social-Class Influences Upon Learning* (Cambridge, Harvard University Press, 1948).

DE GROAT, Albert F., and THOMPSON, George C., "A Study of the Distribution of Teacher Approval and Disapproval Among Sixth-Grade Pupils," *Journal of Experimental Education,* Vol. 18 (1949), pp. 57–75.

PARSONS, Talcott, "The School Class as a Social System," *Harvard Educational Review,* Vol. 29, No. 4 (Fall, 1959), pp. 297–318.

WAGENSCHEIN, Miriam, "Reality Shock: A Study of Beginning Elementary School Teachers," Unpublished M.A. thesis, Department of Sociology, University of Chicago (1950).

III

MEANS AND MODELS
FOR SOCIALIZATION

9

Social Structure
and Self-Emergence

Introduction

People live in a world of objects, animate and inanimate, human and non-human. These objects exert significant influences as they act upon or are reacted to by those who come into contact with them. Initially, the child is powerless in the face of the objects surrounding him, and if he is to survive he must look to human objects for care, protection, and instruction. Although he soon comes to react selectively to the objects around him, it is the human objects, who from the very beginning react toward him and thereby exert significant and lasting influence upon him.

For the new-born, people as objects, do not exist. Although he is an object to others, the infant does not exist as an object to himself. With the passing of time, gradually at first, then more rapidly as he grows older, he comes to react toward others with a recognition or awareness of their separate identities; and concurrently, he is conditioned to behave in somewhat like manner toward himself. In essence, this is the beginning of his self-emergence, of the process whereby he is enabled to distinguish himself from others and to react toward himself as well as toward those around him.

The importance of the *self* is partially that it is an ever-present consideration in the life experience of the person. As a mechanism through which one becomes aware of certain expectations and evaluations made by others, the self acts as a criticizing and regulating agent impelling the person to conform to those expectations whereby he merits the consequent and personally satisfying evaluations made by others. Ultimately, therefore, the self functions toward integrating the person into the group; and viewed collectively, it facilitates social control and promotes community consensus.

129

Essentially, the self is a complex of reflexive attitudes that arise in the process of socialization. The self is, therefore, a social product. As such, the course of its development is dependent, in large measure, upon the persons and social structures involved in the socialization of the child. "The self, as that which can be an object to itself, is essentially a social structure, and it rises in social experience." [1] This conception of self-emergence clearly implies that the self is no mere bundle of physical attributes, that it is not the organism or physical structure. Rather, in terms of its existence, it is preceded by the physical structure and arises only in social interaction.

Cultures, it should be remembered, vary widely. This means that the feelings, expectations, evaluations, and satisfactions persons experience regarding themselves vary also. For example, the members of a given society might be characterized by self-assurance or self-doubt, by self-esteem or self-abasement, by self-advancement or self-denial. Whatever the self-pattern of the person, it can be expected to be related to his culture and, in some significant respects, be consistent with the self-patterns of those who are important in his life.

THE SELFLESS NEONATE

At birth, the infant is organismic-centered. He is subject to the control and direction of his inner drives and impulses. Primarily, he responds not to external social forces but to internal personal drives. Unaware of the limitations and expectations of the social world into which he has entered, his responses to his inner needs and impulses are imperative, unrestrained, and unsocialized. He is devoid of awareness of the objects about him, unaware of the limitations of his own body, and without attitudes toward either. For him there is neither self nor other. Yet, if he is to learn, both must come to be. The process whereby he becomes aware of self and of others occurs through the same interactional process and within the same general social context.

Social life, by its very nature, requires limitations and restraints upon the automatic and organically regulated functioning of the human infant. Thus, the infant's organic and inherited traits which impel him toward organismic-centered behavior are soon superceded by culturally determined and socially imposed interests, techniques, and activity. Although this transition might never result in the complete and continuous submission of the organic to the cultural, the emerging dominance of the latter can be clearly observed in the growing child. Perhaps the principal product of this emerging dominance of the social and the cultural over the organic is the development of the self.

[1] George H. Mead, *Mind, Self and Society*, Charles W. Morris, ed. (Chicago, The University of Chicago Press, 1934), p. 140.

The first step in the rise of the self lies in the anticipatory reactions which the child builds up with respect to his mother or some other person. For example, in the course of learning to use the mother as the intermediary in the satisfaction of hunger, the child develops a host of anticipatory reactions to her. In satisfying this want, the mother performs a series of acts. Very shortly, therefore, in addition to the systematic pains or tensions, shown by crying, the child, in expectation of having his demand fulfilled, acquires bodily postures and gestures of lips, tongue, and hands. Moreover, these movements become increasingly correlated with the corresponding actions of the mother: her presenting the breast [or bottle, *authors' insert*], her tone of voice, her smile, the pressures of her hands and body on the child.

Out of this interactional matrix an essential identification arises. Just as the mother interprets the infant's cries, manual gestures, and bodily tensions as evidence that he wishes to be fed, so his own gestures take on significance because they lead to his taking her breast and ingesting her milk. He cannot get his reward, in fact, unless he adjusts his own acts to hers. He learns to control or direct his acts in terms of what another expects of him. That is, the first meaning of hunger and its satisfaction comes from his mother's actions toward him as well as from his toward her.

This process of identification of the child with his mother—that is, the linkage of his drive and his response to her reactions toward him—is an example of the earliest phase of self-development.[2]

As the infant grows older, he gets larger and stronger. At the same time the various parts of his organism, including the central nervous system, become highly coordinated. As a result, he becomes more aware of and begins to respond to aspects of his environment. Gradually, he shows signs of greater and more consistent responses to cues, such as outstretched hands; to things, such as the bottle and his rattle; to persons, including those who are unfamiliar as well as those who are familiar.

The Self and Word Symbols

This initial phase of self-development is soon followed and supplemented by the development of language facility.[3] Thereafter, as the child is exposed to contacts with siblings, other members of his family, his peers, and non-family adults, he comes to interpret and respond to their reactions to him. In this way, his context of meaningful interaction is enlarged. Just as he anticipated and responded to his mother's behavior in the nursing act, so he does with regard to others. As he develops facility in the use of word symbols, he experiences increasingly greater understanding of his own behavior and that of others. As the child's area of

[2] *Social Psychology*, 2nd ed., by Kimball Young. Copyright © 1944, F. S. Crofts and Company, Inc., pp. 133–134. Reprinted by permission of Appleton-Century-Crofts.

[3] A detailed discussion of word symbols or language is presented in Chapter 14.

interaction expands, his identifications with and imitation of others increase. Through this increase and his growing ability to communicate, he comes to accept their definitions of himself and of others. Thus, when he is approximately two to three years of age, he may be heard to say, "I Jimmy," or "Jimmy good boy," or "I no baby," depending on the definitions made of him by significant others.

This learning of word symbols in the initial phase of self-emergence is interestingly illustrated in the story of little Jocelyn, age, two and a half. She, like many children, seemed to enjoy hearing herself talk. She apparently made a game of asking anyone who would listen, "Wha' you' name?" Then, without waiting for the answer: "I Zoshlyn." When asked pointedly "What is your name?" she would reply "I name 'Zoshlyn'." Several weeks later she was heard to say pleasantly and teasingly to a service man, "Hi, wha' you do my house?" Increasingly, thereafter, words seemed to have a strange and satisfying fascination for her.

At about the age of three or four, the child's verbalized imaginings illustrate Mead's contention that the self is essentially a social structure which arises through social experience and which "in a certain sense provides for itself its social experiences. . . ."[4] In such situations, the child is his own companion and he converses with himself. For example, Jimmy speaks to himself in the words and the simulated tone of his mother; then he responds in his own words and voice. Such communication with self can be carried on through the involvement of a variety of persons, but usually with persons with whom the child has had significant relations. In its essence, this communication with self involves "taking the role of the other."[5] Later, and in situations involving others, especially at play, the child is aware of the attitudes and actions of his peers toward himself and toward other objects. At this point he seems constrained to behave in accordance with these attitudes and actions. Because of this, he is enabled not only to anticipate the behavior of others, but also to make his own behavior consistent with their expectations.

THE INDIVIDUAL ASPECT OF THE SELF

It may well be that the personality, more especially the self, is much more than the sum total of that which is internalized from others. This is clearly suggested in Mead's comment that "the 'I' is the response of the organism to the attitudes of the others; the 'me' is the organized set of attitudes of others which one himself assumes. The attitudes of the others constitute the organized 'me,' and then one reacts toward that as an 'I.'"[6] That the self is completely social in origin and content is certainly by

[4] George H. Mead, *op. cit.*, p. 140.
[5] *Ibid.*, see especially Part III.
[6] *Ibid.*, p. 175.

no means a generally accepted conclusion. For some, the notion that the self develops from the internalization of social norms, or from role-taking is not a sufficient explanation. In this connection it is said that although man is a social being, he is never completely or fully socialized. The mere internalization of a norm, according to this position, does not affirm the acceptance of it, nor does it assure conformity to it. Thus, it is necessary and instructive to distinguish between "social demands, personal attitudes toward them, and actual conduct." [7]

In social-psychological literature, the uniqueness of the individual has not been completely overlooked or denied.[8] That individualism is a sig nificant trait in the person is suggested by Wrong:

. . . socialization may mean two quite distinct things; when they are confused an oversocialized view of man is the result. On the one hand socialization means the "transmission of the culture," the particular culture of the society an individual enters at birth; on the other hand the term is used to mean the "process of becoming human," of acquiring uniquely human attributes from interaction with others. All men are socialized in the latter sense, but this does not mean that they have been completely molded by the particular norms and values of their culture.[9]

This distinction between socialization as "transmission of the culture" and as "process of becoming human" has much to recommend it. Certainly it is clear that the acceptance of and conformity to social norms and values cannot always be assured. Widespread or even consistently deviant behavior on the part of many people is mute testimony to this. Therefore, even though the present discussion of socialization places emphasis on the child in relation to the expectations, interaction, and impact of persons and social systems, this is not intended to imply that he is *fully socialized*. In fact, it seems clear that

no matter how thoroughly the persons who compose a society have been trained, they remain individuals, distinct physical and psychological entities. They may have a store of associations and emotional responses in common and reduce most of their complementary activities to matters of unconscious habit, yet they retain the capacity for independent thought, feeling, and action. Although the individual is dominated and shaped by his social environment he is not obliterated by it.[10]

[7] Dennis H. Wrong, "The Oversocialized Conception of Man," *The American Sociological Review*, Vol. 26, No. 2 (April, 1961), p. 187.

[8] Although they are not discussed here, the Freudian and various other psycho-analytic views relevant to the self have considerable merit. This is clearly recognized by Wrong in his discussion of the "oversocialized" conception of man. Among the many references to the origin of the self to be found in the literature of theoretical psychiatry, (broadly defined), perhaps Harry Stack Sullivan's comes as close to the view followed here as any. See his *The Interpersonal Theory of Psychiatry* (New York, W. W. Norton & Company, Inc., 1953), pp. 158–171.

[9] Wrong, *op. cit.*, p. 192.

[10] *The Study of Man* by Ralph Linton. Copyright © 1936, D. Appleton-Century Company, Inc., p. 95. Reprinted by permission of Appleton-Century-Crofts.

The Self as A Plurality Pattern

A personality cannot come to exist apart from other personalities. This observation necessarily implies social interaction or group behavior, which, in turn involves explicit and implicit patterns of procedure of social systems. Therefore, social systems loom large in the development of the personality. Since the self, which might well be regarded as lying at the core of the personality, is a social self, groups and social systems are indispensable to its development. "The self has a character which is different from that of the physiological organism proper. The self is something which has a development; it is not initially there at birth, but arises in the process of social experience and activity, that is, develops in the given individual as a result of his relations to that process as a whole and to other individuals within that process." [11]

Ultimately, the self is not the mere totality of one's experiences, nor is it derived from any single group participation, the alleged dominance of the family notwithstanding. In reality, the self results from experiencing many groups and systems. In a sense, then, the person has many selves. For example, there may be a family self, a peer-group self, a school self, and even a self self (activated when one talks to himself). Ideally, the person's several selves are integrated into a composite or unified self. "There is usually an organization of the whole self with reference to the community to which we belong, and the situation in which we find ourselves. . . . The unity and structure of the complete self reflects the unity and structure of the social process as a whole; and each of the elementary selves of which it is composed reflects the unity and structure of one of the various aspects of that process in which the individual is implicated." [12]

Mead's concept, the "unified self," does not necessarily imply a completely integrated whole. As a matter of fact, he calls attention to the possibility of relinquishing part of the self, or of the dissociation of the self.[13] The possibility of the lack of integration, or the fragmentation of the self is further suggested in the fact that the self emerges in a context of multiple group situations which are sometimes relatively unintegrated and even conflicting in terms of their dominant values and norms and their characteristic behavior patterns. When, therefore, reference is made to the integration of elementary selves into the unified self, the referent is the ideal rather than the real.[14]

That the *complete self* is a complex of *elementary selves* is perhaps best illustrated in modern, pluralistic, open-class societies such as the United

[11] George H. Mead, *op. cit.*, p. 135.
[12] *Ibid.*, pp. 142–144.
[13] *Ibid.*, p. 143–144.
[14] See Ralph Linton, *op. cit.*, Chapter 16.

States. In societies of this type, opportunities for multiple-group involvements as well as for social mobility make it probable that the individual's complete self will be composed of many significantly different elementary selves. This is less likely to be the case in less complex societies. Another significant facet to the emergence of the self in societies such as the United States has to do with the considerable social and cultural conflicts and divergences in values, norms, attitudes, and behavior which exist. Because of conflict and divergences in such social and cultural components and because the individual frequently finds himself involved simultaneously in multiple groups which manifest these conflicts and divergences, it can be expected that the integration of his elementary selves into a relatively complete self might well be problem-creating and even unachievable. To determine the probability of such difficulty, it might be instructive to examine certain apparently conflicting contexts for self-development such as the family and the gang, the slum neighborhood and the church, or, the non-middle class family and the public school.

THE UNIFIED SELF AND MULTIPLE CONTEXTS

The self, as already indicated, arises in social interaction. This social interaction always occurs within certain contexts. Any given context involves a determinable number of social relationships and a recognizable configuration of culture components. Included in these are social structures, models, statuses, roles, values, and attitudes. In the final analysis, it is the significant context with its social and cultural components that sets the stage for and largely determines the course of self-development.

In a study of "good boys" in a high delinquency area, Walter Reckless and his associates have directed attention to certain considerations which relate significantly to this whole process. In their conclusion regarding self as an "insulator against delinquency," they [15] pointed out that

while this pilot study points to the presence of a socially acceptable concept of self as the insulator against delinquency, the research does not indicate how the boy in the high delinquency area acquired his self image. It may have been acquired by social definition of role from significant figures in his milieu, such as a mother, a relative, a priest, a settlement house worker, a teacher, etc. It might have been a by-product of effective socialization of the child, which had the good fortune of not misfiring. On the other hand, it may have been an outgrowth of discovery in social experience that playing the part of a good boy and remaining a good boy bring maximum satisfactions (of acceptance) to the boy himself. Finally, there is a strong suspicion that a well-developed con-

[15] Walter C. Reckless, Simon Dinitz and Ellen Murray, "Self-Concept as an Insulator Against Delinquency," *American Sociological Review*, Vol. 21, No. 6 (December, 1956), p. 746.

cept of self as a "good boy" is the component which keeps middle- and upper-class boys, who live in the better neighborhoods, out of delinquency. The point is that this component seems to be strong enough to "insulate" the adolescent against delinqency in the unfavorable neighborhoods.

No context for self-development, be it an "unfavorable neighborhood" or a middle-class area, is likely to be a totally unchanging situation. Often, a given context expands or becomes more complex to the child as he grows older and moves about more freely within it. In addition, the number of these contexts is increased as he gets older. For present purposes, however, the emphasis will be upon the stable rather than the dynamic aspect of the context. Thus, the time factor (the changes over time) will be considered only as it is implied in references made to the several different contexts in which the growing child comes to be involved.

Initially, the context or social and cultural limits for self-development are coextensive with the limits of the child's immediate family relationships. The patterns of parent-child relationships and the relevant values, norms, attitudes, models, and behavior are the principal components in the initial stages of the child's self-development. Principally, the child imaginatively observes his parents' reactions to and evaluations of his behavior. Because he is dependent on, emotionally attached to, and identified with his parents, their definitions of his behavior and verbalized expectations regarding what he should or should not do, as well as how he should or should not feel, all tend to become his own definitions. To a somewhat lesser extent, other members of his immediate family might have the same kind of impact on him.

That the standards of evaluation applied to the child by others come to be the standards he applies to himself can be supported, at least inferentially:

The individual and his environment constitute a dynamic configuration all of whose parts are so closely interrelated and in such constant interaction that it is very hard to tell where to draw lines of demarcation. For the purpose of the present discussion, personality will be taken to mean: "The organized aggregate of psychological processes and states pertaining to the individual." [16]

If, as indicated above, "the individual and his environment constitute a dynamic configuration" and if his personality is "the organized aggregate of psychological processes and states," then clearly the self, which lies at the core of the personality, cannot be viewed apart from the environment, which for present purposes may be equated with the context for self-emergence.

The configuration of social and cultural elements which the child

[16] *The Cultural Background of Personality* by Ralph Linton. Copyright © 1945, D. Appleton-Century Company, Inc., p. 84. Reprinted by permission of Appleton-Century-Crofts.

experiences within the context of his immediate family is likely to be marked by a relatively high degree of consistency; although exceptions are perhaps to be found in the psychologically broken and the structurally incomplete home. Excluding the latter situations, the course of self-emergence is likely to be facilitated by the consistency involved in family relationships. But when the child begins to be involved in additional contexts, the probability of having to adjust to conflicting situations is increased.

The consistency in the child's experiences referred to here is not intended to include experiences that necessarily lead to the development of a personally satisfying or socially approved self. Indeed, it is possible that such consistent experiences can contribute to the lack of self-confidence, to a tendency toward self-rejection, or to a self image marked by feelings of superiority and of disdain for others. What is important in this connection is that experiences which are consistently repetitive with regard to ends and means are likely to facilitate development in the directions chosen or followed, whatever they may be.

Patently, the configuration of social and cultural elements found in the child's non-family experiences may be similar to that which he finds at home. In such instances, his self-conception derived through family interaction is likely to be supported and further crystallized. If, however, he is subjected to contrasting or conflicting situations in the non-family contexts in which he becomes involved, the possibility of uncertainty, confusion, or modification in his earlier defined conception of self is increased.[17]

As the child grows older and as his social contexts become more complex and increase in number, he can be expected to develop an increasing number of selves and at the same time to feel the need to develop a unified self. As this process continues, the child is likely to become less and less open to significant modifications in his self-conception, so that major changes will tend to occur only under unique circumstances or when more significant others are involved.

MOBILITY AND SELF-EMERGENCE

Reference has been made to the fact that the complete self is a complex of elementary selves and that this has implications for modern, pluralistic, and open-class societies such as the United States. At this point, some comments regarding some of the more significant of these implications are in order.

[17] The concept "differential association" which is applicable to becoming a delinquent is pertinent here. See E. H. Sutherland and Donald R. Cressey, *Principles of Criminology* (Philadelphia, J. B. Lippincott Co., 1960).

The relatively large degree of freedom to move in space, to make personal decisions, and to choose one's companions which is enjoyed by the urban child leads him into involvements in multiple contexts. With increasing age and maturity, he progressively enjoys more of this freedom. As a consequence, he is likely to be influenced by many different persons and groups. Moreover, in many of these situations or contexts, he is expected to identify with, become and remain loyal to, and learn from or emulate the persons with whom he associates. For example, the Scouts, school chums, or the gang might well exert a significant and even lasting influence upon the child. Depending upon the extent to which he is impressionable, each of these contexts or situations is, along with the family, a context for the development of an elementary self.

The notion that the complete or unified self is a complex of elementary selves, implies an integration of the latter into the former. As already indicated, such integration will be facilitated if there is a high degree of consistency among the elementary selves. If, however, there is considerable inconsistency, problems of self-integration may arise. The probability that this latter consequence will develop is rather high in modern American society, especially in the more highly developed urban sections; for there one finds conflicting groups frequently working at cross purposes.

In the United States, many children are exposed at an early age to situations conducive to the development of conflicting self-conceptions. As a case in point, consider the middle-class Negro child in certain southern urban communities. At home he may be taught to regard himself as a unique and worthwhile person. He may be stimulated to move and act with self-assurance and poise. In his contacts with others, at home or in school, he may be encouraged to stand up for his rights, to insist on taking his turn, and to examine carefully the reactions of others toward him in the light of his own self-conception. When, however, such a child comes into repeated contacts with lower-class Negroes or with members of the dominant white community, as he is almost certain to do, the integrity of his already developed self-conception might well be threatened or questioned. In this situation, the expectations of the dominant white community are perhaps such that the middle-class Negro child must almost necessarily come into close and continuing contact with children of his race who are of lower-class status. Furthermore, the prevalence of and pressure toward racial identification might operate as a powerful force leading such a child to think of himself, first and foremost, as a Negro and to accept whatever limitations and imputed characteristics such a pressure toward racial self-identification implies. Yet, for this child, the toleration of the limitations implicit in this situation and the acceptance of the expected racial identification do not coincide with the self-feeling he has developed at home. As a result of these latter experiences, such a child might find it extremely difficult to develop a fully integrated or unified self.

Another example or illustration of the development of conflicting elementary selves can be found in the dual context of the lower-class home and the school. A number of research studies give evidence that the social and cultural character of these two contexts are considerably different and conflicting.[18] It can be expected that by the time the lower-class child enters school he will have developed a self-concept consistent with the values and attitudes, the models and norms, the statuses and roles that prevail in his lower-class situation. Thus, his aspirations, expectations, and evaluations regarding self are likely to be firmly rooted in his lower-class background. In school, however, this child is likely to find that his standards of self-judgment are no longer approved and do not bring him acceptance and reward. As a consequence, he may begin to lose his confidence in self—even in others; or he may actively resist the school personnel's attempts to modify his self-conception, preferring, rather, to follow the self-pattern laid at home. Conceivably, he might reject the home-determined self for that promoted in the school. But whether the home or the school prevails, the likelihood of conflicting elementary selves remains.

In addition to the examples cited, there are other types of social and cultural contexts in American society which might contribute to the development of conflicting and inconsistent self-images. These include formal groups such as the Boy Scouts, for example. Also included are informal groups such as those experienced by children at the movies, on playgrounds, and in casual play. In the final analysis, however, participation in these contexts leads to difficulties in self-development only to the extent that the child interacts simultaneously in two or more contexts that are significantly incongruent, or to the extent that he becomes involved in a context which disturbs his pre-established self. Ultimately, the influence upon the development of the self exerted by these various contexts are related to the intensity of emotional involvement and the repetitiveness of contacts which the child experiences within them.

SUMMARY

In the discussion in this chapter, certain broad generalizations regarding the social and cultural contexts in which the self emerges have been set forth. Although the immediate family is the initial context for self development, other contexts usually exert some influence in the totality of this process. As indicated already, the several contexts available for interaction on the part of the child are potential situations for the emergence

---

[18] See Allison Davis, Burleigh B. Gardner, and Mary R. Gardner, *Deep South, An Anthropological Study of Caste and Class* (Chicago, University of Chicago Press, 1941).

of elementary selves. To the extent that these contexts are characterized by basic differences in social and cultural patterns, to that same extent is the child exposed to the likelihood that he will develop different elementary selves. Since these elementary selves must necessarily undergo a degree of integration toward the development of a complete self, the extent to which this integration is achieved will be related to the degree of inconsistency among the contexts which contribute significantly to self-emergence. Finally, because societies such as the United States provide widely conflicting contexts for self-development, the integration of elementary selves into the complete self may be, for many children, a difficult and even unsuccessful experience.

READINGS

COOLEY, Charles H., *Human Nature and the Social Order,* rev. ed. (New York, Charles Scribner's Sons, 1922).

DAI, Bingham, "A Socio-Psychiatric Approach to Personality Organization," *American Sociological Review,* Vol. 17, No. 1 (February, 1952), pp. 44–49.

GOFFMAN, Erving, *The Presentation of Self in Everyday Life* (Garden City, N.Y., Doubleday & Co., Inc., 1959).

KINCH, John M., "A Formalized Theory of the Self-Concept," *American Journal of Sociology,* Vol. LXVIII (January, 1963), pp. 481–486.

PIERIS, Ralph, "Speech and Society: A Sociological Approach to Language," *American Sociological Review,* Vol. 16, No. 4 (April, 1951), pp. 499–505.

10

Parents: Key Models
for Socialization

INTRODUCTION

Concurrent with growing awareness of himself, a child discovers the existence of others. While many older people seem to come and go in his life, certain people seem to remain longer and re-appear frequently in his expanding world. Most likely, he becomes familiar first with an adult woman, whom he will ultimately address as mother. Later on, an adult male makes himself known to the child as father. While other kinship ties will become known and identifiable as the child emerges slowly from infancy, such relationships seldom ever reach the significance or magnitude associated with his parents. They alone will be able to observe his metamorphosis from a helpless, inadequate bundle of life to adulthood and a place among his fellowmen. Their investments of time, energy, hopes, and thought will yield a product in the form of a human personality. Certainly, they will exert conscious effort to shape the life of their offspring. One young man defined parenthood in terms of "to have and to mold." But, subtle and not-so-obvious effects must also be considered if the full import of parenthood for children is to be understood. Essentially, these matters concern models placed before children.

The variety of parents is striking. Practically every adult is a parent, or will be one, and there is no single type that represents all possibilities. One cannot select some idealistic configuration for parenthood and insist that this pattern fits all persons. After all, realistically, convicts, racketeers, alcoholics, confidence men, ambitious politicians, conniving businessmen, sadistic tyrants, and thoughtless braggarts are, or have been, parents. These types are found in company with the timid recluse, the lazy employee, the confused youth, the defeated middle-aged, the impulsive gambler, the vain social climber, and the disorganized coward. All of these, and many other types, are parents and set models for children. In the ensuing discussion of parental models, this variety of parents should be kept in mind. When generalizations are made, one can then reflect and profitably say, "Yes, but, on the other hand. . . ."

THE MEANING OF MODELS

Children acquire increasing skill in linguistic communication with their associates. In time, cultural symbols take on added meaning. Children become better able to deal with items somewhat removed from their own immediate environment. Symbols, however, stand in the place of reality. In the world of children, real objects, tangible things, living people, and their own experiences are most meaningful to them. Of course, the adult world will urge children to distill some meaning out of these gross matters, but the down to earth nature of their lives continues to hold them in a firm grip. Mothers and fathers are not understood in terms of nebulous qualities, but as "my very own mother" and "my very own father." These are the people who personally attend to them every single day and every single night. Words that stand for such qualities as gentleness, devotion, concern, indulgence, responsibility, or thoughtfulness would fall on uncomprehending childish ears. Instead, ask children to point out the parents who feed them, clothe them, comfort them, and protect them, and they are quick to recognize which adult man and woman serve in these capacities.

It has been said that some children are born hero worshipers. They will follow a hero or heroine like puppies trotting contentedly after their master, and they will harbor few grudges. Without question, without comment, without ill will,[1] they tend to accept these people as their own and strive to be like them. They will mimic such personages down to the minutest details. It is not so much a desire to become a carbon copy of other people that this occurs, as it is the restrictions imposed by the fact that comparatively few people enter children's lives at the outset. Later on, there will be rivals for the parents' primacy and the competition will most likely become intense and complicated. Note how many parents feel neglected when their children begin to look to their playmates, their school chums, their teachers, their ministers, and their friends as possible models to emulate. Nevertheless in the early years, parents have a clear field and can consolidate this advantage by working with children throughout their formative period.

Models are finished products and children see them as possible goals in

[1] In this connection the following fragment of a case history is pertinent: A little girl, who had been unmercifully beaten by her mother to the point of losing one eye and becoming partially blind in the other, was asked what she thought of her mother. She replied, "I still like her, but I can't see her as well as I used to."

their own, unsettled lives. What one shall be and how one should conduct one's self can often be answered long before one actually takes a given role. Models point the direction and children use them to tell where they are going.

Models, are not automatically copied. They may serve chiefly as examples of what to do and what *not* to do. Or, they may act as points of departure from which one may choose to modify, deviate, enlarge upon, or tone down. Models can suggest certain objectives, but the tailoring of the suit will come from the person who will eventually wear it. Thus, parents may never be too sure that the models they set for their children will be repeated in the future. Many a pious parent has been surprised by the irreligiosity of his offspring. Many rural parents are distressed that young people are highly attracted to city life. Many honest parents are dismayed that their own children have become dishonest. Following in the footsteps of one's parents, is never guaranteed. The action that follows after an observer has observed is part and parcel of the impact of models.

A Theory of Models

Because much of what is discussed and illustrated here rests upon a theoretical framework, it will help if a brief description of the structures and functions that relate to parental models in the socialization of children is offered. Mothers and fathers are viewed in this chapter as *the middle generation,* the link between the examples provided by older generations of grandparents and the new generation of children. The middle generation has already developed a fairly stabilized pattern of life which they now carry out by words and actions. This pattern will involve intra-parental relationships such as how they regard each other, how they handle power relationships, and how each conceives of self; and will involve inter-generational relationships such as how they regard their children, how they regard their elders, and how they deal with family and non-family members.

Children are viewed as observers of their parental examples (and, indeed, other parents of the middle generation). They adopt all or part of these models, and interpret them in their own distinctive way. Depending on their subjective judgments of parental models, children will move closer or farther from these models when other powerful forces come into play. These forces may be the greater appeal of their peers as models or changes that alter the entire pattern. Changes in the family cycle, for example, will move the child out of infancy into increasing understanding of the significance of parental models. Previously unnoticed power structures can now be observed and evaluated. They may be found to be greatly appreciated or somewhat repugnant.

Finally, the entire family structure is immersed in larger class, community, and culture complexes that strengthen or weaken various relationships. Children internalize this matrix into their personalities. Parental models are either chosen as guides to conduct or as counter-models. Like a pendulum does not stand still between the extremities of its swing, children tend to waver between models until they can ultimately choose a stabilized, mature way of life for themselves.

PARENTAL MODELS: POSITIVE AND NEGATIVE INFLUENCES

1. Manhood and Womanhood

Most societies have prescribed definitions of what an adult male or an adult female should be. Children of each sex look closely at their respective parents for guidance in this matter. Adult womanhood is equated with their mothers and adult manhood with their fathers. A child of a college professor once called all male visitors "Doctor," because he thought his father and his father's associates were typical of all men. It is not uncommon to witness a child rushing up to some strange man or woman and shouting, "Daddy!" or "Mommy!" to the embarrassment of the innocent party. Fathers represent masculinity and mothers represent femininity as defined by their society and children spend years absorbing their ways.

Clifford Kirkpatrick[2] has contributed the term "POSS," which means "parent of the same sex," and the term "POOS," parent of the opposite sex, as objectifying devices in discussing parental models. The use of such terms has the advantage of removing some degree of sentimentality which the terms father or mother seem to convey.

Kirkpatrick and others have wisely noted that children not only note carefully the model of manhood or womanhood presented by their POSS, but they also look to their POOS to try to understand members of the opposite sex. A boy's conception of the feminine world is strongly colored by the model of womanhood offered by his mother. A girl's knowledge of manhood springs largely, at first, from the model offered by her father. To overstate the matter somewhat, if one parent or the other has particularly greater influence, the result may be a feminized male or a masculinized female as a child. It will require much maneuvering at a later date to change the individual enough to more approximate the masculinity or femininity attributes regarded as appropriate by his culture. In some cases, the re-adjustments or basic re-alignments of personality attributes appear to be almost impossible to achieve. At best, great effort

[2] Clifford Kirkpatrick, *The Family, As Process and Institution*, pp. 207–213, Copyright 1955. The Ronald Press Company.

can lead to some modifications of personality qualities to meet cultural limits. These modifications are achieved or are possible within societies such as America provided highly skilled professionals are employed over an extended period of time. Such professionals are neither abundant nor available to every person, even in America. For other societies, arrangements to handle individuals who have somehow failed to meet sex-typed role requirements can vary from expulsion to complete acceptance of role reversals. The *berdache* or squaw man complex of the Blackfoot Indians is a notable example of the latter arrangement.

Because children will spend most of their lives under special circumstances ascribed to them by their sex, parents are generally expected to make every effort to personify manhood or womanhood as idealized by their society. Failing to do so is to suggest that their children defy social pressures and to aid and abet the career of the social deviant. Because manhood and womanhood are generally complemental and supplemental, efforts to be true to social types are crowned by successful marriages in which the two sexual worlds can live in harmony and accord.

It is possible to interpret this discussion as seeming to advocate complete agreement with whatever a society demands of its men and women. What if some individuals judge that there is some injustice in the roles ascribed to men and women in a particular society? Is it suggested that such matters be overlooked and that people should acquiesce to such practices as the subordination of women or the exposure of men to hazardous situations? Such meek submission to the status quo is not the central issue under discussion. What is paramount is that social changes come about because people act in concert. That is, as increasing numbers of people adopt ways that vary from the past, there is bound to be the eventual acceptance of new social systems. Once again, social conformity to the newer systems is demanded. It is to the power of social controls that attention is directed and not necessarily to the forces that bring about social change. The stability of social systems may be upset, but they are replaced by new social systems, which again require some degree of acceptance.

Cultural inertia is a compelling force and it seems especially so in the case of manhood and womanhood. Even today, fragments of feudalistic attitudes towards women or Victorian conceptions of proper decorum still exist. When suffragettes demanded voting privileges for women, their strongest opponents were not so much men as other women. Ideas as to the nature of manhood or womanhood have evolved slowly in history. In the foregoing analysis, it has been suggested that children are exposed to well established conceptions of manhood or womanhood. Experimentation with deviant forms in childhood guarantees an inevitable clash between individuals and the society in which they must live. If this is the goal of parental models, then such may be achieved by doing whatever one pleases. If this is not the purpose of parental models, then parents need become more sensitized to what their behavior does to their developing children.

2. Husband and Wife

Carrying the manhood and womanhood models out to full fruition, parents also present to their children a close-up view of at least *one husband* and *one wife* in their society. Marital roles may be far removed from the lives of children, but sooner or later, depending upon cultural patterns, they might assume these roles. Other marriages may be closed off from view except for gross, external observations. Being participant observers within the family structure, however, children can make detailed, internal observations which can be stored away for future reference. How do men treat women in marriage? How do persons in subordinate positions achieve certain satisfactions despite such handicaps? What is required of married women? These, and many more questions, are answered as children watch the behavior of their parents.

Husbands and wives who daily display before their children such qualities as affection, devotion to duties, responsibilty, thoughtfulness, and courtesy build a model that might well endure throughout the lifetimes of their children and, indeed, well into other generations. A longitudinal research study that would be most revealing would be one in which the traits displayed in one generation are traced back to as many past generations as possible or projected into the future by noting successive generations reacting to specific role characteristics. There are numerous hints that parental models have deep personality effects when, for instance, wives or husbands have thrown up their hands in despair and said, "He's just like his father was!" or, "This has been going on for generations in her family."

There can be negative influences derived from the manner in which husbands and wives conduct themselves. They possibly may be disloyal, inconsiderate, uncommunicative, angry, disgusted, quarrelsome, and generally contentious. If the union survives in this atmosphere, children could almost interpret as normal this type of marital "bliss." If the alienation proceeds to the breaking point, then children may be plunged into a closer relationship with one parent to the comparative neglect of the other. Still another result is derived from research data which suggest that children of divorced parents are prone to accept divorce as an alternative when confronted with baffling material problems themselves.[3]

[3] See Clarence W. Schroeder, *Divorce in a City of 100,000 Population* (Peoria, Ill., Bradley Polytechnic Institute Library, 1939); Lewis M. Terman, *Psychological Factors in Marital Happiness* (New York, McGraw-Hill Book Co., Inc., 1938); Lewis Terman and Melita Oden, *The Gifted Child Grows Up: Twenty-Five Years' Follow-Up of a Superior Group* (Stanford, Stanford University Press, 1947); Jessie Bernard,

On this latter result, the precedent of divorce is set and prepares the way for repetition. "If Mother can do it, so can I," says the disgruntled spouse who experienced the dissolution of her own home in childhood. After all, such a woman has survived the impact of divorce as a child and she can conclude that she emerged unscarred in any manner.

3. Provider and Homemaker

Aside from the roles of masculinity or femininity and husband and wife, parents also enact economic functions that help set the home environment of children. Men, as providers, sustain the family with their daily work. Their homes reflect their economic successes or failures. Women, as homemakers, commonly supplement the income and its management by their own home production and management patterns, which, in turn, have repercussions in the world of children. Children thus inherit an economic and its accompanying social atmosphere which will vitally affect them by the provision of social advantages or disadvantages. Some will live in hovels and others will live in mansions. Some will endure a subsistent existence, while others will regard luxury as commonplace.

Again, the reaction to such models may be positive or negative. A classic type dramatized in many novels or plays is the person who as a child experienced grinding poverty because of the ne'er-do-well he had as a father. A spark is thus kindled in the tinder of youth which emerges as a fire in the years of maturity. Such a person vows never to live in poverty again and takes, if necessary, any step that leads to wealth and economic power.

Turning to the homemaker model developed by the wife and mother, an ideal type has been described in Proverbs:[4]

A woman of character, how wonderful she is to find!
She is worth far more than the most precious jewels.
Her husband can trust her confidently,
His wealth shall not be diminished through her.
She will do him good and not evil, all the days of her life.
She provides an ample supply of wool and flax,
And willingly works with her hands.
She is like a merchant ship, bringing her food from afar.
She gets up before daybreak to serve her household its food.
Even cares for the needs of the maidens who wait on her.
She judges the value of a field that is for sale,
And completes the purchase.
With what she earns she plants a new vineyard.

Remarriage (New York, The Dryden Press, 1956); William J. Goode, *After Divorce* (New York, The Free Press of Glencoe, Inc., 1956); Paul H. Jacobson, *American Marriage and Divorce* (New York, Holt, Rinehart & Winston, Inc., 1959).
[4] Proverbs 31:10–31.

She ties her apron about her body firmly
And rolls up her sleeves to work vigorously.
She senses how valuable is what she has to offer,
And does not mind burning the midnight oil.
She busies her hand at the spinning wheel,
Yet the same hands stretch out to the poor,
And are busy for those who are in need.
She has no fear of the snow for her household,
For her family is clothed in warm, rich garments.
She makes her own raiment, and dresses in materials
Both durable and becoming.
Her husband has an admirable reputation when he
Sits among the elders of the land.
She makes and sells fine garments
And delivers to the merchants embroidered sashes.
Her clothes are worn in dignity and good taste.
She lightly accepts the prospect of advancing age.
When she speaks, it is wisdom
And kindness governs her tongue.
She carefully administers her household programs,
And never eats the bread of idleness.
Her children grow up to make her happy
And her husband can constantly praise her.

The biblical ideal homemaker is viewed as important as her husband in his role of provider. Modern counterparts may still be found and hymns of praise are still sung in their name. The work of the chief provider is balanced by the work of the homemaker and the consequences of doing this, or not doing this, are felt in the lives of all the family members. Certainly children are most conscious of the homemaker model as they witness her activities more often than they do those of their father. One small child replied when questioned about this matter, "My mother works. I don't really know what Daddy does."

Less poetic and more realistic appraisal of the role of the mother from the point of view of children suggests that children's criteria for evaluating parents are fairly self-centered. That is, their appreciation of their mother is based not upon her own intrinsic value, but rather upon what services she renders for them. The work of mothers, then, is more taken for granted by children. It is not until they are adults that children begin to introspect and find that their mothers merit far more honor than they rendered as little children.

Women may not play just the roles of homemakers, but may become co-providers with men. They may even become greater providers than men. Nevertheless, the traditional function of reproduction continues to haunt them. Clifford Kirkpatrick[5] has summarized some of the variations

5 Clifford Kirkpatrick, *op. cit.*, pp. 166–167.

that may occur for women as they attempt to meet both their reproductive and work functions. These are expressed as follows:

1. Reproductive Function . . . "excess"
   Problems: Loss of Work function
   Unable to participate in other social activities
   Treated as a "brood" animal
2. Work Function . . . "excess"
   Problems: Denial of marriage or motherhood
   Work may be excessive or unsatisfactory to self because of amount or quality
   Others may be dissatisfied as well
3. Reproductive Function . . . "deficient"
   Problems: Both marriage and motherhood are threatened
4. Work Function . . . "deficient"
   Problems: Lack of satisfactory work
   Failure to use capacity and training
5. Reproductive Function and Work Functions . . . "excess"
   Problems: Double burdens of childbearing and work drudgery
6. Reproductive and Work Functions . . . "deficient"
   Problems: Parasitic situation
   Failure to be useful either in home or at work
7. Reproductive and Work Function . . . "unfair balance"
   Problems: Man provides and woman forced into childbearing against her wishes
8. Reproductive and Work Functions . . . "lack of proper distribution"
   Problems: Reproduction and work may be ample, but too widely separated for smooth transitions
   Not enough time to do both well
9. Failure to balance work and reproduction as social pressures fail to allow woman to use her best resources
10. Free but uncertain choices as to balance between work and reproduction
    Problems: Role confusion
    How is one to behave if left to one's own devices?

There are many potential models from which to choose when women attempt to deal with their reproductive and work functions. The choices made will rest upon individual circumstances and social settings. Children are affected by whichever model is finally selected. Their reactions to these models ultimately become reference points for future behavior.

4. Friend or Enemy

The unconscious image presented to children by parents also includes friendship or enmity towards given persons or groups of people. Children may not comprehend the words that are spoken in kindness or in anger, but they grasp quite readily the overt action of being considerate or inconsiderate to outsiders. In general, the tastes of their parents are transmitted to the children by means of deeds that are clearly generous or clearly hateful. In this area, children are much more prone to mimic their parental models since they lack the experiences in time that have led their elders to treat other people as they do. Love and hates are not so much discussed as they are enacted. Only after the passage of much time, when children have reached more adult levels and are equipped to consider the bases for likes or dislikes, can new directions be taken which may differ from those of their parents.

5. Religious or Non-religious

In this area, as in the area of friendship or enmity, children are most likely to pursue the religious practices of their parents. Choices are rarely offered, if at all, and children are exposed to religious or non-religious conditioning as soon as feasible. If there is some form of piety, the mysteries of a given faith may not be crystal clear to children, but they tend to identify with it. If parents do not include religion as part of their interests and activities, then the child tends to follow suit and may judge religion as some foolish superstition that somehow has survived from darker, more benighted, times. In either case, the religious model of parents is duplicated in the lives of the young. Conversion to some faith or the acceptance of some non-religious philosophy usually awaits a more mature stage, if the impact of parental models is to be reversed.

6. Worker and Player

Societal conditions will vary, but it would be fairly accurate to note that generally children are first initiated into play activities and are delayed in the ascription of work responsibilities. Going out to play and preoccupation with toys are typical experiences of all children. Later on, these will be translated in terms of leisure, avocations, rest, and sheer pleasure in adult life. But, once again, parental models are carefully watched by children for the cues that will suggest just what the play or work shall be. Donald Pierson [6] tells an intriguing story of how children in Brazil play a game called "Capitao do matto." This is a form of hide and seek in which those in hiding are presumed to be slaves and the seekers are led by a "bush captain." This is based upon the historical cases of slaves who fled into the Brazilian jungles to escape their harsh taskmasters only to be pursued by organized parties of hunters. In brief, the implication is that the activities of older people in their serious moments become fit subjects for play among the younger set.

[6] Donald Pierson, *Negroes in Brazil* (Chicago, The University of Chicago Press, 1942), p. 48.

Little girls are quite serious about their play activities with their dolls and their housekeeping, again a direct interpretation of parental models. Two little girls recently remarked to a passer-by while they were cautiously allowing some mud patties to dry on a large rock near their home, "We'll have some of these cakes left over from our party, so if you don't want them, we'll have them for another day." Or, boys will play at being soldiers, a role all too familiar to many of the world's children. In these instances, the work models of the adult world become the play objects of the children's world. A most interesting thesis would be to study the toys of children to discover just how frequently adult ways are commandeered by children and re-expressed in their play. The hypothesis suggested here would be that the relationship would be most direct.

Parents might contemplate just how far they are removed from the play activity of children. Noting that children appear to be oriented around play and parents are oriented around work, then it might be wise to inquire just where along the course of one's life did the preoccupation with play convert to preoccupation with work. Rather than to do one or the other, it might be worthwhile to bring work and play into better balance. Certainly there is growing evidence that the work of men is less and less paramount because machines assume former burdens. A shortened work week, the idealization of the weekend, the numerous holidays and annual vacations, the increased mobility of populations to reach parks, forests, and other recreational locations, and the commercialization of fun are some of the factors that conspire to press parents to pay far greater attention to leisure activities than was ever possible before in human history. An even more compelling reason to consider the importance of play lies in the earlier retirement of people from the work world and the increased number of years that have been granted older citizens. Such people frequently have to relearn how to play because they have lingered too long at work.

Within highly industrialized societies like the United States, a polarity between children and parents has been traditionally one of play for children and work for parents. The adolescent period represents a crucial time when some transition ordinarily occurs for individuals between the play world of children and the work world of adults. This transitional period merits attention and will be discussed at greater length in an ensuing chapter on adolescence. An extended discussion on play, games, and work may also be found in Chapter Fourteen. Within the context of this chapter, however, play and work are treated as both antithetical and synergetic.

The contrasting elements of children's play, which is concerned with sheer pleasure, non-productivity, expressiveness, and self-rewards, and parental work, which is concerned with routine, productivity, fatigue, and service to others, may possibly come into conflict. On the other hand, there are adults who have found that their earliest child play were faint hints of their future vocations. For such adults, their work is still pleasure, a means for personal expression and creativity, and enjoyable in and of itself. Work and play can thus be at odds or can operate together.

All work is not necessarily pleasurable and it may need to be learned that hard work is sometimes required. Thereafter, or separate from the work place, recreational needs can be met. Children whose parents find their work is a labor of love, have a model to follow which is attractive and highly desirable. One potential pitfall is the over-zealous parent who attempts to lead his children into work or professional services in which he alone is enthusiastic. There are numerous fields of endeavor and parents who have found work and play compatible may be more successful with their children if they do not persist in advocating a single, preselected vocation.

7. Citizenship

Children observe the direction in which parents look and how closely they affiliate themselves with kinship members or with members of the larger society. Some parents can weave both of these elements into their lives. Others seem to confine themselves only to kinsmen. Still others concentrate their energies in civic enterprises that take them far afield from family life. The affairs of the country, or the region may become part of a family atmosphere or may be kept in a separate compartment to be brought out only on special occasions. The political philosophy of parents enters the lives of children when they observe partisan quarrels of older people, discussions to convince compatriots that a given political doctrine is correct, the voting habits of parents, and the support given to community needs. The relationships appear to be positive and direct. The influence of parental models of citizenship is evident in the commonly heard statement, "Why, we have been members of the ———— Party for generations!"

PROBLEM AREAS

Other than the actual personification of *roles* which children may eventually take, parents present models of *qualities* that may be called into play in meeting various social situations. These are characteristics which may serve children as assets or liabilities. They pose thorny problems for conscientious parents. Only a few can be suggested within the limits of a single chapter.

Honesty or Truthfulness

This quality is a verbalized virtue, widely subscribed to by parents and is representative of the possible entanglements that can come from trying to move children in *acceptable* directions when the culture itself is inconsistent. "One should always tell the truth." "Honesty is the best policy." "One lie leads to another." "Liars never win." "The truth will always be revealed." These are folk statements that illustrate the common concern for truth-telling. Yet, parents can anticipate a serious problem in children who are utterly frank to the point of being blunt, painfully accurate, and, even tactless. One little boy once turned to a house-guest when he saw a break in the conversation and blurted out, "You have buck-teeth, don't you!" Obviously, the overall lesson that one should be honest had been well taught, but the subtleties, the extra finesse, the special polish that should have accompanied the major lesson had not yet been adopted by the child.

Like many rules, there are exceptions and special circumstances in which the general rules do not apply. These specific conditions are not easily grasped at a youthful level. Just how does one have a child understand that there are certain untruths or fabrications which are devised to shield persons from the anguish or unhappiness that complete truth might bring. A classic case is one in which a parent, who has made a strong case for honesty, instructs her child to tell a salesman at the door that she is not at home. The child blithely tells the man, "My mother told me to tell you that she is not home!"

If the complete truth were told forthrightly, there is a strong possibility that the fabric of society would be seriously torn. One may think all kinds of things, but it would be extremely unwise to reveal one's innermost thoughts too freely. Bitter enmities would possibly replace current friendships. Employees would possibly be extremely vulnerable if employers would choose to vent their anger upon their completely honest underlings. Currently cordial student-teacher relationships might collapse. The examples are almost unlimited, but the principle would remain the same. There are amenities and other special civilities that must be observed to avert a clash between personalities. Parents often labor at teaching their children to say "Thank you." and "Please. . . ," and "How do you do?" when full comprehension of these expressions may be lost. The lessons of courtesy and thoughtfulness may not be deeply understood, but children are quick to imitate the examples set by their parents. Even then, the tendency to be direct on the part of children will often emerge at the most inopportune times. Witness the case of the child who asks the visiting minister, "Why did Mummy and Daddy tell me not to swear in front of you?"

Independence

Parents certainly do not desire a helpless child to remain with them forever. The day will eventually come when he will be independent and able to stand alone. Yet parents often find the weaning process unpleasant and make considerable effort to cling to their offspring or to have their children cling tightly to them. Mothers, particularly, having attained status and satisfaction from being wanted and needed, frequently find the growing up process to be sad and unappealing. Philip Wylie[7] has written, almost with an acid pen, about "Momism" in his *Generation of Vipers*. The failure to cut the "Golden Cord" has apparently crippled many children and yet the pattern is repeated over and over again.

Parents who are themselves independent find enough resources to satisfy their social cravings and do not have to utilize their children to these ends. Instead, they will offer increasing opportunity for their children to depend on themselves to get things done. Their satisfactions come from the fact that the young lives in their care have flourished and grown sturdy. On the other hand, parents who are dependent and who seek outside support for their own inner shortcomings unconsciously produce a kindred soul in their children who are unused to freedom and its responsibilities. They savor, instead, the warm assurance to be found exclusively within their own small family circle.

The case for independence can be made too strong—or too early in life. Parents may find that they have been unwise when they find that their children look to no one including the parents for any guidance or assistance. Independence may be a worthy objective, but there is always the possibility of unintended consequences.

Sexuality

The models of manhood and womanhood discussed previously also involve ability to deal adequately with matters pertaining to sex. These are important for both boys and girls, but sex and sexual behavior weigh heaviest upon females. Their bodies and bodily functions are closely associated with sex and sexual development throughout their lives. At first, their femininity is treated in a perfunctory, matter-of-fact manner which excites minimum comment on such matters as dress or adornment. But, the potential is always there, latent motherhood. The girl's body will begin to change and she will dramatically leave childhood behind with the onset of puberty. The coming of age for boys is far less momentous, although it may be the signal for elaborate rites of passage if

[7] Philip Wylie, *Generation of Vipers* (New York, Holt, Rinehart & Winston, Inc., 1942); see also Edward A. Strecker, *Their Mothers' Sons* (Philadelphia, J. B. Lippincott Co., 1946).

males are held in esteem in given societies. The girl will bear the babies in the far off future and her body will signal how near or far that time may be. Her older female models can suggest what will happen to her in due time, but she alone will deliver and spend a maximum amount of time rearing both males and females.

It is vital for girls to receive an appropriate amount and special kind of sex-education. The female's body may be her greatest asset or her greatest liability, depending greatly upon her sexual training. Such socialization does not come as dramatically as biological development, but demands patience, thought, effort, and great skill to result in a young woman who is aware of the significance of her sexuality within her own society.

If there is greater concern for the sexual training of females, this does not imply that boys can be treated in some offhand manner when sexuality is involved. They too have their share in future responsibilities. It may well be true that the need for female sex education exists because of the comparative ignorance and unconcern of adult males. Excellent techniques have been developed for an intelligent sex education for children.[8] They are intended for use by both boys and girls and are often treated in mixed company; that is, boys and girls are instructed together rather than kept apart.

The foundation for such co-education is laid in the home. It should be continual and accurate at every age level. Parents set examples in their normal household routines and can accomplish much by the emotional tone with which they act their sexual roles. Shame is a subtle matter acquired by a child by means of its treatment by others and its constant observation of others. For instance, a little girl will proudly display her pretty bouffant petticoat to any passerby until she acquires some sense that such an under-garment is not to be displayed for the edification of everyone. Ideas of modesty are slowly acquired, and can be quite confusing to children who catch glimpses of a not-so-nice adult world which conducts, for example, beauty queen contests, sells cars with girls wearing bathing suits, or places lurid magazines on drugstore stands.

Kindness

Kindness can be equated with compassion, consideration, unselfishness, and love, even though these have shades of meaning all their own. The quality of dealing thoughtfully, and having empathy is an important need

[8] See Lester F. Beck, *Human Growth* (New York, Harcourt, Brace & World, Inc., 1949); Alan F. Guttmacher, *Having a Baby* (New York, Signet Books, 1950); Milton I. Levine and Jean H. Seligman, *A Baby Is Born* (New York, Simon and Schuster, Inc., 1949); Frances B. Strain, *New Patterns in Sex Teaching* (New York, Appleton-Century-Crofts, 1951); Lester A. Kirkendall, *Helping Children Understand Sex* (Chicago, Science Research Associates, Inc., 1952).

in social living. Children may not incorporate it into their personalities immediately, but working towards this objective is begun in the home with parents serving as working models. Children's egos, for the most part, appear to be strongly tied to self-concern and self-interest. Children usually come into contact with comparatively few people who are generally overly concerned with the well being of the children. The numerous people outside this immediate circle will eventually make themselves felt. Much of children's success will hinge on whether or not they have developed social sensitivities that will win them favor and esteem in the eyes of others.

Children may develop qualities of independence or honesty, but failure to respect the feelings and ideas of others may prove to be a most serious shortcoming in their makeup. Often one hears that children are cruel towards other children unintentionally. Their direct approach to what they see may cut deep enough to leave psychological scars that are not easily overlooked. Hurting someone, without intending to hurt, still hurts. Parents are wise to catch the side-remarks, the thoughtlessness, and the insensitivity of children quite early before it grows to such proportions that only psychiatric care or police action can be effective. Their own model of consideration and displays of kindness and gentleness can suggest patterns that might be followed with great profit by their children.

SUMMARY

Parents have a great impact on their children, not only in their words, but more importantly by their actions. The models they present are frequently unconscious examples or enactments of what they want their children to become. Because children have not yet acquired skills in dealing with abstractions, they are most impressed by the living models set before them by their elders. These they may mimic, follow in part, or possibly reject, depending upon circumstances. Other models will eventually be followed, but parental models are central. Models may be of a positive nature, contributing to an effective life within the limits set by a society, or they may be negative, socially crippling or harming the young when they reach adulthood. Seven roles were discussed, with applications toward male or female behavior. These were (1) Manhood and Womanhood, (2) Husband and Wife, (3) Provider and Homemaker, (4) Friend or Enemy, (5) Religious or Non-Religious, (6) Worker or Player, and (7) Citizenship. While all these had their problems, the most difficult areas pertained not so much to roles as they did to the development of personality attributes. A few qualities were suggested, such as honesty, independence, sexuality, and kindness, as far as challenging parents to set the patterns for their acquisition by their children. These traits are applicable to many social roles and may be assets or liabilities depending upon how well they are understood.

READINGS

ANDERSON, Nels, *Work and Leisure* (New York, The Free Press of Glencoe, Inc., 1962).

BOSSARD, James H. S., and BOLL, Eleanor, *Why Marriages Go Wrong* (New York, The Ronald Press Company, 1958).

DAVIS, Kingsley, "The Sociology of Parent-Youth Conflict," *American Sociological Review*, Vol. 5, No. 4 (August, 1940), pp. 523–535.

FARIS, Ellsworth, "The Concept of Imitation," *American Journal of Sociology*, Vol. XXXII (1926–1927), pp. 367–378.

KAGAN, J., HOSKEN, B., and WATSON, S., "Child's Symbolic Conceptualization of Parents," *Child Development*, Vol. 23 (1961), pp. 625–636.

LINTON, Ralph, *The Cultural Background of Personality* (New York, Appleton-Century-Crofts, 1945).

MACCOBY, Eleanor, "The Taking of Adult Roles in Middle Childhood," *Journal of Abnormal Social Psychology*, Vol. 63, No. 3 (November, 1961), pp. 493–503.

MEAD, George H., *Mind, Self, and Society, from the Standpoint of a Social Behaviorist* (Chicago, University of Chicago Press, 1934).

MURPHY, Lois B., *et. al., The Widening World of Children: Paths Towards Mastery* (New York, Basic Books Inc., Publishers, 1962).

PIAGET, Jean, *Language and Thought of the Child* (New York, Harcourt, Brace & World, Inc., 1926).

PUTNEY, Snell, and MIDDLETON, Russell, "Effect of Husband-Wife Interaction on the Strictness of Attitudes Towards Child Rearing," *Marriage and Family Living*, Vol. 22, No. 2 (May, 1960), pp. 171–173.

REDL, Fritz and WEINMAN, David, *Children Who Hate: The Disorganization and Breakdown of Behavior Controls* (New York, The Free Press of Glencoe, Inc., 1951).

RIESSMAN, Frank, *The Culturally Deprived Child* (New York, Harper & Row Publishers, Inc. 1962).

ROSE, Arnold, "Parental Models for Youth," *Sociology and Social Research*, Vol. 40, No. 1 (Nov.–Dec., 1955), pp. 3–9.

ROUCEK, Joseph S., *Social Control*, 2nd ed. (New York, D. Van Nostrand Company, Inc., 1956).

RYERSON, Alice, "Medical Advice on Child Rearing," *Harvard Educational Review*, Vol. 31, No. 3 (Summer, 1961), pp. 302–303.

STROUP, Atlee, "Marital Adjustment of the Mother and the Personality

Adjustment of the Child," *Marriage and Family Living*, Vol. 18, No. 2 (1956), pp. 109–113.

VINCENT, Clark, "The Loss of Parents and Psychosomatic Illness," *Sociology and Social Research*, Vol. 39, No. 6 (July–August, 1955), pp. 404–408.

11

Families, Siblings,
and Socialization

INTRODUCTION

The family embodies a network of relationships and interaction marked by continuity, cooperativeness, and emotionality perhaps
not duplicated in any other relational system. Viewed from the perspective of the total society, the principal and two-fold function of the
family is the bearing and rearing of children, or, reproduction and socialization. Although the family institution is to be found in all societies,
the composition of the group and the nature of the social system
through which the family institution is manifested differ from society
to society; but families everywhere include and involve children.

Since the nature of the family institution differs from society to society,
the structures through which family life is carried on differ also. Hence,
some family structures are composed of more relationships than are others.
This point can be illustrated by comparing the three-generation family
unit with the two-generation family. A three-generation family unit which
includes members of two adult generations, six or seven children, along
with an aunt, uncle, and/or cousin of theirs will have a much greater
number of possible relationships than the family unit composed of parents
and their three or four children.

In modern, highly industrialized, and urbanized societies such as the
United States, the family structure tends to include three sets of relationships: parent-parent, parent-child, and child-child. These can be sub-
divided so that each member of the family could have a different relationship with every other member. Despite this, the family structure
in the United States has a comparatively small number of possible relationships. One of the consequences of this is that American children are

likely to have only limited opportunities for intense affectional relations with adults. Furthermore, their early years are likely to be marked by only minimal opportunities for variety in identification and imitation of adults. Largely because of this, sibling relationships loom large in the socialization process, especially in the earliest years of life.

CHILDREN AND FAMILY STRUCTURES

For children, the great importance attached to the structure of the family in the United States is derived from two principal considerations. The first is the value that every child has a right to the love, care and protection of both of his parents. The second consideration relates to the small size of the family and the consequent limited number of affectional ties. As a result of these considerations, the maintainance of a structurally complete family is a dominant value.

The family setting or the home may be regarded as the *nursery of socialization.* Aside from the care and protection provided, it furnishes the child with his initial and basic instruction regarding attitudes, values, norms, and skills. Ideally, it offers him models to be emulated, aspirations to be pursued, and security when he feels threatened. In addition to the affection and reward he gets from his parents, the family often provides companions (siblings) whom the child may regard as his very own.

A principal and widely held goal of the nursery of socialization is to raise healthy and happy children. To do this, many parents rely mainly on the prevailing psychological theories of child rearing; some still rely on traditional practices or on advice from grandma; and perhaps others do what they can and hope for the best.

Ideally, the current structure is perhaps adequate to the task of socialization, at least in the child's earliest years. However, the structure of the family is such that it can never do the complete job of socializing the child. Even with its structural limitations, however, it can do its job well, if the necessary knowledge, insight and techniques are applied.

To illustrate, the family group is not made up of a man, woman, boy, and girl; rather, it includes a father, mother, brother, and sister. Yet, it is conceivable that these latter status-role components of the family are sufficiently close to man, woman, boy and girl so that the child can eventually come to understand and react to the more inclusive statuses more effectively. In this same connection, it would seem that the sibling relation might be used for the learning and promotion of effective and satisfying peer relations.

Families: Ideal and Real

If the family is to perform its function well, the continued completeness of its structure is a necessary condition. Only through the continued existence of the total family unit can the complete range of the unique relationships and interactions of the family be maintained. Only in such a unit can certain types and degrees of emotional attachments be continuously available. When the structural completeness of the family group is broken, certain readjustments in relationships, distortions of reality, or deprivations of various sorts are likely to result.

The results of breaks in the family structure, that is "broken homes," are not always the same; neither are they always clearly nor immediately detrimental to the child. Some of these results are unknown, or even unknowable. When a break does occur, its effect upon the child might be directly related to a number of considerations such as the psychological climate prevailing in the family prior to the break, the personal characteristics of the members who remain within the group, and the resources for adjustment which are available to those who must carry on. Furthermore, since the social definitions and objective consequences of family breaks by separation, divorce, desertion, and death are not the same, the child's reactions to such breaks can be expected to differ widely.

In addition to breaks in the family structure, certain break-like impairments frequently occur. These impairments result principally from occupational roles which require parents, especially fathers, to be absent from the home regularly during the child's waking hours. When both fathers and mothers work outside the home, the completeness of the family structure might be diminished.

As already indicated, the precise results of breaks in the structure of the family cannot be anticipated. This is no less true of occupationally or otherwise induced impairments. One thing is certain, however: whenever siblings are left more or less alone their interaction continues and might be intensified. More commonly, however, they are not alone, but have other adults in quasi-parental roles.

Family structures, viewed as households, may be modified other than through breaks and impairments. Sometimes, uncles or aunts are members of the child's household; or sometimes these, or other relatives, live in close physical proximity, so that they have frequent contacts with the child. Structurally, this situation has the effect of expanding the arena of family interaction and increasing the number of possible relational combinations. From the point of view of the child, the presence of such a relative may provide an additional source of authority, of competition, of conflict, or of emotional security. Moreover, these same possibilities exist for the child's parent and the result of the operation of any one of these forces is likely to have some influence upon the parent-child relationship, as well as upon the relations of siblings.

SIBLING RELATIONS

For many children, developmental experiences may be characterized as *from only child to sibling*. Every family in which siblings are present was once a family with an only child, except those cases involving multiple first-borns. Whether or not such an only child is to be equated with the only child who has remained, or is believed by his parents as destined to remain, an only child is not altogether clear. Conceivably, the parents with one child who expects to have others react differently toward that child than do such parents who do not expect to have other children. Subject to the possibility of such differential reactions to the only child, then, certain observations regarding the only child seem to be in order at this point.

Often the parents of an only child are extremely concerned about him. They may overprotect him. They may shower gifts upon him and apply few disciplinary measures to him. They may regard him as their last and only hope for the continuity of the family line. Other people often regard the only child as, or expect him to be a "spoiled brat," a "lonely child," or "a child too old for his years."[1] Whatever the reality of his situation, the only child does not enjoy the intimate and continuing experiences found among sets of siblings and a disproportionate number of his contacts is with adults.

Despite his probable disadvantages, the chances are that the only child will have superior educational advantages, economic security, and material comforts and possessions. On the lighter side, his toys, clothes, and spending money are likely to be quite sufficient for his needs. As compensation for these advantages, however, parents are likely to hold great and exacting expectations of their only child.

The "First-Born" Sibling

The first-born of a family approaches the sibling relationship with a developmental experience more or less characteristic of the only child. Possibly, he is a product of over-protection, over-indulgence, and/or over-solicitude. Or, he may be a lonely child who vaguely feels the need for the companionship of someone close to him in age and kinship. With the birth of a brother or sister, the first-born or older child is

[1] See Norma E. Cutts and Nicholas Mosely, *The Only Child* (New York, G. P. Putnam's Sons, 1954); Ruth B. Guilford and D. A. Worcester, "A Comparative Study of the Only and Non-Only Child," *Pedagogical Seminary and Journal of Genetic Psychology*, Vol. 38 (1930), p. 411.

faced with the necessity of making readjustments with his parents and adjustments to his sibling. No longer is he the center of his parents' attention. He must now share their attention and affection with another. This means that he now has a competitor for all those things that were once his for the asking.

The first-born and his sibling are not only competitors; they soon become allies. "In championing their cause, as children, against the powerful adult parent, they join hands and tricks. It is an excellent kind of skirmishing, in which all the children stand to gain both emotional release of their pent-up resentments, and also a weakening of parental dominance, by keeping a thin, wavering, but common front of children against adults." [2] As the sibling relationship crystallizes, they play one parent against the other, protect each other from parental wrath, and conspire to gain parental approval, or to minimize parental control. Once firmly established, the sibling relationship comes to be a powerful force in the socialization experiences of children.

Models of Sibling Relationships

Usually, brothers and sisters have opportunities to observe, either directly or indirectly, certain adult models of sibling relationships. These models may be found within their own extended families, within their neighborhoods, or through indirect sources such as publications, television, and the movies. By observing these models, children can learn the appropriate behavior in the brother-brother, brother-sister, or sister-sister relationship. In their efforts to imitate such behavior, however, they must distinguish between the adult and the sibling aspects; for certain elements in these models are derived from the adult status and are not inherent in the sibling relationship as such.

From the point of view of child siblings, certain aspects of the adult-sibling model may be unacceptable. This may be because of generational differences. For example, it may be that the older generation of siblings were reared to follow and continue to follow a pattern whereby the senior sibling exerts authority or is clearly dominant over the others. Again, the older generation of siblings, being of the same sex and separated in age by only one or two years, might still share confidences, use each other's personal effects, or do things together as often as they can. In some cases, elements of the adult model of sibling relationship such as these may have little or no appeal for the younger siblings.

Sometimes, parents regard certain adult-sibling models as undesirable for their children. Although these models are often found outside their respective families, this need not be the case. For example, the mother

---

[2] W. Allison Davis and Robert J. Havighurst, *Father of the Man* (Boston, Houghton Mifflin Company, 1947), p. 120.

who has habitually, although not gladly, submitted to the dominance of an older sibling, and who continues to do so, might go to great lengths to make sure that her children are not involved in such a dominance-submission pattern. Or, a mother and her siblings may follow a pattern which they find satisfying, or that they accept as ritualistic, yet she may regard that pattern as unsuitable for her children. Apart from its manifest function as a control device, the admonition, "Don't do as I do, do as I say" may serve the latent function of protecting children against certain parentally defined undesirable aspects of adult models for sibling relations.

Siblings Against Parents

The great majority of children live in families in which there are two or more children. Therefore, the sibling relationship is an almost ever present facet of family life and of childhood. It is manifest that much of the child's family life is spent in association with his siblings. Although the specific content of the associational experiences of siblings within a particular family is somewhat unique, certain broadly defined patterns of sibling relations are widely experienced.

On the whole, sibling relations are intimate, all-inclusive, and recurrent. Although these characteristics apply to the family as a unit, they tend to have special meaning for the siblings involved. Because of status-role differentials in the family based on age, children are limited in the extent to which they have access to certain areas of family life. This limitation is implied in the reactions: "Speak when you are spoken to," "Children are to be seen, not heard," and "Now, don't worry your little head about that." Furthermore, even in those situations in which older children exercise authority over their younger siblings, that authority is usually delegated, limited, conditional, and subject to immediate revocation by parents.

Even as parents have a special area of family life reserved to them, so it is with their children. Perhaps the exclusiveness of parents contributes to a counter-exclusiveness of siblings. More likely than not, the exclusiveness of children is closely related to age, interest, responsibility, and skills. These somewhat common characteristics impel them to activities which are generally looked upon as inappropriate for adults. As a matter of fact, because they are children they are permitted, encouraged, pressured, and sometimes even forced to engage in children's activities.

Before they reach school age, brothers and sisters spend many hours at or near their homes. This they do day after day, and quite frequently, in each other's company. "You and your brothers can go out and play now" is an announcement of a concession or a reward often granted

children. Not infrequently, this concession or reward is given in response to the question, "Mama, can Jed and me go out and play?" Sometimes, however, going out to play is engineered by the mother who sometimes finds that children "get in the way." Indeed the keen sense of
anticipation felt by some mothers as the opening day of school draws
near might not be due totally to the educational value involved. After
all, when children are sent to school they are "out of the way."

Siblings: In-group Against Out-group

For at least several years after reaching school age, siblings still
spend considerable time in each other's company. Frequently, they go
to and return from school together. They go to, and return from the library, the playground, the corner store, or the neighbor's house—together.
And, of course, they seldom ever miss the Saturday morning movie—
if they can help it.

The gamut of feelings and reactions in the sibling relationship is indeed a wide one: "Mama, can we go to . . ." "We didn't go any place
but next door." "Mama, make Jed leave the T.V. alone; he knows we
always watch 'Huckleberry Hound' at seven o'clock!" "Must I take
Jed with me, Mama; must I?" "You can't play ball with us; you're a girl."
"Now Jed, you stop that this minute; Mama, will you make him—stop
it, now!" "You leave my brother alone; you big bully!" Such requests, en-
treaties, threats, and warnings, attest to the continuity and uniqueness of
the sibling relationship—to the "happy to be together twosome"; to the
ever-present and unwelcome little brother; to the *girl* who "can't" or
"shouldn't play with boys." Probably the most famous statement of the
uniqueness and solidarity of the sibling relationship is the alleged Boys-
town expression, "He ain't heavy, Father, he's my brother."

As already indicated, the contacts and interactions of siblings within
the family constitute a relatively all-inclusive relationship. Brothers and
sisters tend to reveal much more of their total personalities to each
other than they reveal to outsiders. Although it is true that certain aspects
of siblings' personalities which are not displayed among themselves are
shown to non-siblings, these latter aspects tend to be of a more clearly
defined and limited character. A case in point is "puppy love" behavior.
Among siblings, however, it is expected that various kinds and greater
degrees of interests, responsibilities, obligations, and activities shall prevail. This all-inclusiveness of the sibling relationship is pointed up and
indeed facilitated by the long and recurrent face-to-face contacts in
which they are usually involved.

Among the elements of the sibling relationship—elements which facilitate socialization—companionship, imitation, instruction, cooperation,

and competition stand out. More specifically, brothers and sisters eat together, learn together, and often share the same sleeping quarters. They also tease, quarrel, tattle, and fight. Some of these same situations are experienced among non-siblings; when shared by siblings, however, there is a qualitative difference which is significant. The character of family relationships, which are marked by deep and continuing emotional involvement, by close and highly personalized identification, and by socially expected and sanctioned solidarity, all give a qualitatively different character to the interactional content of the sibling relationship. Quite obviously, sibling interaction is not always harmonious. Frequently, there is conflict among them. For example, siblings do fight among themselves. When they do, however, such fighting tends to be a thing of the moment, and is not as deeply emotional as in the case with non-siblings. This is clearly shown in the abruptness with which such fighting ends when outsiders intervene or when siblings at war are threatened by others.

Generally, the sibling relationship provides for unity and mutual support, especially in the face of opposition or threats from outsiders. Parents encourage their children to combine efforts and to defend and protect each other when necessary. Therefore, when a younger sibling is engaged in conflict or has to resort to fisticuffs with a child who is not a sibling, his brothers and sisters can be depended on to make sure that it is a fair fight. In some instances they intervene in his behalf if things are not going well for the little brother.

Sometimes the solidarity of siblings is broken or impaired, temporarily, when contact with non-siblings is made. For example, when an older sibling is at play with his peers he may attempt to exclude his younger brother or sister. Or, the older girl may seek to get away from a younger sister who insists on "hanging around" when she is expressing a developing interest in boys. As a rule, however, these exclusions are not categoric; they are selective and short lived.

Sibling Rivalry

The competition which involves siblings takes many and varied forms and is directed toward the achievement of a variety of goals. "Whether a child is a first child, who has been replaced by a new baby, or whether he finds older and therefore more privileged brothers on the scene when he arrives, he certainly will have to come to grips with jealousy and rivalry. To make the situation worse, his parents unconsciously will train him in contradictory fashion concerning this rivalry. For they will urge him both to compete with his brothers and sisters in some ways, and not to compete with them in other ways." [3] Some of the more common goals

[3] Davis and Havighurst, *op. cit.*, p. 120.

of sibling competition include parental attention, approval, affection, praise, encouragement, and rewards.

As pointed out by Davis and Havighurst,[4] children do not always consciously choose such a rivalry; nor need they be aware that they are competitors or rivals. Frequently, they are encouraged or almost forced into the process. For example, parents sometimes press their younger children to live up to the scholastic achievements of their older siblings. "Why can't you get good grades like your sister?" is a question commonly asked by parents. Perhaps teachers also contribute to this process when they welcome the new pupil with the comment, "We're glad to have you in our room, John. I know you'll be a good student like your brother Henry."

Sibling rivalry may result when the child feels neglected because he is replaced by another. It may also result from subjectively defined invidious comparisons. In the first case, the overt response might be to retreat; in the second case, fantasy-level rivalry sometimes results. The child who retreats—often a three or four year old—"may revert to a wetting or soiling, infantile speech or sucking on the bottle in an attempt to be once more the baby on whom his mother will lavish time and affection."[5]

Fantasy-level sibling rivalry is perhaps sometimes expressed by the distain of one sibling for the other. In all probability, however, the widespread distain shown among siblings is not the result merely of the retreat from competition into fantasy-level rivalry. The differentials in the cultural definitions of the privileges and interests of children according to age are perhaps relevant considerations. This is suggested in situations in which older children seek to separate themselves from their younger siblings—and often, with parental approval or at least tolerance. Thus, Bobby may be defined by his older sister as "just a younger brother"; Julie may be looked upon, even by a younger brother, as "nothing but a scared girl." Disdain, such as expressed in these reactions suggests that children are aware of differential definitions based on age, as well as on sex. The utilization of these definitions, however, may be a response not only to the impact of culture; they may also be a manifestation of a socially derived personal need.

The net effects of sibling rivalry may be upsetting to the child, disturbing to parents, or disintegrating to the sibling relationship. Because of the variables involved, the precise effects cannot be predicted. It is safe to say, however, that sibling rivalry is a natural phenomenon, especially in situations involving the birth of the second child. For the

[4] *Ibid.*
[5] William E. Martin and Celia Burns Stendler, *Child Development: The Process of Growing Up in Society* (New York, Harcourt, Brace and Company, 1953), p. 397.

intervention of a third party into a dyadic relationship (considering the mother-child relationship) is always likely to be a disturbing force.[6]

Non-Peer Siblings

Frequently, children in the same family are widely separated by age, size, and emotional and social maturity. These differences often stimulate or are associated with certain interests, knowledges, skills, and activities. Children thus differentiated tend to experience or react to the sibling relationship in ways different from those of their younger, less developed brothers and sisters. As a result, they tend not to spend long periods of time in direct and intimate contact with their younger siblings. They are usually less intensively or less directly involved in competition or rivalry with them.

In the sibling relationship involving children who are widely separated by age, the older child, especially the female, sometimes acts as parent substitute. This is probably not as common in the United States as it is in certain less complex societies. In many parts of the world this substitute-parent role is performed by older siblings as a matter of course. It is a socially expected and sanctioned pattern of behavior. In the United States, as compared to certain other societies, it is not a widely nor firmly institutionalized pattern; therefore, the pressures toward this kind of behavior tend to be relatively minimal.

Perhaps this relative lack of emphasis on the parent-substitute role for siblings in the United States is partly because of the prevailing system of age differentiation which leads older siblings into a life-space in which home-oriented activities are minimized and the process of emerging independence from the family is facilitated. Thus, it is common for older siblings to begin early to make protestations against the presence of a younger brother or sister. "Do I have to take Junior, Mom?" "Scram!" "You're not big enough to go with us"; "Why are you always tagging after me?" are but few indications of the tendency on the part of older children to get away from the responsibility of looking after their younger brothers or sisters.

The rejection of the parent-substitute role by older brothers is perhaps frequently stimulated by their interest in *the gang*. Since the gang is an age-graded association, younger brothers are often rejected. Thus when a member permits his younger (too young) brother to tag along, he anticipates the group's displeasure at the latter's presence. What is more, he knows that if he persists in letting this young aspirant tag along, his own membership might be placed in jeopardy.

[6] For a discussion of such structural changes see Howard Becker, *Systematic Sociology on the Basis of the Beziehungslehre and Gebildelehre* (New York, John Wiley and Sons, Inc., 1932), pp. 506ff.

The role of parent substitute is more likely to be expected of an older sister than of an older brother. This is consistent with the prevailing division of labor whereby females are directly and primarily responsible for child-care. Initially, an older sister might accept willingly, or at least tolerate, the responsibility of taking care of a younger brother or sister. With increasing age, however, difficulties and conflicts tend to arise. Frequently, a proprietary or domineering tendency may come to characterize the older girl's reactions to her younger charge. For example, having been made responsible for looking after a brother or sister at play or when on the way to school, the older child may now attempt to extend her authority by trying to boss her younger sibling in other situations. In such instances, the younger child may rebel and appeal to the mother. If the appeal is rejected, the older child is likely to be encouraged to go to extremes in the exercise of her delegated authority. If the younger child's appeal is upheld by the mother, the older sibling, regarding her authority as having been undermined, might resolve not to exercise any responsibility at all. In either event, a problem situation is likely to develop.

The romantic complex which characterizes youth culture in the United States is perhaps one of the most effective deterrents to the continued performance of the parent-substitute role by older siblings, especially females. This is sharply pointed up in the family situation when the older sister reaches her teens. By this time, girls have developed an interest in the opposite sex. They increasingly become involved in school dances, in parties held in the homes of their peers, and in other heterosexual contacts involving the movies, picnics, hay rides and the like. These aspects of youth culture tend to have a divisive effect upon siblings who differ widely in age. Because of social differentiations based on age and the resultant expectations and behavior, as older siblings approach their teens they tend to identify and associate less closely with their younger siblings and to become less and less involved in the parent-substitute role.

But this is not the whole story of the parent-substitute role of an older sibling. Sometimes—perhaps even frequently—the older child manifests a real interest and concern for his or her younger charge. Although the attachment may be merely expressive of the acceptance of duty, some such parent substitutes apparently enjoy their work. For the latter, little brother or little sister may be held in high esteem and regarded with such great affection that looking after him or her comes to be and remains a great joy.

As a matter of fact, the avoidance or intolerance which is expressed by many older siblings in the United States toward identifying too closely with their younger brothers or sisters (or with younger children generally), is not always the case, and of course, is not universal. In France, for example, it is reported that children quite readily play with those younger than themselves. In contrast to the American boy who is often intolerant of a little brother or a younger child, "French children appear interested in younger children and ready to accept them in their games. A boy of eight or nine will play ball with a smaller boy, a five-year-old or even a two-year old, without showing any impatience at the ineptitude of the younger one. The two children may be brothers or may belong to families who know each other" [7]

Although the sibling relationship is characteristically a relationship involving age mates, the latter must not be construed too narrowly; for rather than chronological age, in some cases, reciprocal identification and acceptance are of the essence.

Given a sibling relationship with a parent-substitute role which involves reciprocal identification and acceptance, the end result is likely to be satisfactory and beneficial to all concerned. First, parents may be relieved of, or at least aided in, carrying out certain responsibilities in child-rearing. Second, the parent-substitute sibling may experience a sense of responsibility, adequacy, and maturity which will facilitate his or her own personality integration and growth. As for the sibling being cared for, he or she may profit by continued access to a role model; by the security of of an ever-present protector; by a constant source of help and instruction; or by the knowledge that someone who understands and cares is always there.

When viewed within the context of the family, the sibling who plays the parent-substitute role as described here can be seen to occupy a significant position in the family structure. For once this role is accepted, along with the reciprocal emotional involvement implicit in it, there is relative assurance that the parental function can continue, even in the face of long periods of absence by the parents themselves.

It is perhaps accurate to state that whatever the difficulties or shortcomings involved in the parent-substitute role of a brother or a sister, this role involves certain mutually compensatory features. It may be, for example, that Tori is "just a younger sister," or even a "nuisance" to her older sibling; yet, to her parents, or at least to her mother, she may be "the baby" or "just a little girl." Moreover, even though an older child rejects his younger sibling, that rejection is likely to be for certain purposes or in specific situations; it is perhaps seldom ever complete. For the final analysis, the sibling bond tends to be strong and lasting.

Finally, the intermittent isolating of siblings from their parents, such as that experienced in the sibling parent-substitute role, is functionally related to the growing up process. For the younger sibling it is protective and potentially instructive, for the older sibling provides the experience

---

[7] Martha Wolfenstein, "French Parents Take Their Children to the Park," *Childhood in Contemporary Cultures,* by Margaret Mead and Martha Wolfenstein (Chicago, The University of Chicago Press, 1955), p. 103.

in the exercise of authority and in the acceptance of responsibility. On the whole, the sibling parent-substitute situation is an aspect of growing up. But this does not mean growing out of the sibling relationship. As an integral part of family structure and interaction, the sibling relationship is a highly permanent one.

SUMMARY

The sibling relationship is a special and significant part of the complex of family relationships. As such it is significantly involved in the socialization of the child. Excluded from certain aspects of family life available only to adults, siblings engage in behavior which is intimate, recurring, and all-inclusive. The solidarity thus developed by siblings sometimes leads to protective conspiracies against their parents. In addition, siblings often combine to present a united front against members of other families.

Despite the unity implied in the sibling relationship, there are two divisive forces which appear to be an integral part of that relationship. The first is sibling rivalry; the second is implicit in the parent-substitute role of the sibling. Rivalry among siblings is widespread among children and sometimes upsetting to parents, although they often stimulate or tolerate it. As for the parent-substitute role of the older sibling, it is functional for purposes of child rearing and it contributes to the older child's movement away from childhood toward adulthood.

Finally, it is axiomatic that the nature of social life is such that contact, communication, and interaction are necessary vehicles for the integration of newcomers. The family and peer-group relationships are, of course, two such vehicles. Although they are effective and therefore important in their own right, the work they perform is complemented by the unique contribution of the sibling relationship. As a relationship which is qualitatively different from parent-child and peer-group relationships—and sometimes prior in time to the latter—the sibling relationship assures the child of an early and relatively continuing opportunity to develop his potentials for personal growth and socially productive behavior.

READINGS

BROWN, L. Guy, "The Development of Diverse Patterns of Behavior among Children of the Same Family," *The Family* (April, 1928), pp. 35–39.

DAMRIN, Dora E., "Family Size and Sibling Age, Sex, and Position as Related to Certain Aspects of Adjustment," *Journal of Social Psychology* (February, 1949), pp. 93–102.

HILGARD, Josephine R., "Sibling Rivalry and Social Heredity," *Psychiatry* (November, 1951), pp. 375–385.

KOCH, Helen L., "The Relation in Young Children between Characteristics of Their Playmates and Certain Attributes of Their Siblings," *Child Development* (June, 1957), pp. 175–202.

KOCH, Helen L., "Some Emotional Attitudes of the Young Child in Relation to Characteristics of His Sibling," *Child Development* (December, 1956), pp. 393–426.

OSTROVSKY, Everett S., *Children Without Men,* New Revised Edition, Collier Books (New York, Crowell-Collier Publishing Company, 1962).

ULLMAN, Frances, *Getting Along with Brothers and Sisters* (Chicago, Science Research Associates, Inc., 1950).

12

Peer Groups

Introduction

Although the child's early family training is fundamental to future learning and interaction, it does not fully prepare him for the multiplicity of experiences that are almost certain to be his. Indeed, the nature of the family is such that this cannot be done. Moreover, when it is recalled that the family is but a part of a larger functional whole, such complete preparation is not to be expected. The function of the family, as is the case with any unit of society, is significantly related to and limited by its structure. The definitions of family members, for example, are such that, for members of the family, the female child must be experienced only as *daughter* by her father and only as *sister* by her brother; for outsiders, however, she is a *girl*. As a result, in order to experience persons in terms of the multiple statuses they occupy, one must move outside the family.

The Nature of the Peer Group

In the process of preparing to participate in the full range of possible social interaction, one must necessarily learn to interact with his equals. Such preparation may occur to some extent within the family. Later, this occurs in other social structures such as the school. In the family, however, there is little chance to put this learning into practice, except in those families where there are siblings of relatively the same age. Such equalitarian relationships are nonetheless affected by the factor of kinship, and as a result are to be differentiated from those involving age mates who are not bound by family ties.

Children of relatively the same age who associate together in response to their own interest constitute a peer group. For the child whose contacts have been confined to members of his family, the peer group represents a situational change in both the locus of his activity and the persons to whom he relates. The peer group represents a situation that is rather distinctly different from the family and other situations involving children and adults, such as the school and the church or synagogue.

The child's peer group can be distinguished from his family by a number of significant characteristics. Unlike his family (1) membership in his peer group is voluntary, and changing; (2) he and his associates are age mates, equals, and sometimes of the same sex; (3) interaction tends to involve momentary behavior rather than a fixed routine; (4) the cultural content of interaction is supplemental to and sometimes in conflict with that of the family; and (5) the relationship is one that is essentially based on mutuality.

LEVELS AND DIVERSITY OF PEER GROUPS

Two important considerations in the structuring of peer groups are age and social access. Children who are much the same age tend to have equal ability and opportunity for freedom of movement. Thus, they are likely to have approximately the same chances of making contacts with each other. Two sets of limitations may intervene to reduce or direct the mobility and contacts of the child: family rules and social class considerations.

The first level of peer-group participation is that which involves the very young child. As early as two years of age, children come into contact with their age mates. At this time, however, there is little in these contacts which can be characterized as clearly peer-group interaction. Because such contacts tend to be confined to the child's house and yard, and sometimes next door, they are likely to be continuing. These children grow up together, get to know and perhaps like each other, and soon they constitute a unity for purposes of play. Such play groups remain relatively permanent, engage in activities, and move about together at the will and upon the instructions and approval of their parents.

Play for the very young child begins when he is around two years old and is an activity in which he alone is involved.[1] As he grows older and makes contact with other children, the interest expressed in his solitary play is continued or modified in his relations with age mates. When he played alone, he was in full command of the situation; things went according to his wishes. Now that others are involved in his play activities their interests and wishes must be taken into account. It is no wonder that children's play groups do not always involve harmonious interaction.

[1] See George H. Mead, *Mind, Self, and Society,* Charles W. Morris, ed., (Chicago, University of Chicago Press, 1934).

That conflict is commonplace among people is an obvious, easily observable fact. It occurs even among the play groups of the very young. "Many parents complain that their pre-schoolers . . . cannot play with other children . . . for any appreciable length of time without hitting, biting, destroying playthings, crying."[2] However, conflict as it exists within groups of children tends to be intermittent, short lived, and easily forgotten. It represents the child's response to the need to come to grips with the problems and difficulties inherent in cooperating and sharing with others.

For those children who attend nursery school and kindergarten, the play group continues to be and perhaps becomes a more vital force in their learning experiences. Play groups in these situations, in contrast to those in the child's home and neighborhood, can be seen to differ in certain respects. First of all, many children do not attend nursery school or kindergarten. Second, those who do attend are subjected to a more formal regimen of play than in their homes and neighborhoods. Third, they are likely to meet and associate with more children, some of whom are from significantly different social and cultural backgrounds. Fourth, the content of their play is likely to be predetermined for them and to involve a greater degree of supervision than they receive at home.

Although the play group is an association of children, it is not totally devoid of adult influence. Ideally, it excludes adults from membership and participation, but because very young children are still largely dependent upon adults for care and protection and because their movement is limited and supervised by adults, children's play-group activities cannot completely exclude their adult elders. Hence, adults are functionally involved in the play activities of children, as protectors, as supervisors, or as observers who are prepared to intervene when necessary. Despite the intervention of adults, the play group is usually the first situation in which the child interacts with others on a basis of equality. It is the first relationship in which performance rather than kinship is the principal criterion upon which he is assessed.

As the child grows older, his freedom to move in geographic and in social space tends to expand, his contacts increase, and his peer relationships multiply. Soon, he may be involved with peers from different neighborhoods, different social and cultural backgrounds, and in different situations, both formal and informal. Opportunities to become involved in gangs, in cliques and in clubs are likely to be open. Because of the changing character of his social situation or of his interests, he may come to belong to a gang, a clique, and a club, or clubs, concurrently or successively. Or, he may affiliate with only one of these.

[2] Francis L. Ilg and Louise Bates Ames, *The Gesell's Institute's Child Behavior* (New York, Dell Publishing Company, Inc., 1955), pp. 258–259. With the permission of Harper & Row, Publishers, Inc.

The Gang

In the literature of social science, gangs are differentiated from cliques. Gangs are usually regarded as conflict groups, although violent and non-violent gangs have been distinguished. "Youth gangs of the twenties and thirties were basically friendship organizations in which boys helped one another. In addition to illegal or occasional violent activity, these groups carried on comparatively harmless gang behavior—including sports and social activities. They were not organized essentially around violence—the core spirit of the modern gang." [3]

Whether gangs are viewed as violent or non-violent, they tend to be regarded as peer groupings comprised of children and adolescents from lower- or working-class families.[4] However, one notable exception holds that the gang phenomena is not class-connected.[5] For present purposes, there is no need to choose between these contrasting views of the gang, except to indicate that, as used here, the character of conflict is regarded as a distinguishing feature. The conflict referred to, although overtly expressed, does not necessarily include violent or destructive behavior. It does include any one or combination of disobedience to parents, such as staying out too late; associations in defiance of parental approval; overtly expressed disdain for adult authority, including parents and teachers; and violations of sex taboos through action or overt discussion.

Implicit in these characteristics of the gang is the fact that they tend to be self-controlling and to determinedly avoid adult intervention or supervision. Generally, the members of the gang are boys who live near each other and bind themselves together for the pursuit of shared interests. These interests are often diffuse and transitory and they range from mere *hanging around* to predatory or marauding activities. Some gangs are no more than a group of peers whose activities are unorganized, spontaneous, and, at best (or worst) irritating to parents and school authorities. Others, however, are more formally organized, purposely anti-social, and threatening to the community. The first type is usually composed of younger boys; the second type usually involves adolescents.

By and large, the nine year old member of the gang divorces himself to some extent from the control of his parents. He also strives to avoid control and supervision from teachers and other adults. In the gang he develops a new set of loyalties, subscribes to a different pattern of values, conforms to a circumscribed system of norms. He acquires new informa-

[3] Lewis Yablonsky, *The Violent Gang* (New York, The Macmillan Company, 1962), p. 6.

[4] See Albert K. Cohen, *Delinquent Boys: The Culture of the Gang* (New York, The Free Press of Glencoe, Inc., 1955); Frederick Thrasher, *The Gang* (Chicago, University of Chicago Press, 1936).

[5] Herbert A. Block and Arthur Niederhoffer, *The Gang* (New York, Philosophical Library, Inc., 1958).

tion and new skills. As a result of his membership in the gang, not only is his area of interaction expanded beyond the family, play group, neighborhood, and school, but his whole life organization is likely to be affected. Of course, the extent to which the gang leads to his isolation from his family will depend on a number of factors, including the precise nature of his gang, his family background, his prior experiences, and his own personality at the point of his entrance into the group.

The Clique

The clique is less distinctly and overtly in conflict with adult society. In some respects it approaches the non-violent gang, for it is an unorganized, informal, self-determining, intimate participation group. As with the non-violent gang, its conflict with the larger community tends to be expressed in behavior that is irritating rather than destructive or threatening. As a matter of fact, the behavior of these two types of peer groups is sometimes overlapping. Thus the *wild* automobile rides, the boisterousness, and the sexual escapades of some cliques are not too different from the behavior of some gangs.

From much of the literature dealing with the behavior of young people, the terms *gang* and *clique* do not refer to distinctly different social structures. Rather, it seems that whether one or the other term is used depends to some extent upon the social class status of the children in question. Bossard and Boll hold that "cliques operate primarily as an instrument of the class structure." [6] Apparently, there are those who agree with them on this point. When they add, however, that "lower-class boys and girls, it is significant to note, do not participate in cliques as a rule, having neither the time, leisure, social graces, social interests, nor home opportunities" [7] the agreement seems to be less widespread and explicitly stated. [8]

Rather than focusing on these criteria as characteristics of the clique, the present writers choose other criteria. Thus: (1) the clique tends to use the school as its base of operation or point of departure for its activities, (2) it tends not to be in open and continuing conflict with the adult community, and (3) its deviant behavior is generally more tolerated, excused, or overlooked by adult authorities. Generally, the clique is a relatively small, intimate, face-to-face group. In addition to being age-graded, it is often comprised of one sex. Boys and girls tend to form and maintain their respective cliques, although they merge temporarily for certain activities. Usually, the child becomes involved in the clique

[6] James H. S. Bossard and Eleanor Stoker Boll, *The Sociology of Child Development* (New York, Harper & Row, Publishers, 1960), p. 519.
[7] *Ibid.*
[8] See August B. Hollingshead, *Elmtown's Youth* (New York, John Wiley and Sons, Inc., 1949).

as a result of the acquaintances he makes at school. By the time he reaches junior high school his clique relationships are rather clearly formed.

The interests and activities expressed in these clique relationships are quite varied and differ according to the sex and age of the participants. Girl cliques characteristically engage in activities appropriate to their sex. In contrast to the relatively restrained and circumspect behavior in girl cliques, the behavior found in boy cliques tends to be of greater, although intermittent, concern to school, parental, and even police authorities. Frequently, there is interaction or joint activity involving male and female cliques. Usually they meet at school where parties and the like are planned. Later their plans may be implemented at mutually agreed upon meeting places or hangouts.

Membership in a particular clique is often not permanent. Since the school has a relatively large and culturally diverse child population; discrimination, selection, and change with regard to one's clique associates are quite possible. Therefore, the child's clique affiliation is often a shifting phenomenon. Because of this, he gets to know and to interact with children from different neighborhoods, some of whom may be of different racial, religious, ethnic, or socio-economic backgrounds.

The Club

Ideally, the peer groups discussed up to this point are formed by children, composed of children, and directed by children. On the whole, they involve a minimum of adult control and intervention. In addition, they tend to be informal groups in which behavior is considerably spontaneous. Because these groups are child dominated, loosely structured, and characterized by spontaneous behavior, they sometimes irritate or offend adult authorities. It is largely for this reason that adults, especially teachers, church leaders, and recreation workers, often seek to devise ways of increasing their control over such groups. This is frequently achieved by stimulating and encouraging these children, either as groups or individuals, to engage in formally organized activity.[9] So it is that much of the free floating energy of children has been harnessed and channeled into the Boy Scouts, the Campfire Girls, the Future Teachers of America, and various school-sponsored organizations.

For present purposes, the term *club* is applied to these children's groups. Although they are usually sponsored and supervised by adults, they are defined here as peer groups. Apparently this definition is not

[9] In recent years such efforts have been extended to include boys' gangs. See Lewis Yablonsky, *The Violent Gang* (New York, The Macmillan Company, 1962), pp. vii–xiii; Paul R. Crawford, Daniel I. Malamud, and James R. Dumpson, *Working with Teen-Age Groups: A Report on the Central Harlem Street Clubs Project* (New York, Welfare Council of New York City, 1950).

altogether accepted by some writers. After listing certain peer groups, Bossard and Boll add that "perhaps we should include here such character-building agencies as the Boy Scouts, Campfire Girls, and so forth. However, since the latter are not constituted and operated entirely as peer groups, they are omitted from consideration, although this is not to be interpreted as a lack of recognition of their very great importance." [10]

Despite this observation, it seems reasonable to include organizations such as the Boy Scouts in the peer group category. Perhaps the above-named authors' use of the term "agencies" in referring to the Boy Scouts and Campfire Girls was intended to refer to the total organizational patterns of which scout troops are only component parts. If this is their rationale, it is an understandable and reasonable exclusion. As used here, however, "boy scouts" and "campfire girls" refer to units of interaction comprised of the participating children. Granted that adults do exercise supervisory prerogatives, the participating children regard *themselves*, and not their adult supervisors, as boy scouts or as campfire girls.

SOCIETY'S STAKE IN CHILDREN'S PEER GROUPS

Viewed from the perspective of the socialization process, peer groups are functional. Initially, peer-group activity is usually an enjoyable event or series of experiences for children. Later, in adult-supervised peer group activity, there is still enjoyment in the pursuit of childhood interests. Yet, from the very beginning, peer-group behavior has meaning beyond that which it has for the children involved. While thus engaged they are acquiring new information, developing new skills, and acquiring new values and attitudes; all of which contribute to their growth and development.

The recognition that peer-group activities are functional in the socialization process is perhaps the principal justification for adult intervention in these activities. Although some types of peer groups are less subject to control or pressures from adults than others, none is completely free from such influence. Ultimately, these associations of children must take into account and somehow deal with the influences exerted on them by adults. For example, in the play group, young children frequently seek to influence their peers in accordance with the wishes of their parents by expressions such as, "My mother says we shouldn't play in the streets," or "Let's play in the yard; I can't go to the movie today." It is not uncommon for fathers to intervene in the ball games of young boys. At times, intervention such as this happens repeatedly and eventually comes to be expected and accepted by both the boys and the participating fathers.

[10] Bossard and Boll, *op. cit.*, p. 499.

From this it is not a giant step to the more formally structured adult-supervised children's groups, such as Little League baseball for one.

An interesting and significant variation on the theme of adult-supervised children's peer groups is found in the Kibbutz or Collective Settlements of Israel.

In most of the Collectives, children live apart from their parents and are attended mainly by members assigned to this task. From their birth on they sleep, eat and study in special houses. Each age group leads its own life and has its autonomous arrangements. Almost every activity in the age group is supervised by an elected committee and many issues are settled by open discussion between the youngsters and the adults in charge of them. Committees work under the guidance of adults but children are given some experience in self-government and get some preparation for active participation in adult institutions. . . .

The age groups lead their own social and cultural life. On festive occasions they do not participate in the general celebration but arrange special festivities in which parents participate as passive observers. The only important exception is the culminating feast of the year (Passover) when parents and children participate alike. It is mainly through the age group that children come into definite and structured relations with the adult world.[11]

Except for the adults in charge of the children, the Kibbutz is a unique situation in which the peer group occupies a position of prime and central importance. So it is, then, that children serve as agents of socialization. In contrast to the United States where children's peer-group activities tend to be play-oriented, at least the peer-group activities in Israel involve far more than play. They are concerned with the direct preparation of children for the assumption of adult roles. Although the collective decision-making, cooperative study, and ceremonial activities of the children are carried on apart from adults, this separation is temporary and preparatory. For when adulthood is reached, the newcomers, by virtue of childhood experiences, are likely to be rather well prepared for the new status-role requirements.

This contrast between the orientations of children's peer groups in the United States and Israel suggests that there are wide variations in the character, specific purposes, and results of peer-group participation cross-culturally. Obviously, the fact of cultural variation would lead one to expect this. Despite such observed differences, there are common features to be found in all peer groups. These groups tend to be age graded, to involve relative freedom from or a minimum of adult control and participation; they provide security and support from equals; and they are contexts in which children can experience among themselves new ideas, attitudes, and relationships.

Whatever the nature of peer groups in terms of structure, activity,

11 Yonia Talmon-Garver, "The Family in Israel: The Kibbutz," *Marriage and Family Living*, Vol. 16, No. 4 (November, 1954), p. 348.

autonomy, or social-class differentiation, they are expressive of generational differences and the consequent structuring of society. They thus serve a useful and necessary purpose. Without them, the ascription of roles consistent with physical competence, especially for younger children, would pose great difficulties in the socialization process. Moreover, they provide mutual psychological support by age mates who are recognizably and socially defined as "inferior" to adults.

THE DYNAMICS OF PEER-GROUP MEMBERSHIP

Membership in the peer group does not necessarily imply complete and continuing involvement. The individual members of any particular peer group vary in their degree of interest, activity, and participation. Frequently some members of a given peer group are strongly interested, highly active, and relatively permanent in it. In contrast, other members are slightly interested, moderately active, and only temporarily involved. In terms of these polar positions, the remaining membership falls at varying positions in between.

Affiliation in peer groups is, on the whole, voluntary but not permanent. Although the child may be a member of several peer groups simultaneously, he may experience successive membership in a series of such groups. Thus, a boy scout may belong to a junior high school clique and to one or two clubs. Later, he may drop out of any or all of these and spend much of his time as a participant in a gang.

Sometimes children are not wholly satisfied with their peer-group affiliations. They may be involved with a particular group of age mates because of parental pressures. For example, a boy's mother wants to be a *den mother*, so she insists that he become and remain a cub scout. In other instances, some children may feel that they are more mature than their age mates or they have interests significantly different from them and strive to become attached to older children; until they are able to do so, however, they may hold onto the associates they have. Finally, some may find that their peers engage in behavior contrary to their own inclinations, but because they are fearful of being left alone, they stay with the group.

Peer-group membership is, to some extent, the result of the actions and influence of parents. The residential locations of families and possibly their social-class status are significant factors in determining their children's access into certain groups. Usually, children attend schools in the areas in which they live. This tends to limit the number and even the types of peer groups available. Furthermore, children whose families experience economic deprivation may not be able to afford membership in peer groups associated with organizations such as the school and fraternal orders.

It is highly probable that some children do not affiliate with certain peer groups of their choice, or are only peripherally associated with them because of parental opposition or prohibition. Not uncommonly, parents forbid or suggest that their children should not associate with certain other children because of the latter's racial, religious, ethnic, or class identity. Equally common is the parental admonition to avoid "bad company." Whatever the considerations, be they residential location, rejection of a particular category, or protection against exposure to "bad company," parents are likely to influence their children's membership in peer groups. Moreover, this influence, whether it be positive or negative, might be compounded by their children's own reactions to these barriers to peer-group participation.

The Socializing Impact of Peers

In order to understand more clearly the importance of the peer group in the socialization of the child, attention is directed to some of the more specific and characteristic experiences associated with these groups. These experiences range rather widely in quality and include many new and different values, attitudes, expectations, and overt activities. Furthermore, the extent to which these characteristic experiences prevail varies in accordance with the type of peer group, the character of its individual members, and the circumstances surrounding its operation.

As the young child gains physical autonomy and language facility he is increasingly involved with persons other than his parents. If he has a sibling or siblings, his experiences with them are likely to open up new vistas for free and independent action. Witness the three-year old who insists: "No, let me do it by myself!" In this relationship he learns what it means to interact—to compete, contend, match wits—with someone more like or equal to himself. He recognizes that in this relationship he is not bound to obey, and he perhaps enjoys it; he finds that he has greater opportunity to behave in accordance with his own wishes, and he perhaps finds the experience intriguing. Gradually the young child becomes more and more accustomed to and satisfied by his relations with those of his own age level.

Although the child's early relations with non-adults tend to begin with siblings (except first-borns) these relations soon come to include non-sibling age mates. As a consequence, the free and independent action facilitated by the sibling relationship is continued and promoted. First, his physical space for interaction is enlarged, because he is now likely to spend much more time away from home. Next, his freedom from strict parental control is increased, and he is more or less on his own. As a result of this new freedom and these new contacts, he is introduced to new values, attitudes, and behavior patterns.

In the peer group, children find a context in which they can experience a considerable degree of independent and self-determined action. The routine expectations of family life are to some extent left behind. During the many hours children spend together, the places they go and the things they do all tend to result from their own interests and decisions. One child's objection to a group decision which is not sanctioned by his parents is relatively ineffective because there is little consensus among families regarding what their children may or may not do. Thus, when Johnny says, "My mother doesn't want me to play in this old building," the other children are not likely to be dissuaded; in fact, Johnny may find himself going along with the gang.

For many children the peer group provides a refuge from the authoritarian impositions of the family. "Do this," "Don't do that," are commands not easily ignored when given by parents. Such commands are examples of authoritarian impositions which sometimes lead to feelings of frustration and resentment. Because these feelings may not be expressed openly and directly against the parents who stimulate them, they may be directed toward others or turned inward.

Generally, the peer group constitutes a situation in which such authoritarian impositions and their probable consequences are less likely to occur. Usually each peer group member has a voice in deciding what the actions of the group shall be. His is a voice to be heard. "What shall we do?" "Let's do this." "I don't want to play field; I wanna pitch." "You pitched last time; it's my turn now." These suggest the approach of decision-making as it occurs among peers. Complete freedom of choice for each child in the peer group is non-existent; obviously situations sometimes arise in which someone has to give in. However, the final decision is usually determined collectively. Generally, this process of decision-making is unlike that experienced by the child in his family. It is a decision-making process in which, while his idea might not be accepted today, it might have been accepted the day before—and, of course, he has another chance tomorrow.

Leadership in the Peer Group

The influence exerted by the peer group is not equally distributed among its members, it varies widely with each individual. The influence exerted by any particular member is related to a variety of considerations such as "whose bat it is," "who owns the car," "who has the money," "who thought of it first," or even "who can lick whom." Despite considerations such as these, some children do tend to wield continuing and considerable influence upon the members of their peer groups. These children may be regarded as leaders of their peer groups.

Leadership in the peer group is a formally defined status only so far as the group itself is formally organized. Generally, one comes to occupy this status not through any formal measures, but because he has greater access to certain resources, or because he is personally outgoing and generally liked, or because he is physically superior to or more inventive than his peers. In the more formally organized groups, however, one may be elected, or otherwise chosen, to be the leader for any of the above reasons. Under certain circumstances, perhaps, adult supervisors sometimes manipulate the prevailing situations so that the children will choose certain of their members as leaders.

The children's peer group usually varies in permanence, solidarity, and formal structuring. Such variation is reflected in the component parts of the group, including leadership. Thus, the leader himself and the specific expectations of leadership as a status-role component may undergo changes from time to time. For example, at a given point in time, the leader and leadership in a particular group may be highly important in determining the interests, the activities and the resultant satisfactions experienced by the members. At another time, however, these considerations may be less involved with the role of the leader. This may be the result of the emergence of a new type of leader, a decline in group solidarity, or a transition in the nature of the group itself.[12]

The extent to which leadership is a significant element in the structure of the group differs with respect to the age level or formal organization of the group. In the play groups of young children leadership tends not to be a clearly defined or permanent status; rather, it is usually nebulous. However, in the more formally structured groups such as clubs, leadership is a more clearly defined and important status. Regardless of the presence or absence of a clearly defined leadership status, the performance of the leadership role—formal or informal—is almost sure to make some impact upon both the leader and the led.

Trying the Old and Learning the New

By and large, the child's peer group serves a twofold purpose. It is a testing ground for the lessons learned at home and is a situation in which new lessons are learned. When the child enters the peer group he must

12 See Ronald Lippit and Ralph K. White, "An Experimental Study of Leadership and Group Life," Theodore M. Newcomb and Eugene L. Hartley, eds. *Readings in Social Psychology* (New York, Holt, Rinehart & Winston, Inc., 1947), pp. 315–330.

adjust rather quickly to new persons and circumstances. To this end, he utilizes the language facility, the attitudes, and the skills acquired through experiences with the members of his family. In the young children's play group, for example, such expressions as "That's a bad word you said," "I'm gonna take my bat and go home if you let him play," and "I can do that, see!" all attest to the efficacy of his prior training and experience in his home.

Among children at play, conflicts and disagreements are almost sure to arise. How they deal with such situations initially, is determined largely by what they have been taught at home. For some children, to "stand up for your rights," or not to "let anybody push you around," or to "hit 'em back if they hit you" are often parentally inculcated guidelines for handling disputes and the like. For other children, however, conflict in the form of quarreling, using unacceptable words, or fighting are reactions which, according to parental admonition, should be avoided. Here again, the child tends to rely on his family training for appropriate responses to peer-group experiences.

But the peer group itself is a learning situation. Through direct instruction, observation, and imitation the child acquires new ideas, attitudes, values, information, and skills. He may learn the accepted stereotypes of his social class, the appropriate attitudes toward the outgroup, and the expected reactions to adult authority as represented, for example, by teachers and the police. Furthermore, for children from families where certain subjects of discussion are treated as closed areas, such as sex, race, and religion, the peer group may be the principal source of information.

Aside from the transmission of specifics in the learning process, the contacts with various personality types which may serve as models to be emulated also make their impact upon the peer-group member. The "good guy" and the "bully," the "pal" and the "cry baby," and the "smart guy" and the "dope" are all personality types or models frequently encountered in the peer group. In the give and take which characterizes the collective behavior of children, all of these personality types are likely to communicate something of themselves to some of their fellows.

Finally, the peer group experience constitutes a situation which competes with the family and other agencies for the loyalty of the child. Because of the freedom and independence found among his age mates, the child may sometimes turn away from the family and look to his peers for support and security. At other times, he may be ambivalent and not know which way to turn. On occasion, he may reject family and all adults and rely completely on the approbation of his peers, as is sometimes the case with the member of the gang. Whatever the nature of a particular peer group, the circumstances surrounding the child's involvement in it, or his specific reactions to that involvement, his experience as a member is almost certain to play an important part in his social development.

SUMMARY

In this chapter, the discussion has been directed toward the peer group as an interactional context in which children of relatively the same age collectively examine, explore, and learn about themselves and their world. Compared to other interactional contexts, the peer group is qualitatively different. To some extent, it improves upon and promotes the early teachings of the family. Because of its distinctive nature, however, it often counteracts and even supplants these family teachings. Despite this latter tendency, the peer group constitutes a connecting link in the chain of group situations which facilitates personality development and societal continuity.

Peer groups differ in several respects including the degree to which they are formally structured, the extent to which they are subjected to adult intervention, and the nature and diffuseness of their activities. In addition to being age- and frequently sex-graded, membership in the peer group is often shifting and of relatively short duration. Moreover, the child may be involved in several peer groups simultaneously. Apart from the relative freedom from adult supervision and the opportunity to pursue self-determined ends, children's peer groups represent a generational division of society and as such are significant carriers of culture.

READINGS

GORDON, C. Wayne, *The Social System of the High School* (New York, The Free Press of Glencoe, Inc., 1957).

HALLER, A. O., and BUTTERWORTH, C. E., "Peer Influence on Levels of Occupational and Educational Aspiration," *Social Forces*, Vol. 38, No. 4 (May, 1960), pp. 289–295.

HARTLEY, Ruth E., FRANK, Lawrence K., and GOLDERSON, Robert M., *Understanding Children's Play* (New York, Columbia University Press, 1952).

JENNINGS, Helen Hall, *Sociometry in Group Relations* (Washington, American Council on Education, 1948).

NEUGARTEN, Bernice L., "Social Class and Friendship Among School Children," *American Journal of Sociology*, Vol. LI (1942), pp. 305–313.

PARSONS, Talcott, "The School Class as a Social System," *Harvard Educational Review*, Vol. 29, No. 4 (Fall, 1959), pp. 297–318.

SEIDMAN, Jerome M., ed., *The Child* (New York, Holt, Rinehart and Winston, Inc., 1962), especially chapter 7.

ZILLER, Robert, and BEHRINGER, Richard D., "A Longitudinal Study of the Assimilation of the New Child in the Group," *Human Relations*, Vol. 14, No. 2 (May, 1961), pp. 121–133.

13

Parent Supplements

Introduction

While families occupy a paramount place in the socialization of children, other agencies act in a supplemental capacity. Some of these have been previously noted in the discussion about adult non-family participants. Distant relatives, friends, neighbors, nigh-dwellers, acquaintances, guests, servants, functionaries, and passers-by were cited as having marked effect on the developing child. These individuals, however, offered rather *informal* contacts with children. It is with the *formal* contacts that this chapter is concerned. These are supplemental or further extensions of parental prerogatives. They can sometimes attempt to act in *loco parentis*, in place of the parents, but they cannot easily substitute for the parents. At best, the formal agencies aid and abet homelife. The base of operations for most children, however, remains within their homes. In a sense, children oscillate between their homes and these formal agencies to enlarge their societal outlook.

The initial experience of many children with formal agencies, probably, begins with compulsory attendance at some public school. Thereafter, parental supplements may be encountered in churches or synagogues. Some children may have need for the specialized services of welfare angencies. The injured, handicapped, or seriously ill may have to enter community hospitals for professional attention. Or, the well, the interested, the healthy, active children may enter organized recreational programs. Such agencies do not necessarily involve every child in a community, but they do reach the lives of many children, and aid and abet parents in bringing children into closer touch with their society. With the exception of certain welfare agencies which may displace parents temporarily or permanently, these agencies render services beyond the abilities of parents, but, ideally, in such a manner as to strengthen the hands of the parents. In general, children spend only a portion of their time with these agencies and are returned to the care of their parents for a greater part of their daily or weekly routines.

CHARACTERISTICS OF FORMAL AGENCIES
WHICH SUPPLEMENT THE FUNCTIONS OF PARENTS

1. The structure in which children work tends to be formal rather than informal.

The organizations involved are forthrightly brought into existence because it is their purpose to handle large numbers of children. They may have provisions to treat each child as an individual case, but the general effort is to process as many children as possible. The result may be neglect of certain highly individualistic needs, but their services spread to many children. The presence of large numbers of children requires that they be processed in a routine, planned, scheduled manner. An imposed regimen eliminates inefficient use of personnel and confusion concerning requirements on the part of children.

2. Frequently, the leaders have had specialized training calculated to enable them to deal effectively with children.

Laymen are generally disqualified in these agencies, although their voluntary help in carrying out established policies is welcomed. To be interested in children constitutes an underlying motivation to work with children, but that alone is insufficient to be employed within these agencies. What is desired and needed is professional training which certifies that personnel command the basic essentials of knowledge and skill within a specific field.

3. Financial support for many of these agencies is community-wide because a single family unit could not afford the cost of the services rendered.

By drawing upon some of the financial resources of family units within a community, chiefly through public taxation, the children of the community can be accommodated. No single family would have the burden of paying for the professional services given to its children. Support, other than that of a financial nature, is also desired, but the community-wide financial base remains the chief means by which these agencies may be extant.

4. The child-centered agencies free parents enough so that they may attend to other responsibilities aside from child-rearing.

These agencies do not operate merely because parents have defaulted or abandoned their children to substitutes. Parents simply have other responsibilities in addition to the socialization of their young. Fathers must make a living and mothers generally must tend to household tasks. Both mothers and fathers have to attend to civic duties if their community is to prosper. They may have to care for aged parents or handicapped friends. They may need educational or professional training to perfect their skills. Fathers may be called upon to defend their lands. Mothers may be called upon to nurse the ill. Total attention to children is practically impossible for those who have taken on adult responsibilities.

In addition, parents have some need for rest, relaxation, and enjoyment of leisure time. This may be accomplished mainly away from the company of demanding children. It is not so much a desire to escape the presence of children, but that there is the need to deal with children when one is refreshed, in good physical and mental health, and in an accepting mood.

Thus, parent supplements take over where parents must let go. Social changes in traditional patterns move parents to give their *divided* attention to children rather than their undivided attention. This does not mean that parents are released from their duties. Quite often, these agencies will call on parents to assume their fair share of whatever burdens may develop as a result of children's association with the agencies. In short, the relationships between parents and parent supplements are rarely unilateral, but tend to be more reciprocal and mutually gratifying.

The foregoing characteristics may be applied to numerous agencies which act as parental supplements, but for purposes of brevity, only schools, religious organizations, and welfare agencies, will be presented as adjuncts to the families of a given community. These should provide some insight into the relatively important services of these parental supplements.

Schools

Nursery, primary, and secondary schools probably constitute the greatest single parental supplement in the lives of children. Beginning as early as three and four years of age at the nursery level for some children, at the kindergarten level for many children, or at the first grade for most children in the United States, there is instituted a process of transmitting attitudes, knowledge, and skills calculated to fit children into society.

All the instructional process of the school does not occur in the formal classroom. While much is made of the acknowledged courses of study, school officials regard extra-curricular activities associated with school life as important phases of the educational process. Schools may be viewed as communities in miniature. That is, they are for all practical purposes somewhat self-contained in meeting the needs of their participants. Ostensibly, the main work of a school is in the classroom. But there are also prominent facilities such as a dispensary, a cafeteria, a gymnasium, an auditorium, administrative offices, maintenance rooms, and a surrounding campus with possible parking or play space provided. In addition, there may be a school newspaper, a school annual, a school orchestra and band, a school choir or chorus, a series of school teams, a fleet of school buses, and a school print shop. Possibly a school government in the form of a student council exists as well as corridor guards or safety patrols. And, there is a seemingly endless parade of entertainment and instructive offerings during the school year such as assemblies, films, songfests, dramatic presentations, concerts, sporting events, speakers, dances, carnivals, drives, and special field trips.

In brief, children, while still closely tied to their homes and families, experience a new world in the course of their formal schooling. It pre-empts greater amounts of a child's time as he progresses through the various levels of instruction. It introduces him to children in the vicinity of his home whom he would ordinarily not meet or come to know. It places before him a wide range of subjects from arithmetic and spelling to history, geography, science, literature, and fine arts which he may have missed in the circle of his immediate family. It stimulates his mind, enlarges his vision, and brings him into contact with a wide distribution of personality types which he may easily have missed or overlooked.

The child's status in the formal educational system is that of a learner. It is a subordinate role in which conformity to school norms is expected. What he studies, when he studies, how he studies, where he studies, and why he studies have all been somewhat pre-determined. The young student, himself, is rarely consulted. The one person who looms largest in the child's world is his teacher. Some qualities reminiscent of his father and mother become evident in this person and the learner finds he must yield to this authority.

Ideally, the teacher's role is a most delicate one. In the earlier grades, the elementary teacher typically acts as a continuity of the feminine models already set down by mothers. Only recently have men been added to elementary school staffs. They help to balance the preponderantly feminine models so commonly experienced by smaller children. A teacher brings to the classroom years of training which has culminated in graduation from a college or university. The teacher weds his formal training to his personality, and by drawing upon these inner resources, makes the most of his training to instruct children at any given moment. He must be conscious that beyond the children temporarily under his jurisdiction stand numerous families. "Touch a child and you touch his family" is a fragment of educational folklore which makes a great deal of sense to a teacher. Furthermore, the teacher must be aware that above his status in educational systems stand even more powerful individuals, such as principals, supervisors, superintendents, and school boards of trustees. These represent not just the families of his particular set of students, but all the families within the community. Depending upon the wisdom and tact he can muster, a teacher must go about his business, above reproach, setting a model that is worthy of imitation. No one must be offended. No one is to be harmed. All must be helped, cajoled into cooperation, and made satisfied.

How, for example, should teachers grade children for their efforts in the classroom? Does the child understand what is wanted of him? Is there anything hampering his mastery of a subject? Are there extenuating circumstances that should be taken into account? Are the examinations given to a child valid measurements of his ability? How will a passing or failing grade be taken by a child, his family, or the school officials? These questions sorely puzzle a conscientious teacher because no one claims that grading is an exact science, and yet, grades are accorded considerable attention in evaluating individuals. Will a high grade encourage a learner to loaf and rest on his laurels? Will a low grade send a learner into despair so that he will not even make an attempt to improve his work? Grading is not to be taken lightly, and in a sense, is the pay check children bring home to share with their families.

Exact science or lottery, the subjective experience and symbolic value of grades are important. From the point of view of the recipient, grades contribute to the self-judgments of a child. Some children may view themselves as capable of mastering whatever subjects suit their fancy. Some may judge themselves as just average or one of the crowd. Others may decide that they are inadequate academically and expand this judgment into inadequacy in most of their life's experiences. From the point of view of the larger community or society, academic records have been taken into account in determining whether or not individuals will be granted further opportunities for further study, awards, promotions, specialized work, or honors. When one student presents a grade record that is consistently excellent, regardless of subject or instructor, this will open doors that remain closed to another student who has a grade record that is below average.

The reactions of parents to the grades of their children are fertile grounds for sociological investigation. Some will, no doubt, become defensive and fail to comprehend why their "Egbert" or their "Alice" did so poorly at school. Some will take great pride and consider the talents of their child to be inherited from their side of the family. Others may be noncommittal. Still others will become excited enough to call school officials and demand the immediate dismissal of the teacher involved. The reactions will certainly vary, but all will reflect the family's appraisal of the educational process which has been turned over to parental supplements. The various reactions will also reflect the general character or personality attributes of the parental generation.

School officials constantly engage in self-criticism and self-evaluation. There may be educators who regard their work as above reproach, but these are relatively rare. There are, however, many families who are either unwilling or incapable of self-evaluation. It is this type which are uncritical of themselves, but are over-critical of their children's formal school instruction. These families may well ask if they encouraged good study habits. Did they try to undermine the image of the teacher in the child's mind? Is the emotional atmosphere within their home conducive to the best study conditions? Have they socially crippled their children by thoughtless, but nevertheless significant remarks? The child, after all, is a joint project of the school and the home and they may operate as effective or ineffective partners.

Aside from grades, home-work seems to loom large as an area of joint interest to schools and families alike. In the lower grades, home-work does not seem to be a matter of contention because the bulk of the formal training is confined to the classroom and dismissal from school at the end of the day closes the door on formalized study until the next morning. But as children advance into higher grades, home-work does become an issue because school work spills over into family life well beyond the dismissal hour. It is a standard bit of humor, used widely by cartoonists, to poke fun at unwitting parents who "help" their children with their assignments. Typically, a school-age child enters the living room, report card in hand, and says, "Dad, you passed Geography of South America this semester, but you sure flunked fifth grade arithmetic. Teacher says that she hopes you will do better next year."

The major source of possible irritation between homes and schools appears to be the increasing preoccupation of children with their formal education and its concomitants which tend to lead children away from their original home environments. This may be a part of the process of weaning children to independence, but the transition may not always be tranquil and placid. The teachers can become more important to children than their parents. School-mates can become more interesting to a child than his own siblings or relatives. School activities take larger blocks of time from activities formerly held exclusively by the child's family. The child has found a larger world outside his immediate family and this world seems to promise much more for him than his earlier acquaintance with his family. The extent to which schools and families are in agreement about objectives and the ways to reach these objectives explains the smooth or stormy relationships that can develop between educational authorities and parents.

Liaison between homes and schools has been attempted by organizations called PTA's or PTO's, Parent-Teacher Associations or Parent-Teacher Organizations. These organizations have both their antagonists and their protagonists. Some have said that they are very ineffective in what they set out to do. That is, they become polite channels to show off children or to explain school policies to parents. Others, however, point out that they serve as necessary links between schools and homes and are effective channels of communication. Some PTA's have conducted vigorous, enlightened programs, while others have been halfhearted, inept efforts. In one sense, these organizations can be very useful if parents and teachers are seriously interested in their common project, the further growth of children. In another sense, these organizations become the arenas for an inevitable clash of interests between schools and homes if they choose to pull in opposite directions. Homes, which treat children on a personal, intimate, individualistic basis, simply do not face the same problems as schools, which treat children on a community, impersonal, general basis. A home will deal directly with a few children. A school will deal directly with many children. That they have worked together is to the credit of those who have looked beyond their immediate conditions for the sake of the larger society, as well as for their children who will live in it.

RELIGIOUS ORGANIZATIONS

Not only do schools impinge upon families, but so do religious organizations. Like schools, churches and synagogues tend to dictate the direction parental action should take and seek the wholehearted cooperation of families to provide the necessary follow-through if religious instruction and activities are to have meaning. Children, then, are not the sole concern of religious organizations, but the families from which they come are of paramount concern.

There are many children who do not experience any religious institutions. Their families are part of the roughly one third of the American population that is unaffiliated with any religious organization. Even within the approximate two thirds of the American population which is affiliated with some form of organized religion, there are numerous families who are somewhat marginal. The children in these families can understandably regard religious organization as some vague social activity which people attend on rare occasions over the period of a year. It is for those children who do participate in the activities associated with religious organizations that this discussion is concerned.

There is one point of view that holds that children cannot be "middle-of-the-road" when it comes to religious faith. The disparity and variety of philosophies require either an acceptance or a rejection of religious ideologies. To be liberal in religious viewpoints is admirable when it is a matter of respect for differences, but, to be liberal in the sense of concluding that one faith is just as acceptable as another is to ultimately accept none or reject all of them. Most religions require a loyalty that implies acceptance of a single dogma and the rejection of all other religious formulas. It is true that some faiths require strict attention and devotion to their maxims because they regard their own ideas as above reproach and, in fact, the only true religion. Other religions do not take such a stand, but choose to say that there are elements of truth and value for the followers of a variety of religions. They only require, for their own followers, that these individuals adhere to the organized faith of their families.

For a time, children tend to follow the religious philosophies of their parents without question. If the parents are anti-religious in some form or another, then their children acquire familiarity with this point of view. If the parents are highly in favor of a particular religious system, then this becomes the context of initial, and often lasting, experiences of children. Shifts away from the religious convictions of parental generations will usually not occur during childhood. Only an inkling or a hint of future disenchantment with a particular religious system may be found at this time. The seeds of discontent will possibly be sown during childhood, but the power of parents will not permit their germination until adolescence or beyond.

Like schools, religious organizations tend to require larger blocks of time and attention from children as they grow up. They are involved in activities such as Sunday or Sabbath Schools, worship services, financial drives, congregational suppers, bazaars, choir or dramatic rehearsals, weekday evening sessions, retreats, brotherhoods, sisterhoods, and special study groups. All these may strengthen the church or synagogue, but may or may not strengthen the home. Each family unit generally has the freedom to decide for itself just how much they will invest in religious activities. The decisions will vary from making religion the be-all and end-all of family life to token attendance at major religious festivals.

Parochial schools represent another area of common ground between families and their religious affiliations. Not satisfied with what the child may experience religiously in company with his parents or with what may be gained from attendance on Sundays, Sabbaths, or special Holy Days, there are faiths that urge attendance on week days in a school which presents secular subjects, but couches them in a context of religious thinking and emphasis. It is not sufficient, then, for some to learn spelling by itself, but rather it is regarded as important to learn the spelling of religious words. It is not sufficient, from this point of view, to learn history, but one should study historical material which is steeped in religious traditions. One may learn subject matter as in any other school, but in the parochial school the major theme is clearly a religious one.

In some societies, sacred-secular dichotomies are practically nonexistent. Children are taught that religious ideology and daily routines are inextricably woven together. They cannot be separated from each other without serious damage to both. Parochial schools in these societies are unnecessary. It is only within societies that have attempted to separate spiritual matters from secular matters that certain faiths feel the need for a parochial school system.

In the United States, it is a Constitutional principle to divorce religion from political life. The chief device has been an announced policy of separating "church and state" in the name of religious freedom for all. Much of this vaunted separation, however, has not been achieved in reality. Among the predominant faiths, the religious events of Christians, such as Christmas and Easter, are observed in secular schools as national holidays. Cities, streets, stores, and businesses are decorated and prepared according to the *holiday* season. Non-Christians are either disregarded or urged to join in the festive spirit of the religious occasion. The songs that proclaim the birth of the Messiah or His Resurrection are sung in community schools, despite the recognition of religious diversity. Many are amazed that minorities are offended when Christmas trees or Nativity scenes are placed in or around public schools or facilities. Even when Christian minorities, such as the Amish, favor an elementary education for their children without extra embellishments, their religious convictions have clashed with civil authorities. The ideal of church and state separation has been frequently enunciated. These pronouncements, however, are not necessarily statements of reality as much as they are repetitions of satisfying slogans. They may point out a direction, but they are not followed very far in that direction.

The key figures in religious organizations are such functionaries as priests, ministers, and rabbis. Through their sermonizing, their interpretations of religiosity, their religious zeal, their daily religious devotions, and their enactment of their religious convictions, they may have a powerful impact upon children. Their very person is sometimes surrounded by an aura of compelling religious spirit that command not only respect, but possible emulation. They may not be as close to children as teachers or parents, but their exalted position may sometimes overshadow the prosaic images of these persons with whom they deal daily.

Religious experience involves a specific morality. Its appeal may be through the intellect by the use of authority and logic. More often, it involves emotions which are not easily handled by reasonableness. Thus, arguments calculated to change moralities may fall upon deaf ears. An approach to newer morality via emotionality, however, has some chance of success. Those who are parental supplements in religious organizations exert their influence, therefore, chiefly through the encouragement of certain feeling-states. Stories, songs, symbols, and dramatic presentations have a telling effect upon youngsters. The more dramatic a religious event can be made, the more chance that its emotional overtones will remain a longer time. In this connection, it is noteworthy that many of the rites of passage marking the growing up of children have a religious ceremonial tied to them. The experiences may be terrifying, extremely pleasant, drawn out or brief, humbling or uplifting, but the excitement and stirrings engendered are almost branded into a child's memory.

As in the case of schools, parents are somewhat side-lined to give as much power and authority to parental supplements as possible. By and large, parents accept this demotion to permit representatives of their religious organizations as much chance as possible to promote the religious development of their children. They have vacated or stepped aside in the formal training of their children in this respect and lend credence to the idea that others are far better qualified to do the specialized work of religious instruction. It is only in folk societies or societies emerging from a folk background that parents assume greater responsibility in the religious education of their youngsters.

WELFARE AGENCIES

A multitude of social agencies may be subsumed under the title of welfare agencies. The specific organizations that are herein treated are orphanages, boystowns, homes for disabled children, homes for delinquent children, organizations for dependent children, and juvenile centers which take roles ordinarily held by parents. Children become involved with welfare agencies because, for one reason or another, parents are not functioning as effectively or as is normally required by their society. Whatever the circumstances, children cannot be left to fend for themselves and are, accordingly, turned over to paid professional workers.

There are many children who have never seen a social worker or been handled by a social agency. In their case parents do not need or are not known to need supplemental help. They meet their normal responsibilities to the best of their ability. It is for those children who could profit from parental supplements or surrogates that this discussion is concerned.

Parents have typically sought the supplemental help of schools and religious organizations, but may or may not voluntarily seek aid from welfare agencies. In some instances, parents have abandoned their children. Welfare agencies step into the breach at this point. In other cases, parents themselves are in need of care and so cannot render it to their children. In any event, welfare agencies help provide whatever parental functions are missing for deprived children.

One of the most common criticisms of these systems of caring for children in need is that they may prolong dependency more than necessary. It is a widely held belief that taking burdens off the shoulders of parents encourages them to continue to heap their normal responsibilities on others. Furthermore, if parents are excused from meeting their obligations to their children, what incentive is provided to change their ways? Welfare agencies, however, exist for *all* cases of children in need and not for those particular cases in which parents may be deliberately trying to escape their respective tasks. Parents die or are accidentally injured. Parents may not be employed because there may not be as much need for manpower as in the past. Illness may occur requiring prolonged convalescence or hospitalization. Welfare agencies take care of these legitimate cases until such time as parents or parent substitutes can become operative once again.

Social workers are conscious that their immediate task is not to remove the causes that lead to case loads, but is to deal with the unfortunate results. They must make the best of a situation as it exists. It is the responsibility of individuals, families, schools, churches, synagogues, and communities to creat healthy atmospheres which will prevent the development of welfare cases. However, human failings do create less than optimum conditions and the work of social welfare agencies is sometimes necessary.

One central thread that runs through many cases handled by welfare agencies is the apparent lack of love or concern for others. Some parents lack normal affection for their children. If they do care for their children, then they may be unconcerned for their spouse, their employers, or the general community. Frequently, the lack of concern with which they were treated by their parents or by others is carried over into their own lives by unconcern even for themselves. In numerous cases, the unifying force of concern for others is absent and the result is a family which cannot and does not hold together. When someone cares, there may be found the security upon which children rely.

Many welfare agencies find that their facilities are inadequate to meet the needs of growing numbers of children. Facilities originally planned to care for a limited number become crowded and inefficient under the press of too many people. Home-like atmospheres simply cannot be offered when large numbers of children must receive at least the most rudimentary attention. The result has been a formalizing, an increasing of routines, a standardization of procedures, and a relatively impersonal handling of children in order to perform even minimal tasks. Less time and little room may be found for individual attention and warm relationships that may reshape warped lives. The instances of rehabilitation are a credit to social workers who are performing what is often judged to be a thankless task. That others are recidivists in such agencies is mute testimony, however, that there is much more to be done.

There are cases of children who are shifted back and forth between parents and welfare agencies. The efforts of one may be nullified or reinforced by the other. Children who can find some consistency between their parents and the work of parental supplements are in a position to be helped. Those who find an inconsistency between their parents and parental supplements can easily emerge confused and impeded in their acquisition of social skills and insights. If both parents and parental supplements fail in their repective areas of responsibility, then children are inevitably marked by these circumstances.

Welfare-agency workers face a dilemma in choosing between a *professional approach* to children and a *non-professional approach* to children. By a professional approach to children, social workers mean that they must efficiently handle youngsters as so many young persons in need of professional care. They must acquire some skill in avoiding emotional involvement with individual cases. To carry the emotional burdens of each child would become intolerable and would handicap the professional services of the social worker. The same applies to teachers who cannot emotionally share the educational problems of each pupil or to medical doctors who cannot suffer the agonies of each patient. A sympathetic approach is needed with children but rarely can it be employed at such an emotional depth that the social worker is professionally blinded in whatever decisions are needed.

Because specialized training is necessary for social workers, there is usually a minimal amount of qualities required to reach that status. However, there is a wide difference between those who are top-rated in their work and those who lag far behind. Obviously, the personalities of professionals will vary and account for the verve with which some approach their duties and the lackadaisical manner with which others handle themselves. There are social workers and there are *social workers*. There are teachers and there are *teachers*. There are ministers and there are *ministers*. Far too many professionals wear their labels superficially. The responsibility of graduating professionals, such as social workers, who are supposed to possess in common the minimal qualities that will enable them to handle children, rests with the professional schools who certify their abilities. Unfortunately, some children are penalized because chance has brought them into contact with those who seek only to get by.

It is the *whole* child who has come for treatment by a parental supplement, not a fragmented personality who needs help in only a single area of his life. Thus, children are not necessarily only delinquent, dependent, or deficient. Those who treat them as if they were may be useful because of their special abilities, nevertheless, it is the total personality that requires consideration. A possibly useful parallel may be found in the situation in the medical profession in which specialists have somewhat displaced the general practitioner. Instead of treating the whole patient, a patient is segmentally handled by a urologist, radiologist, anesthetist, serologist, or cardiologist. There are benefits to be derived by persons becoming specialists in their field. Those who object to specialization point out that the process leads away from consideration of the total human being, a consideration of paramount concern to both individuals and the society in which they live. The *team* approach in which specialists pool their knowledge for each case under the guidance of an able executive gives promise that some of this segmentalization might be minimized.

Summary

There are times when children are in need of supplementary services that parents cannot offer. It is not that parents are unable to render these services but that they must turn their attention and energies to areas other than the rearing of their children. The parental supplements specifically discussed were schools, religious organizations, and welfare agencies. They share in common the characteristics of some degree of formal organization, the use of trained professionals, and community-wide financial support. The relationships between parent supplements and parents are reciprocal and mutually beneficial.

Schools are probably the most common parental supplements within the reach of most children. Religious organizations reach fewer children than schools do. And welfare agencies handle even fewer children than either religious organizations or schools. All have profound effects on the children they process. All have special problems with which to cope. None of these problems is insurmountable, each lends itself to further study and intelligent effort.

Readings

Bettelheim, Bruno, *Love Is Not Enough: The Treatment of Emotionally Disturbed Children* (New York, The Free Press of Glencoe, Inc., 1950).

Bisno, Herbert, "How Social Will Social Work Be?" *Social Work,* Vol. 1, No. 2 (April, 1956), pp. 12–18.

Brookover, Wilbur B., *A Sociology of Education* (New York, American Book Company, 1955).

Bush, Robert N., *The Teacher-Pupil Relationship* (Englewood Cliffs, N.J., Prentice-Hall, Inc., 1954).

Edwards, Newton, and Richey, Herman G., *The Schools in the American Social Order* (Boston, Houghton Mifflin Company, 1947).

Hutchinson, Dorothy, *In Quest of Foster Parents* (New York, Columbia University Press, 1943).

Kramer, Judith R., and Leventman, Seymour, *Children of the Gilded Ghetto* (New Haven, Yale University Press, 1962).

Robbins, Florence G., *Educational Sociology* (New York, Holt, Rinehart & Winston, Inc., 1953).

Ross, Murray G., *Religious Beliefs of Youth* (New York, Association Press, 1950).

TEETERS, Negley, and REINMANN, John, *The Challenge of Delinquency* (Englewood Cliffs, N.J., Prentice-Hall, Inc., 1950).

THURSTON, Henry, *The Dependent Child* (New York, Columbia University Press, 1930).

WALLER, Willard, *The Sociology of Teaching* (New York, John Wiley & Sons, Inc., 1932).

14

Play, Games—and Work

INTRODUCTION

At various points in the chapter on the peer group, references or allusions were made to the play and games of children. Because play and games are characteristic of childhood and because they are significantly functional for socialization, they will now be discussed in some detail. Close observation of the life cycle of the person indicates that some of the elements of children's play and game activities, including derivative values, attitudes, knowledge, and skills, are continuous through childhood and indeed through the total life-span. Of special interest here is the fact that these elements come to be expressed in the occupational roles of adulthood. Because children's play and games are in some respects continuous phenomena which come to be significant components of the world of work, both will be viewed and discussed together.

PLAY

Generally, *play* refers to mental or physical activity for non-utilitarian purposes—for sheer amusement. It may involve the individual child or groups of children, and is usually either minimally regulated or wholly random. *Games*, on the other hand, are organized play. They are contests which are carried on according to fixed or pre-determined rules, and they involve two or more persons. Play, therefore, is a more general term; the game is a particular form of play.

The world over, play is a commonplace activity for children. In fact, play seems to be a necessary outgrowth of the physical and social nature of man. At birth, the infant is impotent and immobile. Gradually he engages in random, undirected movement. This leads him to explore, to examine, and to manipulate his immediate environment. These activities, initially guided by sheer impulses, soon lead to the development of certain elementary interests on the part of the infant. Through trial and error, with parental encouragement and facilitation, the child experiences more and more success and pleasure from the manipulation of objects and situations.

Children actually experience play long before they experience playmates. The beginning, certainly the antecedent, of play occurs in the mother-infant situation. It begins with the mother playing[1] with the infant. Gradually the infant responds—joins in the play.

The child is for a long time dependent upon moods and emotional attitudes. . . . He responds to facial expressions earlier than to most stimuli and answers with appropriate expressions of his own, before he makes responses that we consider significant. He comes into the world highly sensitive to this so-called "mimic gesture," and he exercises his earliest intelligence in his adaptation to his social environment.[2]

Therefore, when instances of play occur in his social environment or between his mother and himself, his responses mimic the play gestures of his mother.

At first, the play gestures of the child are mere smiles, gurglings, or other apparently gleeful antics. In reality, it is the mother whose play is consciously motivated. Initially, the infant is like the passive spectator at a game who enjoys and applauds; soon, however, somewhat like the passive spectator he feels like getting into the act, and finally he does. As these play experiences multiply, the child becomes sensitive and conditioned not only to his mother's moods and emotional attitudes, but also to her words and actions. As actions become possible for him and as words take on meanings, the child is increasingly able to respond to the play actions of his mother with play actions of his own. Thus, for example, he uses his hands to play "peek-a-boo" and "patty-cake."

As the child comes to understand and use words, and as he is learning to walk and manipulate objects, he is less and less the passive spectator and more and more the active participant: now, he *plays with mother*. By this time, mother has gained a degree of freedom from the incessant demands of child care, and may not always feel like playing when the baby wants to play. Perhaps she has other pressing things to do now that the baby is growing up. Nonetheless, since the child has been conditioned to the pleasures of play, he will perhaps seek to repeat the experience over and over again. At this point a substitute mother-playmate is necessary. To find this new playmate the child turns inward to "the imaginary companions which a good many children produce in their

---

[1] Strictly speaking, this is not play. The activity is somewhat functional for mother: it keeps the baby quiet and perhaps makes him feel secure.

[2] George H. Mead, *Mind, Self, and Society,* Charles W. Morris, ed. (Chicago, University of Chicago Press, 1934), p. 368.

own experience. . . . Play in this sense . . . is a play at something. A child plays at being a mother, at being a teacher, at being a policeman; that is, it is taking different roles, as we say." [3]

Such play activity in which the child takes the role of the other is part of the process whereby he acquires a self; at the same time, however, he is preparing himself for collective and organized play, for the game. This solitary play is no mere repetition of mother-child play. As a matter of fact, it is probable that the child's memory, his imagination, the prevailing situation, and even the power of choice all combine to facilitate variety in solitary play. Therefore, at one time he plays at one thing; at another time, his play is directed toward something else.

If the child has siblings, or when he contacts other children, they serve as playmates. They become the others whose roles he takes. If he derives pleasure from playing with them, as he did from playing with mother and playing alone, he can be expected to keep them as playmates. Once he becomes accustomed to playing with other children he will perhaps like to play with some but not with others; he may reject particular children as playmates but he is not likely to cease having playmates. In fact, the apparent importance of playmates at this stage suggests that "the play is *not* the thing" for he comes "to regard himself as a playmate who must share his toys with other children if he is to keep them as playmates. This compels him to see other characters in the playthings besides their immediate attraction to his play impulse and to that of possession. The plaything becomes a composite object; it is not only that which gives expression to his own impulse but something that keeps with him his cherished friends." [4] Viewed in this perspective, play becomes not merely an enjoyable personal experience stimulating body or mind, it is a device whereby the child gains access and acceptance in the world of significant others.

Close observation reveals that not all children are equally involved in collective or group play. Indeed, some are so involved only minimally. Attention has already been called to the solitary play of the child as the phase of play which follows immediately after mother-infant play. It was pointed out that solitary play involves taking the role of the other. Through this process the child is prepared for effective interaction in situations involving other people, including other children. To translate and apply the learning derived in solitary play to interactional situations involving playmates, the child must have access to other children. The prospect that this transference or application—which is necessary for effective socialization—might not be made fully or at least easily is a very real consideration in the lives of the only child, the over-protected child,

[3] *Ibid.*
[4] *Ibid.*, p. 371.

and the child who is withdrawn. Not uncommonly, children of these types continue to play more or less by themselves. As they grow older they tend not to establish firm or relatively permanent peer-group relationships. They tend not to participate in organized play or in games. It may be that as these children continue to grow toward maturity, their play and recreational activities will become increasingly solitary and sedentary and that such activities will come to be their substitutes for companionship.

During the earliest stage of childhood, up to the child's entry into school, play is a central and time-consuming activity for most children. For those who attend nursery school and kindergarten it still continues to be so, except that these systems provide for organized and supervised play. Apart from these latter situations, however, practically all very young children devote practically all of their waking hours to play. Obviously, they enjoy it; perhaps equally obvious is the enjoyment—and the release?—parents get from knowing their children are at play.

The Game

As indicated in the above reference to the nursery school and the kindergarten, some play activities of children are organized and supervised. Some of the organized play activities of children, by their very nature, require collective and cooperative behavior; hence, organization becomes necessary. Playing "hide 'n' seek," "tag," or "skipping rope" are examples. Play activities such as these require only a minimum degree of organization; others, however, require a more complex pattern of organization. It is this organization, this interconnection and playing out several roles, that distinguishes the game from mere play. The child at play can take a series of roles but they need not be interrelated: he can move from role and situation to a distinctly different role and situation as his whim or fancy dictates. In the game, however, he must take a set of interrelated roles and must respond, and be prepared to be responded to, according to the rules of the game.[5]

Viewed in terms of the socialization process, the game is a significant context for social interaction. It involves norms, acts, and goals which are defined in terms of specific rights, privileges, and duties. These, in turn, are combined into status-role components which are differentially assigned or are achieved by the participants in the game. Interaction in games is carried on not in terms of the whim or fancy of the individual, but in accordance with the prevailing expectations resulting from the status-role relationship in which the child is engaged. In a game of base-

[5] *Ibid.*, p. 151.

ball, for example, a youngster might feel like taking a turn at bat, but whether or not he may do so depends upon where he is in the batting order. Furthermore, if he is the umpire, he may not expect to get a turn at all. In the game, then, the child learns to take his turn and to let others take theirs.

The child who is often pampered and permitted to have his way at home, learns that playing games requires that the rules be followed. He learns also that the game is comprised of parts (of roles) and that each player has a part. As he comes to know the rules well and as he gains experience in the different parts of the game, the understanding and experience thus gained facilitate his successful participation. Equally important, he is thus better prepared to participate in other interactional situations.

To a considerable extent, games constitute the principal activity of children's peer groups. Especially for the younger ones, they are the answer to the question, "What do children's peer groups do?" These same activities by children continue not only because of their interest, but largely because of adult approval and promotion. Perhaps remembering their own childhood, adults often insist that children should be carefree and gay: so parents send their children out to play. Sometimes this gets them out of the way. Frequently, especially in the United States, adults organize and direct large-scale play and game activities for children, such as Little League baseball, for example. To some extent, Cub Scouts, Boys Clubs, and Brownies reflect this adult interest in the promotion of children's activities. Thus it is that patterns of play have become institutionalized.

In the United States, this institutionalization of children's play and games is largely a twentieth-century phenomenon. Earlier, children were not generally encouraged to play. An idle mind was "the devil's workshop"; thus, early in their lives, children worked hard in field and factory. Frequently, boys as young as ten or twelve were to be found at work for employers who were exacting and even harsh taskmasters. Furthermore, children were sometimes indentured for varying periods of servitude. In Colonial New England, for example, the system of indenture was early extended to include homeless children as well as children of the poor. In Rhode Island the workhouse overseer "had the power to bind out for a period, not to exceed four years, anyone who was unlikely to maintain himself through work in the institution. This provision also held for children." [6] Childhood in the United States, therefore, has not always been regarded, ideally, as an idyllic period filled with pleasure and play.

The secure status of children in present-day American society, with its

[6] Herbert Hewit Stroup, *Social Work* (New York, American Book Company, 1948), p. 62. Second edition, 1960.

emphasis on personal development and the full enjoyment of life, is largely a reflection of the general social reform movement which flourished in Europe and America during the nineteenth and twentieth centuries. Out of that movement, various social and cultural changes have emerged. Greater personal freedom, a higher level of living, expanded educational opportunities, and increased leisure have all resulted from these changes.

An increase in leisure time and the patterned and to some extent institutionalized use of that leisure, are two changes in life in the United States which are significantly related to the subject of children's play and games. While this new emphasis upon leisure is significantly involved in the lives of children, it represents but one aspect of an all-inclusive approach to the enrichment of childhood experiences. It is generally accepted that today's children should enjoy every opportunity for healthy and creative living. They have been guaranteed the right to live as children, that is, to be free from care and responsibility not befitting their years. The ideals and rights of children as set forth in the Children's Charter of the 1930 White House Conference on Child Health and Protection [7] guarantees, at least by implication, that their only "work" shall be to grow up in healthy surroundings, to learn to the extent of their capacities, and to spend the rest of their time joyously at play. In this same report [8] it was noted that

there is a strange paradox in the recent-day program of recreation and physical education. The efficiency of the program diminishes as one follows it back to its application from the youth of eighteen years . . . to the infant. It is better in the secondary school than in the elementary school, and for the pre-school child it nearly disappears. . . . The neglect of the pre-school child is held even more serious than neglect at a later age. With the young child, his work is his play and his play is his work. Habits of mind and muscle are formed in this impressionable age which endure for life. Until recently the pre-school child was left to the home. In modern life, however, supplemental aid is found necessary. So we have the nursery school and kindergarten. We find progressive playground supervisors setting aside special space for young children and supplying suitable play implements and good leadership.

Since this report was submitted many relevant changes have taken place. Significant among these changes have been the promotion of hobbies, the expansion of various play programs both in the school and in the neighborhood, the increase in club organizations, and the development of athletic activities, including those sponsored by church organizations, fraternal lodges, and police departments.

[7] *White House Conference, 1930, Addresses and Abstracts of Committee Reports* (New York, The Century Company, 1931).
[8] *Ibid.,* p. 216. Reprinted by permission of Appleton-Century-Crofts.

The Game: Socialization or Success?

"My boy is a Little Leaguer," the father proudly announced. The pride in this announcement is frequently observed. Is this expression of pride stimulated by the father's belief that his boy's association with Little Leagues contributes to the physical and moral development of his son? By the superior achievement of his boy at bat, on the base path, or in the field? By the fact that as a Little Leaguer his son moves in select circles? Conceivably, any or all of these might have been the conscious stimulants of this father's pride. But is there perhaps another, underlying and deeper reason behind this bursting with pride? Perhaps a brief examination of Little League ball will suggest the answer.

In the United States baseball for boys eight years and over is a highly organized game. Little League Baseball, Junior-Pony-Colt Baseball, National Hot Stove League, and Babe Ruth League, Inc. are organizations which systematically sponsor baseball for these boys. Although these sponsoring groups are interested in boys and in baseball as a recreational and educational service rather than an economic enterprise, there are nonetheless certain aspects of this organized activity which are reminiscent of professional and commercialized sports. It has a structure which involves a chain of authority and a division of labor. Thus, there are boards of directors, national officers, state and regional directors, coaches, managers, umpires, official scorers, and of course players. Incorporation, chartering, and contracting are also involved. Rules of eligibility and of play are formalized and followed. Systematic scheduling of play, the publication of official rosters, and state tournaments are other elements of the system.

The manifest function of these games is well illustrated in an official statement in the National Hot Stove League Junior Baseball Program:

Its object is to promote, promulgate, and perpetuate non-commercialized baseball, throughout the United States for pre-teens and teen-agers; to surround it with proper safeguards; to aid and assist in the fostering, developing and regulating of local chapters in accordance with the spirit of sportsmanship, honesty, and fair play; and to aid and assist in the furthering of championship tournaments.

While we train our boys to win, and desire to win, we must prepare them to accept defeat when it comes and profit by its lessons. It is repeatedly emphasized that less emphasis be stressed on winning at all costs, bearing in mind that the attainment of exceptional skill or winning of games is secondary. The moulding of future men is the goal.

One would perhaps grant the likelihood that these baseball activities are functional in the directions stated in the purposes above. Like other social organizations, however, organized baseball for boys can be expected to have latent as well as manifest functions. The manifest functions have been judged to be important; otherwise, the activity would not have been organized. Since the latent functions are not explicitly stated or perhaps even recognized, they too become important, at least objectively so. Conceivably, the latent functions could negate or neutralize those functions that are manifest.

Stated succinctly but generally, the game of baseball is functional, manifestly, in the socialization process. The multiple roles and the emphasis on the rules which are part of this game are suggestive of the instructive analyses of socialization presented by Mead and Piaget.[9] Mead pointed to the function of play and the game in the development of the self, and Piaget called attention to the crucial significance of the rules of the game in the moral development of the child. If the game had been as highly institutionalized when they examined it as it is now, they might well have discovered and followed certain leads relating not to the child, but to the adult. They might have been struck, for example, by that aspect of the symbolic nature of the game whereby adults are enabled to strive to recapture glimpses of their selves of bygone years when they were children. They might have found that some fathers who missed the childhood joys of the game now seek to compensate through their sons; or, that those fathers who enjoyed the game are seeking to relive their past through their promotional efforts in baseball for boys.

Despite the formal claims of the game's potential for child development, the adults' observable reaction of delight at winning or disappointment at losing, and even their rabid rooting at the game, all suggest a concern beyond that of the development of the players. Relevant to this,

the consumption of sports may have the latent function of bringing continuity into the personal lives of many Americans. Team loyalties formed in adolescence and maintained through adulthood may serve to remind one, in a nostalgic way, that there are areas of comfortable stability in life—that some things have permanence amid the harassing interruptions and discontinuous transactions of daily life.[10]

It need only be added that whatever the reactions of adult sponsors, supervisors, or supporters of these children's baseball games, such reactions are likely to influence the children who are the active participants.

In organized baseball and sports generally, an extremely high priority is placed on winning. It is not enough to "go down swinging" or even to "give it your best." The overridingly important criterion of success is the affirmative aswer to the question, "Did you win today?" The disclaimer notwithstanding, it is quite probable that winning is an important con-

[9] George H. Mead, *op. cit.*, Part III; Jean Piaget, *The Moral Judgement of the Child*, (London, Kegan Paul, 1932).

[10] Gregory P. Stone, "American Sports: Play and Dis-Play," *Chicago Review*, Vol. IX, No. 3, pp. 83–100.

sideration in the minds of coaches and players, and perhaps parents of players of organized baseball for boys. More than a contest, organized baseball for boys is a display—a display of skill, of speed, of courage, of the will to win. In some instances, it is a diminutive spectacular in which the little players are aware that hope, confidence, pride, or reward is "riding on every pitch." To the extent that this is so, the burden may increase, tension may mount, and failure or a single misstep or error may prove damaging to the self.

PLAY AND THE RECREATION COMPLEX

The cultural conditioning centering in the play activities of children in the United States has a continuity which is manifested in various patterns of adult behavior. Thus, play is not confined to childhood; rather, it is widespread and takes many forms among adults. Apparently the axiom "All work and no play makes Jack a dull boy" is taken seriously by many Americans who have long since left the status of childhood. Their interest and participation in play is perhaps largely the result of their childhood orientation to play.

Understandably, and from the economic point of view, adults regard work as more important than play. Moreover, the less play-appearing the job, the more like *real* work it is. Hence, the frequently expressed reaction, "I *work* for my money." Despite this priority which is usually given work, most Americans experience the urge to get away from it all, for, as already suggested, they take seriously the saying "All work and no play makes Jack a dull boy." Perhaps even those who say ". . . makes 'jack' and plenty of it," tend to use some of their "jack" for play purposes. Apparently, then, the play orientation and the play experience gained in childhood have a carry-over into adulthood, for groups of adults often get together for relaxation, for an evening of fun. On these occasions it is not uncommon for them to indulge in children's games such as guessing games, riddles, puzzles, and cards or other play or game activities that hold their attention.

Aside from these special occasions for play, many adults play with their children. They teach them games, they fill-in as substitutes on children's teams, and on occasion they initiate children's play in order *to get some exercise.* Manifestly, parental (or adult) participation with the children in their play and games is for the purpose of facilitating wholesome childhood experiences; yet, the avidity with which many fathers play with, or *show* their sons how to play with, their electric trains suggests that children are not the only beneficiaries in such situations. Long after Christmas, and hours after sons are in bed, some fathers are still *showing* their sons how to play with their (the fathers'?) electric trains.

The childhood interest in play continues into adulthood and is perhaps reflected in how adults spend their vacation periods. Handball, tennis, horseshoe pitching, sack racing, swimming, and dancing are but some of the activities in which they engage. To be sure, they read, listen to music, and just relax, but to a considerable extent they behave in accordance with the suggestion "Why don't you go out and play!"—a parental suggestion made to them when they were growing up. Of course, this is not a conscious response; rather, their play is rationalized in terms of its potential for relaxation, its contribution to the physique, its facilitation of good fellowship, or its promotion of popularity. In any event, for many adults on vacation the "play is the thing."

FROM INFORMAL PLAY TO INSTITUTIONAL PLAY

The continuity from children's play and games to the informal play activities of adults does not stop there. It has permeated almost the entire social structure of the United States. Practically every institutional pattern includes provisions for play both for children and adults. Schools, religious organizations, governmental agencies, and business and industrial concerns all support and include in their programs provisions for play, leisure-time activities, or recreation.

Perhaps the outstanding example of formal provision for regulated play is to be found in institutionalized education. In the school system of the United States recess is, for many, perhaps one of the most highly valued parts of the curriculum. To some extent, this assessment is shared by teachers as well as students. As viewed by teachers, recess is important because it gives most children an opportunity to relax, to exercise, and to engage in cooperative enterprise that is almost certain to be enjoyable for most school children. Recess is also valued by teachers as a social device which compensates for loss in learning due to the limited attention-span of the children. And, of course, the play and games during recess are frequently regarded as learning experiences.

It is because play and games are potential learning experiences that recess is here regarded as a part of the school curriculum. The range of attitudes and skills and the proliferation of roles required by children's play and games have great potential for personality development. Perhaps a few examples will illustrate this point. Playing tag, skipping rope, and ball games all contribute to bodily coordination and growth as well as to the development of manual dexterity. Other activities such as "follow the leader," which requires imitative behavior; "blackboard relay," which involves collective sentence construction; and "ball tag," which provides opportunities for taking the role of the other are ultimately, though not necessarily by conscious intent, activities which facilitate learning. Many of these games, and others like them, are played during recess. Even those which are not outdoor games, "blackboard relay," for example, are sometimes played during recess times spent indoors because of inclement weather.

In addition to recess, other aspects of the school system which facilitate play activities include after-school use of the playground, gymnasia, and the games of the schools' athletic teams. Perhaps the most widespread and highly organized play pattern of the school system is to be found in the athletic team. Today, thousands of these teams involve tens of thousands of children—mainly boys—who develop various socially approved skills and attitudes as a consequence of their participation. Although much more than personal enjoyment is involved in these team activities, for many of the participants, the "play is the thing."

Although children are the principal participants in school-connected play and games, many adults participate in these activities through the performance of peripheral roles. Classroom teachers, physical education instructors, playground supervisors, and athletic coaches all have important parts in the promotion of these activities. To be sure, this is required of them by the very nature of their jobs; yet, they reap benefits resulting, not so much from a job well done, as from the sheer joy of seeing happy children at play or having a winning team. Actually, these adults share, at least vicariously, in the thrills and satisfactions which their charges experience directly. Furthermore, this same enjoyment is widely felt by adults who stand on the sidelines as spectators.

Adult interest in and enjoyment of play and games are not limited to directing and observing children at play. For many adults, play is a part of their regular routine of living. It may be experienced in connection with their occupations, their religious organizations, or their friendship groups. Aside from these sources, however, adults frequently satisfy their play interest through participation in various activities especially established for this purpose. Thus, bowling alleys, pool rooms, golf courses and dance halls are widely patronized. Obviously these examples of play activities do not exhaust the list of diversions through which adults get their enjoyment and relaxation.

For the American adult, productivity in the economic sense is one of the principal social expectations. Moreover, if one is to enjoy the good things in life and get ahead, he must work. Laziness, or idleness, or wasting one's time is to be shunned. Therefore, because adult play is non-productive, it has to be justified. This justification of the economically non-productive activities of adults is implied in reactions regarding the need for relaxation, the creative use of leisure time, and the physical benefits derived from play and exercise. Since opportunities for play are widely commercialized, it is also justified in the fact that such play constitutes an economic enterprise. The widespread participation of adults in play activities and the social sanctions which support this participation combine to make play a significant part of American social life.

The continuity of the play orientation developed during childhood does not end in the play activities of adults; rather, it is increasingly regarded as desirable and even necessary in the life experiences of the aged. Thus, persons who have passed the prime of life and are no longer productive can sometime spend much of their time in play or the pursuit of pleasure. Consistent with this emphasis, adults are encouraged to prepare for old age by developing hobbies of various sorts. In an effort to promote this kind of preparation, settlement houses and other agencies conduct classes in arts and crafts, and they continually point up the virtues of being able to play and relax throughout life.

PLAY AND MASS COMMUNICATION

The mass media of communication provide a service which is based largely on its entertainment, excitement, and escape potential. The extension of lines of mass communication into the homes of many people perhaps adds a new dimension to the socialization process. In addition to its play or entertainment value, mass communication probably exerts some influence upon the child's total personality. Just what that influence is, however, is a question which has not yet been answered. One study has been designed to test the hypothesis that "children will spend more time watching television if they are highly frustrated in real life than if they are not." The findings were, at best, suggestive of further study. The two principal findings were

1. In the upper-middle class, the children who are highly frustrated in their current home life . . . spend the most time viewing television programs.
2. In the upper-lower class, there is little or no relationship between frustration and TV viewing in children.

In commenting upon these findings, the researchers [11] observe that "in the upper-lower class, where the parents spend a good deal of time watching TV, there is more positive motivation for a child to watch television, so that a child will be drawn to it even in the absence of frustration because it is a dominant activity of the family circle. In the upper-middle class, the effects of frustration may be seen more clearly, because, in the absence of frustration, the child is drawn away from television."

Whatever the precise effects of television, or any of the other mass media, they have subjected the people of the United States to a barrage of information, ideas, models, and suggested courses of behavior. This

[11] Eleanor E. Maccoby, "Why Do Children Watch Television?" Jerome M. Seidman, ed., *The Child* (New York, Holt, Rinehart and Winston, 1962), pp. 349–355. By permission of *The Public Opinion Quarterly*.

has been true of children no less than of adults. For children, the comics, the movies, radio and television have increasingly come to be important media of instruction and entertainment. Although the nature and degree of influence which these forces exert on children have not been determined, it is clear that they appeal to them. This is due not only to the direct impact of these media but perhaps also to the fact that adult society gives great prestige and support to them. For example, children often observe that their parents and other adults follow the fashions set by movie and television stars, look to news commentators for political direction, and rely upon physical education experts for weight control and other health measures.

Another indirect influence exerted upon children by mass media is that many parents rely heavily upon advice on child-rearing given through books, newspapers, radio, and television. Instead of relying on tradition for knowledge about feeding schedules, handling sibling conflicts, allotting allowances, or teaching sex information, some parents depend on these communication media. These indirect influences, along with those which result from the child's direct involvement in reading, listening, and viewing, are forces which might help greatly in the determination of the course of his development.

Apart from their individual interests and consumption of the contents of mass media, children are collectively, systematically, and selectively served these contents by the public school system. In many schools throughout the country regular use is made of movies and television both for purposes of teaching and recreation. In addition, magazines and newspapers are widely used as supplemental teaching materials. Finally, the drama classes and clubs, the school newspapers, and the public speaking programs in many schools, provide many children—sometimes even younger children—with countless opportunities for learning and enjoyment.

CONTINUITY IN PLAY, GAMES, AND WORK

The differentiation of people into various statuses has implications for the principal activities in which they are expected to be engaged. Ideally, the male is the breadwinner and the female, the homemaker. These roles are complementary and therefore both are important. But what of the child who is non-responsible and non-productive—who spends his time at play? As already indicated, the manifest function of play is to build sound bodies and minds and to promote the enjoyment of the period of childhood. It is obvious, however, that children will eventually assume adult roles and this requires preparation.

Even a casual examination of children's play and games reveals that they have something in common with the work activities of adults. Play and games involve values, attitudes, norms, roles, and skills as do adult work activities, and these are sometimes transmittable to work patterns. Some of the tools with which children play are often used in work performed by adults. Finally, children often play in teams, and quite commonly adults work in teams; children play with trucks, tractors, trains, model planes, and chemistry sets—and dolls; adults work with these—and babies. These parallels in the play patterns of children and the work patterns of adults differ quantitatively and, of course, are not qualitatively identical. Furthermore, the possible connection or continuity between play and work patterns is not consciously considered by children; nor is this connection emphasized by adults. Yet, it is there.

The parallel or interconnection between play and work has been widely noted and discussed.[12] Since work is de-energizing and play is restorative, this interconnection is to be expected. It is evidenced in various areas of commercial recreation and in amateur athletics, including college football which has at times been defined as "play for pay." The mutual penetration of work and play has recently become especially evident. "Work tends to be permeated with behavior formerly confined to afterwork hours. Play conversely tends to be measured by standards of achievement previously applicable only to work. One asks oneself not only in personal relations but now also at work: Did they like me? Did I make a good impression? and at play, no less than at work, one asks: Am I doing as well as I should?"[13]

Children are introduced to the work world of adults in their play and games. Through their make-believe, they indicate a knowledge and, to some extent, an understanding of the nature and implications of certain occupational activities. At first, young children frequently say they want to be or play at being firemen, policemen, and cowboys. Later, they begin to talk of being engineers, doctors, and lawyers. It is perhaps significant that the play of young boys seldom involves the lower-job levels, such as garbage collector, street cleaner, and handy man. Significant also is the fact that young girls play at the occupational roles ascribed to females. The little girl who says she wants to be or plays at being even a doctor would probably cause raised eyebrows or the statement "She'll grow out of it."

It is no coincidence that the work roles chosen by children for their occupationally-oriented play activities are consistent with the division of labor based on sex. Neither is it coincidental that the more prestigeful jobs are more frequently chosen. Since sex differentiation is an essential

[12] See David Riesman, *et. al.*, *The Lonely Crowd* (New Haven, Yale University Press, 1950).
[13] Martha Wolfenstein, "The Emergence of Fun Morality," Eric Larrabee and Rolf Meyersohn, eds., *Mass Leisure* (New York, The Free Press of Glencoe, Inc., 1958), p. 93. By permission of the Macmillan Company.

objective of the socialization of the child, such choices are facilitated by adults who teach children the play-work activities appropriate to each sex and reward them when they learn. Fathers sometimes permit their sons to watch them at work and even let them help; mothers do the same for their daughters. On the other hand, children are dissuaded from engaging in play-work activities not appropriate to their sex. Thus, early in their lives little boys are discouraged from playing with dolls, from "cooking," or from "housecleaning." In like manner, little girls are not encouraged to have paper routes, climb trees, or build houses.

The child playing alone or in a game with other children is having fun and enjoying himself, but he may be doing much more than this. He may be acquiring experiences, insights, attitudes, and skills which will, to some degree, serve him well in some future occupational endeavor. He may not be conscious of this, and sometimes neither are his parents, but the transfer of learning from today's play to tomorrow's work is much more than a possibility.

The connection between children's play and adult work as it occurs in the United States is not altogether by design, nor is it generally recognized or emphasized. Whatever contributions children's play activities make to their occupational choices and preparation may at best be regarded as a latent function. This is suggested in the widely expressed view that children should not concern themselves with family problems. Thus, parents tend not to discuss their financial difficulties within earshot of their children. If, however, a child should hear such comments and express concern, parents usually attempt to reassure him with responses such as, "Now don't worry your little head about that." In most family situations children are to be protected against such concern or involvement, and the concession or the subterfuge "You can go out and play now" is frequently used to bring about such protection.

In contrast to the situation in the United States, where children's time is consumed largely in school and in play and games, some societies make definite provisions for work experiences for children. Furthermore, such experiences are not regarded as mere training devices, rather they are designed largely for the utilitarian purposes they actually serve.

Samoan children do not learn to work through play. . . . Nor are they permitted a period of lack of responsibility such as our children are allowed. From the time they are four or five years old they perform definite tasks, graded to their strength and intelligence, but still tasks which have a meaning in the structure of the whole society. This does not mean that they have less time for play than American children who are shut up in schools from nine to three o'clock everyday.[14]

[14] Margaret Mead, *Coming of Age in Samoa* (New York, William Morrow and Company, Inc.), p. 133. Copyright © 1928, 1955, 1961 by Margaret Mead.

Work patterning for children, such as reported to have existed in Samoa, can have both immediate utility and training potential. Thus, while the child is performing the work role appropriate to himself, as a child, he is perhaps acquiring a sense of responsibility which might well continue into his future work role as an adult.

In the United States, the work done by children is, by comparison with Samoa, significantly different. Generally, very young children do not have home-job assignments. From time to time, however, the five- or six-year old might be asked to do something for his mother. Some older children do have regular home chores to do, however, the definitions of these chores tend to vary. Thus, finishing the chores first is a prerequisite to being permitted to go out to play. Again, having to wash dishes is sometimes regarded by the boy as an onerous task which does violence to his maleness. Or, to have to work at home when the kids next door do nothing but play might be defined by the victim as a gross injustice.

Often older children who work regularly, do so for pay: for an allowance if the work is done for the family, or for a wage if the worker is a newsboy or a babysitter. Ultimately, however, the end in both situations tends to be the accumulation of spending money, and work as a value is perhaps secondary, if important at all.

Summary

Participation in play and games is a personally and socially significant aspect of childhood experiences. Initially, the young child tends to be rather completely absorbed in individualized play. As he matures and becomes more autonomous, he engages in collective play or games. Except for attendance at school, the activities of children in the United States are oriented principally toward play activities. But even in the school system, play is widely utilized both as an end in itself and a means to learning. Thus, the interests and energies of children—especially the young—tend to be directed mainly toward play, while those of adults are directed principally toward work.

With regard to play activities, children appear to be the principal participants and adults the principal promoters. As a result, children come to be oriented to play and this orientation continues into and throughout adulthood. During adulthood this same orientation is expressed through the promotion of play among the new generation of children. But adult interest in play is not confined to promoting play among children; it is also manifested in overt behavior involving play and games adapted to adult needs and interests.

Finally, children tend to be preoccupied with play activities. Nonetheless, adults also participate in—and provide supporting sanctions for—

their own specialized play activities. As a consequence of this cross-generational continuity, play has come to be a firmly established and socially significant component of the social structure of the United States.

READINGS

ALPENFELS, Ethel J., "Work and Play as Seen by an Anthropologist," *Childhood Education,* Vol. 25 (1948), pp. 149–152.

CLIFT, Virgil A., "Recreational and Leisure-Time Problems and Needs of Negro Children and Youth," *Journal of Negro Education,* Vol. 19 (1950), pp. 333–340.

COHEN, John, "Ideas of Work and Play," *British Journal of Sociology* Vol. 4 (1953), pp. 312–322.

FRANK, Lawrence K., "Play in Personality Development," *American Journal of Orthopsychiatry,* Vol. 24 (1955), pp. 576–590.

HAVIGHURST, Robert J., *et al.,* "Leisure Activities and the Socio-economic Status of Children," *American Journal of Sociology,* Vol. LIV (1948), pp. 505–519.

PIAGET, Jean, *The Moral Judgment of the Child* (New York, Harcourt, Brace & World, Inc., 1932).

ROBBINS, Florence Greenhoe, *The Sociology of Play, Recreation, and Leisure* (Dubuque, Iowa, Wm. C. Brown Company, Publishers, 1955).

SEAGOE, May V., "Children's Play as an Indicator of Cultural and Intra-Cultural Differences," *Journal of Educational Sociology,* Vol. 35, No. 6 (February, 1962), pp. 278–283.

SULLENGER, T. Earl, *et al.,* "The Leisure Time Activities of Elementary School Children," *Journal of Educational Research,* Vol. 46 (1953), pp. 551–554.

WERTHAM, Fredric, *Seduction of the Innocent* (New York, Holt, Rinehart & Winston, Inc., 1954).

IV

*HAZARDS, OBSTACLES,
POTENTIAL DIFFICULTIES
IN SOCIALIZATION*

15

The Child
and Culture Symbols

INTRODUCTION

The path of socialization is strewn with obstacles, hazards, impediments, or potential difficulties that make the process far from easy, or free from awkwardness. Children are being introduced to a strange, often baffling, society that has accumulated intricate structures and seemingly devious ways. Even to the adults in the society, there are puzzling and troublesome procedures, and they find their way frequently only by reason of bitter experience or sheer good fortune. Experience and awareness have forewarned them of cultural inconsistencies and complexities, the twists and the turns, the bypasses and shortcuts, the subtleties and the innuendoes, the consequences and repercussions, as well as the essence of appropriate actions with all their nuances. Children do not have the advantages of experience and often move ahead blissfully unaware of complicated matrices until such time as an encounter with cultural intricacies converts their naïveté into chastened and wiser maturity. Often lessons come in the form of failures and deep emotional hurts which may cripple them for life. Mental illness is too frequently the price of imperfect socialization. Sooner or later, children are expected to meet cultural expectations or suffer the consequences of being identified as misfits.

Herein culture symbols are examined as the first of a series of topics characterized as hazards, obstacles, or potential difficulties in the process of socialization. Chapters to follow will deal with selected sensitive areas, such as sex, race, and religion, autonomy and emerging responsibility, and finally, some deviant end-products of socialization. No implication is intended, in this array, that culture symbols constitute an area of greater importance than the topics that follow. The use of culture symbols constitutes simply a context of general significance and probably should,

221

therefore, be given first consideration before more specific matters are studied.

Learning A Language

The vehicle or device that carries much of the cultural content and conveys it to young learners is language. Familiarity and mastery of language is one of the characteristics that differentiates between children and their elders. It is not strange that elementary or fundamental education is concerned with the three "r's," reading, writing, and 'rithmetic. The greater the skill linguistically, the greater the chances are that the individual has come to grips with whatever the culture contains. Language is the essential connecting link between the learner and much that is to be learned. The acquisition of language, however, often may not be easy.

Sturtevant[1] succinctly defines language as "a system of arbitrary vocal symbols by which members of a social group cooperate and interact." Among the key words in this definition is the word "arbitrary." The symbols used vary from group to group and are the end-products of a usually long history of chance circumstances. They are not so sacrosanct that they could not be altered and may conceivably be accorded the same sense or meaning. Probably, the assertion that "a rose by any other name would smell as sweet" covers the capricious nature of linguistic symbolism.

A most insightful or ingenious example of linguistic symbolism is provided by McKee's substitution[2] of a series of geometrical designs for the English alphabet symbols. They appear as follows:

A B C D E F G H I J K L M
+ ⊓ ✕ ⊔ ⊗ △ ⋒ ⊏ ⋃ ⋂ ⅃ ∨ ⊕

N O P Q R S T U V W X Y Z
♂ ✢ = ‖ ⌐ ⊥ ∧ ⊸ ⊶ ⊷ — ⊇ |

Under McKee's system, a sentence such as, "Look, son, I just found a stray puppy," would look like this:

∨⊕⊕⅃, ⊥⊕♂, ⋃ ⊓⊸⊥∧ △⊕⊸♂⊔ + ⊥∧⊓⊕⊇ =⊸∘==⊇.

The symbols look weird and possibly could severely handicap those who may try to memorize the system and put them together in some meaningful way. But this is precisely what happens to children who are expected to learn the arbitrary symbols of the English alphabet! The shape or

[1] Edgar H. Sturtevant, *An Introduction to Linguistic Science* (New Haven, Conn., Yale University Press, 1947), p. 2.
[2] Paul McKee, *The Teaching of Reading in the Elementary School* (Boston, Houghton Mifflin Company, 1948), p. 24.

form of the letters must be memorized laboriously and then put together in some approved grammatical form.

Sturtevant[3] describes a perfect alphabet as one that has one symbol and only one for each phoneme or speech sound. He[4] says that "a number of European alphabets come near enough to it so that children, once they learn to write, need not waste any appreciable further time learning to spell." Nevertheless, there remains enough silent letters or groupings of letters that change their sounds seemingly indiscriminately and these will continue to plague young learners for many years to come, unless some drastic change occurs. Instructing children to spell by sounding a word, that is, phonic spelling, may have its advantages, but it also conflicts with the variant ways a given symbol or group of symbols are sounded in society.

The combination of the letters "ough" is an excellent case in point. The word *bough* sounds this combination of symbols as "ow." The word *though* changes it to sound like "o." Writing the word *through,* the same group of letters now take on the sound of "oo." The word *rough* uses the combination of "ough" to sound like "uff." If the word is *cough,* then the combination is sounded as "awff." Finally, if the combination appears in the word *hiccough,* it can be pronounced as "up." Thus, there are, at least, six different sounds for the combination "ough." These variations exist and require no defense other than to say, "This is the way we do things," and it would be wise if children committed them to memory without probing questions which demand a defensible logic.

Symbols can be described as being in the place of or representing something else. In themselves, they are unimportant, but for what they represent, they are most important in the acquisition of human knowledge. They are abstractions from reality and hence become refined, specialized signs that do not require direct experience to transpire before lessons may be learned. Take the word *war* for example. A student does not necessarily have to have had military duty in combat in order to derive some understanding of the nature of modern warfare and its effects. As a child, he may witness a movie, look at some still pictures, visit a museum filled with guns or armaments, study some models of planes, tanks, or missiles, see a play, or read a story that has a war theme. The symbol, war, once presented and understood, calls to mind all these experiences and their ramifications. If learning is alleged to be acquired chiefly through direct experience, educational pursuits may conceivably be slow and probably accompanied by much greater pain than young learners now pretend to associate with it.

William Graham Sumner in his classic *Folkways*[5] wrote along similar

[3] Sturtevant, *op. cit.,* p. 24.
[4] *Ibid.*
[5] William Graham Sumner, *Folkways* (Boston, Ginn and Company, 1940), Mentor Book, 1960, pp. 126–128.

lines. Excerpts, such as the following, highlight the point of the arbitrary nature of language and the subsequent confusion that can occur for children in their attempts to comprehend and master it.

How can a child understand the combinations of sound and sense when it must know language in order to learn them? It must learn to speak without knowing previously how to speak, without any previous suspicion that the words of its mother mean more than the buzzing of a fly.

Every vocable was to us (children) an arbitrary and conventional sign; arbitrary, because anyone of a thousand other vocables could have been just as easily learned by us and associated with the same idea; conventional, because the one we acquired had its sole ground and sanction in the consenting use of the community of which we formed a part. We do not, as children, make our language for ourselves. We get it by tradition, all complete. We think in sentences. As our language forms sentences, that is, as our mother-tongue thinks, so we learn to think.

Much humor has been found in the fumbling manner with which children try to break through language barriers. From the vantage point of adulthood, these childish attempts to communicate are hilarious, appealing, and delightful because they reflect the innocence of children and their inexperience with various shades of meaning. Whenever linguistic errors are committed by young children, they are accepted, generally, as concomitants of the process of learning. One may possibly laugh about ridiculing children for their almost inevitable linguistic mistakes. Made at this early stage of their social development, these slips of the tongue may be viewed as normal and acceptable. To persist in such errors at later stages, however, could be serious and pressure might be applied to eliminate them before they become habitual through usage. In association with age-grading, naïveté is expected among the young, but beyond childhood, innocence could be appraised as intolerable.

THE MEANING OF WORDS

Just as there is a problem with the failure of an alphabet to provide a single sound for a single symbol or combination of symbols, so there is a problem with the meaning of words. The French have an expression to cover this difficulty by referring to it as *double-entendre*. In the English language, the appropriate term would probably be ambiguity or multiple intent or implications. In maturity, adults deal with the problem by carefully choosing their words. From a vast store of words in their vocabulary, adults have the tremendous advantage of selecting an appropriate word to express their idea. The limited nature of children's vocabulary increases the chances that their choice of words will fall short of the desired thoughts. Indeed, the precision desired between communicants within scientific disciplines is slowly emerging, even in modern times. To expect the precise use of words among children is to expect too much.

There are numerous examples of linguistic ambiguity and the following may serve as examples. No doubt, these examples could be multiplied a hundredfold.

1. "Outside"

In the first grade, a child asked for permission to get a drink of water from the water-fountain located in the hallway. The teacher, apparently disturbed that there would be an interruption of her lesson with the class, reluctantly granted the request, but added the comment, "You will have to stay *outside* until I call for you. I cannot have children going in and out of the room when I am teaching." The term "outside" had only one meaning to the child and that was "out-of-doors" or outside the building. Because it was a cold, wintry day, the child was dismayed that he would have to stand outside the building after getting his drink. Without protesting, however, being accustomed to authoritative commands, the child satisfied his thirst and went promptly outside the building to await the arrival of his teacher. Lacking a coat, the chilly weather became too much to endure and the little fellow ran over to the home of a nearby relative. Shortly thereafter, when the child was missed by the teacher, the whole school was practically in an uproar searching frantically for the lost child.

This incident is not fictitious and illustrates the inability of children to grasp the connotation of words despite some familiarity with their denotative qualities. Words have meaning in context and much depends upon the referent. Had the teacher been specific and said, "Remain *outside* of the classroom and *inside* the hallway," perhaps the child would never have taken the action he did. Referent items with which to associate various words can be acquired in time, but children are handicapped by inexperience.

2. "Cat"

The word "cat" is frequently cited as among the earliest terms understood by many children. Yet, this simple noun does not merely represent or symbolize a small, domesticated, soft-furred, feline, purring, meowing, mice-chasing, lithe creature often observed as a household pet. It could refer to much larger, carnivorous mammals such as lions, tigers, cougars, jaguars, or leopards. It may be used to describe a woman who makes spiteful remarks about a person without that person's knowledge. Construction workers have called their caterpillar tractors or earthmovers "cats." Teenagers have used the identical symbol for a talented dancer. Or, it can have the same meaning as "secret," when one speaks of "letting the cat out of the bag." With so many possibilities, children could easily commit a *faux pas* which could be quite embarrassing.

3. *"Cuscus"*

An interesting experiment has been conducted by Ralph Hall, former Director of the Audio-Visual Center, Kent State University. Taking the noun "cuscus" at random, he copied the full description of this animal as found in a large, standard dictionary. Submitting this description to elementary school children in the vicinity, he requested that they draw a picture of a cuscus in one of their art classes. The sketches followed the description of a cuscus faithfully, but not one drawing was accurate or true-to-life. Far too often, adults regard a dictionary as tantamount to a linguistic bible to be followed faithfully. Of course, dictionary definitions are useful tools, but it does help to have prior knowledge before one attempts to maximize their benefits.

4. *"Post-office"*

A study of an isolated, folk society in the Blue Ridge Mountains yielded the following:

The children were asked to define a "post-office." The majority of those who tried to define this word said that a post-office was a place with a basket of apples in front of it. Some added further details, such as, "and some men sitting at the door." They had seen the post-office in Oakton Hollow which is the general store. Not one directly associated mail with the definition of post-office, probably because mail rarely comes into Colvin Hollow.[6]

5. *"Formation"*

A father, wishing to inform his young son about modern aircraft, pointed to four airplanes flying overhead and remarked, "Look, son, there is a formation of airplanes!" Some time later, the same young boy, proudly proving he had learned from his father, upon seeing two planes flying together, pointed to them and said, "Look, father, a two-mation!"[7]

6. *"Equator"*

No doubt, this a familiar case, but it does illustrate how children can follow their teachers faithfully and still be laboring under a misappre-

[6] Mandel Sherman and Thomas R. Henry, *Hollow Folk* (New York, Thomas Y. Crowell Company, 1933), p. 124.
[7] Sturtevant, *op. cit.*, p. 98.

hension. The incident is reputed to be the reply of a child, when asked to tell what the word "equator" means. The child proudly answered, "An equator is a menagerie lion running around the center of the earth." The child's definition closely followed the sounds uttered by his teacher, but did not quite grasp the symbol as intended.

7. "Upset"

A little girl was tipping her chair back from the breakfast table and her father warned her, "Please, honey, don't tip the chair back so far, you may upset it." The little girl innocently replied, "It's all right, Daddy. The chair won't have a nervous breakdown."

8. "Wrong"

A three year old child was told by her mother that she had placed the slippers she was wearing upon the wrong feet. Sadly, she told her mother, "But, Mommy, these are the only feet I have!" [8]

9. "Yes" or "No"

These words act much in the manner of traffic lights: they convey to children permission to go ahead or to stop whatever they are doing. But children soon learn that "yes" or "no" are not necessarily associated with definite permission or definite refusal of activity. Almost with the ability of a brilliant lawyer, children can find loopholes that provide a reasonable basis for whatever behavior or goals they wish to pursue. Thus, a "No!" can become the signal for such strategy as, "I shall try elsewhere—my other parent, my grandparents, a friend, or an easy-going neighbor." Or a "Yes!" can be interpreted to mean, "I am free to do whatever I please," rather than as it was intended by an exasperated mother who said "Yes" because she meant to say, "Yes, please let me be free from your constant annoyances, your begging, or your nagging."

CONCEPTS

Not only are linguistic symbols ambiguous, but when placed together to express an idea or concept, they can become quite confusing to neophytes. In acquiring languages, quite frequently idioms are lost to learners because they have studied the formal structures and neglected the informal ones. In the process of being socialized, one has first to become

---

[8] Reprinted from *The Secret World of Kids* by Art Linkletter with the permission of Bernard Geis Associates, publishers, © 1959, by Art Linkletter, p. 260.

acquainted with various rules before he may learn just where they may be broken or where they do not apply. Concepts are ideas that are held by members of a particular society. They are the special cultural ways of looking at phenomena and deriving some specific meaning from them. Depending on one's grasp of how a particular society views situations, one is either able to function cooperatively and effectively with other societal members or not. Children, particularly, are somewhat handicapped in their progress towards societal membership because their comprehension of their culture is comparatively minimal.

The following are a few examples taken from the American culture in which those who are unfamiliar with the culture need further experience and understanding before concepts can become clear and/or useful:

1. Being polite and courteous

A foreign student in a major state university came storming into the office of the advisor for foreign students quite indignant and distressed over an experience in the Registrar's Office. The student demanded, "Is it or is it not customary in this country, when someone has done something for a person, that it is proper for that person to thank the other person for his kindness?" The advisor, puzzled, agreed that this was the courteous thing to do. "Then why," asked the unhappy student, "when I thanked the clerk in the Registrar's Office for helping me register for my classes, did she tell me, 'Don't mention it!'?"

Children experience this same confusion of being polite and courteous. Why should a child have to say, "Please" and "Thank you"? Why should a child shake some stranger's hand? Why should a child kiss some strange woman he never saw before who is introduced to him as his aunt? Why should children take turns and share their toys? Reluctance to perform according to the wishes and instructions of their parents is understandable on the part of children. Therefore, much more has to be provided than blind obedience. If the accepted procedure is to submit to the will of older people, then children may be still puzzled but will conform nevertheless. If, however, as in the American society, thoughtful behavior or behavior based upon reason is allegedly preferred to submission, then considerable explanation and patience are necessary to secure the desired action. Deference to culture symbols such as a cross, a flag, a star of David, or a policeman's badge, do not come naturally, but spring from some comprehension, additional background, and continued usage.

2. A case of unusual posture

A little boy named Ricky was walking through an elementary school corridor with his abdomen pushed out. He was intercepted by a teacher who inquired why he assumed this extraordinary posture. Ricky explained that he had a troublesome stomach-ache early that morning when school began. He approached the principal and asked for some relief. The principal told Ricky that he would be able to take him home at noon, but he would "have to stick it out 'til then." This, Ricky was faithfully doing.[9]

3. "I'm going to leave you."

Children depend highly upon their parents for a sense of security. Their absence can pose a real threat to their existence, especially when very young. A nursery school child was found crying on the porch steps one summer day. The teacher tried to console him but without much success. It took much prying to uncover the real cause of his deep grief. His father had deserted his mother and when his mother had left him for the morning, she had mentioned something about "leaving him." His interpretation of this remark was that not only had his father left him behind, but now, the same pattern would be followed by his mother, and he was all alone in the world. The possibility of "leaving" someone and then coming back did not occur to him and he felt that his secure world was now completely shattered.

4. "Stay in line."

While some children will look for loopholes in directives, others will obey quite literally whatever instructions are given them. A teacher, thinking in terms of school efficiency, told her charges that when the bell rings for dismissal at the end of the school day, they were to line up, single file, and "stay in line" until they left the front doors of the school. Further, they were not to loiter, but to return home promptly so their mothers would not worry about them. One little boy arrived home quite promptly, but a bit apprehensive, expecting a scolding or a spanking, because his trousers were wet. He really had to use the washroom before he left school that day, but without protesting, he had "stayed in line" and marched out of school as ordered by his teacher.

5. Going to school

There is a certain joy and anticipation on the part of many youngsters about attending school for the first time. However, the novelty effect, or the "honeymoon period" soon ends when children begin to realize how long they are expected to attend schools. A first grade child told his

[9] Linkletter, *op. cit.*, p. 262.

parents upon his return from his first day in classes, "Well, that's that. I've been to school. I'm finished now!" When the parents explained that there are many more days to follow before he has passed the first grade, he began to wonder about what lies beyond that grade level. "What happens after first grade? Am I finished then?" It took quite a while to make it clear that there were quite a few grades ahead for him, and even after twelve grades, there may be more educational levels to reach. It is no simple matter to make certain that children gain some perspective of the long roads that lie ahead. No doubt, the younger children with older siblings are in an advantageous position to assess what is expected of them because their brothers and sisters have gone ahead and indicated their future path. The only child has no such guides except by close observation of other children in the neighborhood.

6. Going to bed

In infancy, children, generally, welcome sleep or bedtime. There comes a time, however, when going to bed appears to them to be a sign of their youth and that staying up late is the prerogative of older people. Some parents report how versatile children are at stalling the inevitable pressure to go to bed and sleep. They want a drink of water or a good-night kiss. They may want a story or they decide that this is about the strategic time to discuss their plans for the future. Or, they forgot to brush their teeth or wash their face and hands. Finally, they may ask why parents don't go to sleep the same time children do. Don't older people need sleep too?

7. Paying for items

Children have observed how their parents move about a supermarket and place various items in their carts. Of course, there will be cash registers at the end of the line and their parents will have to pay for whatever is in the carts. This latter situation either escapes them or remains, for a time, a mystery or some adult activity of no consequence. What they do remember is the former situation and how the grocery items became their own. Thus, it is not uncommon to find a small child valiantly "helping" his mother with her shopping by placing the nearest available bit of merchandise in the metal cart. It does not matter what the item may be or its cost. It only matters that whatever you place in the cart somehow appears later in your own home and this is the crux of the matter. Explanations of the money system, honesty, and profits and losses are concepts that await a more mature period when dollar and cents symbols take on some meaning.

8. Street numbers and locations

When one of the writers was a little boy, his father happened to see him entering a candy store along one of the major streets of the city. Instead of weighing his words, that is, making certain that his son knew the meaning of his statement, the father asked, "What were you doing on E. 123rd Street yesterday afternoon?" The reply was a puzzled denial, "I wasn't on 123rd Street yesterday!!" The father, thinking he had caught his son in a deliberate lie, proceeded severely to scold him for being a liar. It took a great deal of discussion to bring out the fact that the child, at that age, did not know the numbering system for streets in the city and was completely unaware that the candy store was located on a given street numbered as E. 123rd. There are times when ignorance may be bliss, but in front of a wrathful father, knowledge would have been much more helpful.

The world is a big one to a small child and how to find one's way around presents frequent dilemmas. Landmarks, guidelines, reference points, compass directions, distances, and various twists and turns must become familiar aids rather than perplexing ideas that serve to confuse the young and uninitiated. It is a sign of real progress to be able to walk from one's home to school and back again safely. Prolonged trips over other routes wait until the child has acquired such navigational skills as reading a signpost, observing traffic regulations, or following a highway on an automobile map. Adults can gain some sympathy for children in this matter if they ever become strangers in a city or a foreign land.

QUALITIES NEEDED TO UNDERSTAND CULTURE SYMBOLS

Three qualities seem to stand out as essential in understanding the significance of culture symbols. These characteristics would smooth the process of socialization, and would remove or reduce the hazards associated with culture symbolism or enable children to bypass them without difficulty. These qualities are patience, pondering, and pain.

The first quality, patience, is needed because understanding the fullest possible meanings of a symbol requires time for absorption. Ideas that took centuries for a whole society to develop cannot be digested immediately by little children. A number of children report that an idea introduced to them when quite young finally "dawned" on them later on. The ability to comprehend culture symbols which are foreign to the limited experience of children requires the passage of time. Teachers can merely plant the seed of an idea, but the flowering of that idea may come at a time, place, and circumstance long after the teacher has passed from the scene. Patience on the part of both teacher and student goes a long way towards appreciation of cultural symbolism.

The second quality, pondering, is required because thought must be expended or invested before a given abstraction can acquire significance. Whatever the stimulus and whatever the avenues by which cultural symbols are introduced, they must eventually be intellectually savored. They must be considered along with the store of knowledge already acquired and filed for future reference. They must be called up again and again in order not to lie dormant and useless. Ideas must be sharpened by contact with other ideas before their points can become functional.

The final quality, pain, is suggested not because it must be associated with cultural abstractions, but because learning is not necessarily a joyous, easy examination of interesting phenomena, but often a rigorous, tough, and demanding operation. Sacrifice, hardship, and agony may not be pleasant companions in gaining insights, but knowledge thus attained is rarely forgotten. Whether it be the meaning of money or the gaining of an education, to have received these too easily can make them matter-of-fact rather than deeply appreciated and precious. One does not have to work at making learning difficult, but if it has been difficult, the surmounting of difficulties often leads to appreciation.

SUMMARY

Initiating the first of a series of discussions on the obstacles, hazards, or impediments in the path of socialization, this chapter dealt with the mastery of culture symbols. These symbols are derived or distilled from actual experiences of mankind and are bequeathed to children as part of their cultural heritage. Language was particularly noted for its problems: the development of an alphabet, the combination of various letters into words, and the combination of words into concepts. Their arbitrary nature and the increased chance for confusion were underscored. Selected examples, acknowledged as only a few of the numerous possibilities, were presented and the humorous and not-so-humorous results were highlighted. Finally, it was suggested that patience, pondering, and pain were three qualities that either enhanced the process of socialization or enabled children to avoid or remove difficulties in their progress towards maturity.

READINGS

BLOCH, Bernard, and TRAGER, George L., *Outline of Linguistic Analysis* (Baltimore, Linguistic Society of America, 1942).

BLOOMFIELD, Leonard, *Language*, rev. ed. (New York, Holt, Reinhart & Winston, Inc., 1940).

BLUMENTHAL, Albert, *Small-Town Stuff* (Chicago, The University of Chicago Press, 1932).

MILLER, George A., *Language and Communication* (New York, McGraw-Hill Book Company, Inc., 1951).

MORRIS, Charles, *Signs, Language, and Behavior* (Englewood Cliffs, N.J., Prentice-Hall Inc., 1946).

PEI, Mario, *The Story of Language* (Philadelphia, J. B. Lippincott Company, 1949).

WHITE, Leslie, "The Origin and Nature of Speech," in William S. Knickerbocker, ed., *Twentieth Century English* (New York, Philosophical Library, 1940), pp. 93–103.

WILLIAMS, H. M., McFARLAND, M. L., and LITTLE, M. F., *Development of Language and Vocabulary in Young Children* (Iowa City, University of Iowa Press, 1937).

16

Sensitive Areas:
Sex, Race, and Religion

INTRODUCTION

It is with considerable trepidation that *some* parents and other people associated with the socio-cultural training of children approach certain facets of socialization. There are *other* parents who are confident that whatever *they* do with their children is above reproach or is "right" for them. They proceed fearlessly or, at least, unabashed by criticism from members of the "out-group." A pluralistic, mixed class, highly differentiated society such as in the United States does not necessarily follow a single set of values or norms. It is always a decision for those engaged in sociological analyses to determine if they will draw their data from a specific group and confine their observations to this group or if they desire to describe the maximum number of societal participants, aware that whatever generalizations are developed have notable qualifications. It is with the latter decision that the analyses that follow should be identified. Unless otherwise specified, then, the discussion of sensitive areas in socialization, by conscious choice, applies to what has been popularly called "WUMP" samples; white, urban, middle class, Protestants, the "majority group" in the United States.

The selected sensitive areas of sex, race, and religion constitute the bulk of the ensuing discussion. It should be noted that "race," in this chapter, is not intended to be confined to any single, specific, physical typing, but is broadened to include minority groups on a variety of bases, such as ethnic or religious differences.

No doubt, there are those parents who would say that for them, sex, race, and religion were not troublesome because they dealt with these subjects without trauma, without fear, or without pain. Such persons are fortunate indeed, and a study of their cases might prove to be most instructive. Other parents, however, do encounter considerable grief, anguish, and trouble with these matters. It is the children of these parents who deserve attention and whatever understanding can thus be achieved.

Sex, race, and religion have been at the center of massive social upheavals, unrest, and even bloodshed. In a sense, there has been mutual agreement among some people to close these areas off from any further investigation, any further debate, or any further change. A *status quo* is frequently reached on these topics and becomes practically sacrosanct. Objections to conditions as they exist are tantamount to heresy. But culture changes. Systems that establish certain patterns dealing with sex, race, and religion are generally changed gradually, almost imperceptibly, so that surface appearances are maintained and the guardians of established morality are not alarmed. The changes may be so subtle, that not until children have matured are any departures from established norms detected.

Those who have major influences in child rearing represent not so much the present as they do the past. A generation or more removed from childhood, parents, grandparents, and their surrogates have often acquired views and actions which they attempt to inculcate into their children. But even with adamant older generations in charge, sex, race, and religion can prove to be difficult. In the first place, children experience, within themselves, a slowly awakening interest in the significance of sex in their lives. Secondly, they do have the opportunity in the pluralistic American society to meet people who hold a wider variety of viewpoints concerning racial issues than is available in their own family. And, finally, children may also become increasingly aware of the range of religious faiths that exist in the society. Under such circumstances, the blandishments or exhortations of their elders may not have as strong an effect upon their lives as their parents may desire.

Out of the welter of industrialization, urbanization, and specialization in the work-place, a more pluralistic configuration of moralities seems to be emerging. Change appears to be at the very heart of the configuration. Thus, experimentation can be anticipated as more characteristic of the conditions under which contemporary American children will be reared in the forseeable future. This will undoubtedly become a cause for alarm among those adults who are committed to specific, unchanging values. It suggests that socialization of the young will be in the direction of ability to cope with shifting and variant values rather than with absolute values.

General Characteristics of Sensitive Areas of Socialization

The common denominators that seem to hold for all the sensitive areas are:

1. Appeal to emotions rather than to intellect
2. Personal privacy
3. Children are regarded as "too young"
4. Considerable social control
5. Pride in the past
6. Fear of change
7. Decisions first, facts later
8. Pretense of individualized choice
9. Adult embarrassment
10. Easier to order than to question

Emotional Appeal

One common thread that is identifiable in these sensitive areas is the fact that they touch upon internalized feeling-states and not, necessarily, upon intellect. That is, one is not required to *think* about reasons for conforming to social definitions about sexual, racial, or religious behavior; rather, one is deeply stirred and urged to *feel* anger, love, humility, pride, generosity, or repugnance to appropriate phenomena. Generally mothers and fathers do not sit down with their children and coldly present the nature of sexuality whether it be between boys and girls, men and women, or between members of the same sex. They express their sexual ideas within an emotional context of considerate acts, fond glances, modest movements, caresses, kisses, scolding, raised eyebrows, frowns, and sighs. Similarly, training in racial issues is not a matter of delivering a lecture on the pros and cons of dealing with members of other races. Children are often instructed by catching the emotional fervor generated by the tone of voice employed, by the facial expression, by the casual comments unconsciously dropped in the presence of children. Religious instruction, too, is carried out in such a manner that children acquire feeling-states involving solemnity, dignity, mystery, power, exuberance, humility, fear, acceptance, or whatever moods are revered in a given faith. Often, instruction in "that other" religion or a contrasting religion is also carried on in a subjective, emotional atmosphere. When attempts are made to logically analyze, to seriously question, or to study the details, the expected reaction is often that this destroys the spirit or heart of the matter.

Personal Privacy

Sex, race, and religion are highly subjective areas because they have to do with individual actions and feelings that are highly personalized. Frequently, one cloaks these areas from public view; to reveal one's self in these areas is to fail to reserve something that is exclusively separate and distinct from all others. Of course, it is true that all human beings are involved in some way in these areas; and in many ways, they are not unique or distinctive. Nevertheless, by maintaining procedures that keep others at a distance, the individual is independent, protected, and assured that his inner dignity is secure. By separation of the sexes, by wearing clothes, and by private rooms, persons may maintain their modesty, their mystery, and their integrity. In this connection, it may be worthwhile to point out Harry Golden's comment [1] that one way that the Nazis used to break the remaining shred of personal dignity that Jews retained, despite pitiless persecution, was to strip them of all their clothes and to force them to walk in the streets in the nude.

In societies such as the United States which hold high the ideals of personal dignity and worth, one does not freely divulge his private reactions to race or to racial issues. One may pay lip service to the ideals of the society, but one can hide or disguise his own viewpoints quite easily. Outright prejudice is a serious problem which demands a prompt answer whenever it crops up. However, much prejudice is of the subtle type that is so carefully masked that sometimes even the prejudiced person is convinced of his magnanimous nature. Here, as with sexual matters, one has to be extremely cautious in exposing private thoughts and feelings.

With respect to religion, each adult person in the American society is supposed to deal with spiritual matters as he pleases. Americans carefully circumvent many conversations that would lead to discussion of the whys and wherefores of a given religious creed. One allegedly has freedom of religious convictions, and others are not to intrude or make invidious distinctions regarding religious beliefs or practices. The personal commitments of an individual are his privilege and others may not sit in judgment when it comes to faiths. Once again, individual privacy is allegedly respected and held inviolable.

Children are "Too Young"

A third quality shared in common by the sensitive areas in socialization is the commonly reiterated declaration of the innocence of children and the subsequent desire to protect them from certain harsh realities until they are "ready." Why begin too early to divulge details of sexual differences and behavior and their tremendous significance, some parents say. Children have enough to learn without being confused by matters in which they have no need to participate until they reach physical and social maturity. Despite this, there seems to be an emerging awareness that perhaps the appropriate attitudes can be introduced earlier in chil-

[1] Reprinted by permission of the World Publishing Company from *Only in America* by Harry Golden (New York, Permabook Edition, 1958), "The Shame of Nakedness," pp. 30–31.

dren's lives without shock, without embarrassment, and without connotations of obscenity or repugnance. One is counseled to approach them at their level when it comes to revealing sexual *secrets*.

This same reluctance applies to racial topics. Where racial considerations are significant, as they are in the United States, too forthright an approach by members of either majority or minority groups may instill in their children, behavior that could get out of control. A similar situation exists for religious information. Foundations are carefully laid before there is a hint to young children that other people uphold dissenting religious views from those of their parents. In fact, religious instruction usually begins and continues for many years without references, if possible, to other religions. Not until children are thoroughly grounded in the religious fundamentals of their families are they likely to be brought into contact with the comparative studies of religion or problems of inter-faith relationships.

Social Control

Evidence of the importance of these areas may be found in the painstaking efforts to guard against or ward off any attempts to tamper with ongoing social structures and procedures relating to them. Severe penalties await those foolhardy enough to challenge the *status quo*. The implication here is not that the *status quo* is satisfactory and should be maintained at all costs; rather, it is that these areas are regarded as fundamental enough to merit close social supervision and attempts to challenge them will not pass unrecognized.

Parents and all those associated with socialization approach these areas with a caution born of the knowledge that "society" is looking over their shoulders and is ready to react violently if the "wrong" move is made. To treat sexual topics fully, to specify different ways to handle interracial contacts, to be disrespectful of religious convictions or to be tolerant of other religions is, for some people, equivalent to removing the foundation stones of the social structure, thus causing its collapse. People tend not to regard this with equanimity. The penalties will fall, not upon the children alone, but upon those responsible for creating such qualities.

Pride in the Past

Interested persons explain that none of these sexual, racial, or religious structures or procedures came overnight. They are the final product of centuries of development. This being the case, those who would devise some procedure that would undermine the crust of custom lack a time-tested formula. Certainly, new ideas may question and test the relationships of males and females or the way in which racial membership or religious dogma is handled, but the innovators have the faith of their convictions without real proof that the newer ways actually will work. Older patterns have proved themselves workable, although not satisfactory to everyone. All is not perfection with either old or new ways of behaving, but many have respect for the durability of old techniques which have accomplished so much over so long a period. Newer ways can offer promises and new hopes for improvements and have an appeal when the older ways have thoroughly failed to meet human needs.

Fear of Change

Change implies a threat to certainty. Many people seem unwilling to change when the choice is between the tried and proven over the untried and unproven. Those who rear youngsters have emerged from the past heritage and they do not regard themselves as horrible products. If their children follow their models, elders would be quite pleased. Changes in areas as important as male-female relationships, minority-majority group relationships, and sacred-secular relationships may drastically alter social and personality structures which may not be tolerated by the rest of one's society. Under such conditions, parents proceed cautiously or not at all.

Obedience First, Reasons Later

In the sensitive areas, there is further difficulty because of the imposed morality of sex codes, racial etiquettes, and religious scruples. It is not a question of subjecting these areas to study or investigation. One does not necessarily explain to a child that there is this and that reason for conducting one's self in a socially approved manner. The first requirement is that the morality is to be followed. Later on, when the child is more mature, the basis for these mores might be proffered. Usually, children are expected to obey in the present and to wait for a more propitious time to find the reasons for their conformity. It is true that the *facts* may never be presented or by the time they are discovered or revealed, the behavior may have become habitual. Facts, in these cases, may tend to be overlooked or discounted.

Pretense of Individual Choice.

One does not necessarily command or call forth behavior in children by outright demands. The desired ends are secured by increasing experience. Under such circumstances, ideas appear to be natural or normal. Children are often denied complete freedom in these areas and by cutting off any avenue of escape, except the preconceived goals, their *choices* are highly approved, applauded, rewarded, manipulated and encouraged. The similarity to animals driven into a corral, having made a choice to enter the enclosure because there is nothing else to do, is quite close, if not exact. If the social situation can be structured in such a manner as to convince the child that this is what he *wants* to do, then the training period is likely to proceed unmarred by dissention and antagonism.

Adult Embarrassment

No doubt, many adults are convinced that everything is all right. They find themselves ill-equipped and uneasy if they were to suggest behavior other than that existing in the *status quo*. Their encrusted rigidity cannot tolerate nor comprehend experimentation or tampering with these sensitive areas. How red-faced or embarrassed they become when youngsters suggest other possible arrangements! Adults can easily become exceedingly uncomfortable by childish experimentations and explorations because they have already erected their lives on certain, taken-for-granted premises.

Easier to Order than to Question

In the face of these conditions, adults generally resort to exercising their prerogatives and listen to no further argumentation or protestations. It is so much simpler to insist upon getting one's way than resorting to persuasion, debate, reasoning, marshalling of facts, or trying to convince. Typically, in the sensitive areas, the depth of thinking is minimal or almost absent. Children are required to follow certain procedures and no questions may be asked. Later on, to be sure, a rationale may be provided. Its acceptance, then, is practically assured.

SEX

Despite American preoccupation with sex, there is a certain amount of precaution lest children become too soon and too much acquainted with sexual matters. Perhaps, it is most typical of middle class morality to emphasize such "respectability." For lower-class children, many middle-class admonitions concerning "proper appearances" do not apply. For such children, the facts of life are better known, not so much through thoughtful contemplation, but more by means of increased opportunity to observe people who cannot afford certain middle-class niceties or proprieties. For upper-class parents, the opportunity to take pains when it comes to shielding the young is maximized and respectability is not only expected, but is paramount to keeping family pride untarnished.

Much of this concern and anguish springs from the social systems created and maintained by men. There is no need to paint an idyllic picture of primitive sexuality. There are those who have possibly over-interpreted the relative sexual freedoms found among pre-literates. Every social system encounters its critics because it fails to meet every human being's needs. Nevertheless, there is some justification for the release from fear, shame, and guilt that seems to accompany sexual systems found among so-called uncivilized peoples. Sexual interest is based upon normal biological drives, but Americans tend to suppress, deny, or thwart their sexuality by permissiveness under restrictive conditions. That sex holds a tremendous appeal is evident in the dominant role it plays in advertising, in the entertainment world, and in romantic notions found in abundance on the American scene. Freud and neo-Freudians hold a major place in modern psychologies. The Kinsey and other sexual studies have won widespread attention. American children are being reared before such a backdrop.

What are some of the dilemmas facing parents and others in acquainting children with sex and its ramifications? The following are suggested:

1. Modesty outside the home versus modesty within the home
2. Toilet training versus absence of control
3. Separation of the sexes versus heterosexual living
4. Suspicion of outsiders versus acceptance of family members
5. No discussion of origin of babies versus understanding of origin of babies
6. Minimizing the role of the father versus clarification of father's role
7. Technical sex terms versus familistic, personalized terms
8. Attitudes of repugnance versus attitudes of acceptance
9. Ascribed sex roles versus achieved sex roles
10. Observance of sex taboos versus achieving a perspective on sex
11. Absence of preparation for adolescence versus preparation

While this is not a complete listing, it does indicate some of the questions that American parents and their supplements face in the sensitive area of teaching sex habits to their offspring. The initial concern is with outside appearances. The secondary consideration is for personal and family experiences which are not shared with outsiders. The overall problem is how to provide wholesome experiences within the home that will eventuate in acceptable public behavior outside.

Because some of the dilemmas mentioned above are not self-explanatory, it will help if there is a brief explanation of some of the statements, expressions, and terms employed.

Modesty

The locus of modesty centers upon the genitals for both sexes and upon the breasts of females. Modesty also applies to other parts of the body such as the anus, buttocks, legs, and waist. In other societies, ideas of modesty may be further applied to the face, hands, or feet. In brief, then, exposure of human anatomy is carefully defined by a cultural heritage and children must be led to accept, understand, and practice accordingly. This is a monumental task because children are devoid of all such notions of modesty at the beginning of their lives. The journey to adolescence and adulthood will be a long and puzzling one and just how to bring about the desired social products successfully confronts all parents.

The problem is compounded because, not only is the child innocent of all social definitions, but he begins his social experiences within a home that accepts him completely, naked, exposed, and unashamed. While appropriate clothing is placed on his body, there are numerous instances when modesty taboos are disregarded and rendered null and void within the home. The child, his siblings, or his parents need not be too careful in exposing themselves to each other, as they are, for all practical purposes, one flesh and blood. Certainly, the transition from no modesty to modesty as defined by the greater society must be gradual. Lapses in the transition, however, only serve to delay or arrest the process.

Notions of modesty are closely associated with age-grading in various societies. Regardless of social definitions, very young children may break the modesty taboos with impunity, until such time as they have grown up a bit more and can begin to comprehend what elders expect of them. Then, increasing pressure is brought to bear upon them to expose portions of their anatomy only in great privacy. Dr. Dickinson[2] reported how firm these trainings were entrenched when he had to deal with grown women who came to him for the professional services of a gynecologist. He noted through his many years of medical practice how women resisted disrobing in his offices preparatory to a physical examination, even if it meant the doctor could not properly diagnose their problems. Not until decades had elapsed and the general tenor of the American society had changed to one of greater frankness in the area of sexuality, did his patients cooperate without argument or embarrassment.

Toilet Training

As with so many other areas of childhood, in the matter of toilet training, there is a social acceptance of infants who eliminate waste materials from their bodies whenever the function must be satisfied.

2 Robert Latou Dickinson and Laura Beam, *A Thousand Marriages* (Baltimore, Williams and Wilkins Company, 1931).

Societies differ thereafter in the speed and scope with which they urge bodily control of elimination processes until a proper place, facility, and time can be found. Much socio-psychological discussion has occurred on the significance of toilet training upon the personality. It is certainly an important step in the socialization of children and there need be much surveillance on the part of those charged with such responsibility. Once this step has been taken, however, except for the occasional lapses of bed-wetting or soiling of clothes, children are regarded as having moved well along the path towards acculturation.

An interesting thesis associated with toilet training applies to the interpretations given to elimination which manifest themselves later on in maturity when it comes to sexual expression of emotion. If children are taught that elimination is filthy and immodest, then the transfer of such an idea is made to the sex organs involved in such action. When maturity is reached, this notion is not easily replaced by the feeling that sex and sex relationships are clean, noble, and highly acceptable. Some adults appear to suffer tremendous pangs of guilt and remorse when they attempt to reverse their earlier training in regard to their genitalia and express their love and devotion to their marital partners. Apparently, the greater training given to females in the American society on this matter, does call for much re-adjustment and understanding on the part of their husbands in later life.

Sex Separation

In the home environment, the two sexes live in close proximity and intimacy not found in other relationships. But, originating in the home and carried outside to the neighborhood, school, and larger community, the sexes also acquire some separate sense of identity. Girls and boys play together and enjoy each other's company for many years, but imperceptibly do move apart and enter separate or different *worlds* because of social definitions of sex segregation. There is no doubt but that such separation is not willfully decided by males or females but is a system socially imposed. Many would argue that it is natural, but anthropological data on pre-literate societies and social-psychological data on contemporary societies would suggest that the tenable hypothesis is that males and females move into separate worlds in response to social expectations.

Within each sexual world, the masculinity or femininity of persons as defined by the society may be brought to greater perfection or intensity, untainted by contacts with the "others." In the American society it is almost fashionable to at least pretend a high loyalty to members of one's own sex and to underrate members of the opposite sex. Of course, children soon learn to play the game well enough not to lose complete inter-

est in the opposite sex, despite the unifying effect of "a common enemy."
There are some members of the opposite sex, one may concede without
losing membership in the world of one's like-sexed fellows, who are very
nice. Not until adolescence or beyond, is it regarded as fair to abandon
one's sex world to find partners with whom to share one's life. With the
establishment of a new family unit in matrimony, the cycle begins once
again. The adult male and female, however, do carry with them the
earlier childhood experiences of sex separation and may not always find
them easy to overcome.

Suspicion of Outsiders

In homes that provide warmth and protection, children are likely to
grow up without fear or worry of sexual assaults. However, beyond the
home environment, there is danger and children must be guarded or
shielded from such harm as well as prepared to deal with strangers who
are potential attackers. Physiologically, children are unprepared. Psychologically, they can be disturbed. Sociologically, their future heterosexual
relations are at stake. Certainly, one does not envy the not-so-delicate task
of preparing children to deal with this matter.

Perverts do exist who may victimize young children sexually. Therefore, the warm acceptance of grown-ups can be dangerous if transferred
outside the home among strangers. Children have to be instructed about
such matters as accepting rides, candy, or other enticements to accompany
some unknown person to some unfamiliar destination. There is serious
harm, however, if children are taught that *all* strangers are dangerous and
to be mistrusted. As with so many other human problems, it is the degree
or quality of training that counts.

Origin of Babies

Certainly, in this so called enlightened age, one does not have to repeat
the age-old warnings against concocting weird stories of the origin of
babies. Yet, there is a persistence to folkways that resists modern teachings. One continues to hear about storks, cabbage leaves, angels, and
other assorted deliverymen who are totally credited with the arrival of a
child. One boy, who was told that the stork brought him, his mother, and
his grandmother, cried out in despair, "We haven't had a natural birth
in our family for three generations!

Answers to such queries as to the arrival of new babies are often given
matter-of-factly in many families by replying as honestly as possible, using
words and ideas at the child's level of comprehension. Where else, say
some parents, should children learn such facts if they cannot secure them

within their homes? By default, many American families have failed to discuss these matters and the results are that, as late as the college level, corrections often have to be initiated.

Families differ on such instruction and while children may be cautioned about keeping this information within the family circle and for their own use, they can and often do carry such data to other children in the neighborhood. Differential speeds of training and exposure to certain information, especially that pertaining to sex, have been known to cause the most embarrassment or harassment to already burdened parents.

Most children seem satisfied with explanations that babies grow within the bodies of their mothers until strong enough to develop in the outside world. Further refinements are added as the child's curiosity and understanding are broadened. The fertilizing of the ovum by the father is a most puzzling matter to children and is rarely asked about until they reach more mature years. Of course, circumstances can be present which enable the father's role to be adequately explained. James H. S. Bossard [3] and others have credited female dogs owned by families as being valuable members of any household. Sex-education can be given casually, when in the course of events, the family pet is about to deliver some puppies. Rural families have never had too much trouble with the arrival-of-babies question, because of their frequent observation of animal copulation, birth, and death. The urban family can rely on visits to the local zoo, farms nearby, and a wide array of reading materials set at children's levels.

Technical Terms

What should be the "proper" language to express sexual facts for children? Most terms are not beyond the child's ability to understand if they are used in context and without embarrassment. Far too frequently, one hears a wide assortment of colloquial, folksy, whimsical expressions that are tabu in the non-family relationships. One can understand why these familistic, personalized expressions get started. It is their maintenance and reinforcement that cause the disturbance. Soon enough, they have to be shed and the wisest decision would be not to even start their usage. The inability to express one's ideas as applied to sex originates in the failure to learn terms that may be properly expressed in society under favorable circumstances. Hesitancy or reluctance to discuss sex frequently stems from unfamiliarity with technical terms such as penis, vagina, buttocks, coitus, erogenous zones, breasts, ovulation, menstruation, or gestation. These terms are very frequently misspelled and distorted as late as the college level.

[3] See James H. S. Bossard, "The Mental Hygiene of Owning a Dog," *Mental Hygiene* (July, 1944), pp. 408–413; Nelson Foote, "A Neglected Member of the Family," *Marriage and Family Living*, Vol. 18, No. 3 (August, 1956), pp. 213–218.

Attitudes

In many ways, sex and sexuality become problematic because of the built-in-responses known as attitudes rather than because of difficulty with technical terms. The facts are important, but even more so are accompanying attitudes. Thus, the objective of much sex-education in America has to do with the development of attitudes that regard sex as a normal, healthy part of life and not something that is shameful, guilt-ridden, vicious, degrading, or horrible. Children are recipients of much instruction and they quickly absorb the attitudes of their instructors along with the fundamentals being discussed. It cannot be repeated often enough that words alone cannot convey educational lessons. The *manner* of their presentation, the emotional overtones and implications, frequently play a greater part in the learning process than the actual content.

Sex Roles

Children learn early in life that their sex predetermines which social roles must be played and which are forbidden. Females have ordinarily been the subjects of most prohibitions or proscriptions. Their emancipation while long heralded has not quite been realized as yet. Social barriers still exist. There is a "masculine protest" found among some women who recognize certain advantages conferred upon men. It is a syndrome of defense mechanisms and overt behavior symptoms which some women develop as a consequence of knowledge of the facts of sex evaluation. The male in the American society who recognizes certain concessions granted to women because of their alleged weaknesses, and who adopts a "female protest" is a rarer specie.

Children often rebel against the ascriptions and restrictions imposed on them because of their sex. There is need to know more about the successful parents who have gracefully led their charges into their respective social roles without encountering obstructive behaviors or reluctance to conform.

Sexual Perspective

It is a simpler matter to follow prescriptions or formulas than to seek newer areas of behavior. An over-riding objective of many educated Americans is to acquire a respect for humanity rather than for a given sexual category. While sexuality is not to be minimized, American treatment of persons will hopefully rest upon a more equitable basis than the arbitrary assignment of roles because of sex differences. Boys and girls, and men and women, it is claimed, respond to a common treatment and not to special catering to alleged special interests of each sex. Much that is claimed as basically sexual in origin is really a result of training begun early in childhood. So-called masculine traits or so-called feminine traits can be inculcated in either sex. If socio-psychological attitudes were developed that boys and girls are equally desirable, equally precious, equally worthy, some progress would be made towards elimination of false and gross exaggeration of sexual differences that have been previously maximized and over-emphasized in the American society.

Adolescent Preparation

With the onset of adolescence, full sexual functioning can begin. Far too many children have been permitted to drift into adolescence unprepared and ill-equipped to cope with new conditions. Each stage in life requires preparation for the next stage and the onset of adolescence is no exception. Much of childhood is a preparation period, and regardless of the sensitive nature of sexuality, there is little excuse for wasting time by pretending that childhood will go on forever. Sex drives and sexuality emerge and their final form is readied in the crucible of childhood. Delaying tactics do not help. A positive, accepting, understanding, compassionate point of view on the part of American parents has often gone a long way towards resolving the dilemmas associated with sex differences.

RACE

While delicacy and taste characterize the sexual area, perhaps the adjective explosive best describes the racial area. Here again are some allegations about biological differences which have been academically dismissed by world scholars.[4] *The acceptance of documented facts concerning race is not under discussion. The important thing is the acceptance of a mythology that is nevertheless made real by an adult world.* Many people argue on behalf of established systems and not upon consideration of scientific findings. Racial categories are important and sociologically they must be considered.

From the Viewpoint of the Child

To children, alleged racial distinctions are not so obvious. Most studies made by objective scholars support the contention that children do not instinctively dislike or significantly reject biological attributes such as

[4] See "What is Race?", a publication of UNESCO. Other pamphlets include "Sense and Nonsense about Race," by Ethel J. Alpenfels (New York, Friendship Press, 1957); "The Races of Mankind," by Ruth Benedict and Gene Weltfish, Public Affairs Pamphlet 85.

skin pigmentation, shape of eyes, texture of hair, or size of lips. It is only with the ideas and feeling states of adults that children take on similar attitudes or concepts. As "Bloody Mary" tells about it in "South Pacific," you have to be "carefully taught."[5] Thus, there is no basis for an *innate* contempt or admiration for persons who seem to be biologically different than others. The continuation and promulgation of race ideas is the total responsibility of members of the adult world, not children.

From the "Majority" Point of View

Among those who are in power, there is a strain to maintain the *status quo* that has enabled them to have favorable living conditions. It is imperative to such people that their children continue the pattern under the ominous threat that circumstances would change drastically if variations were attempted in racial treatments. Whether real or imagined, such adults feel impelled to continue in the ways of their fathers lest some calamity fall upon them. The procedure may be by direct teaching of the young or, most likely, through subtle and indirect methods, but there is some satisfaction in noting how one's offspring will follow carefully the parental models. The heritage is thus preserved and all is regarded as "well."

From the "Minority" Point of View

For those, however, who live every day of their lives under the shadow of prejudice, the lessons to children become painfully clear: (1) Conditions in which they live are not necessarily "natural." (2) Their elders did not necessarily create these conditions. (3) One can become resigned to unhappy circumstances. (4) When one is young, there is always a chance to change and improve social conditions. (5) One can fight social injustices by fair or foul means. Instruction may not come only from parents, relatives, and friends, but from daily observation of deprivation and humiliation. The minority child is born into a hostile world and he may not accept his conditions as gracefully as the child of majority parentage.

From an Objective Point of View

As previously noted, minority status is one of the sensitive areas in socialization. There is no simple formula or recipe to settle centuries of experiences with it. Certainly, the present discussion does not pretend to present an answer to racial issues. It is possible, however, to point to a few

[5] From the play, *South Pacific*, part of the lyric of a song sung by a resident of the mythical island of "Bali Hai."

items which may cast some light or offer some guidance to objective thinking: (1) Perhaps no one side of racial arguments is totally correct or without faults. (2) Various people may be guilty of maintaining a stalemate for reasons of their own. (3) The sharing of common values within a common culture may be the one redeeming feature that will eventually result in a peaceful settlement of current antagonisms. (4) Changes are inevitable in social living and the direction and rate of change rest with human beings who try to create their own environment. (5) Danger is ever-present that an atmosphere of good-will can be destroyed and a social upheaval of a violent nature can occur. Socialization on racial issues in America continues under not-so-favorable conditions.

It will help to elaborate upon the items listed above which can or may clarify problems confronting American parents as they attempt to handle data concerning race on a more objective level.

1. CRITICISM FOR THOSE WHO ARGUE EITHER SIDE OF RACIAL ISSUES. If there eventually is to be a reduction of racial tensions and a more satisfactory modification of minority-majority group differences, then it is worthwhile to consider abandonment of assuming that one side or another is either totally "wrong" or totally "right." Antagonism has been engendered by insistence by a group that virtuous action is to be found only to the credit of one select group and to the detriment of that group's opponents. Full consideration of all possibly relevant data from history or from objective study indicates that tactical errors have been committed by both sides of racial quarrels. Exploitation of African people, for example, by white slavers is certainly to be found in historical records. On the other hand, Negro tribal cultures accepted slavery as a norm imposed upon captive people. Slavery, the source of much contemporary white-Negro conflicts in America, can therefore be laid at the door of both whites and Negroes who cooperated in its development.

2. A STALEMATE SITUATION FAVORED BY BOTH MINORITY AND MAJORITY REPRESENTATIVES. For certain individuals in the majority group, the maintenance of current Negro-white relationships is most satisfactory. That is, there are economic and socio-psychological advantages in the retention of present practices. Further, political power lies in the hands of majority group members, a condition they would like to retain. On the other hand, certain individuals in the minority group, such as some race leaders, make a career for themselves out of the *status quo*. The acceptance of Negroes as full citizens, instead of second class citizens would mean, for many, the end of their career. This may also not be regarded as satisfactory by certain ambitious minority leaders. Their "thunder," under such circumstances, would be taken from them. Thus, both sides contribute to a minority-majority group stalemate.

3. SHARING OF COMMON VALUES MAY HELP. Room for optimism may be in order, however, because both Negro and white share much of a common culture. Much has been written about African survivalism, but American Negroes are chiefly familiar with the American way of life and Africanism, at best, is only a remote and vague echo of the past. Almost with deliberation, the social structure with which African slaves were once familiar was removed from their lives. They were treated as chattel who lacked cultural backgrounds. The cultural background of Negro Americans is probably more *American* in many ways than that of white Europeans who claim they are *Americans* despite their comparatively recent arrival. As both minority and majority group members share the American Promise of equitable treatment and "justice for all," there is room for a favorable prognosis that this common ground will eventually bring people to understand each other.

4. BUILT-IN CHANGE. It may safely be predicted that changes will occur in minority-majority group relationships, because stagnation is not typically a characteristic of the American culture. The rate of this change may be slow or fast and its direction may be favorable to one side or another, but a stand-still does not appear likely in dynamic America. As men become increasingly conscious that much of their lives is bound up with situations of their own making, then they may work in directions that will modify their present difficulties. This has been the general trend over much of human history, and as long as men will exist there is little evidence to support the contention that this trend will be reversed.

5. EVER-PRESENT DANGERS. The area of race has been presented as a most sensitive area with which to deal. As previously indicated, a currently descriptive word for racial issues is *explosive*. This is to say that much bitterness has been accumulated over the centuries between minority and majority peoples. The harboring of this bitterness is a most threatening condition that could manifest itself in a variety of ways, including violent ones. People who have been denied full participation in a culture may not be fully placated by the eradication of all social barriers. Undoubtedly, there is a lurking fear on the part of some whites that *fair treatment* after years of rejection may not always result in peaceful, happy conditions. Past humiliations may or may not be forgotten by minority people who may be granted "freedom." Similar to holding a lion by its tail, one hesitates to let go. Even the lion may not be too prepared to deal with its new freedom. Minority-majority group relationship apparently will continue to plague or puzzle the best minds for years to come.

In the meantime, children are being raised under the cloud of race-thinking. The greatest roadblock to a reasonable resolving of racial issues lies with the creation of personality types that are not easily manipulated. Sensitive, bitter, tough, sullen, or angry personalities created in childhood reach fruition in adulthood, and such persons will probably not listen to reason. Creating personalities that are arrogant, conceited, tyrannical, or bigoted maximizes the explosiveness of the issue. If this is vaguely realized by those who socialize the young, perhaps there may be more caution exercised in dealing with children when racial questions occur.

RELIGION AND MORALITY

If there is some hesitancy in American society to lead children to continue older patterns of sexuality and race relations, there is considerably less of this when it comes to faith and sacred beliefs. Parents are more certain that their ideas of worship and conscience are practically inviolable and consciously indoctrinate their children in their religious ways. There is little middle ground on religious morality. One is either for or against a given doctrine.

There can be differences within a given faith. Religious history records numerous cases of religious schisms, splinter groups, and disputes over incidentals of religious dogma. Great care must be exercised when one says that so-and-so group believes in a specific procedure or theology. A recent publication came into the writers' hands which was entitled "What Methodists Believe." Some astute reader had scribbled an appendage so that the title read "What *Some* Methodists Believe." Intra-religious strife and in-fighting may possibly be more vicious than that of the inter-religious variety.

Usually, children are given little choice in religious matters but are heavily indoctrinated to follow a given spiritual philosophy. Those who claim to give children free choice in their faith succeed in fooling only themselves that such really is the case. If the attitude of the parents is negative to religion and religious expression, then the training assumes the character of deliberate omission and neglect. Choices of organized religions are rarely made, from such a background, when maturity is finally reached. Like so many things, roots must be laid early in life if there is to be a final, healthy product.

A Way of Life

Religion is not merely a form of worship or a philosophy; it enters into the patterns of daily living. It spills over from formal services and observances to everyday practice. People speak of a seven-day-a-week religion rather than some overt church attendance on Sunday morning.

Children become the targets for attention in these matters by well intentioned adults who see their previous errors, but can correct them only by re-shaping the lives of the young. Thus, the schooling of many children is deliberately made parochial, sacred, or religiously oriented and adults willingly pay to support such instruction. Church affiliated organizations for youth are created to occupy their time, attention, and energy well beyond the traditional Sunday schools. In school, in the home, in business, and in leisure time, religious ideas are sometimes incorporated and espoused. Children are asked by their religious leaders to *live* their religion rather than to be constantly sermonized about it.

Americans are short of the idealistic goals of religious leaders when churches and synagogues are commonly racially segregated. Some studies [6] indicate that the "melting pot theory" of America does not apply to religious issues. Each religious group remains somewhat aloof from the others and refuses to lose its identity. Children literally grow up in religiously segregated sub-cultures and know very little about variations in religious points of view.

Separation of Church and State

The variety of religious beliefs is related to the "hands off" policy of church and state separation. There could be as many religions as there are individuals if freedom of conscience would be carried to logical extremes. Of course, there are many areas of consensus and like-minded men are often gathered together religiously. The conscientious parent, however, has to try to fit together some incongruent philosophic ideas. He has to support a given religious faith while professing a belief in religious freedom for everyone. Supposedly, this applies to children, too, but parents will not apply religious freedom when it comes to their own families. For others and for themselves, religious freedom is quite desirable. For children, freedom of choice is not granted.

The variety of religions that must live amicably side by side in the American society does pose other questions. How can they insulate impressionable children from too great an interest in a faith different from that of their parents? How can parents maintain religious identity while fostering interfaith understanding? How can parents talk of "right" and "wrong" behavior and not offend their neighbors who hold to a different religion? How can minority parents create a way of life when a majority of people differ from their point of view so drastically? Does the growth of one faith pose a threat to the existence of the others by too vigorous efforts at proselytizing?

[6] See Judy Jo Reeves Kennedy, "Single or Triple Melting Pot? Intermarriage Trends in New Haven, 1870–1940," *American Journal of Sociology* (January, 1944), pp. 331–339.

SUMMARY

In this exposition of selected sensitive areas of socialization, perhaps sex has been over-emphasized. Certainly, race, religion, and other areas could receive as detailed or more detailed discussion. The objective of this chapter, however, was not an encyclopedic inventory of all possible subjects, but an effort to draw attention to these areas of socialization that challenge students of the sociology of childhood. Whether the subject was sex, race, religion, or some other sensitive area, certain common characteristics were noted that made the socialization process very difficult. These were enumerated as emotional appeals, relatedness to personal privacy, the efforts to shield the innocent, the use of strong social controls, the pride in past heritages, the reluctance to make changes, the presentation of supporting evidence only after commitments were made, the presence of individualized choice, the embarrassment of elders, and the tendency to command rather than to debate. The training in sexuality was pictured as one of meeting the demands of society while negating many of these demands within the intimacy of the home and family situations. Racial issues were presented as explosive because modern mythology persists in the face of objective evidence to the contrary. Religious training in a pluralistic society was described as decisively handled despite some puzzling and gnawing dilemmas. No one envies the position of parents in finding their way on these matters with their children. Like the proverbial English, Americans "muddle through" as best they can.

READINGS

BERRY, Brewton, *Race and Ethnic Relations* (Boston, Houghton Mifflin Company, 1958).

DOZIER, Edward, SIMPSON, George and YINGER, J. Milton, "The Integration of Americans of Indian Descent," *Annals of the American Academy of Political and Social Sciences,* Vol. 311 (May, 1957), pp. 158–165.

DRIVER, Helen I., ed., *Sex Guidance for Your Child* (Madison, Wis., Monona Publications, 1963).

ECKARDT, Roy, *The Surge of Piety in America* (New York, Association Press, 1958).

ELLIS, Albert, and ABARBANEL, Albert, eds., *The Encyclopedia of Sexual Behavior* (New York, Hawthorn Books, Inc., 1961).

FRAZIER, E. Franklin, *The Negro in the United States,* rev. ed. (New York, The Macmillan Company, 1958).

GOODMAN, Mary E., *Race Awareness in Young Children* (Reading, Mass., Addison-Wesley Publishing Co., Inc., 1952).

HAVIGHURST, Robert, and NEUGARTEN, Bernice, *American Indian and White Children* (Chicago, University of Chicago Press, 1955).

HYMES, James L., Jr., *How to Tell Your Child about Sex*, Public Affairs Pamphlet, FL 149 (New York, Public Affairs Committee).

PARSONS, Talcott, "Age and Sex in the Social Structure of the United States," *American Sociological Review*, Vol. 7 (1942), pp. 604–616.

POFFENBERGER, Thomas, "Responses of Eighth Grade Girls to a Talk on Sex," *Marriage and Family Living*, Vol. 22, No. 1 (February, 1960), pp. 38–44.

SCHERMERHORN, R. A., *These Our People* (Boston, D. C. Heath & Company, 1949).

SCHNEIDER, Louis, and DORNBUSCH, Sanford, "Inspirational Religious Literature: From Latent to Manifest Functions of Religion," *American Journal of Sociology*, Vol. LXII, No. 5 (March, 1957), pp. 476–481.

SKOUSEN, Cleon W., *So You Want to Raise a Boy?* (Garden City, N.Y., Doubleday & Company, Inc., 1962).

SUTHERLAND, Robert L., *Color, Class, and Personality* (Washington, D.C., American Council on Education, 1942).

WHITMAN, Howard, *The Sex Age* (Garden City, N.Y., Doubleday & Company, Inc., 1942).

17

Autonomy[1] and
Emerging Responsibility

INTRODUCTION

Childhood is characterized by dependency, control of one's life by others, and a generalized acknowledgement that responsibility rests with older persons. The ultimate purpose in socializing children is to enable them to reverse these characteristics and to embrace the adult roles of their society. Thus, children are to be moved from a completely dependent to a relatively independent state. They are to be granted increasing control of their own destinies. Finally, they are to be credited with their own responsibilities and expected to remove all liabilities from the shoulders of others.

In the animal kingdom, of which Homo sapiens is a part, the process of achieving independence may be described as *weaning* to adulthood. In one sense, weaning is an appropriate term for Homo sapiens' experiences, too. In another sense, it is inadequate because the significant differences that distinguish human behavior from the behavior of other animals lie in the area of social and cultural qualities. While the roots of human life remain in the soil of animalistic nature, the nutrients that place mankind above the biological kingdoms are the structures and processes that are the social heritage of every human child. It is these data that are the forte of sociologists. It is to these data that sociologists turn, keeping a mindful eye upon the biological foundations of all life.

The prospect of moving from dependency toward independency may be a most exciting adventure to some children or highly frightening and painful to others. Most likely, children experience degrees between this polarity of feelings and sometimes welcome the events associated with

[1] Autonomy is ordinarily used to mean "a socio-cultural independent personality." As used in this chapter, autonomy means "a socio-cultural absorbent personality."

growing up and at other times reject their impositions. In previous discussions, attention has been focused on the first dozen years of a person's life. Can the socialization process proceed smoothly in twelve evenly spaced steps or are they arranged in blocks of five years, three years, or two years? Or, is the pace highly irregular, sometimes imperceptible and at other times amounting to a fast gallop? Few would pretend to know the answers to these questions. Certainly painstaking research has given some insight, such as that in the work of the Gesell Institute scientists with their development of growth curves. Much more can and will probably be done. All that can be accomplished for the present is to seriously probe into the processes to learn more about matters known to possess great portent in the lives of individuals and, subsequently, for all humankind.

BIOLOGICAL FOUNDATIONS FOR AUTONOMY

It is interesting to contrast the weaning period of selected species of animals with that of Homo sapiens. The general, pervading rule seems to be that the larger the animal, the fewer number born at one time; and the more complicated the creature, the longer the period of time it takes for the animal to reach a state of self-reliance. For example, salmon carefully prepare a nest in a quiet stream and guard it until the eggs are fertilized and covered for protection. The fingerlings are practically on their own immediately after birth. A family life, as such, is non-existent. Cougars, on the other hand, care for their kittens for about one year. Thereafter their family life terminates. Bears will take about two years with their cubs in a fairly patient attachment before they abandon them to adulthood. Elephants will nurse their young for about two years and spend an additional two years tenderly watching over their calves.[2]

Man seems to be the sole creature who cares for, watches over, and carefully trains offspring for the arduous years of self-direction. Approximately the first twenty years in the lives of Americans are utilized to bring youngsters into some state of readiness to assume adult burdens. Even at the end of two decades, some "children" expect their parents to provide for their needs by financing their education, their travels, their entertainment, their homes, their families, and even their own children.

[2] For additional readings on the biological foundations for autonomy see S. C. Kendeigh, "Parental Care and Its Evolution in Birds," *Illinois Biological Monographs*, Vol. 22 (1952), pp. 1–356; J. Bowlby, "The Nature of the Child's Tie to His Mother," *International Journal of Psycho-analysis*, Vol. 39 (1958), pp. 1–24; M. Gunther, "Instinct and the Nursing Couple," *The Lancet* (March 19, 1955), pp. 575–578; J. Bowlby, "Maternal Care and Mental Health," *World Health Organization Monograph* (1958), Series 2; H. F. Harlow and R. R. Zimmerman, "Affectional Responses in the Infant Monkey," *Science*, Vol. 130 (1959), pp. 421–432; R. A. Hinde, "The Early Development of the Parent-Child Relationship," *Discovery* (February, 1961), pp. 48–55.

One might wonder when a human being can be safely said to be grown up if his dependency is continued for a lifetime.

Some students of biological phenomena can see much significance in the fact that human females can bear children up to about age forty-five. This would grant a child born at approximately the end of a woman's fertility period the fairly normal expectation of twenty years of dependency. Thereafter, a child would be seriously deprived of maternal care and relationships that seem to be his birthright. It should be pointed out, however, that human males remain fertile and vigorous far beyond the years allotted to females. That is, they may not be able to impregnate their older wives, but can achieve fatherhood with younger, fertile wives under an approved polygynous system. The conclusion is that perhaps the fundamental relationship in a family is really the mother-child relationship, and not the father-child relationship. There are numerous instances within the animal kingdom in which the father is dangerous to his offspring and often has to be driven away by a protective mother. Animal fathers are far less solicitous of the well-being of their children. Maternal care, on the contrary, has been notable and variously described as "instinctive" or as a "drive." Among Homo sapiens, the father is needed to support and protect both mother and child and this he seems able to do, in the American society, up to the magical age of 65, at least, and sometimes well beyond this age.

Social Foundations for Autonomy

The child dependency period is not strictly a product of biological conditions. It is highly related to intricate, complicated social structures and processes. Human infants have a longer road to travel than merely gaining control of their bodies to meet their biological needs. Societies have to perpetuate themselves just as surely as individuals seek to transmit their ways in order to achieve a kind of immortality. Thus, societies are well fortified to provide all new entrants with rules and regulations that will enable the relationships between individuals and societies to be cordial and productive. There is much for children to learn before they are accepted as participants in good standing, and adults will painstakingly move children through the approved steps to maturity. By these means, the double objectives of personal competence and societal strength are somewhat reached.

In the rearing process, increasing control is gained over the biological processes such as eliminating, finding nutrition, keeping one's self clean, recognizing dangers that can hurt or destroy the body, finding recreation and exercise, and securing enough rest on one's own volition. In short, a child learns to keep his body in a state of good health without over-dependence upon others. When this happens these matters can be routinized and no longer be of major concern. Thereafter, a maximum amount of attention is paid to acquiring social know-how. It is this socialization process that has been the main stream of the present discourse.

Refusal to "Let Go"

While it has been noted that the final result of rearing children is alleged to be the creation of autonomous individuals acting in concert with members of their respective societies, there are some parents who lose sight of these objectives and consider their dominance over children to be the pinnacle of social success. If such elders have so diligently taken care of youth, then surely, they believe youth must serve the purposes of the elders. Having finally tasted social power, they possess a reluctance to *let go* and permit their children mounting doses of freedom. In other words, there are some parents who have experienced a peculiar form of social status from their parental roles. If they relinquish their control, what will they have in its place?

No doubt, refusal to let go may not be a conscious effort on the part of parents. For example, dominance patterns supported by social sanctions can easily become habitual patterns. Habits built up through a dozen years or more will not be shattered, discarded, and collapsed at the first signs of rebellion against an established authority. Perhaps, it is an error to even think of parental habits as beginning at the birth of a child. Certainly the roots of parental dominance reach far back into the earlier life-history of given parents. Possibly a more realistic picture of parental authority would be a wall of habitual practice supported underneath by a foundation of a whole lifetime of experiences and interpretations.

If this line of reasoning is followed, the real nature of parenthood may present a formidable barrier to independence. What types of personalities do parents possess? Are they weak-willed people who find a degree of satisfaction in exerting their wills against the yet unformed, more vulnerable wills of their children? Are they fundamentally selfish people who egocentrically think of their children as "their property" to be used for parental purposes? Are they given to thoughtlessness and take for granted the iron grip they fix upon their youngsters? Are they stultifying or stifling in their tactics to such a point that they rear children who lack a desire for independence, who have no ambitions, who are listless and dull?

An interesting parallel to the umbilical cord which once was the chief connection between child and parent, is the "golden cord" of mother-child relationships. If one prefers a less earthy description, one could just as well use the more folksy "tied to mother's apron strings" conception of the same situation. In any event, some mothers have been stereotyped as clinging tenaciously to their children and refusing to free them from their childish servitude. The interfering mother-in-law stereotype perhaps contains enough truth to continue to be a disturbing and alarming element in many marriages. Even when their children have "grown up" and are independent, such mothers tend to cling to their fantasies of being in charge of their children's destinies. Because the bond between parent and child is a social one, fathers are not immune to the criticism usually reserved for mothers. In their more masculine ways, certain fathers attempt to assert their prerogatives far beyond the first twelve years of their children's lives. In retaliation, some youngsters flee to campuses away from home to shed parental chains.

Willingness "to Hold On"

As is so often true in reciprocal relationships, all the responsibility for childhood bondage does not necessarily rest on parents. Children, too, are wise enough to note the advantages of parental assumption of authority and responsibility and are content to continue the *status quo*. It is rather attractive to maintain the ease, comfort, and irresponsibility of childhood for a prolonged period of time. Why change habits when others will cater to your needs, will support your wishes, and carry your burdens for you? Not all slaves jumped for joy when they heard the Emancipation Proclamation. Not all women seek equal rights with men. Not all students can hardly wait until they can leave their classes and compete in the economic or professional world. In short, not all children press for autonomy; some tend to relish the carefree days in which others have to pull in a harness and take care of boring, but necessary, routines.

If children have been well schooled in obedience to parental authority, then it is not painful for children to continue in their patterns of subservience. It becomes second-nature or "natural." Given this condition, it is upsetting and radical to even think of challenging the powers of parents. The internalization of parental values may have proceeded so far that the inner, spiritual bonds render outside bonds extraneous. If one has never tasted freedom, how is that person able to make some judgment about its nature? Apropos this theme, would a person who came from an authoritarian background be prone to warmly embrace democracy or would he accept without qualms a more dictatorial condition? Those who come from an individual-centered life could possibly become a bit more realistic about those who adopt authoritarian patterns, because such persons have not had too much experience with a democratic heritage.

Although the American society favors a concern for individual freedom, there are still sub-cultures or particular families that deviate from the ideal norm. Children in either of these circumstances would not be exposed to values calling for increasing autonomy. Like fish in the water, there is no contrasting air to suggest anything other than the present conditions. Children socialized under these circumstances would be highly uncomfortable if confronted with self-direction and self-assertion. They, too, hold on and will not let go of their parents.

A special case exists in the child who is kept a perpetual baby. Regardless of the person's age, reference to him is "he is our baby" or "our youngest one." Special attention and care was granted to such a child because the parents will no longer be privileged to have another life to mold. Such a child may possibly be given everything in keeping with his allegedly helpless state. Gifts come to him not because of what he has *done*, but solely on the basis of what he *is* or symbolizes in his parents' minds. The result can be a child who may not lift a finger on his own behalf, but who feels he has only to make his wishes known in order to have them granted. Or, he is so dependent or submerged by his parents' attentions that he never does achieve manhood or womanhood in the normal sense of the term. Should one bite the hands that feed him? Of course, a plausible answer is "Never;" and so the child is fixated at infantile levels regardless of chronological age.

Just as personality types explain some of the unconscious controls exerted by parents over children, so certain personality types among children reinforce the parent-child relationship or weaken it. Has the child a characteristically timid nature? Could the child be described as curious and explorative or highly inexperienced, inept, and ridiculed? Is the child truly loved or basically rejected? Are the child's capacities brought out or are they frustrated at every turn? Is the child challenged or is the child disheartened and downcast? If rejection is maintained long enough, the child, himself, finds self-denial a quality that best satisfies his parents as well as himself. Autonomy and self-responsibilty do not flourish in such soil. A remote possibility remains that rejection can proceed to the point where the parents would like to see the child "grow up" as soon as possible. If this occurs, then the child may be thrust into adult life earlier than most youngsters his age.

Social Pressure for Autonomy

Whether parents refuse to let go or children are willing to hold on, social pressures bring children safely past childhood into adolescence and final maturity. Children have their place, but every society wants them to become adults eventually. The parents will inevitably have to release their hold upon children, if for no other reason than the ravages or "insults" of time, which weaken them and bring about their demise. Children have to stand on their own feet sooner or later. An individual cannot be kept under surveillance and domination at all times and the self-directed, free-willed person who can and will conform to social patterns once he has left the family nest is a welcome asset to a given society. Perhaps this transition might be viewed as passing from the control of the family into the wider control of a greater society. In the family, the controls would be gross and observable. In the greater society, the controls would be diffused and highly subtle. In the family, the agents of control are the parents. In the greater society, the agent of control is the individual.

Autonomy is "Heady Wine"

The granting of power to individuals, welcome as it may be to children who have been held in a type of servitude, is always accompanied by responsibility. Young people are free not only to do what they consider to be right, but they are just as likely to do what is wrong, inept, poor, or despicable. They are released to take the high road of life, but the trail may be rocky, slippery, surrounded by dangers, and far from well marked. With autonomy, comes the chance to test one's ability or the opportunity to find one's inabilities Is the child really brilliant or is he basically a fool? Autonomy will bring his qualities out in the full light of his society. The dreams of his childhood can now be realized, or shattered by harsh realities. It is, therefore, quite understandable to find children a bit apprehensive as real autonomy is conferred on them.

Gradual Autonomy

Because the step from childhood into adulthood is a big one, there appears to be a need for gradual transitions. Children accustomed to parental propulsions do not blithely assume the responsibilities of self-propulsion. They are led to such a condition slowly, step by step, not abruptly. One may take a lesson from the mountaineers who do not conquer a mountain in one big drive up a sheer cliff face. They take it gradually, step by step, moving up an incline, often at angles away from their destination. They rest in base camps between climbs. They sustain each other and encourage each other as they move along. They train. They take the easier slopes first. They do not run up the mountain, they walk up the mountain, cautiously.

Frequently, children are asked, "What will you be when you grow up?" With the granting of more and more personal freedoms, children may begin to realize that they may not be able to be all things, but only *one* thing. A specific career, a specific job, a specific status awaits them and they, themselves, will be among the determining factors in the outcome. They must first master the broad, general, elementary knowledges. As in school, life demands movement beyond the elementary levels into junior and senior levels. The older three "R's" of Reading, 'Riting, and

'Rithmetic" must now be converted into the newer three "R's" of "Responsibility, Reliance, and Regard." They can not be altogether satisfied with broad general targets, but must have particular objectives.

The former juvenile cannot ask others to shoulder his burdens and to protect him if he falters. The child who has walked with the parental crutch must now throw it away and depend on his own young back. The youngster who was the center of the universe, now finds he is a small satellite held in orbit by greater forces to which he must now pay attention. If he has acquired a degree of self-esteem, it will now be tested for durability as he learns to regard the numerous others in his life.

One should be conscious of the magnitude of this transition for children and prepare them as best one can for the journey. At no time is the child so alone that others cannot be of assistance. It is not a sign of weakness to seek and find help. Everyone needs guidance, even the guidance counselor. It would be unwise to think of autonomy as a pure state in which others cannot reach a person or help that person.

Parental Responsibility in the Achievement of Autonomy

Parents have the maximum responsibility to lead children into a wide variety of experiences which can enrich their lives. An exposure to a multiplicity of things typifies those alert parents who seek to strengthen their children for the autonomous years ahead. The narrow, less concerned parents neither care nor make efforts to ready their youngsters for their future. With their eyes on the ground, they rarely lift them to the mountain tops. Their children will probably remain in the safer and easier valleys of life. This is not to deplore such conditions, because societies do need the masses of people who do no more than repeat the pattern set before them by their parents and past generations. Societies also need those individuals who can rise above mediocrity and provide some form of societal leadership.

As children move toward autonomy, it is important to note those parents who are aware of the impending years of autonomy for their children. They consciously expose their children to many things and do so patiently and gradually. If they desire their children to learn to care for their property, they encourage them to clean their room, keep their books, paper, clothes, toys, sporting equipment, and self in good order. If they are sensitive about the amenities, then they give their children a chance to meet guests and to make them comfortable. If they want their children to learn to give as well as to receive, they may provide some pets who require daily attention and care. If money is to acquire a meaning beyond something to spend freely, then allowances are given in varying amounts so they can learn how far money can go before it disappears. If choices must be made in life, then ample opportunity is granted to have the children make choices and learn what the consequences may be. If provincialism is to be dispelled then parents will attempt to give their children some travel experience which takes them far from home. If it is not possible to take prolonged trips, wide reading and other visual stimulation such as pictures and movies may suffice.

The ability to discuss or talk through issues that may prove troublesome, in America at least, is a particular quality desired in the autonomous adult. Its roots can be planted in childhood by those parents who accept their children at their own level and are available when they are needed, who will listen carefully to their children's thoughts and are willing to take criticism, and who give their children an understanding that an ugly side of life exists alongside the beautiful. It probably cannot be made emphatic enough that the channels of communication between parents and their children be left open for the exchange of mutual confidences. If parents close these channels of communication, then, most likely, children will go elsewhere for their discussions and influences. The person with whom one can speak is in the position to make the most profound impression. The person with whom one cannot speak will be possibly the *subject* of a conversation, but rarely the *object* of the exchange. Personalities tend to *expand* in conversation and *shrink* in silence.

It is not implied that children are to engage in man-to-man or woman-to-woman talks at tender ages with their parents solely to achieve autonomy. What has been suggested, to American parents at least, is that there be increasing opportunity for children to have the materials with which to think, increasing opportunity to share or to test out one's thoughts, and finally, the opportunity to be on one's own.

One theme that is intriguing is the depth of thought that comes from being with others or with being alone with one's self. Which produces the deeper results? Do people produce in the classroom, the committee, or in a crowd? Do people think chiefly in silence in the privacy of their own rooms, in their study cubicles, when they sit down alone with a book? Apparently, there are those who can shut out various distractions and can find their personal thoughts without difficulty. But there are others who would be so distressed under such conditions that "they could not hear themselves think." The type that a child may be will determine which procedure or condition can be utilized. In any event, American children have some need for opportunities to think for themselves. It is only after this process that they may possibly be able to contribute to their society.

Throughout this discussion, it is possible to gain the erroneous impression that parents have total responsibility for their children. It is hoped that soon enough children may also take responsibility and thereby assert their own individuality. Many other people, however, have their responsibilities in this matter. By "others," reference is made to friends, acquaintances, teachers, peers, employers, officials, neighbors, and relatives. Parents have received attention because they are central to the socialization of their children. Never, however, are parents to be credited as the sole factors in the socialization of an individual. All along the way, it is quite possible for others to assert themselves and so give a whole new tack to the individual's course in life.

Parents Versus Other Social Forces

Competing for influence upon growing children are *significant others* such as other children and neighbors. It is commonplace to find a number of parents who are not too pleased about what they may call the undue influence of others on their own children. Some parents may desire to insulate, isolate, or build a protective fence around their children in order to maximize their control. Such tactics are not easily carried out in a society which calls for increasing participation beyond the home. Children can and do meet their peers and their neighbors and may find their ways attractive, despite the apparent objections of their parents. In such instances, parents may not be working in the direction of their children's achievement of autonomy, but rather in the direction of slowing the rate of that achievement. Thus, parents may be viewed as being involved in the rate of growing autonomy as well as in the attainment of self-direction by their children.

In the American society, at least, the parental control of the rate of autonomy appears to be a struggle. Mass media, for example, in the form of television programs especially designed to attract children, find their way into children's minds. Television has become an early window on the world for a great many children and not every parent is successful in preventing their children from looking through it.[3]

SUMMARY

Childhood has been viewed in this chapter as a process of moving from a state of relatively complete dependence to a state of relatively complete independence. Both the biological and sociological foundations for this movement were discussed. Some parents were noted as reluctant to let their children become free and children were noted as unwilling to let go of their carefree childhood. Both situations were understandable.

[3] See Irving Merrill, "Broadcast Viewing and Listening by Children," *Public Opinion Quarterly*, Vol. 25, No. 2 (Summer, 1961), pp. 263–276.

Nevertheless, the process of achieving gradual autonomy is encouraged by human societies which seek to develop adults capable of perpetuating social structures and processes. Adults who seek to bind themselves freely to their society are the desirable social products. The movement toward independence will, under optimum conditions, be gradual, thoughtful, and considerate of the children making the transition. While parents are identified as having major responsibilities, other human beings make their influence felt. In the end, the child stands alone and can no longer be called a child, but a responsible component of his society.

READINGS

BAIN, Read, "Needed Research in Parent-Child Fixation," *American Sociological Review* (April, 1945), pp. 208–216.

BAIN, Read, "The Self-and-Other Words of a Child," *American Journal of Sociology*, Vol. XLI (May, 1936), pp. 767–775.

BETTELHEIM, Bruno, "Feral Children and Autistic Children," *American Journal of Sociology*, Vol. 64, No. 5 (March, 1959), pp. 455–467.

BONNEY, Merl E., "Parents as Makers of Social Deviates," *Social Forces* (October, 1941), pp. 77–87.

BRONFENBRENNER, Urie, "The Changing American Child—A Speculative Analysis," *Journal of Social Issues*, Vol. 17, No. 1 (1961), pp. 6–18.

FANDURA, Albert, and HUSTON, Aletha C., "Identification as a Process of Incidental Learning," *Journal of Abnormal Social Psychology*, Vol. 63, No. 2 (September, 1961), pp. 311–318.

GESSELL, Arnold, *et al.*, *The First Five Years of Life* (New York, Harper & Row, Publishers, Inc., 1940).

GESELL, Arnold and ILG, Frances, *The Child From Five to Ten* (New York, Harper & Row, Publishers, Inc., 1946).

HAVIGHURST, Robert, *et. al.*, *Growing Up in River City* (New York, John Wiley & Sons, Inc., 1962).

HOFFMAN, M. L., "Power Assertion by Parents and Its Impact on the Child," *Child Development*, Vol. 31 (1960), pp. 577–591.

KELL, Leone, and ALDOUS, Joan, "Trends in Child Care over Three Generations," *Marriage and Family Living*, Vol. 22, No. 2 (May, 1960), pp. 176–177.

MEAD, George Herbert, *Mind, Self, and Society* (Chicago, The University of Chicago Press, 1934).

MEAD, Margaret, and WOLFENSTEIN, Martha, eds., *Childhood in Contemporary Cultures* (Chicago, The University of Chicago Press, 1955).

MUNN, N. L., *The Evolution and Growth of Human Behavior* (Boston, Houghton Mifflin Company, 1955).

PARSONS, Talcott, BALES, R. F., and SHILLS, E. A. *Family Socialization, and Interaction Process* (New York, The Free Press of Glencoe, Inc., 1955).

RIESMAN, David, *et al., The Lonely Crowd* (New Haven, Yale Univerity Press, 1950).

WHITING, John, and CHILD, Irvin, *Child Training and Personality: A Cross-Cultural Study* (New Haven, Yale University Press, 1953).

18

Some Deviant End Products
of Socialization

INTRODUCTION

Children reared in the same society tend to have similar social experiences, and in some significant respects their behavior is much the same. Although some societies are characterized by rather sharp social class and/or caste distinctions, there is still a residue of socio-cultural experiences in which most children become involved. In the United States, for example, class and caste-like relations prevail to a significant extent; despite this, most American children have a considerable number of similar experiences and characteristics. They are in close and continuing contact with their mothers (or mother-surrogates) during the first five or six years of their lives. They play with toy guns or dolls. They are permitted to go to the movies, but are *sent* to school. Finally, they all receive some instructions regarding socially approved attitudes toward God and country, authority and discipline, property and competition. These are but few of their many common social involvements.

In some respects, therefore, most American children are alike. But they are different, too. Aside from individual differences, certain categories of children display relatively the same configurations of personal-social traits largely because they have had similar experiences. This fact warrants their being classified into social types.

As children grow older, their needs and interests change, their knowledge and skills increase, and their contacts and interaction broaden. As a result, their life organizations become more complex. Such is the typical growth pattern of the normally developing child. Although there is no precise and generally accepted standard for determining the optimum rate of the social development of children,[1] there are certain broadly

[1] See Arnold Gesell, *The Child from Five to Ten* (New York, Harper & Row, Publishers, Inc., 1948).

267

defined behavior patterns which tend to be expected of them. To illustrate, the well-known admonition "Act your age" means that a child of
ten should not act like a six-year old. When he does—and persistently
—he is regarded as not developing in accordance with age-level expectations and requirements.

The socialization process implies that the behavior of children is expected to change as they move from one age level to the next. The
logically expected result of this process is that by the time the child
reaches adulthood he is prepared for personally satisfying and socially
productive participation in the life of the group. Ralph Linton [2] points out
that "each society has a series of ideal personalities which correspond to
the various statuses which it recognizes. . . . The status personality is a
social phenomenon, the psychological type an individual phenomenon."
It is this status-personality, as a social phenomenon, which is relevant
to the particular interest of this chapter.

If a society is to have the status personalities it requires, the personal
and social qualities necessary to constitute such personalities must be
stimulated and transmitted to persons as they develop toward adult
maturity. When, therefore, the typical behavior of children is systematically examined in terms of sex and age, some measure of their social development is possible. Such an approach would lead to the identification
of those children whose development is proceeding at a normal rate. In
like manner, children whose development is retarded or precocious can
be recognized also.

The focus in this chapter is not upon the normally developing child,
but upon the child who is deviant, even though his deviation is short-
lived. The deviations of these children vary considerably in seriousness
and duration. They affect the children themselves and others in varying
degrees. Therefore, in order to point up these distinctions, a dichotomy
of the less serious and the more serious deviants is employed.

The Less Seriously Deviant

In this context, the word *deviant* refers to the child whose behavior
"departs significantly from the norms set for people in their social
statuses." [3] While it is recognized that childhood is not clearly differentiated into functionally important statuses, it must also be remembered
that certain patterns of socially-expected child behavior are clearly re-

[2] *The Study of Man* by Ralph Linton. Copyright © 1936, D. Appleton-Century
Company, Inc., pp. 477–478. Reprinted by permission of Appleton-Century-Crofts.
[3] Robert K. Merton and Robert A. Nisbett, eds., *Contemporary Social Problems*
(New York, Harcourt, Brace & World, Inc., 1961), p. 723. See also Merton's discussion of deviant behavior, *Ibid.*, pp. 723–731.

lated to sex and age. Therefore, the deviant types referred to here are those children who in their interactions with others display configurations of traits which depart significantly from the social expectations applicable to them by reason of their sex and age.

Some Deviant Types: Attributes and Impact

Representative of the deviant types of children under consideration are the "mama's boy," the "cry baby," the "spoiled brat," the "tattle tale," the "sissy," the "tomboy," the "bookworm," and the "bully." The qualities and behavior that constitute these types should be seen and evaluated in terms of whether or not they are appropriate to the sex and age of the children who display them. Thus, the three-year-old who habitually cries in order to have his way could with far less justification be defined as a deviant than the six-year-old who behaves in the same way. And, lest she be defined as a deviant, the eight-year-old had better divert her interests from baseball and climbing trees to things more ladylike.

Like other children, these types grow to maturity. They get older, bigger, and they develop additional skills and acquire greater knowledge. Eventually, they assume the roles of adulthood. But, whether they are none the worse for having been "cry babies" or "tomboys" is related to the extent of such behavior, both in time and intensity.

. . . it is nowadays recognized that a certain amount of petty pilfering occurs among many children around the age of six or seven and is to be expected as part of the process of trying their wings. Children appear to be no worse for very occasional and slight experimental deviations from socially accepted norms of conduct. Since they soon voluntarily abandon such behavior, their misconduct or maladaption cannot be deemed either habitual or symptomatic of deep-rooted causes.[4]

The deviations of some children are not merely experimental; they tend to be habitual. In some cases, these deviations are injurious principally to the children themselves; in other instances, they are a threat to peers, parents, or others. Whatever their extent, or the object of their impact, when such deviations continue beyond the limits of family or community toleration, the effects might be lastingly harmful. And this is perhaps no less the case with the "sissy" or the "bully" than with the "pilferer."

Among these deviant types, the rates of movement through the different age levels of childhood vary widely. In some instances the pace is slow but progressive; in other cases development occurs in spurts; and a few seem to never relinquish completely the behavior which marked them as deviant types. This last category is rather well illustrated in the "tomboy" who grows into a woman who is noticeably masculine in some

---

[4] Sheldon and Eleanor Glueck, *Delinquents in the Making* (New York, Harper & Row, Publishers, Inc., 1952), p. 7.

respects; or the little "bully" who grows, gets older and is still a "bully."

Essentially, these deviant types point out some of the effects of discontinuity in socialization. Generally, patterns of behavior appropriate for one age level must be relinquished when the next age level is reached. But some children do not adapt readily or easily to some of these prescribed changes. Conceivably the relatively intimate, exclusive, and continuing interaction between mother and "mama's boy" might well create a dependency relationship which grows stronger as he grows older. And at ten, mother's implied suggestion "Don't you want to go to camp this summer?" might fall upon deaf ears. Such, then, is a case in which prescribed discontinuity is distorted into continuity, to the detriment of effective socialization.

The Model Child: Model or Deviant?

It is generally recognized that the child who is too aggressive, unduly submissive, too autonomous, or over-protected might be headed for trouble if his situation remains unchanged. Ideally, the child should be aggressive, submissive, autonomous, and protected in just the "right" degree; there should be balance in the variety of his experiences. Such, it appears, are the essential attributes of "good" children. But this is the ideal, and most children do not achieve the ideal or even approach it very closely. But what of the few that do? These are the children who, when they are good, they are very good—and, they are good all the time. These are the model children.

Generally, the model child is too good for most other children—and frequently even for adults. To other children, they are "never any fun"; to adults, they may be objects of pity: "poor child, he's missing all the joys of childhood." And it might well appear that he is. He gets into no scrapes, he pulls no childish pranks, and he violates no parental rules. As a result, his peers tend to shun him and he, in turn, tends to react unenthusiastically to mother's implied wish, "Why don't you go out and play?"

The model child may be not only a conforming child, but intelligent and sensitive—and lonely. If he is lonely, the rejection of his peers and the inability of his parents to fill the resultant void may lead to a progressive decline in his self-concept. This, in turn, may reduce his self-confidence, stimulate self-pity, and lower his regard for people generally. At this point his plight is a manifestation of what Cavan [5] calls "contra-culture."

In her formulation of delinquent behavior in terms of "public tolerance, intolerance, or outright condemnation," good behavior and bad behavior

[5] Ruth Shonle Cavan, *Juvenile Delinquency* (Philadelphia, J. B. Lippincott Company, 1962), p. 18.

are placed at opposite ends of a continuum, and in their extremes both good and bad behavior are socially suspect, even rejected, This is "contraculture." As set forth by Cavan, the "good" end of the continuum ranges from "minor overconformity" to "extreme overconformity," to "contraculture" (extreme goodness). The model child, then, is deeply involved in the contraculture of extreme goodness. Because of this he is apt to experience difficulties in his attempts to relate to others. The difficulties he experiences are likely to affect his family adversely, or at least cause them to be apprehensive regarding his life-chances.

DEVIANTS AND OTHERS

Deviant types of children tend to pose problems not only for themselves, but often antagonize or disturb their siblings, age mates, and parents. The "cry baby," the "tattle tale," or "mama's boy," for example, is likely to be regarded disdainfully by his siblings, especially if their parents seem to treat him preferentially. Not uncommonly, sibling rivalry in the home is intensified by the presence of these types, so that disharmony and even hostility sometimes intrude into the family setting.

In the world of his peers, the deviant type is almost certain to meet difficulties. Required, as he is, to adjust to a variety of children in varying situations, the tolerance or slight sanctions which he faced at home may now be compounded. Thus, the "sissy" may be ridiculed by the boys and giggled at by the girls. The "tattle tale" is to be avoided, the "bookworm" to be shunned, and the "bully" is given a "wide berth."

Children such as these are often embarrassing, exasperating, or puzzling to their parents. The inability of "mama's boy" to stand on his own among his peers, the "tomboy's" unladylike conduct, or the failure of any of these types to act their age is sometimes a source of disappointment and despair to their parents. Yet, these reactions are likely to be tempered by rationalizations or the urge to defend. For in the child-rearing process, parents may consciously or unconsciously find pleasure or satisfaction in certain intermittent deviations toward which they react with the well-known comments "Boys will be boys" or "She'll outgrow it." "Children who have been helped by their parents to *escape* the normal tasks of growing older," say Davis and Havighurst,[6] "seldom 'grow up' in their later personalities." Implicit in this observation is the incontrovertible fact that not only must the child act his age, but one day he must "put away childish things."

The process of socialization rarely results in the creation of completely virtuous individuals. It does lead, however, to the development of certain

[6] W. Allison Davis and Robert J. Havighurst, *Father of the Man* (Boston, Houghton Mifflin Company, 1947), p. 194.

deviant types. These types are, by the very nature of the socialization process, largely the result of the malfunctioning and dysfunctioning of the agencies, instruments or processes involved in socialization. They are problem types to the extent that their normal development is retarded or arrested and to the extent that their personal qualities and behavior mar their development into and during adulthood.

The More Seriously Deviant

In turning to a consideration of the more distinctly deviant types of children, the context for discussion is changed to include the local community as well as the over-all society. In contrast to the preceding section, the focus is now shifted from the children to the social and cultural context in which their deviation is centered. This is warranted by the fact that the presence of these types tends to be correlated with the character of their effective environment. Furthermore, the impact of their behavior or condition is not limited, as in the case of the minor deviant types, but extends to the community and the larger society.

Among the deviant types now under consideration, "the delinquent," "the academically retarded," "the habitual truant," and "the drop-out" are prime examples. The personal-social characteristics of such children, their general conditions, or immediate environments are such that the community—and indeed the larger society—is often impelled to show general concern, to express censure, or to take official action. By and large, the community regards the deviant behavior or the social circumstances of these children as permanent. This behavior is seen as threatening to the children and to the community. At the same time, many persons and groups hold the community responsible for the plight of these deviant types, while others accept the notion that, although the community may not be at fault, it does have the responsibility to do something about it.

The involvement of the community in the development of deviant types has been recognized—even dramatized—by a number of writers. As Goodman [7] sees the situation, one should question the view of social scientists that ". . . 'social animal' means 'harmoniously belonging'. . . ." He says that in this view, fighting and dissenting, rebelling and initiating fundamental social change are not regarded as proper social functions. Furthermore, when things do not run smoothly, improper socialization or failure in communication is the social scientist's explanation. Goodman

[7] From the Introduction to *Growing up Absurd,* by Paul Goodman. © Copyright 1960 by Paul Goodman. Reprinted by permission of Random House, Inc.
   Also see James B. Conant *Slums and Suburbs* (New York, McGraw-Hill Book Company. Inc., 1961).

suggests a different explanation when he asks the question, "Is the harmonious organization to which the young are inadequately socialized, perhaps against human nature, or not worthy of human nature, and *therefore* there is difficulty in growing up?" [8] Goodman's answer to the "why" of deviant behavior is not inadequate socialization but inadequate opportunity ". . . to meet the appetites and capacities of human nature, in order to grow up." [9] That the problems of growing up are rooted in the social order is implicit in his comment that ". . . with all the harmonious belonging and all the tidying up of background conditions that you please, our abundant society is at present simply deficient in many of the most elementary opportunities and worth-while goals that could make growing up possible." [10]

In view of the significant relationship between these deviant types and their social and cultural contexts, and since the literature of social science is replete with studies of these types,[11] major attention will be given to the contexts rather than to the deviant types of children within them.

In this section of the chapter the more distinctly and seriously deviant types of children are discussed. The types already discussed were characterized as children marked by configurations of personal-social traits which depart significantly from the socially-sanctioned age and sex norms applicable to them. Further, it was indicated that, by and large, these types do not represent terminal points in the development of these children; rather, they tend to be types involving retardation or arrested development. Principally, the behavior and the relationships of these children were described as irritants or sources of embarrassment, rather than threats or problems of grave social consequence.

Obviously, however, some of the traits of the "spoiled brat" or the "bully," for example, might be continued into the years of later childhood, adolescence, or adulthood. When, therefore, such traits, in combination with others such as aggression, hostility, emotional and economic deprivations, are experienced under pressure conditions of various kinds, deviant personalities of a more serious nature often emerge.

In discussing seriously deviant types, no attempt will be made to ferret out the causes of the relevant behavior of these children. Since the interest here revolves around the concept of status personalities, it is important to refer to certain aspects of the social structure. As presently employed,

[8] Paul Goodman, *op. cit.*, p. 11.

[9] *Ibid.*

[10] *Ibid.*, p. 12.

[11] See Albert K. Cohen, *Delinquent Boys: The Culture of the Gang* (New York, The Free Press of Glencoe, Inc., 1955); James B. Conant, *Slums and Suburbs* (New York, McGraw-Hill Book Company, 1961); Gerhart Saenger and Harry M. Shulman, "Some Factors Determining Intercultural Behavior and Attitudes of Members of Different Ethnic Groups in Mixed Neighborhoods," *Journal of Psychology* (January, 1948), pp. 365–380.

status refers to the person's "position with relation to the total society." [12]
Because the child's status in relation to his society is of central concern,
his definition as a deviant implies that his behavior leads or is likely to lead
to social disapproval and censure.

It is axiomatic that many people deviate from some norms and therefore might be subject to censure if the norms violated are of sufficient social concern or if the deviants are detected. These "deviants" are not the
concern here. The present interest is in children whose behavior tends to
involve *patterned* deviation from the more significant social norms. Also
included are children who are socially defined as deviants although their
deviant acts are few and minor. The inclusion of the latter category of
deviants brings attention to the present interest in the deviant in relation
to his society or his community. Furthermore, it implies that deviation,
although perhaps not caused by, is, nonetheless, a function of society.

THE DEVIANT AND HIS ENVIRONMENT

To some extent, every society is subjected to forces of disorganization.
The sources of this disorganization might be in the structural arrangements or malfunctioning of the society or they may lie in the society's
response to non-social forces in the natural environment. Whatever the
source of this disorganization, its impact is felt by its people, both adults
and children.

Manifestly, disorganizing forces do not exist to the same degree in all
societies; neither are they the same throughout all social-class levels
within any given society. To illustrate, the economically deprived person
is frequently disproportionately affected by these forces while the
privileged person tends to be secure against them. Even within a single
social-class setting, the forces of disorganization are not similarly felt
throughout. For example, in areas where culture conflict prevails, where
family discord is widespread, or where institutional controls are lax, some
childern come into open conflict with the law while others grow to maturity with minimum difficulty. [13]

Ultimately, the disorganizing or disruptive potential of a society is
related to its values and norms. If, for example, children are regarded as
economic assets, work roles will be ascribed to them and child labor will
not pose a problem. However, if childhood is defined as a status involving
non-responsibility, the gainful employment of children will be socially

[12] Ralph Linton, *op. cit.*, p. 113.
[13] This is implicit in the works of many researchers. See Clifford R. Shaw and Henry
D. McKay, *Juvenile Delinquency and Urban Areas* (Chicago, University of Chicago
Press, 1942); and Walter C. Reckless, Simon Dinitz, and Ellen Murray, "The 'Good
Boy' in a High Delinquency Area," *Journal of Criminal Law, Criminology and Police
Science* (May–June, 1957), pp. 18–25.

rejected. These contrasting examples are well illustrated in the history of the United States: the first situation prevailed prior to the twentieth century; the second has prevailed throughout most of the twentieth century, up to the present.

The Family Setting

An examination of various family structures reveals significant implications regarding the relationship between socially disorganizing situations and social values. The characteristic family form in the United States in contrast with that of Samoa presents a case in point. In the United States, the child—especially the young child—tends to be bound to his parents. If he is separated from them permanently or frequently, this tends to be looked upon unfavorably. Such a child is said to be disadvantaged. This is reflected in the fact that the courts are reluctant to separate children from their parents, even for good and sufficient cause. Furthermore, such reluctance is widely supported by social workers.

In contrast to the situation in the United States, the people of Samoa do not regard close and continuing contact between parents and children as of paramount importance.[14] The child is free to move back and forth from his parents to other relatives. Thus, to the Samoans, the expression, "I live with my parents," frequently heard in the United States, does not carry any overtones of a secure and necessary relationship. Indeed, it might well indicate that the speaker was being denied the opportunity for rich and varied emotional involvements. Because of this, such a child might be regarded with pity and concern.

Obviously, the United States and Samoa are vastly different societies. The first is comparatively large and complex; the second is relatively small and non-modern; and, as such, is less likely to be faced with disorganizing or disruptive forces of the same character and magnitude found in modern societies. In the United States large scale, complex social organizations, sharp divisions of labor, economic deprivation, impersonality in social relations, and high rates of mobility pose certain difficulties with respect to stability and specialization in the child's expanding relationships. Thus, the child needs to be involved in a relationship with his parents that will be permanent and secure. Because his relatives may be widely dispersed over the country, he may not have even physical access to many of them. Moreover, the concept of individualism in the United States is such that, by and large, parents alone have rights and responsibilities in the care, support, and protection of their children.

[14] Margaret Mead, "Coming of Age in Samoa," in *From the South Seas* (New York, William Morrow & Company, Inc., 1939).

Deviation and Disorganization

The literature of social science is replete with discussions of social disorganization. Implicit in these discussions is the view that growing up under conditions of disorganization constitutes a risk factor in the life experience of the child. Among the disorganizing forces which merit consideration, the clash of cultures stand out. Such a clash tends to occur within modern, urbanized and highly differentiated societies. In a world of international conflict the consequences of war might well lead to externally imposed clashes of culture. Such was the case in Japan after the war between that country and the United States.

With the occupation of Japan by the Armed Forces of the United States and in the years immediately following, the process of disorganization in Japanese society was accentuated. This was partly because of the dislocations of war and the attempts of the victorious Americans to facilitate and influence the re-organization of Japanese life in accordance with certain democratic values and norms. That the consequences of the aftermath of war exerted an influence on the children of Japan is clearly suggested in the following report:

Educational Reforms also abolished the morals course—the course which had indoctrinated children in the virtues of filial piety, loyalty to Emperor, submission to elders, and proper conduct in the community—and replaced it with a social studies course. This marks a sharp break between the school and family in the sense that the school now teaches individualism, freedom, and democracy. In this situation school teachers are the target of attack from conservative elements of the society as well as from family members.[15]

In a culturally heterogeneous society such as the United States, the probability that culture conflict will prevail is perhaps ever-present. As a matter of fact, this society has a long history of such conflict in which immigrants from many parts of the world as well as migrants within the society have been involved. During the first half of the twentieth century sociologists and other social scientists devoted considerable attention to the presence of immigrants in the United States.[16] By and large, this concern had to do with problem situations involving these newcomers. Viewed in a larger perspective, many of the immigration studies by social scientists deal with the assimilation of immigrants into the social structure of the United States. Yet, the immediate theme of many of these works was related to culture conflict including crime, delinquency, and other problems indicative of maladjustment.

[15] Edna Cooper Masuoka, Jitsuichi Masuoka, and Nozomu Kawamura, "Role Conflicts in the Modern Japanese Family," *Social Forces,* Vol. 41, No. 1 (October, 1962), p. 4.
[16] Outstanding among these works is William I. Thomas and Florian Znaniecki, *The Polish Peasant in Europe and America,* (New York, Alfred A. Knopf, Inc., 1927).

The culturally marginal position of some immigrant families exposed them to a considerable degree of parent-child conflict. As newcomers to a land culturally distinct from their own, but a land in which the assimilation of immigrant peoples is highly prized, they (particularly their children) found it desirable, even necessary, to adjust to new and different patterns of behavior. Except for work and other necessary cross-cultural contacts, adult immigrants tended to lead a relatively self-contained life and thereby experienced only minimal pressures to conform to the dominant culture patterns. This was not so with their children. Compulsory school-attendance laws, organized youth activities, the popular appeal of the movies and the radio were some of the forces exerting pressure on the children of immigrants to become Americanized. Since many of these children were native-born and since they began to attend public school along with so-called American children, they often felt compelled to be, act, and "talk American." Moreover, they often took on patterns of self-determinative behavior which tended to lead to conflict with and isolation from their parents. This differential pressure upon the immigrants and their children often resulted in strained parent-child relations, in intergenerational conflict, and sometimes in the child's repudiation of the old parental ways.

Not uncommonly, especially for older children, bickering and disagreements between parents and children were centered around such widespread youth activities as keeping late hours, using the family car, dating, and decision-making. Given this culture-conflict situation and the resultant parent-child conflict consequent to it, the process of family interaction often became less than satisfying both for parents and their children. Furthermore, these intra-family difficulties were sometimes expressed in, or contributed to, the child's difficulties in adjusting to the expectations of the larger community.

In a discussion of Polish immigrants in the United States, one author shows how conflict between value systems may interfere with the acculturation process and how such conflict may lead to parent-child difficulties. Because these children often mediated between their parents and the community, they came to enjoy a degree of authority and dominance over their parents which was at variance with the group's traditional parental prerogatives. "Since it was possible to have a separate life outside the home, the desire for recognition or 'getting even' with parents gave rise to defiant behavior in seeking new experience that was often illicit." [17] Apparently, therefore, such conditions of life were reflected in disproportionately high rates of juvenile court contacts for delinquency, dependency, and neglect; excessive school drop-outs; and a significantly higher incidence of scholastic retardation.

[17] R. A. Schermerhorn, *These Our People* (New York, D. C. Heath & Company, 1949), p. 286.

In the late nineteenth and the earlier part of the twentieth centuries, the impact of social disorganization and the deprivation which characterize slum living had their principal effect on the children of European immigrants and children of lower-class, native-born parents, both white and Negro. Today these influences are felt to some extent by children of white migrants into the larger industrial areas of the country, but perhaps to a much greater extent by non-white children, mainly Puerto Ricans and Negroes. In addition to the difficulties associated with slum living, these latter categories of children, especially Negro children, are subjected to color discrimination, residential, recreational, religious, and school segregation and to other forms of differential treatment based on race.

The impact of these race-related experiences would seem to be correlated with and is said by some to give rise to the disproportionately high rates of deviant behavior among these children.

Whereas the problem of delinquency before 1930 was mainly a problem of the native-born child of foreign parentage, notably European, the problem has shifted, since the curtailment of immigration in 1924, to the new "migrants" and the new marginal groups on the American scene—the urban-drifting Negro, the Puerto Rican, and the Mexican. This shift, of course, does not indicate any tendency inherent in these groups toward youthful lawlessness. It is almost wholly a consequence of the barriers of adjustment on social, cultural, and economic levels placed in their way, the ecological concentration and cultural segregation they experience, and the development of a peculiar "delinquent subculture" . . . into which many of their children, marginally excluded as they are, are inevitably drawn.[18]

It is highly probable that this relationship between depressed living conditions and juvenile delinquency prevails with regard to other types of deviation, including academic retardation, habitual truancy, and dropping out of school.

The School and the Deviant

Becoming academically retarded, habitually truant, or a drop-out is presumably related to the success of one's experiences in school. This success may depend not only on the child's capacity to learn, but on his will or motivation to learn. Furthermore, the extent to which the child is motivated to learn is not unrelated to the rewards he gets from, and during, the learning process. The rewards given children in the school take various forms including teacher's approval, praise, ascribed roles of leadership, membership in select groups, special assignments,

[18] Herbert A. Bloch and Frank T. Flynn, *Delinquency: The Juvenile Offender in America Today* (New York, Random House, Inc., 1956), p. 45; see also Harry Manvel Shulman, *Juvenile Delinquency in American Society* (New York, Harper & Row, Publishers, Inc., 1961), pp. 206–213.

and the like. Because of his culturally impoverished background the child slum-dweller is disadvantaged in the competition for such recognition; consequently, a potentially potent stimulus to learning is lost.

In the schools it is commonplace for students to seek the approval of each other. With reference to this tendency, Coleman [19] observes that

As long as meaningful social rewards could be directly supplied by adults, there was little need to be explicit about them in educational theory, for they were naturally provided by the very process of interaction between parent and child, or student and teacher. To be sure, these rewards were often distributed in ways that reinforced the stratification system and took away the lower-class child's meager chance for equality; as some authors have shown very well, the middle-class backgrounds of teachers often made them unable to hold out reasonable reward for reasonable achievement to lower-class children.

In continuing his discussion, Coleman takes the position that adolescents today look mainly to their peers for social rewards. If there has been a shift in the source of these rewards (from parents to peers) this does not mean that lower-class children now have greater access to rewards that stimulate learning. The fact remains that in the school the teacher is still the dispenser of the rewards that stimulate the child to try to learn.

Frustration or failure in school is probably a crucial factor in academic retardation, habitual truancy, and dropping out of school. Frequently these types of children become involved in delinquencies. As a matter of fact, in many jurisdictions the habitual truant is, by definition, a juvenile delinquent. When it is recalled that there is no precise or generally accepted definition of habitual truancy, the implication that the school experience might, in some cases, stimulate children to become delinquents emerges rather clearly.

Today, juvenile delinquency constitutes one of the serious problems in many societies. The United States is no exception. The delinquent is perhaps regarded as the most seriously deviant child in America. Despite this, however, no special discussion of this deviant type is presented, for the interest here is comprehensive rather than specific. The main intent of this section is to direct attention to the relationship between the more serious deviant types of children and the social and cultural context in which they tend to be involved. But it should not be inferred from this emphasis that these social and cultural factors are the cause of deviation. Indeed, many useful and highly successful people were reared in the slums where socially disorganizing forces were widespread. Doubtless, many more such citizens are even now growing up in these slum areas. Despite such successful socialization, however, the available evidence points clearly and dramatically to the fact that slums are areas in

[19] James S. Coleman, *The Adolescent Society* (New York, The Free Press of Glencoe, 1961), p. 11.

which disproportionately high rates of children who constitute what is here referred to as the more seriously deviant types are to be found.

SUMMARY

This chapter is concerned with certain types of deviant children who are defined as end-products of socialization. The significance of the deviant behavior of these children varies in accordance with the nature and persistence of that behavior. Mainly because of this, these deviant types are designated, the "less seriously deviant" and the "more seriously deviant."

Those children who constitute the less seriously deviant group tend to interact in a rather circumscribed context, including home, peer group, and school. As a result, and because they tend to be the younger children, the impact of their deviations is felt principally by themselves and those with whom they come into more direct contact.

The more seriously deviant children tend to become involved in situations which frequently extend beyond their homes and immediate environs. Usually, their deviant behavior is more persistent, defined as more threatening, and often results in community-wide concern or action. In addition, the various types of the seriously deviant are apparently concentrated in the more disorganized or slum areas of cities. This relationship, which has been widely noted, has been a source of considerable concern, of numerous research studies, and of some social action. Implicit in these reactions, therefore, is the notion that the effectiveness of the socialization process is inextricably tied to the social and cultural context in which that process occurs.

READINGS

ALLPORT, Gordon W., *Becoming* (New Haven, Yale University Press, 1955).

GREEN, Arnold, "The Middle Class Male Child and Neurosis," *The American Sociological Review*, Vol. 11 (February, 1946), pp. 31–41.

MEEK, Lois Hayden, *The Personal-Social Development of Boys and Girls* (New York, Committee on Workshops, Progressive Education Association, 1940).

NIMKOFF, Meyer F., "The Relation of Parental Dominance to Parent-Child Conflict," *Social Forces*, Vol. 9 (June, 1931), pp. 559–563.

OSTROVSKY, Everett S., *Children Without Men* (New York, Collier Books, 1962).

SHORT, James F., TENNYSON, Ray, and HOWARD, Kenneth, "Behavior

Dimensions of Gang Delinquency," *American Sociological Review,* Vol. 28, No. 3 (June, 1963), pp. 411–428.

SLOCUM, Walter, and STONE, Carol, "Family Culture Patterns and Delinquent-Type Behavior," *Marriage and Family Living,* Vol. 25, No. 2 (May, 1963), pp. 202–208.

WALTENBERG, William W., "Normal Rebellion—or Real Delinquency?" *Child Study,* Vol. 34 (Fall, 1957), pp. 15–20.

V

PERSPECTIVES
FOR THE FUTURE

19

Adolescence:
Port of Entry to Adulthood

When I was a child, I spoke as a child,
I understood as a child, I thought as a child,
but when I became a man, I put away childish things

I Cor., 13:11 (Paul)

All men are destined to be, but never to remain, children. They grow in age, in size, in skills, and in knowledge. They "put away childish things": the interests, activities, relationships and statuses of childhood are supplanted by those of adulthood. Putting away childish things is a time-consuming process which necessitates preparation and involves trial and error behavior. This process is adolescence.

VARIATIONS IN THE DEFINITION OF ADOLESCENCE

The precise character of adolescence—of growing from childhood to adulthood—varies from society to society. This variation includes a time factor: at what age the process begins, how long it lasts, and the clarity with which the terminal point is defined. It is to be seen in the kind, degree, and methods of preparation. Another variation lies in the extent to which adult rights, privileges, duties, responsibilities, obligations, and immunities are enjoyed fully or partially in the initial period of adulthood.

The variations in the process of becoming an adult are sharply illustrated in the different approaches taken, generally, in primitive and modern societies.

In primitive society the puberty rites are rites of passage from childhood to the next stage—manhood. Adolescence among such groups, if it can be said to exist at all, may actually encompass a very short span of life. In our society

285

adolescence has been lengthened until now it often covers a period of ten years or more. Extreme examples of delay in conferring adult status may be found in East European villages where, until the birth of the first child, the Jewish father, for example, is not considered a real man. The Irish system of delaying marriage until the father of the prospective bridegroom makes economic provisions for him is still another example of the prolongation of adolescence. Thus, because of this prolongation, we are faced with a situation in our modern western culture which is very different from the brief period of adolescence found in preliterate cultures.[1]

The differences between adolescence in primitive and modern societies are significantly related to the prevailing value systems and levels of technology. In terms of inherent capacities, physical, mental, and emotional, children the world over are much the same. They reach puberty at roughly the same time. They tend to develop physical strength and body coordination at about the same rate. Therefore, when adulthood is viewed as involving principally the roles of reproducer and producer, all children are capable of being adults at approximately the same time.

Everywhere, the power to reproduce and the ability to produce are principal role components in the status of the adult. These are the objectively necessary and minimum requirements for the occupancy of that status. Generally, humans do not settle for the merely necessary, for the minimum requirements of the situation. In addition to the job to be done, there are values to be preserved, norms to be observed, and often, rituals to be observed; these often become as important as the job itself. Furthermore, a given behavior which is directed toward a particular function often has consequences which contribute significantly to the performance of other functions. For example, the family sitting around the dinner table are there for physical sustenance; yet, prayer, conversation, and decision-making may become a vital consideration for all concerned.

Perhaps nowhere is the minimum preparation or readiness for adulthood a sufficient basis for being admitted to that status. The extreme in adding to the minimum requirements for entry into adulthood is illustrated among the Aruntas of Australia where "some twenty years are required before the rituals to make a man from a boy are completed."[2]

ADOLESCENCE AS PROCESS

In the United States, the passage from childhood to adulthood occurs on different planes of life and at different rates. As a case in point, religious adulthood is reached rather early. The Jewish boy, for example,

[1] Herbert A. Block and Arthur Niederhoffer, *The Gang: A Study in Adolescent Behavior* (New York, Philosophical Library, 1958), p. 109.

[2] Felix M. Keesing, *Cultural Anthropology* (New York, Holt, Rinehart & Winston, Inc., 1958), p. 248.

becomes "a religious adult" at age thirteen. Generally, one is an adult for political purposes at twenty-one. Other levels of adult status tend also to be reached at different ages. These include the privilege of marriage, the right to enter into contracts, criminal responsibility for law violations, driving a car, dropping out of school, and going into the work force.

In addition to long-standing customs and certain relevant values, the high level of technological development is a significant consideration underlying the American approach to the ascription of adult status. The vast, complex, and bureaucratized character of the technologically-based economy of the United States often requires workers with highly specialized skills and knowledge. To meet these requirements, long years of training beyond the point of puberty are required. Although there are still many jobs that can be performed without an extensive training, persons who have long since passed puberty, but who have not graduated from college, are often forced to work at menial, low-paying, terminal jobs. As a consequence, such workers delay marriage, are only partially self-supporting and, are thereby, something less than full adults.

The process of adolescence—of growing from childhood to adulthood —may be profitably viewed from three perspectives: 1. separation; 2. transition; and 3. incorporation. These represent three interconnected phases of adolescence which, according to Van Gennep,[3] are the essential components in "rites of passage." Separation, transition, and incorporation, viewed as a frame-of-reference or as interconnected phases for analyzing adolescence, raise certain logically-connected questions. Among these, the following will be used as a more detailed framework for the ensuing discussion: "What are the forces that stimulate separation?" "What characteristic forms does separation take?" "What are the significant reactions (child and adult) to the forces that stimulate separation and to separation itself?" "What are the social and cultural forces that facilitate or impede transition?" "What are the time elements—starting point, rate of movement, duration, and terminal point—involved in transition?" "Is incorporation an 'all or none' phenomenon?" "To what extent, and how, are institutional, symbolic and ritualistic components involved?" At best, the responses to these questions can only be expected to point up certain socially and culturally significant aspects of adolescence. Nonetheless, such a result might furnish a potentially fruitful point of departure for further study, discussion, and analysis.

Phase One: Separation

Separation does not begin at any definite point in time. In later childhood, when children are approximately ten to thirteen years old, changes

---

[3] A. Van Gennep, *Les Rites De Passage* (Paris, Nourry, 1909). As used here separation, transition, and incorporation do not imply the rituals and the degree of institutionalization emphasized by Van Gennep.

in body size, contour, coordination and functioning begin to be noticeable. Generally, these changes occur earlier and more rapidly in females than in males. Along with these changes, new feelings, sensations, and impulses begin to be felt. These modifications in the child's make-up are essentially sexual and they signify the emerging power to reproduce. This power, which is symbolized by the word puberty, is finally reached roughly between the thirteenth and fifteenth years. At this point the child may be said to have reached the threshold or the port of entry into adolescence—he is no longer a child in the physical sense.

In large measure, separation begins as a reaction to puberty. It is a response to being different. Since he has changed physically from the child he was, he finds it necessary to depart somewhat from his former childlike behavior. Frequently, however, parents do not recognize this necessity; or upon recognizing it, they sometimes ignore or stifle the child's attempts in this direction. Again, some parents insist that the child should change his ways, but do not specify what ways should be changed. When the child attempts to make changes of his own choosing, he often incurs wrath or resistance from his parents. Caught in the web of misunderstanding or inconsistency, the child tends to seek escape to the freedom of his peers.

In modern, urban, and highly differentiated societies, many situations outside the home facilitate separation. The gang, the clique, the various youth organizations make it relatively easy to get away from "the folks." In these situations, new attitudes, values, skills, and knowledge are acquired. New relationships are formed and new interests begin to develop. Consequently, the old self-concept, "I am a child," begins to blur and fade away.

Meanwhile, parents and adults have observed and reacted to the child's emerging physical changes. Sometimes, by their thoughtless or tactless remarks concerning the boy's high-pitched voice or the girl's rapid but uneven growth, for example, adults compound the child's difficulty in understanding and accepting these changes. Parents are usually apprehensive regarding the so-called pitfalls in the paths of their children, and in their efforts to guide and protect them, they sometimes become more rigid and demanding. When this happens, the child often responds with greater efforts to escape the restraints placed upon him.

Separation of the child from the home means that he has left the familiar for the relatively unfamiliar. He can no longer expect protection and security as he did at home. Now he must fend for himself. He must compete on an equal footing in the world of his peers. If he fails, he may not retreat; if he succeeds, victory is sweet. In any event he can't go home again; he can never again be the child he was. He must continue on his way—an adolescent in transition to adulthood.

Phase Two: Transition

Now that he has "put away childish things," the no-longer-child-not-yet-adult person is in a state of in-betweenness. ". . . children and adults constitute clearly defined groups; the adolescent does not wish to belong any longer to the children's group and, at the same time knows that he is really not accepted in the adult group. In this case, he has a position similar to what is called in sociology the 'marginal man'." [4] The use of the concept "marginal man" to characterize the person in transition is at best an analogy. For Park,[5] the "marginal man" is a person who is "a cultural hybrid, a man living and sharing in the cultural life and traditions of two distinct peoples; never quite willing to break, even if he were permitted to do so, with his past and his tradition, and not quite accepted . . . in the new society in which he now seeks a place." The adolescent in the phase of transition is neither child nor adult. At times, he is viewed and treated somewhat as a child: the decisions he makes are countermanded by his parents. At other times, he is expected to behave as a grown-up: his failure to act on his own results in his being called irresponsible or childlike.

In the transition phase, the adolescent may be ambivalent toward the prospect of being defined as an adult. He may aspire to the rights of adulthood, but he may be reluctant to relinquish the privileges of childhood. The known security of childhood might have greater appeal than the not-yet-known freedom of adulthood. In his thoughts, his feelings, and his actions he sometimes vacillates; but unlike Park's "marginal man," he is likely to want to make the break from his past.

The inevitability of the assumption of adult status is perhaps the determining force in the adolescent's ultimate, though halting, development toward adult maturity. Although at times movement in this direction is impeded or discouraged by adults, and although at times he might be fearful of the responsibilities of adulthood, he, and his elders, know that adulthood is the direction in which he must necessarily travel.

Universally, the ascription or achievement of the more important social statuses tend to be marked by appropriate rituals and ceremonies. In the United States this is illustrated to a limited extent in confirmation, graduation, and marriage ceremonies. In some societies, the occupants of such statuses have undergone a period of preparation prior to induction. In effect, because the society has a vital stake in the role-performance in these statuses, the players are prepared, then inducted formally and publicly.

In contrast, adolescence in the United States does not involve such

[4] Kurt Lewin, "The Field Theory Approach to Adolescence," Jerome M. Siedman, Editor, *The Adolescent* (New York, Holt, Rinehart and Winston, 1960), p. 39.

[5] Robert E. Park, "Human Migration and the Marginal Man," *American Journal of Sociology* (May, 1928), p. 829.

institutionalized procedures and practices. As a consequence, the person in transition is left more or less with a goal but without a guide. The rate of his movement is not predetermined for him, and the practices he is to follow are not spelled out. Thus, trial and error is the most available method of movement.

In the absence of socially prescribed behavior which is clearly communicated, the adolescent tends to rely not upon adults but upon other and often older adolescents for direction and support. They, like he, have no assurance that their way is effective or that it will lead to acceptance by their elders. Thus, "the blind" lead "the blind." In this process, however, even this type of collective support provides a measure of security that is perhaps necessary and helpful. In this connection it has been hypothesized that:

. . . when a society does not make adequate preparation, formal or otherwise, for the induction of its adolescents into adult status, equivalent forms of behavior arise spontaneously among adolescents themselves, reinforced by their own group structure, which seemingly provides the same psychological content and function as the more formalized rituals found in other societies. This the gang structure appears to do in American society, apparently satisfying deep-seated needs experienced by adolescents in all cultures.[6]

This support, it would appear, is to be found not only in the gang, but also in the informal high school clique, in the college fraternity, and even in the casual collectivity of fellow adolescents.

Viewed in terms of overt behavior, the transition phase of adolescence involves adult-like activity. Because the overt action associated with a status is more readily discernible than are the feeling states, adolescents tend to seek first to emulate the actions of adults. The responsibilities and obligations of adulthood, being less observable and measurable, are often ignored or minimized by them. As a result, the behavioral manifestations of adulthood by adolescents, especially in the beginning state of transition, are likely to be the more symbolic equivalents of adult behavior. Smoking, shaving, and swearing are examples of this.

In the transition phase of adolescence, two types of apprenticeship training for adulthood might be profitably examined. The first are situations which are fashioned, maintained, and controlled by the younger generation themselves. One example of these situations is the adolescent gang. Because of its peculiar characteristics, however, the gang is perhaps not an effective instrument of apprenticeship training for adulthood. Characteristically, the values, norms, and activities of the gang are contrary to those of the adult community. Therefore, continuing conflict tends to characterize relations between the two. In recent years, however, a movement has been underway whereby adults seek to utilize the gang

[6] Block and Niederhoffer, *op. cit.*, p. 17.

as a mechanism for rechanneling the energies of the young into more socially acceptable activities.[7]

As popularly conceived, the gang is a conflict group involving principally children and adolescents of the lower classes.[8] Frequently, however, the informal, collective activities of boys between approximately eight and twelve years old are referred to as "gang behavior" or "ganging." In terms of the apprenticeship training under discussion, however, the function of high school cliques, friendship groupings, and other informal collectives is not altogether different from that of the gang. These groups, too, often exasperate, frustrate, antagonize, or alienate the elders of the community.

The second type of apprenticeship-training situation involves the more formally organized adolescent groups. In contrast to the gang, the continued existence of these organizations depend ultimately on their adult sponsors. Some examples of this type of apprenticeship-training situations are scout troups, student government organizations, and college fraternities. Situations such as these represent the closest approximations to socially prescribed and sanctioned mechanisms to facilitate movement into adulthood. Generally, the members of these groups engage in decision-making, formulate plans, and implement them. Activities carried on in these situations usually have the approval of the general community. However, participation in these groups is highly selective; therefore, the vast majority of adolescents are excluded. Although these groups are said to be autonomous, their decisions are sometimes subject to veto by their adult sponsors, and the security thus provided protects them against the consequences of misdirection.

The transition phase of adolescence offers no assurance of adequate preparation for incorporation into adulthood. By and large, the symbolic equivalents of adult behavior are, for purposes of playing the adult role, still mere child's play. While gang behavior sometimes involves knowledge and skills required for adult functioning, more often than not these are utilized for ends that are at cross purposes with the requirements of responsible adulthood. Finally, in the more organized, adult-sponsored youth activities, the relatively few adolescents involved, tend to enjoy a contingent autonomy, and the responsibility they bear and the accountability they face are tempered by the ever-present adult willingness to step in and take over.

Inevitably, the transition phase ends. Its end, however, is not necessarily abrupt; nor need it always occur in an absolute manner. Furthermore, even though induction into adulthood is not heralded—at least

[7] See *Reaching the Unreached: Fundamental Aspects of the Program of the New York City Youth Board* (New York City Youth Board, 1952); and Lewis Yablonsky, *The Violent Gang* (New York, The Macmillan Company, 1962).

[8] For a different and provocative discussion of the concept of the gang, see Block and Niederhoffer, *op. cit.*

not widely—by rites or rituals of community import, there are nonetheless some unmistakable signs of arrival or impending incorporation. "Transition into the adult institution of marriage formally terminates membership in youth culture . . . it is at this point that the sociological requirements of adulthood—economic independence and the family of procreation—are satisfied. Although parenthood and an independent domicile are further criteria of adulthood, it is the formal rite of marriage that symbolizes movement into adult culture." [9] It should be pointed out, however, that there are other signs of the break with adolescence and of the actual intrusion, penetration, or acceptance into adulthood. These include permanent and independent residence away from the family domicile and self-support within the family domicile but with parental acceptance of independent action. Whatever the approach to incorporation, such action is likely to represent not the enjoyment of full adult status but more probably a mere beginning. In the final analysis, the incorporatee and the corporate body of adults must both come to recognize and accept the change in status. And this is likely to be a time-consuming process.

Phase Three: Incorporation

Just as separation changes gradually into transition, so it is that transition becomes, in time, incorporation: the last phase in the process of achieving adult status. Despite the failure of major institutions to provide adequate tutelage for adulthood, adolescents in the United States eventually achieve this status. To reach it some of them find it necessary to re-order their characteristic expressions of their commitment to certain adult values. Such adolescents are likely to be incorporated into adulthood with a background marked by the manifestation of dominant adult values in non-adult ways. Perhaps their competitive spirit and effort were directed mainly toward the proliferation of dates and the pursuit of popularity. Or, their reactions to adult-prescribed sex types might have been reflected in the "slack-pack," "pony tail" and "bobby sox brigade" and the "dungaree," "black jacket" and "sneakers" gang. Their responses to the dominant norms of heterosexual behavior might have included deviations ranging from the first-date kiss to heavy and habitual petting. They might have become accustomed to the corner drugstore, the snack bar, and the drive-in movie as havens from home. They might have diverted the automobile away from its principal function as a means of transportation to a symbolic but nonetheless utilitarian device in the pursuit of popularity and dates. Finally, dating itself might have become for them a means that had no end, a means that was itself an end, or just the

[9] Ernest A Smith, *American Youth Culture* (New York, The Free Press of Glencoe, 1962), p. 207. By permission of The Free Press of Glencoe.

modern version of the western frontier practice of putting another notch on one's six-shooter.

An adolescent entering into adulthood may have been involved in any one or any combination of these experiences and reactions. When he is incorporated into adulthood this experimental background constitutes part of his preparation and equipment for the adult role. Because such a background is inconsistent with the ideal definitions and demands of adult society, the adolescent, now a novice adult, may experience difficulties in his efforts to fit into his new status. These difficulties may relate to different aspects of adult culture and their precise expression may depend on the particular person and the particular situation involved. For some, difficulties may center around the responsibility for self-support and the obligations to support their dependents. For others, the freedom of movement experienced in adolescence may continue to be expressed in the practice of "going out with the boys." For still others, their mode of dress, manners of relating to others, or general public decorum may lead others to be critical of them because of their "immaturity."

One dramatic example of the difficult and indeed lack of smooth incorporation into adulthood, ideally viewed, is found in the case of the adult novice who has an adolescent background which includes juvenile delinquency. In some such instances this violative behavior continues to be followed well into the adult years and constitutes a personal as well as a social problem.[10] As a consequence, adjustment to the requirements of responsible adulthood may be long delayed and in some cases never fully realized.

Apart from any considerable personal inadequacy, incorporation into adult status is not an easy or simple process. It is a matter of progression; generally by stages. "Every individual has a series of roles deriving from the various patterns in which he participates and at the same time a role, general, which represents the sum total of these roles and determines what he does for his society and what he can expect from it."[11] The actual assumption of the adult role (general) is time-consuming, and different people accomplish it with different degrees of difficulty and at different rates. Thus, incorporation includes stages or steps in which one tends to be ascribed (or to achieve) one adult status, then another, then another, and another, until he runs the whole gamut of adult statuses (and roles). For example, one may be old enough to fight for his country, but not old enough to vote. Again he may contract a valid marriage but continues to be dependent on his parents, at least until he "gets on his feet."

[10] See Sheldon and Eleanor Glueck, *Later Criminal Careers* (New York, The Commonwealth Fund, 1937), and, by the same authors, *Juvenile Delinquents Grown Up.*
[11] *The Study of Man* by Ralph Linton. Copyright © 1936, D. Appleton-Century Company, Inc., p. 114. Reprinted by permission of Appleton-Century-Crofts.

To adapt to the role requirements of the status of the adult requires knowledge, skills, and a degree of personal maturity which may be lacking in some adolescents who enter into the phase of incorporation. Furthermore, their efforts to adapt may meet with resistances of various kinds and in different situations. In such cases the role performance of the novice adult may include the intermittent intrusion of some of his old adolescent ways.

REFLECTIONS OF ADOLESCENCE IN ADULTHOOD

In studying the process of socialization, the focus is usually on the transmission of the culture from the old to the young. As a rule, the interest centers on the influences exerted upon children by parents and adults, by older children, or by peers. What the child gives the parents is a consideration that is not widely discussed.[12] The point to be considered here is not what the adolescent gives the adult; rather it has to do with the probable influence of adolescence upon adulthood. Put differently, the question is "Does the novice adult express certain residual adolescent traits and interests which are incorporated into or which stimulate changes in the adult culture?" The answer to this question should be regarded as being based on reasonable inference, not empirical evidence.

The inference that certain residual adolescent traits and interests of the novice adult are incorporated into or stimulate changes in the adult culture is derived, in part, from the following observations:

1. The generalized role of the adult involves multiple roles, for example, spouse, worker (or homemaker), and parent.
2. Generally, the assumption of these roles does not occur concurrently, nor with equal competence.
3. When faced with the necessity of performing a role for which he is relatively unprepared, the novice adult tends to draw upon his past adolescent experiences.
4. Adolescents and adults share some common values, but their expressive forms differ. In some instances the adult may regard the adolescent's expressive form as more effective, efficient, or attractive.
5. The novice adult's contacts with other adults open the way for communication, for the expression of contrasting patterns of behavior, and for the opportunity to imitate each other.

In much the same manner as immigrants who come into a new land, the adolescent who is incorporated into adulthood continues to hold on

[12] James H. S. Bossard and Eleanor Stoker Boll, *The Sociology of Child Development*, 3rd ed. (New York, Harper & Row, Publishers, Inc., 1948), p. 130–144.

to some of the values, attitudes, and behavior patterns characteristic of adolescent culture. Again, like the immigrant, the novice adult not only holds on to part of his culture, he shares it actively and passively with those with whom he is now associated.

Because of the lack of information, it is not yet possible to enumerate definite, empirically verified elements of adult culture which have been significantly stimulated by elements of adolescent culture. It is possible, however, to point to certain cultural parallels which are in most instances dominant components in adolescent culture, but which have been or are being taken over into adult culture. It should be noted, that the time-and-place origins of these cultural parallels are not within the scope of this discussion. Any or all of them might have originated among an earlier generation of adolescents. For example, one cultural parallel might have started during the period of "flaming youth" or the "roaring twenties." Then, it might have been transmitted directly to the succeeding adolescent generation, and then to the adult generation into which the "flaming youth" were incorporated.

Reflections of adolescence in adult culture take various forms. Some must be inferred; others can be easily observed. Some are quite general phenomena; others are quite specific. Perhaps it is well to begin the examination of these "reflections" with the inferred and the general.

American adult society has been called child-centered and youth oriented. "Think young," "Act young," "I like to be around young people"; statements such as these are frequently made by adults. Perhaps they imply something of a socially derived urge to be perpetually young. Or, perhaps, they are but expressions or reflections of an unconscious fear of growing old. Whatever the reason, this interest in youthfulness is attested to by a great number of character-building child agencies and by a greater number of people who support and maintain these agencies through professional, philanthropic, and voluntary efforts.

This interest in or positive orientation towards youth is often reflected in various facets of adult culture. Class reunions at which adults sing the songs of their college days and recall the memories of their own youth are common occurrences, at least among the higher classes. Many times an adult is said to be acting like a child or reverting to infantile behavior. Not uncommonly the parlor games of the young and the dance craze of the current adolescent generation are adapted to adult use. Behaviors such as these may have been picked up by adults as they observed adolescents' behavior. It is highly probable, however, that some elements of adolescent culture are transmitted in direct contact situations by novice adults who continue to manifest certain components of their erstwhile adolescent culture.

Historically, work has been a widely cherished value, an end in itself for Americans. "Thou shalt earn thy bread by the sweat of thy brow."

"Hard work never hurts anyone." "A good day's work for a good day's pay." "Honest labor." "Work, for the night is coming when man's work is done." Expressions such as these suggest that work has a redemptive quality, that it is of paramount importance, that it is necessary, satisfying, and laudable.

The present American scene reveals that changes regarding the conceptions of work are in the making. These changes are related to the increasing development of automation which is rendering work—the expenditure of physical energy—less necessary and less important. It is probable that these changes are related also to an emerging reconception of work as an intrinsic good. Apparently, this latter development is being facilitated by a concurrently developing interest in leisure. More and more, people are concerned about the need for and the importance of leisure. Increasingly, writers are exploring the many implications and possibilities of leisure.[13] In these works, more leisure is not pictured as necessarily a blessing to the person who has leisure time. It is recognized that some people use the leisure time resulting from shorter work hours to work on other jobs. In such instances, this perhaps represents a clinging to the traditional conception of work. Of course, the difficulty of making ends meet may be an important consideration also.

It may well be that the adolescent culture is one of the principal sources of stimulation toward the declining sacredness of work and the increasing importance of leisure. Usually, adolescents and children are kept out of the work force and away from work models. Understandably, therefore, they are not likely to have an unusually high regard for work, especially when fun looms so large in their world. In addition, when adolescents who do not have a deeply internalized positive orientation toward work are incorporated into adult culture, they are likely to maintain and manifest a relative indifference toward work. The life history of the "relief chisler," for example, might be a pertinent subject for study.

A more visible reflection of adolescent culture in the culture of the adult is in clothing, personal grooming, and body adornment. Among adolescent girls, unique styles of dress are commonly found. Slacks or jeans, man-like shirts, socks, and sneakers are frequently standard wearing apparel. Casual or minimum use of cosmetics, distinctively different hair styles, such as the pony tail, are often in vogue. Frequently, the charm bracelet, the scatter pin, or the anklet chain adorns an otherwise unadorned body.

Practices among adults, many of whom can no longer be reasonably defined as novices, which parallel these adolescent habits of dress and

[13] See Mortimer J. Adler, "Labor, Leisure and Liberal Education," *Journal of General Education*, Vol. 6(1951), pp. 35–45; and, Ernest W. Burgess, Editor, "Aging and Retirement," Special issue, *American Journal of Sociology*, Vol. 49 (January, 1954); Eric Larrabee and Rolf Meyersohn, Editors, *Mass Leisure* (New York, The Free Press of Glencoe, Inc., 1958).

adornment can easily be observed in the suburban shopping centers and the laundromats of a thousand communities across the country. Except for the anklet chain, which tends to be missing, the resemblance of the generations is remarkable—at least from a distance. Upon further examination, other similarities likely to be found would perhaps include tastes in music and musicians, the frequenting of drive-in restaurants and theaters, watching television, and perhaps even the reading of "children's literature"—the comics, that is.

Other more important, more positive and perhaps even more lasting reflections of adolescence in adult culture can be observed. The similarities just referred to may be nothing more than mere culture parallels; for this kind of sharing is to be expected of people who are in contact and communication, especially when the culturally prescribed differentials in certain expectations are not rigidly enforced. Yet, the tendency to imitate is still likely to operate. The extent to which practices initiated by adolescents are imitated by adults indicates the extent that the former influence the latter.

From time immemorial young people have borne perhaps the principal burden in war. In some countries various social and political movements have been advanced through the singular efforts and energies of the young. In the United States, the role of the adolescent has not generally required or encouraged him to participate in social and political affairs. In war, however, the American adolescent has perhaps done more than his share.

The present-day American scene is marked by evidence of the emergent social and political impact of adolescents. This impact is manifested most significantly and dramatically in two emergent phenomena; one is directed immediately toward the world arena; the other directly influences the national situation.

The first of these, popularly known as the Peace Corps, is an instrument of American foreign policy which has caught the fancy and has elicited the approval of much of the world. In the Peace Corps, hundreds of adolescents are engaged in responsible, productive, and creative activity. These youth—male and female—have turned to good account the vigor, the enthusiasm, and the spirit of adventure said to be associated with them. Even though this represents a new venture for youth and for Americans, it is already apparent that the results of their participation in this program will almost surely be lasting.

The second of these emergents of adolescence, the techniques of non-violent protest, has already impelled many people to re-examine their appraisals of youth. The daring, dedication, and self-discipline displayed by the youngsters who participate in *sit-ins*, for example, is a dramatic display of the adolescent's capacity for commitment to a cause in which he believes. In pursuing their ends through selected non-violent means, adolescents have worked along with adults and sometimes they have rushed in where adults fear to tread. All in all, the techniques of non-violence, which have been employed largely by adolescents, have left their impact indelibly upon the entire American people.

In time, when the potentials, the practices, and the productivity of adolescents are again assessed, it will perhaps be necessary to look beyond any particular generation of adolescents. For the impact of the Peace Corps and the non-violent protest movement will perhaps be clearly seen. At this point, questions might be raised regarding the impact which adolescents exert in the direction of social change.

Summary

Throughout this chapter, the recurring, though sometimes implicit, theme has been the relatively unique and difficult problem of becoming an adult in American society. Adolescence, that ill-defined status between childhood and adulthood, tends to be defined differently in different cultures. These differences which relate to clarity of status and role, to preparation for adulthood, to characteristic adolescent behavior and to the terminal point of adolescence are the principal sources of difficulty for American youth and for Americans.

Adolescence refers to that process—and age-level period—in which children become increasingly sensitized to, and more or less prepared for, the assumption of the rights, privileges, and responsibilities accorded the adult. This process may be profitably divided into three phases. These are: (1) Separation—the child's first wide and consistent venture into the world of his peers and other non-family persons; (2) Transition—the phase of deep and continued involvement in a configuration of values, attitudes, and behavior which is not altogether consistent with childhood nor adulthood; and (3) Incorporation—a step-by-step induction into adulthood, which involves self-support, marriage, and parenthood.

After induction into adulthood the erstwhile adolescent—now novice adult—may resort from time to time to adolescent behavior. Sometimes this creates problems for him. At other times, however, such behavior may be imitated and accepted by older adults. The contact between the novice adult and other adults tends to influence certain adult culture patterns. This, it appears, is one possible source of stimulation to social and cultural change.

Readings

Broderick, Carlfred B., and Fowler, Stanley E., "New Patterns of Relationships Between the Sexes Among Preadolescents," *Marriage and Family Living*, Vol. 23 (February, 1961), pp. 27–30.

COLEMAN, James S., "The Adolescent Subculture and Academic Achievement," *American Journal of Sociology*, Vol. 65 (January, 1960), pp. 337–347.

DAVIS, Kingsley, "Adolescence and the Social Structure," *Annals of the American Academy of Political and Social Sciences*, Vol. 236 (November, 1944), pp. 8–16.

HOLLINGSHEAD, August B., *Elmtown's Youth* (New York, John Wiley & Sons, Inc., 1949).

PARSONS, Talcott, "Age and Sex in the Social Structure of the United States," *Personality in Nature, Society, and Culture*, Clyde Kluckhohn and H. A. Murray, eds., (New York, Alfred A. Knopf, Inc., 1949), pp. 269–281.

REUTER, Edward B., "The Sociology of Adolescence," *American Journal of Sociology*, Vol. XLIII (November, 1937), pp. 414–427.

20

Education and
Research on Childhood

INTRODUCTION

In this final chapter, it seems useful to turn attention to two separate but related perspectives regarding childhood. The first is education, or the application of data gathered over the years. The second is research, which may consist of either a re-checking of older insights or further exploration. Taken together, education and research appear both to offer the conservation and further growth of knowledge concerning the nature of childhood.

EDUCATION AND CHILDHOOD

The difference between *education* and *propaganda* is sometimes indistinguishable. Ideally, education is characterized by the presentation of all available and relevant information, devoid of all attempts to eliminate data or points of view which are unpalatable. Propaganda, on the other hand, tends to involve selectivity in its information and grows out of preconceptions regarding the ends to be served. Another difference lies in the specificity of the goals of propagandists versus the more generalized goals of educators who value the freedom of full inquiry instead of preconceived, narrow targets. Yet, there are times when educators have unconsciously slipped into the roles of propagandists or propagandists have appeared to be willing to keep an open mind by widening the scope of their information base. The study of childhood particularly has been one field of inquiry which seems to be fertile ground for imaginative work by educators and propagandists alike. It is a challenging task for those con-

300

cerned with the study of childhood to keep the two at least somewhat identified and separate.

While the term propaganda has a connotation of cleverness and an aura of manipulation of others, education appears to have the mantle of respectability, honesty, and soundness. When there is a desire to solve a problem, some people turn to education. Education is often said to be the panacea for all social ills and allegedly has special relevance for the rearing and handling of children. If there is doubt about the socialization of children or there is hesitation about what specific paths should be trod, education is commonly called upon to supply directions.

Confusion In A Period of Instability

In societies where there is no doubt as to what roles children, parents, or adults are to play, the task of socialization is made easy. One has merely to do what all others who are playing fixed roles are doing and he will be socially correct. At least, a parent will have the comforting support of his peers that he is doing "the right thing" and his children will thank him for it in the end. But a society that is sometimes unsure of itself, that is unsettled or instable, that is growing and experimenting, and that even encourages a variety of behavior patterns, gives way to growing doubt and confusion as to goals and procedures. In this type of social climate, which is represented by the American society, there are many contrasting voices heard in the land. Which bit of advice should be put into practice and which suggestion is unsound? Which course of action is wise and which is foolish?

It would be reasonable that in an era of confusion and rapid change caution would be exercised. It is obvious, however, that caution is not the predominant theme of modern times. Rather, there appears to be a willingness to explore, to experiment, and to suggest new ways of doing things. The sources of information concerning children are abundant. While the following list is not regarded as complete, it represents the prodigious production of information concerning various aspects of child rearing in the United States:

Sources of Information Concerning Children

Popular Periodicals

Parents Magazine	Hearthstone Magazine
McCalls	National Parent-Teacher
Woman's Home Companion	Better Homes and Gardens
Redbook	Ladies Home Journal
Saturday Evening Post	The Child
Reader's Digest	Coronet
Life	Look
Boy's Life	Woman's Day

Professional Journals

American Journal of Orthopsychiatry
American Sociological Review
American Journal of Sociology
Sociometry
School and Society
Annals of the American Academy of
  Political and Social Science
Sociology and Social Research
Social Forces
Social Problems

Journal of Home Economics
Marriage and Family Living
Journal of Abnormal and Social Psy-
  chology
Quarterly Journal of Studies on
  Alcohol
Psychological Bulletin
American Psychologist
Child Development
Eugenics Quarterly

Organizations

National Council on Family Relations
National Congress of Parents and
  Teachers
The American Eugenics Society
The Planned Parenthood Association
The Family Service Association of
  America
YMCA
YWCA

Young Men's Hebrew Association
Young Women's Hebrew Association
Red Cross
Travelers' Aid Society

Boy Scouts of America
Girl Scouts of America
Campfire Girls
4-H Clubs
Future Farmers of America
Parents Without Partners
Marriage and Home Committee (Na-
  tional Council of Churches of Christ
  in America)
Future Teachers of America
Family Life Bureau of the National
  Catholic Welfare Conference
Committee on Marriage, Family, and
  the Home (Central Conference of
  American Rabbis)

United States Government Agencies[1]

Women's Bureau
Office of Education
Government Printing Office
Bureau of Public Assistance
Bureau of Employment Security
Bureau of Old Age and Survivor's
  Insurance

Social Work Service, Veterans Ad-
  ministration
Bureau of Census
Bureau of Labor Statistics
National Office of Vital Statistics
National Institute of Mental Health
Federal Extension Service
Children's Bureau, U.S. Department
  of Health, Education, and Welfare

University or College Courses

Child Psychology
Sociology of Childhood
Children's Services
Human Nature and Social Organiza-
  tion
The Exceptional Child

The Handicapped Child
Marriage and the Family
Family in Various Cultures
Juvenile Delinquency
Adolescence
Child Development
Social Gerontology

[1] See *Marriage and Family Living*, Vol. 20, No. 3 (August, 1958), "Government Services Affecting American Families."

This list does not include the numerous newspaper articles or the array of books which have won wide audiences. Donald Brieland[2] has recently summarized such sources, and notes that over thirty-eight syndicated features on children are available to newspaper publishers. Names like Benjamin Spock and his *The Pocket Book of Baby and Child Care,* or Arnold Gesell and his characterizations of children from birth to adolescence are almost too well known to mention. Perhaps not as well known, but nevertheless rather familiar to students of childhood, are the *Public Affairs* pamphlets and the *Better Living* series published by Science Research Associates. The largest single source seems to be the 1,016 page *The Encyclopedia of Child Care and Guidance* edited by Sidonie M. Gruenberg.[3] Finally, there is the famous perennial which has been issued since 1914 by the United States Children's Bureau entitled, *Infant Care.* These and many more constitute a wealth of material dealing with children.

These sources are cited because there is so much information, so many points of view, so much conflicting data, that selecting an intelligent position is a difficult task. Despite the plethora of information, it is possible to hold the view that perhaps there should be *more* and not *less* materials available to interested parents and children who want to find their way in a complicated social matrix.

In view of what appears to be an abundance of data concerning childhood, it would seem advisable to adopt some standard in terms of which one may formulate some judgment concerning the flood of information pouring from mass media. It is this to which attention is now turned.

CRITERIA FOR APPRAISING SOURCE INFORMATION

1. Goals or Purposes

Probably one of the best means to judge the productions of students of childhood would be to question what ends are being served. Childhood data are assembled to help whom? Perhaps some writers and agencies are prompted by their own interests and only by coincidence developed some new insight or new bit of information. There is nothing derogatory in a person pursuing his chosen profession to the best of his ability. Nevertheless, there is some danger in a "publish or perish philosophy" extant among certain professions that stress quantity of output rather than quality of productivity. Certainly there is outstanding work being done by some who are concerned with childhood. The problem is always how to identify those works which are truly significant over and above those which are

---

[2] Donald Brieland, "Uses of Research in Recent Popular Parent Education Literature," *Marriage and Family Living,* Vol. 19, No. 1 (February, 1957), p. 63.

[3] Sidonie M. Gruenberg, ed., *The Encyclopedia of Child Care and Guidance* (Garden City, New York, Doubleday & Company, Inc., 1954).

ordinary. If attention is focused principally on being read or being active in the field, then the end results are not necessarily bona fide gems of wisdom. How many students have wished that authors would digest their materials, get to the point, and save valuable time? Instead, it is more commonplace to observe a steady out-pouring from the presses of mountains of data with a minimal impact in the long run.

Not many years ago, Elijah Jordan [4] wrote a critique of the philosophy of business which, he insists, pervades American social institutions. In his thesis, he portrays "the contaminating influence" of profiteering in industry, politics, religion, law, art, and *education*. Jordan does feel that educators are least prone to submit to such "contamination," but, nevertheless, there remains a clear suggestion that self-aggrandizement has already entered the ranks of professional scholars and there is the inevitable watering down of scholarship and the short-changing of the gullible public. It is not the current purpose to impugn the motives of students of childhood. It is the objective of this present discussion, however, to suggest that the interested reader note carefully if materials on children are merely repetitions of well known data or if they truly reveal information which stimulates the mind, excites the imagination, and opens new vistas previously ignored.

2. Timely or Timeless Information

Certain educational materials on children and childhood apply current, *run-of-attention* philosophies. That is, they respond to or parallel that which interests the public *at the moment*. This approach gives the general public what it wants and not necessarily what it may need. Following public tastes is frequently safer than attempting to lead or direct public preferences in new directions. Thus, there is usually an abundance of educational childhood information which caters to popular opinion and so may be judged as *timely* and *acceptable*. Of course, public tastes may shift and timely information may become dated. Students of childhood may profitably examine advice concerning children published many years ago.[5] From their present vantage point, they may be amused over the naivete or quaint nature of the advice disseminated in those "ancient" days. But students of childhood might also profitably ask if current childhood theses are also too time-bound to be seriously followed in future years. In other words, are childhood data timely or timeless? If it is the former, it may still be worthy because individuals live within their own social and temporal space and not in some future social climate. If it is

[4] Elijah Jordan, *Business Be Damned*, by permission of the publishers, Abelard-Schuman, Ltd. (New York, copyright 1952).

[5] See B. G. Jeffers and J. L. Nichols, *Light on Dark Corners* (Toronto, Ontario, J. L. Nichols and Co., 1895).

the latter, however, then enduring bedrock has been tapped and future generations can operate on a firm foundation.

3. Room for Growth or Expansion

Still another criterion to apply to materials alleged to be education for childhood is to test the resiliency of the data. By this procedure, the limited or restricted nature of the materials may be highlighted or, on the contrary, the unlimited or expansive quality of the information can be ascertained. For example, if it can be demonstrated that a child should be punished for some error in social finesse, then does it necessarily follow that there be punishment for any or all failures in behavior calling for tact. There is, also, the logical error, "the particularistic fallacy," which overgeneralizes from particular information. Thus, action based upon one's own life experience or one's own children may be sensible within a specific framework, but not applicable in a broader context. The constant plea of sociologists for representative samples reflects this desire to expand their theses to other segments of the population. The careful scientist clearly identifies the bases of his contentions and warns against sweeping applications to everyone or under any circumstances.

4. Opinion, Fact, or Fancy

Those who write, speak, or study about childhood have the prerogative of summarizing their ideas to identify what they consider to be the connecting threads of their discourse. There may profitably be, however, a deliberate effort to identify *opinions* of authorities as separate and distinct from their *facts*. The consuming public probably would be wise to distinguish between *what was found* and *what it means*. Data may be interpreted in many different ways and not particularly in the way a given scholar views his materials. Far too often, some anticipate this reaction and proceed to block off any other point of view which negates or differs with their so-called scientific judgment. There is value in imaginative ideas because these become the springboards to new investigations. There is little value, however, in playing the part of a Pied Piper who attracts others to follow sterile or questionable pathways.

5. Source of Data

Scientists are particularly critical of those who base their ideas on scattered, haphazard collections of data. They demand painstaking research as the minimal foundation upon which to operate. Every step of empiric inquiry is usually described by the research worker to the best of his ability and he subjects himself to the closest scrutiny of his colleagues. Unfortunately, and this seems to be the major criticism of much of the material which deals with childhood, there is far too much which rests chiefly upon assertion, declaration, and claim.

Part of the confusion stems from differences as to the meaning of research itself. There are those who consider research as principally the reading of the works of certain authorities and quoting minutely what was published in the past. This library research or research of the literature is mainly a beginning step in more total research work. Such work does not *terminate* at that point but merely *begins* there. Critics of these procedures have referred to them as the incestuous technique of quoting each other's footnotes. Of course, this technique is not plagiarism if sources are credited.[6] The overreliance on this procedure is not only time-consuming, but too often it masquerades as scholarship. Knowledge concerning children should at least rest on research in the fullest sense of the term and not on quoting or parroting authorities in endless succession.

6. Assumptions or "Axes to Grind"

Tacit assumptions buried within research or theoretical frameworks have often proved to be the chief sources of the failure to come to grips with the necessary information. While specific premises are required in order to initiate study, they may be the undoing of the total effort because they orient the study in the direction of dubious judgments. One has to start with the right foot, so to speak, if one is to get into some coordinated step with reality. The person who wishes judiciously to study childhood educational materials will probably do well to pinpoint what assumptions were made at the outset to see if they were sound points of departure.

Most obvious of all assumptions are those which entail "axes to grind" or preconceptions which *must* be achieved regardless of the exposed data. One does not set out to *prove* an hypothesis. One sets out *to test* the validity of an hypothesis and sets no value on what the outcome may be. One processes data, if one is a scientist, not to force them into some favored pattern, but rather to permit data to be observed from every angle possible so that their full significance may be savored.

7. Application

The final criterion might be the translation of the reported data into appropriate action. This is the ultimate test because application might result in utter absurdity or in effective results. It is much easier to propose

[6] See Winifred Lynskey, "Who Will Bell the Cat?" *AAUP Bulletin,* Vol. 41, No. 2 (Summer, 1955), pp. 324–327.

action than to carry it out. While *how-to-rear-your-children* books or articles are interesting, they may prove to be harmless if subsequently they are ignored or they may prove to be harmful if carried out conscientiously by naive laymen.

Seven guidelines have been suggested as possible criteria to consider in appraising *educational* materials concerning childhood. They are:

1. Goals or purposes
2. Timely or timeless information
3. Room for growth or expansion
4. Opinion, fact, or fancy
5. Source of information
6. Assumptions or "axes to grind"
7. Application

Of course, these guidelines for arriving at judgments can also be applied to the present writing. While the materials contained in this text were solely designed for a presentation of the sociology of childhood and not a conscious attempt to be an advice-giving, all-encompassing source of information concerning children, there are probably many who may choose to evaluate it as an *educational* effort after all. The objective of this writing is not advice, but to sensitize and stimulate thought, to encourage analysis, and to generally promote deeper consideration of sociological aspects of childhood.

It might be useful at this juncture to be as clear as possible concerning the observations that have been made which pertain to evaluating "education for childhood" publications. No veiled intention is implied in the suggestion that legitimate profit derived from rendering services to a consuming public may occur. Those who are sincerely attempting to enrich the thinking of their readers are not being reviled. It may be noted as well that those who draw upon personal experiences or unique occurrences to highlight their points are not necessarily suggesting that these events are universal models to be followed or disavowed. Further, researchers are typically cautious about going beyond their data. Perhaps the problem of disseminating information concerning children is more a responsibility which rests with those who seek to popularize empiric findings than those who carefully attempt to locate significant data.

The tools and attitudes characterizing the sociological approach to childhood involve a strong orientation to documentation via social research methodology, a constant vigilance toward the achievement of an objective frame of mind, and the willingness to seek out all factors which channel or affect human interaction. Where there is failure to adhere to these qualities or characteristics, the pressures of being participants in a single ongoing society may be presumed to have been too much for human frailties.

CURRENT RESEARCH EFFORTS IN CHILDHOOD

To keep in touch with or informed regarding voluminous research efforts in the study of children is a monumental task. The quantity of publications produced by modern presses has achieved a bewildering abundance of literature. Its presence is, perhaps, long overdue as a part of the main stream of social scientists' productivity. There are literally thousands of studies and hundreds of publications in the the area of childhood alone. Whether they are speculative or empirically oriented, they add welcomed knowledge about childhood. It is their overall impact and the tedious sifting and weighing of their meaning that puzzles and challenges. The existence of this extensive literature constitutes the growing edge of the study of childhood and gives promise that the rearing of children will be eventually rooted in sound knowledge rather than in the loose soil of fond hope, trial and error, or iron-clad rules.

Viewpoints Concerning Child Research

Critics of research efforts would perhaps be less quick to criticize if they themselves were subjected to the rigors of research. It is far more difficult to make a painstaking, constructive effort than it is to simply find fault with the pitifully small increment of knowledge gained. Yet, to the credit of research scholars, they are typically in the forefront of potential critics by noting most carefully where they may have failed, why certain results were found, and what new work must be done before conclusions are reached. A thesis that might be empirically sustained would be that it is the over-enthusiastic claims and assertions of those who have *read* research reports that have led to the clouding of issues, rather than anything done by those who have *performed* the research studies.

It is equally true, however, that research concerning children must stand the probes of those to whom it is addressed. If certain research findings are found to be lacking, then those responsible may experience the humbling effects of rejection, revision, or neglect. The success of one research may be erected on the site of the failures of others. Sound research has been done, is being done, and will be done, but each effort may be given its *relative* place alongside other studies. In such company, the merits of some research are highlighted and the shortcomings of other research become painfully clear.

The following viewpoints concerning research dealing with children represent three possible positions. The first holds that the scientific study of childhood has not begun. The second consists of unqualified acceptance of child studies. And the third consists of a more cautious, qualified acceptance of child research efforts. An examination of each of these viewpoints follows.

1. **THE VIEW THAT THE SCIENTIFIC STUDY OF CHILDHOOD HAS NOT BEGUN.** In his insightful text, *The Family, Society, and the Individual,* William Kephart presents a point of view that judges child research to be either lacking or at the stages of minimal beginnings. After presenting a series of statements from a number of authorities in the psychological and sociological field, Kephart [7] states

The above statements have been quoted at length and for a purpose. The purpose is to impress upon the reader the unmitigated fact that in the areas of infant-training and child-rearing *no scientific body of knowledge exists.* Few reputable social scientists would make any claim to the contrary, although what popular writers have to say on the subject is another matter.

The bases for maintaining such an appraisal are explained by Kephart [8] by pointing to the numerous difficulties encountered by research workers when they attempt to probe into childhood. They are

1. All children are different and therefore procedures that are effective with some are not effective with others.
2. Parents are different and tactics employed by some are ineffectual with others.
3. Experimentation with children can be objectionable. Cooperation is not easily secured when parents believe their child is being treated as a guinea pig.
4. Study within a home or family setting is frequently denied and if access is gained, the presence of the research worker becomes a factor which accounts for certain results.
5. Interpretation of parental action is confused by failure to distinguish between actions, per se, and children's perceptions of these actions.
6. Current measurements of personality are far from adequate.
7. Criteria are lacking upon which to judge specific child-rearing tactics. Each investigator may assert his own or follow those of an identifiable group, but consensus is lacking.

It should be noted that the difficulties cited by Kephart apply to "action" research with children. That is, they constitute practical problems

---

[7] William M. Kephart, *The Family, Society, and the Individual* (Boston, Houghton Mifflin Company, 1961), p. 522.
[8] Kephart, *op. cit.,* pp. 522–524.

which are encountered when study is made of child-rearing tactics. They are not necessarily applicable in other types of research which consist of empirical testing of theories of childhood which deal with such considerations as childhood status, childhood as a developmental process, or childhood as a category within a population. There are, indeed, formidable difficulties which confront those engaged in action research, which focuses upon child-rearing procedures. However, research workers are not oblivious to such obstacles and conscientiously have attempted to cope with them.

Certainly, if research effort is seeking to develop an overall theory concerning childhood or child rearing, then generalizations must be cautiously evolved. To be applicable to *all* children at *all* times in *all* circumstances, common denominators must be located painstakingly. Much research, as Kephart correctly observes, focuses upon *specific* children within *specific* situations and carefully avoids overgeneralizations. This is not to the discredit of research workers, but rather it is to their credit that they seek to stay within their data. It is the popularizer of research data who makes the assumption that what has tentatively been indicated by the findings of a given study may now be widely publicized as final and conclusive evidence that certain procedures are now in order if childhood is to be understood and enriched.

Of course children may not be treated as laboratory animals in the fashion and tradition of psychologists dedicated to experimentation with mice, rabbits, pigeons, or dogs. There has long been opposition to making the leap from laboratory animal behavior to human behavior because of the numerous variables which must be taken into account including the tremendous impact of social or cultural conditions. Nevertheless, experimentation has been made possible by close observation and the development of control groups which lack the experimental variable under investigation.

Within the home or family setting, experimentation is probably more a household word than many realize. Parents and siblings alike seem to be constantly trying out this or that technique to determine if desired goals can be achieved. If they fail, the behaviors tend to be discarded in favor of more effective measures. If they succeed, they become part of the family setting. It is precisely to these matters that research workers direct their attention.

The remaining criticisms of modern research with children are much more valid, namely that the interpretation of research data is too superficial, that current measurements of personality are far from satisfactory, and that consensus is lacking on criteria. However, the presentation of research reports before professional audiences may help to assure that they will receive close scrutiny. That this is an ongoing process is evident in the numerous journals, conferences, seminars, and papers that are shared by professionals associated with childhood study. More careful or adequate measures of the elusive nature of human personality await refinements which may not be present at the moment but which certainly can be anticipated as scientists apply themselves in this direction. Finally, consensus is being reached, or is in a state of becoming, because criteria have been offered and have met with little opposition from those who have considered them.[9]

2. UNQUALIFIED ACCEPTANCE OF CHILD STUDIES. While the conclusion that scientific study of children has not even begun represents one extreme position, the uncritical acceptance of child studies represents the opposing polarity of views on child research. Brushing aside all warnings that a given study did employ a specific *sample* of the universe, that a particular *methodology* and *technique* were employed, that *unknown variables* were probably operating in the study situation, that the findings are chiefly *suggestive*, and a whole host of other cautions familiar to research scholars, certain professionals and many laymen blithely accept empiric study as overwhelming evidence that "the truth" has, at last, been found. Such persons are trying to bring the latest word to the waiting public. They are often trying to render valuable service. The criticism implied, nevertheless, refers to the omission of caution and appreciation of the *tentative* nature of empiric study. Bossard [10] expressed it neatly when he wrote:

To be sure, students of human problems have emphasized causal antecedents for many years. Only recently, however, has come the knowledge that these causal relations are neither so few in number nor so simple in their operation as had previously been supposed. In the study of these relationships, there has been a transfer of interest and emphasis *from the broadly obvious to the subtly effective* (italics ours). It is this that is essentially new in the contemporary approach to the study of behavior problems.

It is the neglect of the subtleties inherent in a given study that underlies the criticism of overzealous popularists.

Categoric rejection of popularists of child studies may be tempered with still another precautionary note. A public exists consisting mainly of parents who wish to do the *right thing* for their children, and of other well-intentioned persons who wish to translate into action the knowledge developed by scientists in their laboratories. A public thirsting for knowledge is an inviting stimulus and rare is the man who can resist informing the audience that he can offer them wisdom. If childhood and parental

[9] See A. R. Mangus, *Personality Adjustment of School Children,* A Report Based on Studies Conducted Jointly by the Division of Mental Hygiene of the Ohio State Department of Public Welfare, The Ohio State University, and the Ohio Agricultural Experiment Station (Columbus, Ohio, July, 1948), pp. 7–8.

[10] James H. S. Bossard and Eleanor S. Boll, *The Sociology of Child Development,* Third Edition (New York, Harper & Row, Publishers, Inc., 1960), p. 634.

roles were clearly defined, there would be little room for doubt about what to do. In the modern context of individuality and decision-making, guidance can and does come into prominence.

3. QUALIFIED ACCEPTANCE OF CHILD RESEARCH EFFORTS. At this juncture, it should be fairly obvious that the two extreme positions just described do not find support in this text. Rather, the point of view the authors find defensible lies at some point between the polar views. Neither a dramatic rejection of modern research on children seems to be in order nor an unqualified endorsement of child studies seems to be justified. There need be a healthy respect for the untiring efforts of research scholars to uncover intricate details concerning the nature of childhood. On the other hand, their shortcomings must be taken into account as reflecting the present state of ability to discern facts relating to complicated human behavior.

Since August, 1948, the United States Children's Bureau has served as a clearing house for research in child life and has periodically issued bulletins and supplements under the title, *Research Relating to Children*. Those wishing to avail themselves of one of the most complete listings of child research would do well to consult this important source. Even a cursory examination of its contents will reveal that a great many men and women have investigated significant areas relating to childhood. The classifications of research dealing with children have varied from year to year but the numerous phases of childhood that are investigated illustrate the diligent efforts of research scientists to uncover whatever gives promise of verified knowledge. Certainly this prodigious output is neither flawless nor worthless. A more tenable position might be described as one which is appreciative, but which maintains reservations as to the adequacy of research of contemporary scientists.

Research trends

Taking into account studies of children since the outbreak of World War II, it is possible to trace some of the chief lines of research development. The following appears to be the central tendencies of research relating to children since about 1941.

FINANCIAL SUPPORT. While other fields have long had the support of major foundations such as the Carnegie Foundation or the Rockefeller Foundation, it has only been in about the past twenty years that costly efforts in child research have been met by private or governmental organizations such as the Ford Foundation or the National Institute of Mental Health. Prior to this, research could be only minimal since it was conducted by a single investigator with limited resources. In modern times, an upsurge in research efforts has occurred thanks to the willingness of generous organizations to see to it that time-consuming, energy-consuming, money-consuming work can proceed without fear that the findings must be immediate, practical, and applicable to a limited group.

CENTERS FOR STUDY. Research centers have been established at many Universities. The Yale University Child Study Center, Minnesota's Child Study Center and the Family Life Center and the Committee on Human Development at the University of Chicago are representative of such centers. In these settings full time staffs of experts can assemble data systematically so that scattered materials begin to display meaningful relationships. Furthermore, the concentration upon some overriding behavior complex has also led to the establishment of specific research centers which have a contribution to make towards understanding childhood. Cases in point are the Institute on Sex Research at Indiana University and the Human Relations Area Files headquartered in New Haven, Connecticut. The latter organization includes sixteen member universities scattered from coast to coast. This network enables scholars to utilize cross-cultural references to compare hundreds of societies in their handling of various situations. The ready availability of such centers enhances the opportunity of students "to uncover the significant" as it relates to their individual or group needs.

INTERDISCIPLINARY RESEARCH. While each field of knowledge concentrates upon specific matters for purposes of analysis, there has been growing recognition that, in the long run, selected subjects of investigation do not exclusively belong in one field. Many subjects, including childhood, cut across traditional subject-matter fields and a complete picture awaits the cooperative efforts of specialists. Team emphasis has come into existence as research has progressed in the past twenty or so years. While individual investigators continue to operate small scale projects from their particular field's point of view, probably giant strides are being made by coordinated effort of teams of experts, each one capable of making its unique contribution without dominating the research work. Thus, while this text seeks to discuss the *sociology* of childhood, it does not lose sight of the fact that eclecticism in research may be rewarding. This approach to new knowledge is highly endorsed by the numerous teams of research workers which have been formed throughout academic communities.

MEASUREMENT TECHNIQUES. In the past, research workers seemed to be satisfied more with the substance of their findings than with the methods by which these findings were obtained. Evidence that this is not completely a relic of the past is found in studies that appear to gloss over their procedures to reach their substantive data. In particular, more precise and valid measurement techniques have been sought over the past decades rather than extreme concentration on "the facts." Similar to the mathematics student who is urged to master the ability to do problems rather than to solve a single problem confronting him at the moment, sociologists have paid increasing attention to scalability or reproducta-bility, profiles or combinations of indexes, multiple-factor analysis, and improved methods of eliminating errors due to chance. Standards are being evolved to permit comparisons when a given test is administered to various populations. Factors are now weighted rather than the earlier equal-weighted procedures of the 1920's or 1930's. In brief, there is more finesse in research measurement to more precisely express the nature of children and their ways. The sharpening of research instruments should improve the accuracy of scholarly work.

USE OF LARGER SAMPLES. The overall trend is in the direction of securing larger samples of the population without sacrificing representativeness. Previously, a well chosen small sample was deemed sufficient to represent a universe and to evoke confidence in applications to the referrent group. More recently, however, studies designed to determine the extent of the phenomena under observation have turned to the use of thousands of cases scattered throughout various cities, regions, or locales. It ap-parently is expedient to take national or regional samples to test a specific hypothesis, rather than the old method of performing a more modest study with a limited sample and then waiting for others to repli-cate the study with different populations. Such change in procedures is evidence of the quickened pace of social research efforts which now em-ploy methods in line with improved technologies. If sociologists seek to generalize about children and their social situations, then they have cer-tainly begun to turn in the proper direction for widening the scope of their studies. The public, to whom these studies are finally addressed, seems to place considerably more confidence in such procedures than the more tentative, suggestive work of earlier scientists.

CONCENTRATION ON LESS AVAILABLE POPULATIONS. One of the fundamental criticisms of social research has been the tendency to take the line of least resistance and study intensively those populations that were im-mediately available to the research worker. Some have characterized these studies as being "WUMP" studies.[11] This is the label placed upon studies which have mainly used White, Urban, Middle Class, Protestant samples and thus have applicability only to such people. By way of correcting this over-attention to a particular segment of the population, new samples have tended to be those that took into account non-whites, rural people,

[11] Credited to Robert Blood, University of Michigan, in remarks at a Groves Con-ference at Merrill-Palmer Institute, Detroit, Michigan, April, 1961.

upper and lower classes, and non-Protestants. Even if it is granted that WUMP samples are regarded as typical of the general population, by widening the base of study many more children are under surveillance and can furnish research workers with newer insights.

It is true that communities surrounding college or university towns have tended to be over-studied and communities well removed from such academic environments have tended to be under-studied. Not only convenience operated in the selection of nearby communities, but also the cooperative spirit of interested persons made the task of research a bit easier. By pushing out into less available and sometimes less cooperative populations, research workers have had to devise new techniques to secure data. The more challenging work has demanded greater patience and greater ability. The fact that studies are being reported of this nature is a tribute to research ingenuity and resourcefulness, and will begin to make amends for the long neglect of important segments of the total population.

SEARCH FOR NEGLECTED AREAS. Not only are new reference groups being secured, but also research problems have been formulated to fill in the unknown places which have existed for so long. It is interesting to note in the literature, studies dealing with children's view of money, the significance of the absence of the father, or children's perceptions in general. Such studies were shunted aside in the past to allow empiric study of that which was deemed more essential. Assumptions which were made in order to probe in selected directions are now being challenged to ascertain their validity.

GROWING CONCERN OVER FREEDOM. In the United States, with traditions once again under attack, as illustrated by the cold war and by so-called extreme rightists, there is a searching examination of conceptions of freedom. While there is faith in American values, there is probably no other single area which is being seriously studied so intensively as the meaning of being free. Americans no longer feel comfortable in merely reaffirming their convictions, but seem to be questioning the very foundations upon which they have erected their lives because so many others have been won over to opposing ways of life. Have Americans been wrong to cherish individualism and to scoff at the bonds which hold people in line? Do men really need direction and strong social systems in order to exist? Have American families and the manner in which child experts have advised parents to rear their young in the United States been grossly mistaken?

Certainly studies dealing with permissiveness versus rigidity in child rearing practices have held an important place in child research. Representative of such studies which try to trace the ramifications of philosophies of freedom for children is the work of Union College begun in 1936 and called "Studies in Character Research." That this concern pervades the total society rather than solely childhood is evident in the work of the Center for the Study of Democratic Institutions at the University of California at Santa Barbara. This Center has called upon the best available talents to promote discussion of the significant issues involved in the maintenance of a free society. Among their recent projects has been a study of American character initiated in the summer of 1960. Referring back to the foundations of character laid in childhood, William O. Douglas, Associate Justice of the Supreme Court of the United States, stated at their Conference on The American Character,[12] "While we give things a practical twist, there is an idealism in the American character that will carry tens of thousands of youngsters through the years of sacrifice abroad." Americans will apparently continue to re-examine the assumptions they have made concerning the preservation of freedom, whether it be at the level of early childhood practices or in their culmination into adult decisions for action. This search will continue well into the forseeable future as long as the American conception of freedom is threatened.

LONGITUDINAL STUDIES. One of the major criticisms of research has been its tendency to sample or, in the fashion of a photographer, to take snapshots which freeze action seen at the moment, but which fails to take into account that which has transpired either before or after the study itself. This criticism is quite valid and it is not satisfactorily answered by simply compounding research studies so that scientists achieve merely more of the same. By turning to longitudinal studies, research workers are beginning to secure an overall, total picture which includes a whole series of variables hitherto neglected. However, longitudinal studies have their own intrinsic difficulties such as the tremendous costs of long-term financing, the possibility of losing subjects as time elapses, and the need for interdisciplinary teamwork to collate a mass of data. Nevertheless, longitudinal studies are increasing as further evidence of the maturing of modern research relating to childhood. A series of such studies is reported in *Longitudinal Studies of Child Personality* by Alan A. Stone and Gloria C. Onque.[13]

Dr. Milton Senn, Director of the Yale University Child Study Center,[14] citing the advantages of longitudinal study, writes in the foreword, "The ideal longitudinal study is a series of observations so spaced as to discover as many of the variabilities as possible occurring during critical periods in

[12] Conference on The American Character, Bulletin (New York, Center for the Study of Democratic Institutions), October, 1961, p. 8.
[13] Alan A. Stone, and Gloria C. Onque, *Longitudinal Studies of Child Personality* (Cambridge, Mass. The Commonwealth Fund and Harvard University Press, 1959).
[14] Stone and Onque, *op. cit.*, p. viii.

the life of an individual so that ultimately predictions of change are possible and correlations between measurements at various ages are valid." Probably one of the most famous longitudinal studies of childhood which has attempted to establish the normative development of children has been the work of A. L. Gesell and his associates at the Yale Clinic of Child Development.[15] In addition, Lewis Terman has continued to study "gifted children" who are now in late middle age.

While longitudinal studies have their peculiar advantages over earlier, short-range studies, there are also certain limitations which must be taken into account. For instance, while key factors or causal relationships are being sought, how certain can scientists be that the correct ones have been located? Further, because of attritional losses due to the passage of time, some longitudinal studies have been forced to rely on a limited number of subjects as a basis for some rather sweeping generalizations. In this case, longitudinal studies can be criticized for their lack of data just as much as brief, short-range projects. Finally, many longitudinal studies have been clinical in nature and the search for relevant variables and hypotheses applicable to normal children are not necessarily found from observations made during therapy. Of course, scientists must work with available and cooperative subjects and practicality dictates some of these restrictions in the search for knowledge concerning children.

PURE RESEARCH VERSUS APPLIED RESEARCH. Prompted by desire to help children, earlier research characteristically emphasized applied or action research. That is, research topics tended to be those which would lend themselves to the solution of pressing problems relating to children. While immediate problems continue to face those dealing with children and their welfare, there has been recognition that fundamental knowledge gained through painstaking research must precede major breakthroughs in application of knowledge. Thus, while practical research continues relatively unabated, paralleling this effort are studies which seek to fill in gaps in the knowledge. Some of this research would appear to have no immediate application. Nevertheless, such work has proven in the past to be just the piece of information which enables therapeutic measures to be eventually truly effective.

Illustrative of this trend may be the renewed and persistent effort to probe deeper into sociological factors which relate to the nature of childhood. Selected studies reported in the *American Sociological Review*, the official journal of the American Sociological Association, just over the past five or six years, for example, include the following:

[15] See, A. L. Gesell, *et. al., First Five Years of Life, A Guide to the Study of the Pre-School Child* (New York, Harper & Row, Publishers, Inc., 1940); A. L. Gesell and F. L. Ilg, *The Child from Five to Ten* (New York, Harper & Row Publishers, Inc., 1946); A. L. Gesell, F. L. Ilg, and L. B. Ames, *Youth, The Years from Ten to Sixteen* (New York, Harper & Row, Publishers, Inc., 1956).

"Relationships Among Child Training Practices," William H. Sewell, Paul H. Mussen, and Chester W. Harris, Vol. 20, No. 2 (April, 1955), pp. 137–148.

"A Comparison of the Chicago and Harvard Studies of Social Class Differences in Child Rearing," Robert J. Havighurst and Allison Davis, Vol. 20, No. 4 (August, 1955), pp. 438–442.

"Adjustment Characteristics of Rural and Urban Children," Lee Burchinal, Glenn R. Hawkes, and Bruce Gardner, Vol. 22, No. 1 (February, 1957), pp. 81–87.

"Social Class Differences in Child Rearing: A Third Community for Comparison with Chicago and Newton," Richard A. Littman, Robert C. A. Moore, and John Pierce-Jones, Vol. 22, No. 6 (December, 1957), pp. 694–712.

"The Child as a Prototype of the Naive Informant in the Interview Situation," Nicholas Babchuk and C. Wayne Gordon, Vol. 23, No. 2 (April, 1958), pp. 196–198.

"Social Class and the Exercise of Parental Authority," Melvin L. Kohn, Vol. 24, No. 3 (June, 1959), pp. 352–366.

"Factors in the Relationship Between Social Status and the Personality Adjustment of the Child," William H. Sewell and A. O. Haller, Vol. 24, No. 4 (August, 1959), pp. 511–520.

"Early Familial Experiences and Bigotry," William McCord, Joan McCord, and Alan Howard, Vol. 25, No. 5 (October, 1960), pp. 717–722.

William M. Smith, Jr., Professor of Family Relationships, Pennsylvania State University, noted, in his address, "The Family Life Movement: Perspective and Prospects" at a conference of the Ohio Council on Family Relations in March, 1959, that there was an increasing *professionalization* in the movement rather than the earlier tone of enthusiasm unsupported by painstaking study. He noted that a 1943 issue of *Marriage and Family Living*, the official journal of the National Council on Family Relations, had only four out of twenty-three articles that were research-based or even related to causal investigations. By contrast, in a recent issue of the same journal containing forty-nine major articles, at least fifty-three percent or twenty-six of the articles were research reports or were based on factual data.

At the 1960 White House Conference on Children and Youth[16] the following was set forth:

Further research into the following was recommended: congenital anomalies; the prolongation of gestation to prevent prematurity; transportation hazards to centers for premature infants; the increasing rate of infant mortality; perinatal casualties; why parents often fail to use child health services; the readiness of the young child for group experience in nursery school, kindergarten, and first grade, in order to establish criteria for enrollment "other than chronological age"; problems of the young child's growth and development, and which cultural demands are *irrelevant* to his optimal mental health and personality developments; the proper balance between creative learning and the assimila-

[16] *Conference Proceedings*, Golden Anniversary White House Conference on Children and Youth, Inc., March 27–April 2, 1960, Washington, D.C., pp. 205–206.

tion of acts in children's education; the optimal range in the number of pupils per teacher that will permit attention to individual differences; the optimal range of pre-adolescent activity; factors that serve to realize the full potential of children and youth for a creative life.

This same group also debated, at length, a resolution for research "to discover what happens to the enormous and universal national resource of creativity that is evident in the infant and preschool child and to trace the changes towards conformity in the preadolescent and the adult." [17] In sociological terms, this group of interested citizens was questioning the socialization process which is the central focus of this text. The answers will come through research and the arraying of research into meaningful patterns. Such work will not be dramatic or spectacular. Based on past record, it can safely be predicted that research will go forward slowly with many possibilities turning out to be false leads and sterile points of investigation.

Fads in Child Study

The danger in child research lies in the possibility of forsaking long-range goals for the sake of the popular and the immediate. Like women's fashions, a climate of opinion changes with the times until one can observe a cycle in which one ultimately returns to an original starting point or a wave pattern in which one shuttles back and forth between action and reaction. Observers of childhood have frequently noted how during certain periods in history, Americans have treated children with love and affection, reverted to a type of neglect or coldness, and then reinstated warm, permissive atmospheres. Riding with this wave have been research workers who document how effective current techniques with children really are. Certainly such students become suspect when they give support and comfort to popular opinion and then change just as quickly when these views are challenged.

While some research scholars appear to draw their hypotheses from the current milieu, there are many others who are not dazzled by the immediate tone of the times and can soberly and calmly punch holes in the convictions held by what appears to be the majority of people. The serious student of child research notes that many studies do not affirm popular opinion. In testing hypotheses, the result that states "no significant differences" renders valuable service and is just as meaningful as those studies which sustain or confirm tentative conclusions.[18] Like the setting up of bowling pins, it is not too difficult to propose certain hypotheses. On the other hand, to knock them down requires a certain

[17] *Ibid.*, p. 206.
[18] See William H. Sewell, "Infant Training and the Personality of the Child," *American Journal of Sociology*, LVIII (1952), p. 150–159.

amount of skill. Frequently those who propose ideas regarding childhood are apparently not willing or able to verify assumptions or suspicions.

Children are not toys to be lightly handled and then tossed aside in some forgotten corner. Far too often, children have been decisively treated without any assurance that what has been done to them and with them has been for their own good. Perhaps whole generations of children have suffered at the hands of adults who, while being a trifle unsure of themselves, still go ahead and shape lives and personalities. It then requires more generations to return to some equilibrium. It takes time for valid research findings to be implemented in the day-to-day process of child rearing. In the interim period, one can predict that some tragic errors with regard to children will continue to exist.

Caution in Research

In summary of this discussion of current research relating to children, one perhaps cannot unduly stress the need for caution. In a delightful passage in *Children in a Changing World, A Book of Charts*,[19] a summary of what the authors call "Implications for the Future," the following appears:

Most people today know the difference between a weather report and a weather forecast. A report describes past and present events; we assume that the statements made in it are true, and we draw implications from them about the future, which is what we are interested in. A forecast is a neat device for making these implications specific. It is not a statement of fact about the future; it is simply a description of what would happen if things continued to change in just the way they are changing now. But things never do. Sooner or later something new appears and alters the picture. The statistical procedures for working out the implications of a present situation are called projections, and they can be directed toward the future or toward the past.

Mark Twain made some projections in *Life on the Mississippi*. He says: "In the space of 176 years the Lower Mississippi has shortened itself 242 miles. That is an average of a trifle over one mile and a third per year. Therefore, any calm person, who is not blind or idiotic, can see that in the Old Ooclitic Silurian Period, just a million years ago next November, the Lower Mississippi was upward of 1,300,000 miles long and stuck out over the Gulf of Mexico like a fishing-rod. And by the same token any person can see that 742 years from now the Lower Mississippi will be only a mile and three-quarters long, and Cairo (he means, of course, Cairo, Illinois) and New Orleans will have joined their streets together, and be plodding along under a single mayor and a mutual board of aldermen. There is something fascinating about science. One gets such wholesale returns of conjecture out of such a trifling investment of fact."

If we are not to drown ourselves in conjecture, we must recognize a forecast,

[19] *Children in a Changing World*, Golden Anniversary White House Conference on Children and Youth, Inc., p. 73.

or projection, for what it is—a valuable scientific tool in the hands of those who know how to use it. But for those of us who do not know how to use it, a scientific projection may be less instructive and much less reliable than the general implications we ourselves are able to draw from the facts. We must also realize that some projections are inherently less reliable than others. Some fields of study, such as weather conditions, are more subject to change than others, such as the movement of stars. And in any one field the longer the projection, the more time it covers, the less likely it is to be borne out by the facts.

Thus, the need to avoid whole-hearted endorsement of current research studies appears to be the wisest course to follow. Headway is being made, and the currents of time influence studies to move in new and more fruitful directions.

READINGS

The Educational Policies Commission, *Public Education and the Future of America* (Washington, D.C., National Education Association of the United States, 1955).

GOOD, I. J., ed., *The Scientist Speculates, An Anthology of Partly-Baked Ideas* (New York, Basic Books, Inc., 1963).

GRAMS, Armin, *Parent Education and the Behavioral Sciences* (U.S. Dept. of Health, Education, and Welfare, Children Bureau's Publication, No. 379, 1960).

JENSEN, Gordon, *The Well Child's Problems, Management in the First Six Years* (Chicago, Year Book Medical Publishers, Inc., 1962).

STANDEN, Anthoney, *Science Is a Sacred Cow* (New York, E. P. Dutton & Co., Inc., 1950).

Children and Youth in the 1960's (Washington, D.C., 1960 White House Conference on Children and Youth).

Reference Papers on Children and Youth (Washington, D.C., 1960 White House Conference on Children and Youth).

Glossary

This glossary includes certain key words used in this text. The descriptive statements that follow these words are not presented as complete or formal definitions. Rather, they are intended as concise explanations of these key words as the authors have used them in the preceding discussions.

ATTITUDE: The person's tendency or readiness to act toward an object (human or non-human, material or non-material), or class of objects, in a particular way.

AUTONOMY: One's own control of his behavior in accordance with the exercise of his volition within the limits of his social and cultural orientation.

CATEGORY, SOCIAL: A plurality of persons socially defined as sharing a set of distinguishing traits.

COMMUNITY: People living within a specified geographic location and carrying on a common, relatively self-sufficient, and interdependent way of life.

CULTURE: The totality of shared, learned behavior (and the products of that behavior) according to which members of a society live, including their values, attitudes, norms, material objects, and overt behavior.

DELINQUENT: A status ascribed to a child by a juvenile court.

DEVIANT: One who does not conform to some specified standard or set of standards embodied in socially sanctioned sources such as law, custom, and religion.

DIFFERENTIATION, SOCIAL: The process whereby categories of people are ascribed differential statuses in society.

FOLKWAYS: The expected or customary ways of behavior that regulate or characterize the people of a society.

FUNCTION: The consequences of a structure for the system as a whole.

FUNCTION, MANIFEST: The intended or expected consequences of a structure for the system as a whole.

FUNCTION, LATENT: The unintended, unexpected, or harmful consequences of a structure for the system as a whole.

GROUP: Two or more persons interacting according to a set of interconnected statuses.

IDEAL-TYPICAL: A construct of a pattern held to be the embodiment of relevant standards.

INSTITUTION: A complex of values, attitudes, and norms directed toward the achievement of a socially significant end.

INTERACTION, SOCIAL: The process of interstimulation whereby persons and groups exert reciprocal influences upon one another.

MATURATION: Changes in body structure and coordination that occur over time.

MINORITY: Social category to which persons are ascribed on differentiating criteria such as race, creed, ethnic characteristics, or alleged loyalties, which results in subordinate status and loss of power to control certain aspects of their individual or group behavior.

MORES: The folkways which are regarded as essential to the welfare of the group, and the violations of which tend to result in the application of informal sanctions.

NORMS, SOCIAL: Social rules designed to regulate the person's behavior. They include folkways, mores, and law.

PEER GROUP: A group of equals in age, status, or power.

PERSONALITY: The totality of a person's traits.

PRIMARY GROUP: A relatively small number of people whose interaction tends to be face-to-face, intimate, non-specialized, and marked by a deep and rather continuing sense of reciprocal identification.

RACE: A category of persons who are ascribed a particular status because they are alleged to have a set of common and distinguishing physical traits.

ROLE: A pattern of expected behavior associated with a particular status within a social structure.

SAMPLING: Selection of a portion of a universe to determine the nature of the entire subject-matter area under investigation.

SECONDARY GROUP: Counterpart of a primary group, consisting of a plurality of people characterized by tendencies to be in indirect communication, formality, concern for the services being rendered, of short duration, and less interested in the total personality organization of participants.

SELF: A set or complex of attitudes that reflect back upon the holder.

SIBLING: A brother or sister to children of the same parents.

SOCIALIZATION: The process by which the human organism acquires human nature, develops a personality, and enters his society.

SOCIAL PROCESS: Social interaction in which sequential steps are taken toward certain ends.

SOCIAL STRATIFICATION: The process by which social groups and categories are ascribed or achieve differential positions in a ranked order of statuses.

SOCIAL SYSTEM: A complex of interlocking statuses constituting the pattern governing the behavior of the people in a group.

SOCIETY: An organized group of people distinguished by a common culture.

STATUS: A position within a social system to which a role or set of behavioral expectations is attached.

UNIVERSE: The complete phenomenon under investigation.

VALUES: The relative worth or importance which people ascribe to objects, both tangible and intangible.

Author Index

Subject Index